Muslim Minorities and Social Cohesion

This book examines various attempts in the 'West' to manage cultural, linguistic, and religious diversity – focusing on Muslim minorities in predominantly non-Muslim societies.

An international panel of contributors chart evolving national identities and social values, assessing the way that both contemporary 'Western' societies and contemporary Muslim minorities view themselves and respond to the challenges of diversity. Drawing on themes and priority subjects from Islamic culture within Euro-Asian, Australian, and American international research, they address multiple critical issues and discuss their implications for existing and future policy and practice in this area. These include subjects such as gender, the media, citizenship, and multiculturalism.

The insight provided by this wide-ranging book will be of great use to scholars of religious studies, interreligious dialogue, and Islamic studies, as well as politics, culture, and migration.

Abe W. Ata is Adjunct Professor at Victoria University and Latrobe University, Australia, and Visiting Professor at Freiburg University, Germany. His publications span 124 journal articles and 18 books.

Routledge Studies in Religion

For more information about this series, please visit: www.routledge.com/
religion/series/SE0669

Muslim Minorities and Social Cohesion

Cultural Fragmentation in the West

Edited by Abe W. Ata

Routledge
Taylor & Francis Group

LONDON AND NEW YORK

First published 2021
by Routledge
2 Park Square, Milton Park, Abingdon, Oxon OX14 4RN

and by Routledge
52 Vanderbilt Avenue, New York, NY 10017

Routledge is an imprint of the Taylor & Francis Group, an informa business

British Library Cataloguing-in-Publication Data
A catalogue record for this book is available from the British Library

Library of Congress Cataloging-in-Publication Data
A catalog record for this book has been requested

ISBN: 978-0-367-48466-8 (hbk)
ISBN: 978-1-003-04452-9 (ebk)

Typeset in Sabon
by Apex CoVantage, LLC

Contents

Figures

Tables

Boxes

Contributors

Jan A. Ali is a senior lecturer in Islam and modernity in the School of Humanities and Communication Arts at the University of Western Sydney, Australia. A religious sociologist, his main sociological focus is the study of existential Islam. Currently Jan is working on three separate research projects. His first project is a study of different aspects of Muslim terrorism, particularly its causes and consequences. In his second project Jan is looking at Rohingyas in Australia, and the third project is a collaboration with a colleague examining Muslim youths in global cities.

Adele Amorsen is a primary school teacher at a large independent school in Brisbane, Australia. She has spent over 15 years teaching in primary classrooms in Queensland, Australia, in both the state and independent systems. Adele also spent many years lecturing in the field of English curriculum at Queensland University of Technology. She has a keen interest in preservice teacher education and the development of positive and productive relationships between schools and universities to facilitate best practices in both contexts.

Craig A. Anderson is a distinguished professor of psychology at Iowa State University, USA. He is also director of the Center for the Study of Violence and past-president of the International Society for Research on Aggression. His 240+ publications have received over 37,000 citations. He is considered by many to be the world's leading expert on violent video game effects. His General Aggression Model has been applied to clinical, social, personality, and developmental psychology; pediatrics; criminology; war; and climate change, among other fields. In 2017 Dr. Anderson received the Kurt Lewin Award from the Society for the Psychological Study of Psychological Issues, its top award. It was presented for "outstanding contributions to the development and integration of psychological research and social action."

Abe W. Ata is an adjunct professor at Victoria University and Latrobe University, Australia, and a visiting professor at Freiburg University, Germany. He is of Palestinian Lebanese Australian background, born in

Bethlehem. He graduated in social psychology at the American University of Beirut, and was thereafter nominated as a delegate to the United Nations' World Youth Assembly in New York. He gained his doctorate at the University of Melbourne in 1980 and has since been teaching and researching at several Australian, American, German, Jordanian, West Bank and Danish universities. His publications span 124 journal articles, 18 books, and 23 entries in the *Encyclopaedia of Australian Religions* (2009), *Encyclopaedia of the Australian People* (2001) and *Encyclopaedia of Melbourne* (2005). Several of his books were nominated for the Prime Minister's Book Awards for which he was nominated Australian of the Year in 2011 and 2015.

Klaus Baumann is a theologian and social psychologist and the former dean of the faculty of theology at Freiburg University. Currently he is the chair of Caritas.

Maria Chisari is a lecturer in student learning and communication at the University of Sydney, Australia. Her research interests are interdisciplinary, covering the fields of cultural studies, governmentality, citizenship, academic literacies and Teaching English to Speakers of Other Languages (TESOL). Her doctoral research consisted of a genealogy of the introduction of the Australian citizenship test and focused on how migrants both negotiate and contest the discourses around what it means to be a model Australian citizen in contemporary, neoliberal Australia. Maria has published book chapters and journal articles on the subjects of Australian values, multiculturalism and Australian citizenship. Her most recent publication explores the possibility of 'reimagining Australia' through the new *Allegiance to Australia* legislation.

Manijeh Daneshpour is a professor and systemwide director of marriage and family therapy at Alliant International University in California, USA. She is also a licensed marriage and family therapist with more than 22 years of academic, research and clinical experience. She is from Iran and identifies herself as a third wave feminist. Manijeh's main areas of research, publications and presentations have been centered on issues of gender socialization, immigration, multiculturalism, social justice, third wave feminism, premarital and marital relationships and Muslim family dynamics. She has spent more than 22 years training therapists to provide multiculturally sensitive therapy and has been an advocate of social justice and equality in all aspects of her academic, clinical and personal life.

Moira Dustin is a research fellow in the Department of Law in the School of Law, Politics and Sociology at the University of Sussex, UK. She has a PhD in gender studies from the London School of Economics, where she is a visiting fellow at the Centre for Analysis of Social Exclusion (CASE). Before joining the University of Sussex, Moira was director of research and communications at the Equality and Diversity Forum, a network of equality and human rights organizations, where she coordinated the Equality and Diversity Research Network. Moira has also worked at the Refugee Council, providing advice and information and developing national services for refugees and asylum seekers. She has worked as a freelance subeditor on the *Guardian* and *Independent* newspapers and was the information worker for the Carnegie Inquiry into the Third Age.

Lucia-Mihaela Grosu-Rădulescu is an associate professor in the Department of Modern Languages and Business Communication at the Bucharest University of Economic Studies, Romania. She holds an MA degree in British cultural studies from the University of Bucharest and an MS degree in English language education and research communication in economics from the Bucharest University of Economic Studies. In 2012, she received her PhD degree in philology from the University of Bucharest for research in the field of Canadian female ethnic writers. She has published three books, collaborated on a textbook on cultural studies and co-authored a monograph on francophone Romanian writers, and she has also published numerous research papers in academic journals. Her research interests range from teaching methods in English for Specific Purposes (ESP) and business communication to socioeconomy and social psychology and to literary and cultural studies.

Andrew Jakubowicz is an emeritus professor of sociology in the School of Communication at the University of Technology Sydney. He is the author of books on multiculturalism, media racism and diversity and cyber-racism and community resilience. His many articles are standard references in teaching around Australia, ranging from his study on media manipulation during the first Iraq War *(The Invisible Ally) to Political Islam in Australia*. He has researched reports for various levels of government on topics ranging from social policy and cultural diversity to human rights and international students (including for Academy of the Social Sciences in Australia). His television work has been widely followed, including projects such as 'Once Upon a Time in Cabramatta', 'Once Upon a time in Punchbowl', 'The Great Australian Race Riot', 'Vietnam: The War that Made Australia', and 'Is Australia Racist?' His web projects include Making Multicultural Australia and The Menorah of Fang Bang Lu. His nearly 50 pieces online in The Conversation have received 250,000 visits and 4,000 comments.

James Jupp is an academic visitor in the School of Demography, Australian National University. He has been researching in the area of immigration and ethnic politics since his first book on the subject, *Arrivals and Departures* (1966). Major works have included the *Encyclopaedia of the Australian People* (1988, 2001), the *Encyclopedia of Religion in Australia* (2009) and *From White Australia to Woomera* (2002, 2007). He also chaired the Hawke Government's Review of Migrant and Multicultural Programs and Services and has served on various government advisory bodies. His most recent book is *An Immigrant Nation Seeks Cohesion* (Anthem Press, 2018). He was made a Member of the Order of Australia in 2004.

Greg Melleuish is a professor in the School of Humanities and Social Inquiry at the University of Wollongong, Australia, where he teaches political theory, Australian politics and ancient history. He has written widely on a range of topics from Australian political ideas and intellectual history, to world history, to philosophy of history. He is particularly interested in the words that we use to describe human beings and their place in the world, such as civilization, religion, secular, the state and commonwealth. His books include *Cultural Liberalism in Australia* (Cambridge University Press, 1995) and *Despotic State or Free Individual* (Australian Scholarly Publishing, 2014).

Andreas Miles-Novelo is a graduate student of psychology and human–computer interaction at Iowa State University in Ames, USA, working under the mentorship of Craig A. Anderson. He received bachelor's degrees in psychology and English at the University of Nebraska-Lincoln in May 2017. His areas of research include aggression, media research, virtual reality, gaming, climate change, sexual harassment, politics and other areas.

Melinda G. Miller is a senior lecturer in the School of Early Childhood and Inclusive Education at Queensland University of Technology, Australia. Melinda is a registered teacher in Queensland and teaches in the areas of cultural studies, Indigenous education and early childhood education in preservice teacher education programs. Her research interests include cultural inclusion, embedding Aboriginal and Torres Strait Islander perspectives in education curricula, sustainability and teacher professional development. Melinda has been twice awarded the Springer Award for Best Paper, for articles published in *The Australian Educational Researcher* in 2015 and 2011.

Susan Millns is a professor of law and head of the Sussex Law School at the University of Sussex, UK. Her research interests lie in the area of European and comparative public law, and she is currently carrying out research into the impact of Brexit from a gender perspective.

Agneta Moulettes is an assistant professor in the Department of Strategic Communication at Lund University, Sweden. She received her PhD from the School of Economics and Business Administration at the university. She takes a special interest in postcolonial perspectives, mainly to expose the dark side of culture and gender issues related to immigration. Her current research focuses on labor market intermediaries' role in integrating immigrants into the Swedish labor market. She has published in the *Journal of Multicultural Discourses*, *Gender in Management: An International Journal*, *Management Learning* and the *Journal of Workplace*

Rights. She has received an Emerald Highly Recommended Paper Award 2007 and a BAM Best Developmental Paper Award 2015, Knowledge and Learning stream.

Sev Ozdowski is director of equity and diversity at Western Sydney University, Australia, and an adjunct professor in the Department of Peace and Conflict Studies at Sydney University, Australia. He was the Australian Human Rights Commissioner and Disability Discrimination Commissioner (2000–2005) and headed the Office of Multicultural and International Affairs in South Australia (1996–2000). Ozdowski is currently president of the Australian Council for Human Rights Education (since 2006) and chair of the Australian Multicultural Council (since 2014). He was recognized through various Australian and international honors, including an Order of Australia Medal (1995), Officers Cross of the Order of Merit of the Republic of Poland (2007), Member in the General Division of the Order of Australia (2016) and Fellow, Royal Society of New South Wales (2018).

Claudia M. Postelnicescu is a lawyer and consultant based in Bucharest, Romania. She is a legal expert affiliated with the Romanian Academic Society (SAR) and has expertise in human rights, constitutional law and European law. Her research interests are focused on European identity, European foreign policy and migration.

Clive Sealey is a senior lecturer in social policy at University of Worcester, UK. Her most recent book, *Social Policy Simplified*, has at its core the aim of making social policy relevant to individuals' lives, and this is a key aim of both her teaching and her research. Her teaching interests are topics related to poverty and social exclusion, welfare ideology, global welfare issues, and wider current affairs in relation to social policy. She has published on a variety of social policy topics such as migration, austerity, social exclusion, and young people.

Thijl Sunier is a professor of cultural anthropology and holds the chair of Islam in European Societies at VU Amsterdam, the Netherlands. Currently he conducts a research project on Islamic authority, religious critique, leadership, and knowledge production in Europe. He also is involved in a European (EU funded) research project 'Mediating Islam in the Digital Age' (MIDA). His latest English books are *Transnational Turkish Islam* (2015, Palgrave Macmillan) (with Nico Landman) and *Islam and Society, Critical Concepts in Sociology* (four edited volumes) (2018, Routledge). He has written several reports on Islam in the Netherlands commissioned by the Dutch government. He is chairman of the board of the Netherlands Inter-University School for Islamic Studies (NISIS) and executive editor of the *Journal of Muslims in Europe* (JOME/Brill).

Acknowledgement

I am grateful to the following colleagues who provided various pieces of advice and ongoing support whenever needed. They are: Dr Wendy Mee, Dr Susanne Davies, Prof. Klaus Baumann, and Dr Debra Houghton.

Editorial feedback from Marc Stratton, Joshua Well and Janani Thirumalai was incredibly meticulous, inspiring, thorough and unwavering. Also, special thanks to Samer Michael Ata for providing precise statistical calculations and alternative ways of interpreting the data.

Acknowledgement

Introduction

Re-examining social, cultural and religious cohesion in contemporary Western societies

Abe W. Ata

Introduction

This publication draws on several themes and priority issues within the framework of Euro-Asian, Australian and American international research. It will address several critical issues and discuss their implications for existing and future policy and practice in this area. Importantly, it seeks to identify the successes and failures of integrating cultural, linguistic and religious diversity; to examine an evolving national identity and social values; and to assess the way contemporary Western democracies view themselves and respond to the challenges of diversity from non-Western cultures with a special focus on the Muslim immigrant communities.

The ongoing debates in Western parliaments, their constituents in the workforce and in the streets are matters of immediate concern. Daily discussions, formal and otherwise, on social exclusion and inclusion, introduction of citizenship tests, on the relative degrees of social participation in secular Western life, on questions of self-identity, government constructions of groups and cultures in policy and on the phenomena of Westerners converting to Islam have produced an unprecedented momentum and concern on the radio and television talk-backs, making this collection both timely and of potential endurance. Indeed, how multicultural Western societies can manage to hold together, how deeply prejudices can run (over religious matters often cutting more deeply in anti-religious quarters than anywhere else), how undercurrent internal hostilities change the way people feel about their own nationhood and social stability and how governments often find themselves without the expertise to forge the best policies to cover socio-religious sensitivities will be perennial issues to address in the West for generations to come.

The current debate in the community presents a range of mixed feeling about diversity and national identity. These are readily aligned to three main camps:

The first believes that cultural diversity + migration is bad as it leads to cultural and religious disharmony, ethnic separatism, racial tension,

"colonising' the country, abdication of privilege, ghettoization, marginalization and taking away of jobs. Claiming that PC 'Political Correctness' stifles public debate, affiliates of this camp are accused *of saying
that Political Correctness is stifling public debate . . . .* and that *'racism is worse in other Western countries, as if talking about the issue is
unpatriotic'.*

(The Age, Tim Soutphommasane, 2018, p. 19)

The second one advocates that it is good, as it embraces cultural and religious diversity, tolerance, cultural richness and close relations with other
nations. On the one hand, they may acknowledge that integration of diverse
groups e.g. Muslims, can be problematic and controversial and struggle
with both Islamic radicalisation and the new wave of extreme-right populism, on the other.

The third camp holds that cultural, linguistic and historical differences
between the two groups are too great to make a complete reconciliation
achievable. Whoever contributes to a push for progress inadvertently triggers more disorientation and often mobilises the undecided and angry by the
demands for change. In the same vein, to be in denial about such differences
can result in having a higher and bigger wall.

Several thematic questions have been raised and duly addressed in the
chapters that follow. A few of them conducted comparative research to
answers the questions that are listed next; others devoted their study to
a particular country: Has the society focused too much on the skills and
achievement of newcomers than their character – an appropriate democratic
qualification?

- Is the characterisation that Western societies have changed beyond recognition related to minorities being a burden or a model of prosperity?
- Are cost and benefits to prioritising active and equitable interaction
between groups over passive tolerance a successful guide to a better
functioning, harmonious society?
- At what point is a country able to preserve its national sentiments and
identity while at the same time promoting diversity and multiculturalism?
- To what degree is a country able to respect the immigrants' cultures
and yet be allowed to practice them, even if their practices are differently perceived from the mainstream and are not harmful for the wider
society?
- It is argued that mutual respect and respect for diversity, learning about
other cultures in order to enhance critical thinking about one's own and
others are essential ingredients to achieve social cohesion and harmony.
It is equally argued by a smaller minority of the society that if this argument is buried, the world will be in the grip of a societal diversity crisis
similar to a biodiversity crisis. It was equally argued that one's moral
upbringing can fundamentally conflict with the ability to respect and

accept the practices of others commonly termed as 'offensive', be they sexual permissiveness and the like. Should community groups acknowledge such limitations and barriers as an existential reality without being accused of intolerance, or shall they be dismissed?

Culture values, integration and diversity

The majority of societies in this monograph have become increasingly diverse. America, Australia, Britain, Germany, Canada, Holland and others show elements of this in the food, religions, people, popular and scholarly forms, environment, school, media, parliament and the like. The extent of such diverse representation at some schools today in Australia, for example, amounts to 159 nationalities. Daily to weekly ethnic newspapers and languages taught at mainstream and community schools are over 74 and 46, respectively. These figures are on par with those from Canada and Britain.

A few of the complex and challenging issues of difference that need to be addressed 'beyond the goals of social cohesion and building unified societies' such as discrimination, social justice and equity will be presented in the body of this collection. Amongst the first writers to explore this issue Terry and Irving (2010) deserve a mention. Several of these are addressed in the body of this collection.

Although different issues, e.g. social cohesion, traditional dresses and curriculum materials, revealed themselves differently in immigrant-receiving cultures, public debate has variously contributed to a tightening of regulations surrounding citizenship tests, choices of immigrants and integration practices.

In recent months the debate surrounding citizenship tests in the United States, Canada, Australia and Germany has dominated the space in social and printed media. For example, justification behind the recent Australian government's proclamation that tougher English language tests are needed to improve integration was announced by Citizenship Minister Alan Tudge in the Parliament on March 7, 2019. He warned that many migrants are living in their own "cultural bubbles" and that Australia's successful multicultural society is at risk, with many migrants failing to integrate and develop proficient English skills. "It is also partly incumbent on the new migrants when they come here that they want to learn English and we want to raise the aspirations in relation to that", Mr Tudge said (Radio ABC News).

A subtle remark related to cultural diversity is that culture is a broad and comprehensive concept that includes all the ways of being, such as values and behavioral styles; family and social network, language and dialects; nonverbal communications; and perspectives, worldviews, and frames of reference (Banks, 2006; Gollnick and Chinn, 2009). These are arguably barriers that are not easy to climb over. It therefore stands to reason, as culture expresses the values, in-group subtleties of meaning, non-verbal communication that most of our behavior connecting with members across the cultural divide can be very confusing, making it difficult to communicate.

Of interest when the government's Citizenship Bill was introduced in 2017, a Senate committee report on the legislation found the language tests were too tough and would exclude many migrants who could contribute to Australian society.

Banks (2006) points out that cultures are always changing, clearly due to persisting changes within subgroups, the environment and participants and that cultural practices are shared within a specific group and may or may not be shared across groups. Muslim communities (as with Anglo-Saxon) may be seen as one group to an outside. But as subgroups they display different physiognomical, cultural, ethnic, political, traditional, value, language and linguistic elements.

The study of acculturation, and by implication integration, and social harmony or lack of it arguably dates back to the 1930s when sociologists and anthropologists coined the term and explicitly explored acculturation at the group level. They were followed in the 1960s by psychologists investigating acculturation at the individual level. Berry (2008) famously developed his influential fourfold model. He identified these as follows: 1. *integration,* which results in the maintenance of existing cultures and behaviours while people engage in day-to-day interaction within an evolving civic framework; 2. *separation,* which leads to avoidance of interaction with the dominant group in favour of holding on to one's psychological and cultural qualities; 3. *assimilation,* whereby minority groups, referred to as 'non-dominant', lose distinctive cultural and behavioural features and gradually absorb those of the dominant ones; and 4. *marginalisation* resulting in cultural and psychological loss, particularly among non-dominant populations, along with their exclusion from full and equitable participation in the larger society.

For all its elegance, however, Berry's model has come under criticism for its static approach. The field is now characterised by lively debate, with more complex, dynamic models competing for relevance. These newer models seek to answer such questions as how acculturation happens and why biculturalism is so hard to sustain. In recent years this debate has largely focused on Muslim migrants integration and social harmony in Western countries.

Schwartz (2006) made his mark in this field for introducing his cultural values hierarchy model as a lens to try to understand different national cultures. It is relevant to several subthemes in this monograph, particularly the newly government-introduced citizenship tests, such as in the United States, Canada and Australia. Some argue that the aim is to test an applicant's knowledge of the English language and comprehension of Australian moral principles, history and national and Indigenous symbols – the foundation of the commitment to freedom, law and order and principles of democracy. Others argue that the requirements of a citizenship test is a method to control immigration – a test for individualism versus family values, mateship, effort-based rewards and being laid back Laid back is a particularly stereotypical of Australians of being barefoot, lying in the sun on the beach with a stubby bear in their hand. How these values have been organised and categorised as distinctly Australian is a question that eludes an overwhelming consensus.

Schwarz draws a fault line between national groups, each with an opposite cultural orientation: autonomy and embeddedness. He points out that *the embedded* are typically those who avoid changes in tradition, conformity with group norms, minimal control over choice, less consideration for outsiders and monitoring of views and publications. In such hierarchical cultures, people accept their position in the social order, whether superior or inferior. They are nevertheless encouraged to show independence, ambition and self-control, both as individuals and in line with their own group goals. The other culture, the so-called *autonomy group*, aspires to inclusion and harmony. They consider everyone to be equal, adjust peacefully to incoming groups and the world at large, show concern to others' rights above self-improvement and accept their own place in the society.

In another study on universal similarities of values across culture, Schwartz and Bardi (2001) switched their research from those who exclusively focus on differences in values across cultures to study average value hierarchies reflecting universal similarities. The study reveals a great variation in what individuals perceive as important and less important with groups. However there was a greater agreement amongst a total of 56 cultures towards different types of values termed 'pan-cultural baseline of value priorities'. Those which were perceived persistently as very important include values such as self-direction and universalism, compared with tradition and power being least important. Those which ranked in the middle were conformity and security.

The questions that underpin this inquiry are: What makes a certain cultural value or values distinctly nation specific? Is it the degree that a specific culture deviates from Schwartz's pan-cultural baseline? What if the degree of deviation is shared by one or more? What politically criteria would be considered legitimate? Are we no longer able to associate being laid back, mateship, informality and easy-going with being Australian, in the same way that being opinionated, nationalistic, direct and nationalistic is associated with being American?

National Identity and Nationalism

National identity, usually defined in the collective, is understood to represent a sense of nationhood originally created by a group of actors with an agenda. It is aimed at projecting its members as a homogeneous group with a common sense of history, ethnic background and shared identity. These attributes ultimately serve as a political construct for nationalism – a sort unified sense of uniqueness that sets them apart from outsiders. The sense of collective identity is rarely static, but may change through interactions with diverse communities such as refugees and migrants through interactions and public debate and both traditional and social media.

The pace and scope of change differ between nations, as presented in this monograph. For example, the United States and German *Leitkultur* have become more suspicious of accommodating the identities of some groups such as the Dreamers and Muslims into the mainstream. The controversies arising from the question as to whether non-Christian identities and national identities of Western countries are compatible have not been fully resolved. At times it was argued that recent Islamic migrants to Western nations face the dilemma of finding their authentic voice in popular Western culture, balanced against their fears of cultural assimilation and loss of identity.

Such a divided and dually suspicious society continues to struggle with being either actively resistant to change or contentedly blind to it. The values nurturing identities, how they are organised in a hierarchy and if they can be incontrovertibly and accurately assessed by mainstream and marginalised groups are issues that still draw layers of interpretations by social scientists.

Several migrant communities, such as Muslims, as a group have had less success compared to other religious or ethnic minorities, like Jews or African Americans, in opening "a window on the multidimensionality of what can be called cultural ecology" (Mowlana, 1996, p. 178). They seek to know how it is possible to move toward the center of Western culture without compromising deeply held religious beliefs and traditions. In the same vein, a sizable proportion of such groups find much in the American and European values and practices that conflict with their own. A few of these readily point to an uncompromising status quo of a clash of civilizations, an idea originally put forward by Samuel Huntington (1993). The idea that cultures are so separate from each other, whether precipitated by voluntary isolation or otherwise at that time, no longer holds much merit nowadays. Advocates of Huntington's thesis often cite religion (or culture) as the main agent that creates such divisions. Islam–West relations reached a new turning point in 2001 with the bombings of the Twin Towers of the World Trade Center in New York and the Pentagon in Washington, DC, and subsequent terrorist attacks in different countries of the West. Islam has been depicted as a global threat on three levels: political, civilizational and demographic. The global 'War on Terror' has reinforced and fuelled an irrational fear of the religion of Islam and its adherents. Europeans fear rising waves of refugees will mean fundamentally two things: more terrorism and fewer jobs.

Based on this and the negative portrayal of Islam and the threatening Muslim 'other' in the Western media, many in the West have come to understand Islam as a religion that inspires terrorism and Muslims as terrorists who are bent on destroying the West in whichever way possible. Many countries of the West such as the United States, United Kingdom, France, Germany and Australia have developed a suite of tough policies, laws and security measures, including targeting Muslims for discriminatory investigation and treatment under their securitisation regimes.

The forces of economic, political or environmental powers in creating perceived divisions are often overlooked or suppressed. For this reason, I choose 'clash of sensibilities' as a more preferred term. This would more expressly shed more light on findings in the two national surveys that were conducted by the editor (chapter 14 and 15).

Ethnocentric attitudes are on the rise in Europe and elsewhere, with varying degree of intensity. It is argued that both self-assertive attitudes and those directed at 'others' revived the crisis of 'Euro-scepticism'. No longer is the idea of social integration a fait accompli. The birth of a collective identity involving several religions, languages and ethnicities was never conceived before. There are more people harbouring ethnocentric attitudes arguably in several major European countries than there were several years ago. Marshall (1981), who founded the idea of European civic identity, found support that full social integration requires certain conditions to be fulfilled (Gerhards and Lengfeld, 2015). For the host society to be fully integrated, the social and electoral rights of diverse communities should be supported in principle and in social interactions. Viewed from a different angle, citizens of the EU should respect the right of the incoming groups in their 'day-to-day' behaviour.

The recent data obtained by the Pew Research Center (2008), however, have revealed that the numbers of EU citizens with unfavourable opinions of both Jews and Muslims have been on the rise, with the latter attracting more negative attitudes. Opinions about Muslims in almost all of Western European countries are considerably more negative than are views towards Jews. Fully half of Spanish (52%) and German respondents (50%) rate Muslims unfavourably. Opinions about Muslims are somewhat less negative in Poland (46%) and considerably less negative in France (38%). About one in four in Britain and the United States (23% each) also voice unfavourable views towards Muslims. Overall, there is a clear relationship between anti-Jewish and anti-Muslim attitudes: publics that view Jews unfavourably also tend to see Muslims in a negative light.

A more recent study by Wike, Stokes, and Simmons (2016) at the Pew Research Center examined the link between a strong national identity and attitudes to 'others'. In Greece, for example, 81% of people who place themselves on the right of the ideological scale have a negative opinion of Muslims, while 50% of people on the left say the same. There are also double-digit right–left divides in Germany (30 points), Italy (29 points), the Netherlands (25 points), Sweden (21 points), Spain (19 points), France (18 points) and the UK (15 points).

Negative attitudes toward Christians in Europe are less common than negative ratings of Muslims or Jews. And views about Christians have remained largely stable in recent years, although anti-Christian sentiments have been on the rise in Spain – about one in four Spaniards (24%) now rate Christians negatively, up from 10% in 2005. Similarly, in France 17% now hold an unfavourable view towards Christians, compared with 9% in

2004. Little data are available about attitudes towards Muslim societies at large than towards Christian and other minority citizens residing in Muslim countries.

A notable parallel between anti-Muslim and anti-Jewish opinion in Western Europe is that both sentiments are most prevalent among the same groups of people. Older people and those with less education are more anti-Semitic and anti-Muslim than are younger people or those with more education. Looking at combined data from France, Germany and Spain – the three Western European countries where unfavourable opinions of Jews are most common – people ages 50 and older express more negative views of both Jews and Muslims than do those younger than 50. Similarly, Europeans who have not attended college are consistently more likely than those who have not to hold unfavourable opinions of both groups.

Negative attitudes toward Christians have been on the rise in a few countries over the last several years, most dramatically in Turkey. The trend in Turkish opinions about Christians has been very similar to the trend regarding Jews. In 2004, about half (52%) of Turks gave Christians an unfavourable rating; today roughly three in four (74%) hold this view.

The trend in negative views toward Muslims in Europe has occurred over a longer period of time than growing anti-Jewish sentiments. Most of the upswing took place between 2004 and 2006, and there has even been a slight decrease in some countries since 2006.

The newly emerged trends are just beginning to project to advance fresh stories about European, Australian, Canadian and, to a lesser extent, American identities, not from the mainstream optic vision, but from the margin. The recent migrants, Chinese, Vietnamese and Muslims alike, no longer feel comfortable or self-conscious about the mainstream Anglo assumptions of what forms national identity. The judgment from the host societies may have steadfastly kept migrants on the margins for decades and stood in the way of full integration. The recent change is interpreting integration as a two-way formula; that is self-identification and being part of the mainstream is an equally legitimate fulfilment of a natural self-acceptance.

The scope of this project is thus deliberately broad, as it is intended to widen the frame of reference and analysis from potential contributors. I believe the subject of this project will stay with us for a long time. One of the premises behind this work is that the cultural, religious and historical differences between the two main national-cultural groups: the mainstream Western cultures and diverse minority/migrant communities, are too great to make a complete reconciliation achievable. Likewise, to be in denial about them can result in having a higher and bigger wall.

Given the alternatives, a creative dialogue must continue, acknowledging that such concerns are often driven by fear and self-marginalization alike. More people nowadays realise that 'clash of cultures' is a reality that needs to be addressed, regardless of what side of the moral fence each of us sits on.

The essays sought for this book will look behind those walls and explore the issues challenging both minorities (particularly Muslims) living in the

West and key Western societies – Americans, Australians and Europeans. We intend to explore these tensions, challenges and complexities in this book. In particular, we are interested in exploring these issues empirically across a varied platform of settings – communities, schools and universities, the media, government and private institutions – in both English-speaking and non-English-speaking contexts.

The book will contain a combination of primary and secondary research papers from 16 contributors worldwide. These contributors, who come from diverse backgrounds and regions, offer insights into significant developments in the relationships and perceptions between mainstream Western host societies and immigrant communities. Three contributors to this monograph will pointedly address crucial questions faced by these two groups in Australia, and a larger number of them will provide an analysis of the same in North America, parts of Asia and Europe

Why the special focus on Muslims? Placing the analysis into a context

Muslims have usually been considered the top suspects for terrorism in the Western world. An example of this would be the Oklahoma City bombing on April 19, 1995. Before investigators discovered that Timothy McVeigh and Terry Nichols were responsible for the attack, it was initially believed that the attack was organised by a group of Muslim terrorists. This information was repeated on several national television networks.

Drawing a similarity with several Western countries under investigation in this monograph, research indicates that Australian Muslims have surpassed Asians as one of Australia's most marginalised religious and ethnic groups. ABC Radio National's *The World Today* program (February 19, 2003) revealed that more than any other cultural or ethnic group, Muslims and people from the Middle East are thought to be unable to fit into Australia, with more than 50% of Australians preferring their relatives did not marry into a Muslim family, and that Australia was weakened because they were 'sticking to their old ways'.

One of Australia's most-read columnists, Andrew Bolt, wrote in an article "Another Win for Hypocrisy":

> There are enough challenges with Muslim immigration – high welfarism, the risk of terrorism, imprisonment rates in Victoria and NSW three times the average – without inventing fake scares. No, you {Senator Anning) were wrong to claim Melbourne's Sudanese gangs are Muslim. Most come from Christian South Sudan. And you were outrageous to claim that for every 1000 Muslims brought into Australia, there are '50 that want to kill us'.
>
> (The Heraldsun Aug 16, 2018, p. 13)

Without doubt this is an oversimplification of diverse interpretations of interfaith relations and cultural harmony – one that makes it difficult for an outsider to come up with a legitimate single truth. It is important to consider the patterns of cross-cultural differences, as one becomes confused and reactive when communicating with participants in the field. This is a challenge in a society like Australia that contains a multitude of cultures with diverse points of view. In communicating with participants from several cultures, the responses may reflect different worldviews in the way they are affected by outside events. For example, one participant rescheduled an interview several times, each time insisting that I meet at another convenient time. When I insisted that he commit himself in earnest, he grumbled, 'Inshallah' – God willing. Finally, he apologised and said that he had no time. Some who agreed to the interview often increased the volume of their conversation as a sign that a loud voice makes a sound argument.

One should pause at this crossing to consider that much of the Western multi-layered culture is complex and variously patterned. It includes Anglo, Spanish, Germanic and Franco nations that escape holding the Anglo-based stereotypes reserved for Muslims. Muslims living in the West, according to Pew's Global Attitudes (2006), escape the negative stereotypes of fanaticism and violence that are typical of their compatriots in their country of origin. In the five main Western nations (the United States, the UK, Germany, France and Spain), more than 60% thought relations between Muslims and Westerners were, in general, bad.

A number of these essays explore the need for new content and procedures in creating an 'anti-bias' curriculum and discusses ways to create an anti-bias environment, learn about differences, teach about differences and resist stereotyping students. However, the reader is reminded that the phrase 'non-Muslim Australians' and other Westerners is not restricted to Christians, even though the book deals overwhelmingly with predominately Western Christian and Muslim communities. The first chapter, 'Of states, commonwealths and "the clash of civilisations"', is about racial tensions between immigrant Muslims and white Australia. It presents the grievances and general perspectives of the Muslim community and the Australian Christian community towards each other. It recognises that the wide cultural and historical differences between the two communities are too wide to reconcile, but given the alternatives, a creative dialogue must continue. Ultimately, each community must ask: How are we going to portray a better image of the other community?

In what way has this publication contributed more to current debate perspectives, assumptions and reactions?

This publication combines theoretical contributions, a multidisciplinary approach, new research perspectives, various methods of analysis and a variety of topics that refer to a large scale of case studies. As such it reflects a good balance of the international scientific literature due to the skills and knowledge of the editors and contributors. It provides a much needed and meaningful plarform to elevate the dialectic, shift the goal post and widen the reference frame.

The themes analyzed are varied. They cover a sufficiently wide range of timely "live wired" questions of religious and social diversity in contemporary societies: from the educational de-radicalization to terrorism, the media to ghettoisation and exclusion, from Islamophobia to Christianophobia and others.

The diverse complex and sensitive topics covered in this work give it an edge of intimacy and topicality that are not commonly broached. The varied perspectives, disciplines and themes that are reflected in these chapters make it differenct from other publications and add strength to its multi-layered perspectives. Several contributors on multicultural issues have looked beyond the wall to sensitive, intimate and irritating, occasionally 'politically incorrect' and often tabooed concepts, that evoke fears and anxieties amongst all of us. Being the editor of this manuscript, I have realised my biases and prejudices towards ethnic, religious minorities are not different form theirs. The list of topics in this manuscript is amazingly similar and includes fears of being misunderstood, being monitored and judjed by government agencies, hurting others unintentionally, miscommunication and exposing awkward hang-ups and dislikes.

That said, presenting assorted topics can be a challenge in securing an exhaustive in-depth analysis of any knowledge domain. The assumptions for example, about the implicit acceptance of Huntington's theory of civilizations by other contributors is far and wide. One reviewer noted that several authors talk of experiences of radizalization of young Muslims (an important theme in the book) but will they explore Oliver Roy's suggestion that youth radicalization as such is not uncommon and that we might actually be better off talking of its *islamization*? he asks.

Another challenging point raised by this editor and contributor in an earlier publication noted these words:

> "*the complexity of covering all ethnic Muslim communities and associated variables, dynamics and reactions by various non-Muslims, including secular communities, is one project makes it impossible to give it complete justice*".
>
> (Ata and Ali, 2018, p.6)

The discussion of the emergance of neo-nationalist and anti -immigration movements is only partly addressed in this book. The emerging new complex social and political realities across various European societies was not the focus of this project, and may be addressed in a subsequent publication.

This introduction is particularly purposed to help the reader grasp how the different thematic areas touched by the authors converge around a single focus. The collection of essays focuses on several themes, including integration, de-radicalisation, cultural pluralism, the media, religious education, civil engagement, interfaith and intercultural dialogue, Islamophobia and Christianophobia, Muslim–secular hybridised identities, tolerance and factionalism, apologists and the faithful and challenges and future directions. They shed a new light on the interactive dynamics between policy processes, the emerging movements and associations and the political entrepreneurship within the overarching frame of Western self-identity and citizenship. The countries chosen for analysis are Canada, Australia, Germany, France, Sweden, Britain, the United States and the Netherlands.

Out of the findings a complex picture emerges – a kind of multi-layered tapestry of the way migrants and nationals alike project attitudes towards cultural diversity, national values, cultural fragmentation and social cohesion in the Western world.

This publication is different from others in several areas:

First, diverse communities and minorities are not defined solely by the province of their faith, but as an emerging group with dual identities – one which is soul searching, self-critical, reflective, continuously evolving and redefined.

Second, given the complexity of the problem, particularly the underlying tensions between the two communities – diverse migrants (including Muslims – citizens or otherwise) and Westerners – it is unsurprising that "approaches to counter-radicalisation vary considerably from country to country" (Rabasa and Benard, 2014, p. 169). For instance, France and the UK differ in their respective policies (Foley, 2013). We recognise that their policies are well researched, and if differences (which in any case were never large) remain between them and Australia, it would not be cost-effective for us to attempt to settle the matter. Instead, we will be constrained by Australian policy settings at state and federal levels.

Although our proposed research will benefit from, and be influenced by, our knowledge of the national policies of several countries, it will be strictly limited to areas over which the governments have direct control. Authorities may differ on the nature, causes and consequences of violent extremism and on their implications for policy, but there remains much common ground, particularly on why radicalisation happens and who is most at risk. As *Living Safe Together: Understanding the Radicalisation Process* states: "there are some common elements in the experiences of most people who have become radicalised in Australia, regardless of their beliefs or motivations". Our proposed research is based on the core consensus. This avoids unnecessary controversy that might prejudice the utility of our conclusions.

Third, a major difference posits the premise that Westerners who are more knowledgeable about Muslims (and by implication the broader diverse communities) would express more favourable opinions of them and that through knowledge, greater levels of awareness come from equal-status interaction between the learner and individuals of Muslim backgrounds. It is thus argued that scale of our knowledge, fashionable or well worn, and negative attitudes are interrelated.

This timely volume will address these issues and will explore the thesis that significant differences between the two religions, Christianity and Islam, are not to be side-stepped. This could lead to a false sense of security. Differences in interpretation of social values and ways of life, individual accountability, consensual decision-making and attitudes towards implementing moral imperatives do exist, subsequently leading to a nuanced analysis. It is feasible that we should be able to acknowledge them, respect them and address them without necessarily aiming for compromise. Dialogue does not always mean compromise. These different approaches have concrete implications to these communities who are living together in a shared place, i.e. the capacity of accommodating many cultural and religious expressions – within a single language, law and polity – as multiculturalism.

This monograph is divided into four thematic sections, as follows:

Part 1: Social harmony, nationalism, and integration unfolds several areas of political and social areas under investigation. Jupp (Chapter 2) launches into the evolution of the idea of nationalism citizenship and integration of diversity. He notes that many societies today experience multi-cultural forces within them which may or may not contribute to their effective stability. The most frequently studied elements are differing religions, races, languages and customs. He notes that some countries like Australia, the UK and the United States have all at various times consciously introduced or excluded newcomers through legal and administrative measures. They have also developed public policies for 'assimilating' or 'integrating' newcomers from previously 'alien' backgrounds. Thus societies become constructed from a variety of peoples, languages and beliefs which are all expected to conform to already established traditions. Melleuish (Chapter 1) anchors his analysis to the emergence of the states, commonwealths and the 'clash of civilisations'. He argues that the idea of the 'clash of civilisations' assumes that civilisations are necessarily connected with the political entities within which they are placed and therefore not only have a political dimension but can also be utilised for purposes of state power. Commonwealths have long existed in history, but the problem is that they have difficulties surviving without the support of state structures which possess the violent capabilities to protect them. Likewise, the modern nation-state was founded on the desire to integrate political and cultural power. The modern Western state sought to homogenise its citizens into a single cultural entity, but this put it at odds with the various commonwealths that cross the border of the state, such as the community of learning. Then, as a consequence of immigration, it invented the idea of multi-culturalism. The modern liberal imagination, following Kant, dreams of humanity living in one vast commonwealth, but what we have really is a messy reality in which the alliance of political power and culture has opened up the possibility not of 'perpetual peace' but perpetual violence. Chisari (Chapter 3) takes a focused approach on national values, declaring that they are not fixed, but are fluid and changing. She traces the return of Australian values in the Australian citizenship test during recent years – a set of core civic principles that are believed to be unique to Australian identity. The test was designed to teach prospective citizens about the Australian way of life and focused on candidates learning about Australia's culture and history, its political system and the rights and responsibilities of Australian citizenship. It was believed that gaining these new orders of knowledge would equip migrants with the ability to integrate and, as a result, ensure that social cohesion is maintained in Australian society. In this way, Australian governments continue to promote Australian values in order to demonstrate their commitment to securing national security, as well as to reassure the mainstream population that the Australian way of life will prevail in these uncertain times. In Chapter 4 Miles-Novello and Anderson argue how the exposure to Muslims in media and support for public policies is harming Muslims in the United States. In recent years, most news and entertainment media portrayals of Muslims in U.S. media have been negative, focusing primarily on Muslims as terrorists or as citizens of anti-U.S. countries with mostly Muslim populations. This chapter explores the effects that such portrayals have on anti-Muslim thoughts, feelings and behaviours and on the underlying psychological processes. Such portrayals increase anti-Muslim hostility, beliefs, stereotypes and actions, including support for public policies that involve bombing primarily Muslim countries and that involve curtailing common civil rights of Muslim American citizens. Conversely, positive news stories and personal contact with Muslims lead to reductions in anti-Muslim beliefs, feelings and harmful action tendencies.

Part II: Education, citizenship, and cultural diversity comprises diverse areas of critical analysis. Danishpur (Chapter 5) examines our gendered identity and its role in shaping perceptions about social groups and the inequities that trouble our nation, their root causes and potential solutions. We are reminded at the outset that human experience has always been a gender-based story of diversity and evolving identity – from the roots planted many generations ago by Native Americans, immigrants and enslaved peoples to the fresh traditions brought by those arriving from all over the world. In order to have a solid understanding of our gendered identity and the history of our immigration and diversity, we must have an awareness of our enmeshed histories. Together these provide a vision of how to examine our experiences fairly and fully within any beat. The analysis is extended by Miller and Amorsen in Chapter 7. This chapter examines intersections, opportunities and implications for social justice in relation to the three cross-curriculum priority areas in the Australian Curriculum for Foundation – Year 6, identified as Aboriginal and Torres Strait Islander histories and cultures, as Australia and Australia's engagement with Asia and as sustainability. The three cross-curriculum priorities are designed to inform a "relevant, contemporary and engaging curriculum" that builds on the educational goals of the Melbourne Declaration on Educational Goals for Young Australians (Australian Curriculum, Assessment and Reporting Authority [ACARA], 2016). Underpinned by two goals, the Melbourne Declaration values the role of education in building a democratic, equitable and just society. How the social citizenship rights integral to being complete citizens have gradually diminished is a subject that Sealey addresses in focusing on Britishness and British values (Chapter 8). It argues that the net migration resulting in a 54% increase in post–World War II Britain, a growth that is higher than the EU average, triggered enormous policy changes. The two key foci of these policies have been reducing net migration and limiting entitlement to benefits for migrants vis-à-vis benefit tourism. The latter is the main focus of this analysis: how these policy changes are underpinned by a retreat from multi-culturalism towards assimilation, consequences of the diminution of social citizenship rights integral to being complete citizens, the depth of their impact on the rights of new migrants and its limitation on the citizenship rights of the wider non-migrant population.

Another main theme this part addresses relates to issues and implications of cultural diversity, cosmopolitan citizenship and education for Australia. Jakubowicz (Chapter 6) directs his attention to education which, he points out, has been at the centre of debates and struggles over the meaning and direction of Australia's ideologies and practices of nationalism. Two fundamental elements, cosmopolitanism and nationalism, offer competing visions and programmes for education in terms of curriculum, learning processes or performance outcomes. This chapter traces the major axes of tension in Australian education between religious and secular, private and state and developmental and functional. It takes a number of key events that reveal how the contradictions, and challenges, in Australian history are being expressed in the real worlds of educational discourse, such as the education ministers' statements on diversity, the place of language education, the struggle over religious definitions of the good life and the online attacks on an Indigenous poet in the aftermath of a senior high school exam that contained one of her poems. Sunier (Chapter 9) builds on the themes outlined previously, stressing that diversity has not only risen to academic prominence but has also become an inherent part of policy reports on a wide range of issues, especially as demonstrated in the Netherlands.

Part III: Civil liberties, multiculturalism and marginalisation outlines the failures, achievements and implications of integrating minorities in select countries such as Canada, the United States, Australia, Germany, Britain and Sweden. A comparison of the trends, approaches and patterns of the growing reality of multiculturalism between Canada and Australia is made by Ozdowski (Chapter 11). This chapter describes its social and political origins, as well as major policy and programme implementation shifts over the previous decades, outlining references to its aims, successes and challenges to national identity. Also discussed are key achievements of Australian multi-culturalism and the emerging challenges resulting from globalisation, changing immigration patterns and redefinition of the Australian concepts of 'fair go' and democracy.

The difficulties and challenges encountered by Germany, and Europe at large, as a result of recent arrivals of sudden waves of refuges and asylum seekers are examined by Grosu- Rădulescu (Chapter 10). This chapter provides a contextual background of the complexities and contradictions related to government policies and community attitudes to a newly emerged melting pot. A cutting-edge reference to Angela Merkel, the German chancellor, announcing that multi-culturalism is "a sham" set the tone for further nuanced meanings to the waves of immigration that had taken the whole of Europe by surprise. Other themes under examination include the genesis *of* multi-culturalism in Europe: how it has acquired nuanced meanings and interpretation in past few decades. To achieve this, Grosu-Rădulescu traces a brief history of the multi-culturalist project and its success or limits in Canada and reviews the European efforts to implement multi-culturalist ideals on a national level and within the broader pluricultural EU policies. The concept of transculturalism or cultural diversity (a melting of cultural markers) is also examined and compared to multi-culturalism (a gathering of multiple and distinct contributions to the mainstream culture).

Moulettes positions her work (Chapter 17) in the realm of immigration, and in particular the discourse of labour market integration. It takes its point of departure in Swedish labour market policy and politicians concerned with how to come to terms with unemployment and how to integrate immigrants into the labour market. With an overall aim to discuss the current labour market policy and how it contributes to transforming unemployed immigrants into commodities, the analysis draws on ideas from critical theory. In doing so it brings to the surface epistemological misinterpretations and power asymmetries between labour market intermediaries and unemployed immigrants.

Part IV: Western values, Muslim migrants and compatibility of identity covers several areas of investigation. Millns and Dunstin (Chapter 13) undertook to reinterpret citizenship and identity in the United Kingdom and Europe, following Brexit, in mid-2016 when the people of the United Kingdom voted in a referendum narrowly in favour of leaving the European Union. This chapter examines the extent to which people living in the United Kingdom risk being marginalised or discriminated against on the basis of their identity – including their gender, religion, ethnicity and sexual orientation. The contribution critically evaluates the UK's changing 'diversity' agenda since the 1960s – through tolerance, multi-culturalism, cohesion and now integration and discusses how this path has been similar or distinct from other EU member states, as well as the impact of the changing agenda on minorities, their beliefs and values.

In Chapter 14 Ata reports on the sense of compatibility of dual Muslim and Australian identities as perceived by mainstream Australian students. The results are based on a large-scale national survey of attitudes of senior secondary students in private and government schools towards Islam and Muslims. Widespread negative stereotypes and the relatively new presence of the Muslim community in Australia tend to interfere with reconciling the Muslim and 'Australian' identities. Variation in responses between boys and girls in terms of religious or non-religious affiliates also revealed a high level of significance. The findings show Australian non-Muslim students agree that acceptance of Muslims does not come easily in Australia, nor does the school emerge as a site for change.

In another national survey (Chapter 15) Ata assesses how compatible Muslim students perceive their dual Islamic and 'Australian' identities. The results of this five-year-long investigation are based on a field research questionnaire involving 430 students in 10 Muslim high schools. A major finding revealed that a percentage of female participants (57%) recognised that the two identities were harmonious. This was slightly higher than male students (43%). Combined, the two groups, however (93%), declared themselves to be first and foremost Muslim. The findings also reflect a wide spectrum of nuanced responses with room for further analysis regarding their ultimate adjustment, wellbeing and ease of living in both cultures. Crucially, the survey found that students were equally divided on statements related to the degree to which Muslim students feel integrated in various aspects of the host society in which they have grown.

Postelnicescu (Chapter 16) examines the European Commission's policy on immigration and asylum and the way Germany and France address the issues of integration, tensions, sources of conflict, justice and identity within an emerging diverse society. Comparative remarks are drawn out between these two societies as appropriate. Two main points are specifically addressed within its pages: whether the term 'integration', mandatory or otherwise, infringes on any fundamental rights embraced in these two countries and the legitimacy of the host states to mandate rules of the immigrants' self-identity and perpetuation of their cultural and ethical core values.

Ali (Chapter 12) broadens the analysis that was explored in the two previous chapters. He addresses the issue of compatibility of Islamic and Western Core Values. He observes that since the events of 9/11 the perception of Islam as the "internal other" and the "external enemy" has lent further weight to the debate that Islam and the West are incompatible. He argues that viewing Islam and the West as a dialectical paradigm is a politically expedient and socially false construct. Several fundamental values such as justice and compassion are shared by both cultures; albeit differences that are crucial to the preservation of cultural coexistence.

Abdelkader devoted his discussion (Chapter 12) to the dynamics of American core values, Islamophobia, Civil Liberties and Human Rights. He traces the American national values, beliefs and principles to the U.S. Constitution, Bill of Rights and Declaration of Independence. Pursuant to such values, Americans prize personal, political and economic freedoms; rule of law; achievement and success; equality and privacy; and a strong work ethic. In tandem with these core values, fundamental American beliefs elevate the individual's right to attain happiness, so long as doing so does not infringe upon the liberties of others. In a nation of immigrants in which so many strive to realize the American dream, this right inheres to all in a pluralistic society, irrespective of how they look or what they believe. To be sure, national divisions, anxieties and tensions surrounding race and religion have repeatedly tested the country's principles and influenced her trajectory throughout the course of history – with less-than-optimal results at times. The successes of the American experiment in liberty are also addressed through the lens of legal and policy developments affecting its minority Muslim community.

References

Ata, AW (2009) *Us and Them: Muslim-Christian Relations and Cultural Harmony in Australia.* Brisbane: Australian Academic Press.

Ata, AW (2014) *Education Integration Challenges: The Case of Australian Muslims.* Melbourne: David Lovell Publications.

Australian Curriculum, Assessment and Reporting Authority (ACARA). 2016. National Education Evidence Base Inquiry. Sydney.

Banks, J (2006) Researching Race, Culture, and Difference: Epistemological Challenges and Possibilities. In *Handbook of Complementary Methods in Education Research.* ISBN: 9780805859324.

Berry, J.W. 2008. Globalisation and Acculturation. International Journal of Intercultural Relations 32 (4) 328–336.

Bolt, A (Aug 16, 2018) Another Win for Hypocrisy. *The Heraldsun*, p. 13.

Foley, F (2013) *Countering Terrorism in Britain and France: Institutions, Norms and the Shadow of the Past.* Cambridge: Cambridge University Press.

Gerhards, L and Lengfeld, H (2015) *Citizenship and Social Integration in the European Union.* London: Routledge, Taylor and Francis.

Gollnick, D and Chinn, P (2009) *Multicultural Education in a Pluralistic Society.* Pearson. ISBN-13: 9780133007947.

Huntington, S (1993) The Clash of Civilizations? *Foreign Affairs*, 72:3, pp. 92–49.

Marshall, TH (1981) *The Right to Welfare and Other Essays.* London: Heinemann Educational Books.

Moore, J (2010) Shattering Stereotypes: A Lesson Plan for Improving Student Attitudes and Behaviour Toward Minority Groups. *The Social Studies*, 97:1, pp. 35–39. doi:10.3200/TSSS.97.1.35-39

Mowlana, H (1996) *Global Communication in Transition: The End of Diversity?* Sage Publication. ISBN: 9781483327518.

Pew Research Center. 2006. *Global Attitudes and Trends.* https://www.pewresearch.org/global/author/noauthor/page/46/

Pew Research Center. 2008. *Unfavorable Views of Jews and Muslims on the Increase in Europe.* www.pewglobal.org/files/pdf/262.pdf (Accessed: 2 August 2017).

Rabasa, A and Benard, C (2014) *Eurojihad: Patterns of Islamist Radicalization and Terrorism in Europe.* London: Cambridge University Press.

Schwartz, S (2006) Theory of Cultural Value Orientations: Explication and Applications. *Comparative Sociology*, 5:2–3, pp. 137–180.

Schwartz, S and Bardi, A (2001) Value Hierarchies Across Cultures Taking a Similarities Perspective. *Journal of Cross Cultural Psychology*, 32:3, pp. 286–290.

Soutphommasane, T (Aug 6, 2018) Challenging Racism Is Patriotic. *The Age*, p. 19.

Terry, N and Irving, M (2010) Cultural and Linguistic Diversity: Issues in Education. *Special Education for All Teachers*, 5, pp. 109–132.

Wike, R, Stokes, B and Simmons, K (July 11, 2016) *Negative Views of Minorities, Refugees Common in EU.* Global Attitudes & Trends, Pew Research Center.

Part I

Social harmony, nationalism, and integration

Introductory remarks

Abe W. Ata

The essays in this section provide a conceptual framework and relevant views on the rise of the clash of civilisations, better phrased as a clash of cultural perspectives. They also provide an overview of the subject of Anglosphere and an extended discussion of the theoretical literature on media influence. Debates on Australian values are addressed in detail, and the pertinent links with evolving notions of citizenship are established as a case in point.

Melleuish (Chapter 1) anchors his analysis to the emergence of the states, commonwealths and the 'clash of civilisations'. He argues that the idea of the 'clash of civilisations' assumes that civilisations are necessarily connected with the political entities within which they are placed and therefore not only have a political dimension but can also be utilised for purposes of state power. Commonwealths have long existed in history, but the problem is that they have problems surviving without the support of state structures which possess the violent capabilities to protect them. Likewise, the modern nation-state was founded on the desire to integrate political and cultural power. The modern Western state sought to homogenise its citizens in a single cultural entity, but this put it at odds with the various commonwealths which cross the border of the state, such as the community of learning. Then, as a consequence of immigration, it invented the idea of multiculturalism. The modern liberal imagination, following Kant, dreams of humanity living in one vast commonwealth, but what we have really is a messy reality in which the alliance of political power and culture has opened up the possibility not of 'perpetual peace', but perpetual violence. Jupp (Chapter 2) launches into the evolution of the idea of national citizenship and integration of diversity. He notes that many societies today experience multicultural forces within them which may, or may not, contribute to their effective stability. The most frequently studied elements are differing religions, races, languages and customs. He notes that some countries like Australia, the UK and the United States have all at various times consciously introduced or excluded newcomers through legal and administrative meas-ures. They have also developed public policies for 'assimilating' or 'integrat-ing' newcomers from previously 'alien' backgrounds. Thus societies become constructed from a variety of peoples, languages and beliefs which are all expected to conform to already established traditions. Chisari (Chapter 3) takes a focused approach to national values, declaring that they are not fixed but are fluid and changing. She traces the return of Australian values in the Australian citizenship test during recent years – a set of core civic principles that are believed to be unique to Australian identity. The test was designed to teach prospective citizens about the Australian way of life and focused on candidates learning about Australia's culture and history, its political system and the rights and responsibilities of Australian citizenship. It was believed that gaining these new orders of knowledge would equip migrants with the ability to integrate and, as a result, ensure that social cohesion is maintained in Australian society. In this way, Australian govern-ments continue to promote Australian values in order to demonstrate their commitment to securing national security, as well as to reassure the main-stream population that the Australian way of life will prevail in these uncer-tain times. In Chapter 4 Miles-Novello and Anderson argue how exposure to Muslims in media and support for public policies is harming Muslims in the United States. In recent years, most news and entertainment media portrayals of Muslims in U.S. media have been negative, focusing primarily on Muslims as terrorists or as citizens of anti-U.S. countries with mostly Muslim populations. This chapter explores the effects that such portrayals have on anti-Muslim thoughts, feelings and behaviours and on the underly-ing psychological processes. Such portrayals increase anti-Muslim hostility, beliefs, stereotypes and actions, including support for public policies that involve bombing primarily Muslim countries and that involve curtailing the common civil rights of Muslim American citizens. Conversely, positive news stories and personal contact with Muslims lead to reductions in anti-Muslim beliefs, feelings and harmful action tendencies.

1   Of states, commonwealths and the 'clash of civilisations'

Greg Melleuish

The modern Western state sought to homogenise its citizens in a single cultural entity, but this put it at odds with the various commonwealths which cross the border of the state, such as the community of learning. Then, as a consequence of immigration, it invented the idea of multiculturalism. The modern liberal imagination, following Kant, dreams of humanity living in one vast commonwealth, but what we have really is a messy reality in which the alliance of political power and culture has opened up the possibility not of 'perpetual peace' but perpetual violence.

The idea of a 'clash of civilisations' has been a common trope since it was first enunciated by Samuel Huntington (1997). It postulates that the key reason for conflict between countries are civilisational differences, and that the foundation of those differences is religion. Peoples clash because of ideas, values, practices and customs. Now, there can be no doubt that people can, and do, murder and oppress other people in the name of ideas, but that they should do so is really something of a puzzle. In less complex societies it was generally the case that conflict, often very bloody and violent and murderous, was generated by such things as the stealing of women and cattle (Keeley 1996). The origins of human warfare lie much more in the competition for resources rather than in the competition of ideas.

This raises the very real issue of how and why ideas and beliefs came to play such a role in human conflict. If one reads accounts of wars in the ancient world, the clash of ideas seems far less important than other matters. Sometimes the Greek-Persian wars are portrayed as a clash of civilisations, but that depiction owes more to modern America than to the ancient world and to a view that the Greeks belonged to the 'West' and the Persians to the 'East'.

One of the few occasions in which those wars were understood in terms of ideas is in Thucydides's (1996) account of the Peloponnesian War in which the war is described in terms of the conflict of the adherents of democracy led by Athens and those of oligarchy led by Sparta. For the Spartans democracy is dangerous because it unleashes innovation, thereby threatening traditional Hellenic values.

It is difficult to see the rise of the Roman Empire as a clash of civilisations, even in the case of the Carthaginian Wars, especially as Rome came to conquer Greece, which the Romans appreciated possessed a civilisation superior to their own and attempted to appropriate what they saw as its superior qualities. The one case in the Roman world which might be construed as a 'clash of civilisations' based on ideas and values occurred in Judea, where the Jewish uprisings can be understood in terms of cultural difference (Goodman 2017).

The Romans most certainly persecuted the early Christians, primarily because they believed them to be subversive of the Roman order, failing, as they did, to offer sacrifices to the emperor. Real persecution does not appear to have become widespread and systematic until the mid-third century when the empire was in the throes of crisis and Christianity was growing accordingly (Moss 2013). It would be difficult to see the relationship between the traditional Romans and the Christians as a 'clash of civilisations', despite some anti-Roman rhetoric on the Christian side.

Rather, it was the development of heresy, and the violent means adopted to extirpate it, which seem to prefigure later 'clashes of civilisation'. This occurred because of the alliance which grew up between religion and state power in the wake of Constantine's conversion to Christianity. Christianity, like Buddhism, was not initially linked to any form of political organisation. It can be argued, however, that both required the protection of an empire if they were to flourish. Without that protection they both could easily have withered and eventually died. This is illustrated best by the ultimate fate of both the Christian Church of the East, which flourished for almost a millennium only to suffer despoliation when the Mongol Empire was destroyed (Jenkins 2008), and Manichaeism, which failed to find a state to protect it. Religions which are a matter of practice, culture and intellect are essentially forms of what are best described as commonwealths (Melleuish 2009). The mode of power which characterises commonwealths is ideological or intellectual power (Mann 1987: 46–48) which may seek to overpower one's opponents but which cannot do so without the assistance of some sort of political and military entity. For this reason, commonwealths tend to be peaceful in nature and more interested in the spread of ideas than in warfare and violence.

Political entities, on the other hand, have been defined in terms of violence; as Max Weber (1970: 77–78) famously wrote, a state has a monopoly on coercion and violence, at least in the modern world. This, in part, is because of the link between politics and military power. Political leaders have always been either military leaders or commanded those in charge of the military. Political entities, or polities, simply have not been able to survive without the means of violence to protect them. The Western Roman Empire collapsed once it had lost the province of Africa and the means to pay its armies. China was unified by a leader who put into practice a violent militaristic philosophy, legalism, although this philosophy was largely dumped by the next dynasty, the Han (Fukuyama 2011: 110–127). Nevertheless, even though Chinese political culture adopted Confucianism and military values were not highly esteemed, this did not change the reality that it was military power which preserved China from the pastoral peoples to the west who occasionally overran the empire.

If commonwealths can be understood as networks, this does not mean that these networks are necessarily pacific. Human beings have a capacity to develop and elaborate any set of beliefs and ideas in a variety of directions, leading to disagreements and to conflict between people holding different views. This process of elaboration, followed by disagreement, conflict and ultimately condemnation of opponents, would seem to be a natural human propensity. Human beings are perhaps puzzled by the reality that the ideas which they hold can be developed in a variety of ways, especially as most human groups would prefer that a consensus exists amongst its members. Hence, there is a tendency for individuals holding similar views to form into schools. Nonetheless, there are considerable advantages to human beings as a group in that the members of that group do not agree and do not always form a consensus. Given the constantly changing nature of the environment faced by human groups, they need to be able to adapt and hence need to be able to create more than a single set of ideas.

The real problem for any society is to manage those disagreements so that they do not lead to significant social conflict. A commonwealth is effectively what Niall Ferguson (2018) has recently described as a network, or more correctly, a set of networks which can be mapped in terms of overlapping Venn diagrams. They are generally more egalitarian than a political or military structure, which more typically organise themselves into hierarchies able to be mobilised for purposes of action. A network has no real purpose beyond allowing for the interaction of its members. It should be noted, however, that commonwealths can become hierarchies especially in their interaction with polities, as occurred to the Christian Church.

One way in which a polity can deal with a variety of commonwealths under its jurisdiction is simply to let all the flowers bloom, such as occurs most readily in a culture which is polytheistic in nature such as ancient Rome or in India. In such circumstances it is possible to create unity through allegiance to a central unifying political figure who takes on a divine status. In a similar vein, the Mughal emperor Akbar created his own religion to sit on top of the various religions of his subjects (Maroney 2006: 150–164). In the Islamic world other religions were tolerated so long as they recognised their inferior status. It is worth noting that small religious groups such as the Mandeans and Yazidis survived in the Islamic world, whereas, with the exception of Jews, this did not happen in Europe (Russell 2014). In Europe, Jews were expelled from many countries during the Middle Ages, including England, of course, the Spanish expelled both Jews and Moriscos from Spain once unification under a Christian monarchy had occurred (Rae 2002:

55–82). Christian Europe traditionally had problems tolerating minorities; for example, even in Venice, which traded with the Islamic world, there was no mosque (Goffman 2007: 135). It is often not fully appreciated that until fifty years ago there was no significant Muslim population living in Western Europe.

It is important to recognise that disagreements within civilisations have led to as much, if not more, conflict than conflicts between civilisations. Until relatively recently it was unlikely that large numbers of individuals from different civilisations would come into contact with each other, whereas they would most likely come into contact on a regular basis with those who were different within their own civilisation.

The most amazing thing about such disagreements is that it can lead to people being killed simply on the basis of their beliefs. It is interesting that all three Abrahamic religions, Christianity, Islam and Judaism, developed the idea that people who had incorrect beliefs and practices within their own religion could be executed as heretics (Ames 2015). All these religions had significant divisions at some stage during their existence, including Judaism, which had the Karaites who rejected rabbinical Judaism. It has generally been the case that religions are more intolerant of heretics than of people from other religions.

How then does heresy develop? In the case of Christianity, the development of heresy is linked to the emergence of a particular church claiming orthodoxy in relation to its rivals. Heresy emerges because of statements of doctrine which define that orthodoxy in the later Roman Empire, from Nicea to Chalcedon. Heresy requires a highly developed intellectual state of affairs in which religious experts can define orthodoxy and hence, lack of orthodoxy.

In this regard, it is worth noting that in less developed Western Europe there appears to have been little in the way of heresy before the eleventh century, as opposed to the more literate and intellectually developed Byzantine Empire. The emergence of heresy in the eleventh century was connected to the creation of a more sophisticated intellectual environment in the West combined with the emergence of a papacy which was simultaneously more bureaucratic and legalistic (Berman 1983: 85–119). To be a heretic, in the West at least, requires a particular intellectual environment with a high level of sophistication. In part, this was supplied by the recursive method which was imported into Europe from central Asia via the Islamic world (Beckwith 2012). Given the natural human propensity to elaborate ideas and practices, heresy – or the differentiation between supposedly correct and incorrect ideas and practices – becomes more prevalent once a culture has attained a highly developed and sophisticated intellectual and legal structure, which Europe only really reached in the eleventh century. Heresy, understood as an intellectual elaboration which is viewed as deviant, is characteristic not only of religious societies but also of modern, supposedly secular, ones. It is a feature not only of modern political ideologies but also of science where those sceptical of anthropogenic climate change and Darwinism are treated with a disdain similar to medieval heretics.

Cultures have their own particular cultural patterning, as Marshall Hodgson (1993: 126–170) argued. It may well be the case that European historical development spawned a persecuting society as part of its cultural patterning, as R. I. Moore (1987) famously argued, but it also developed an ideal of tolerance which tended to mitigate the worst features of that patterning. The Spanish model of expelling those who are different in the hope of achieving cultural and religious conformity established a model which other states could follow, especially in the wake of the Reformation. The last major expulsion was that of the Huguenots by Louis XIV in 1685, although religious conflict continued into the first half of the eighteenth century. The most savage anti-Catholic riots in Britain, the Gordon riots, occurred in 1780. Nevertheless, as Benjamin Kaplan (2007) points out, in the real world, inhabited by real people, accommodations were reached between people of different religions to enable peace and stability. In Ausburg, for example, two separate communities of Lutheran and Catholics co-existed, each with its own churches, institutions and cultures. Holland managed to maintain a plurality of religions (Kaplan 2007: 243–245).

Two events mark the development of the modern European nation-state. The first is the growing power of the state apparatus as it sought to centralise power into its hands (Braddick 2000). This meant the transfer of power from local communities to the central government so that local leaders became representatives of the power of that government as much as protectors of local interests. Part of this process was that law came to be associated with a particular territory rather than with a people so that all people living within a state had to observe the same laws regardless of their culture or religion.

For our purposes, the crucial change came when the state appropriated what can be described as the 'commonwealth' functions once the prerogative of the Church, including education and welfare. This desire to unify education, welfare and even the Church under its umbrella was particularly manifest in the French Revolution (Israel 2014). The nation is a jealous God and became even more jealous once it had appropriated the functions of the commonwealth to it. School instruction would create the common culture shared by all members of the state. But it was not necessarily so simple. In nineteenth-century New South Wales, in the 1870s, the Educational Board refused to teach history in its primary schools; it much preferred geography. The reason was that it was impossible to establish an authoritative historical account (Parkes 1873). In particular, in a colony containing both Catholics and Protestants, history was a contentious matter when it involved religion, and so it was best not to stir up conflict. If the state seeks to control education, and those aspects of human existence which properly belong to the commonwealth, this gives it enormous power to mould the minds of its citizens. In the Australian context, state educational instruction meant the withdrawal of funds from denominational schools. Catholics, who had no desire to entrust the education of their young to what they perceived to be a basically Protestant state, made enormous sacrifices to ensure the survival of their own schools. Nevertheless, it has been the case that over time the state has acquired ever greater capacity to mould young minds through education, especially as the length of time which young people spend in educational institutions has increased and appears still to be increasing.

The second feature of Western modernity has been the development of the liberal idea that beliefs are personal in nature and have no place in determining membership of a political community. Hence the French revolutionaries sought to include both Protestants and Jews within the French political community. In a modern liberal state, the beliefs and ideas of an individual citizen do not matter so long as those beliefs do not lead to that citizen seeking to harm his or her fellow citizens. In theory at least, no one should be prosecuted for holding certain beliefs. At the same time, the state exercises a monopoly over school curricula and thus can heavily influence what views an individual comes to hold. The state can thus prescribe what are, and what are not, acceptable values for its citizens through this monopoly, which explains why certain groups seek to control it.

The modern notion of toleration developed in England in the late seventeenth and early eighteenth centuries when it was recognised that there needed to be a way to deal with the fact that differences in politics and religion led to what was described as the 'rage of party' with the ultimate possibility of bloodshed (Knights 2005). The English took a route which might initially seem to be counterintuitive. Instead of limiting and restricting what one could say in public, they allowed for much fuller public expression of a range of ideas and beliefs. They abolished the need for printed material to be licenced by the state. This allowed a wide range of views to be expressed.

The answer to the prospect of bloody confrontation arising out of a difference of opinion in matters religious and political was not the imposition of conformity, but the ideal of the gentleman who could conduct himself with civility and forbearance. Such a person would keep his passions under control and not be subject to either superstition or fanaticism. This was in line with other developments within England which saw the emergence of an intellectual culture that encouraged practicality and discouraged individuals to push their ideas to intellectual extremes. Living a good life was more important than its intellectual definition; moreover, an excessive concentration on intellectual definitions tended to create the basis for division and difference grounded in words rather than realities.

Toleration was linked to behaviour and action to the detriment of intellectual activity. Empiricism assumed a significant role in English culture, and practicality was emphasised rather than indulging in theorising. An English intellectual appeared to be an oxymoron. A culture attuned to experience and suspicious of abstract ideas is, it can be argued, less likely to engage in discriminatory behaviour than one based on using intellectual distinctions to divide up the world. This does not mean that the English did not engage in discriminatory behaviour, especially in its imperial possessions.

As a set of English colonies, nineteenth-century Australia revelled in its anti-intellectual outlook and belief in practicality. At the end of the nineteenth century an observer described how socialism without doctrines had developed in Australia (Métin 1977). It also had a practical form of liberalism. As with Reformation Europe it contained two major religious cultures, Protestant and Catholicism which was largely Irish in nature. Despite a degree of friction between the two sides, there was very little in the way of violent confrontation, largely because religion was, as far as possible, excluded from the public sphere.

At this point I think that I should attempt to summarise my argument as follows:

- Human beings, by their very nature, possess the capacity to elaborate and develop their ideas and practices such as potentially to lead to conflict. Such conflict is more likely in a culture which has developed its ideas to a highly sophisticated and rationalist level.
- Due to its cultural patterning, the culture of what is best described as Latin or Western Christendom found it difficult to deal with a range of Christian beliefs, either in the shape of medieval heresies or the explosion of Christian expression in the wake of the Reformation and with people from non-Christian religions.
- The birth of the nation-state saw the state essentially appropriating what had previously been the 'commonwealth' functions of the Church for itself and then proceeding to craft vast educational systems which could be used to create a population with a high degree of cultural homogeneity.
- As the establishment of the nation-state was also connected to liberalism, this meant that the nation-state accepted liberal principles which allowed for a range of ideas and beliefs to be expressed freely, so long as they caused no harm. In the British case this free expression of ideas was aided by the fact that the English had a cultural tradition based on practicality and the idea of the gentleman.

This is not to say that in the modern age commonwealths, in the shape of scientific and intellectual communities, religions and other forms of cultural communities, did not flourish. In 1914, just as war broke out, one such expression of a commonwealth, the British Association for the Advancement of Science, was meeting in Australia and that meeting included German scientists (Scheckter 2014). The scientists went home to their own countries to work on ways of defeating, and perhaps causing the death of, their one-time colleagues.

The twentieth century, which was the age in which the nation-state reached its apogee, was also the age of an increasing globalisation which pitted global networks against the more formal hierarchies of the nation-state. It was indeed nationalism which enabled Europe to destroy itself just as it had come to dominate the rest of the world; commonwealths of science, labour, religion and international commerce were powerless to prevent Europe's mad desire to destroy itself. The nation-state, combining military, economic, political and ideological power, strove to become a unified entity capable of clashing with other nation-states. The aim was autarchy in all things.

In Europe, at least, 1945 was seen as the logical outcome of the 'clash of the nation-states' which seemed to lead inexorably to year zero. Of course, this was not the case with much of the rest of the world, which seemingly rejoiced in the demise of Europe while seeking to emulate its nation-state model. The West, understood as Western Europe and its derivative cultures, sought to transcend its nation-state past, especially once the Soviet Union had ceased to be a major threat in 1991. The West embraced the various networks, which can also be understood as commonwealths, which their increasingly globalised worlds seemed to offer. Western countries also embraced the ideal of allowing members of other civilisations to come and live in their countries. This has been an extraordinary experiment unprecedented in world history.

The essential point is that countries of European derivation have an established tradition of bringing state and commonwealth together to produce a population with a fairly homogenous culture. This is quite unlike countries such as India, which are simply culturally heterogeneous, and India suffers from chronic communal violence. In those places where Western countries in the past had to deal with populations of quite different origins, the outcomes were not promising; think apartheid in South Africa and Jim Crow in the South of America.

Even so, Western countries appear to have been caught between the two imperatives of creating a homogenous nation-state on the one hand and a faith in liberal principles on the other. In certain cases, such as Australia, the move towards increasing the diversity of the source of its migrants was driven by necessity. The European moment in world history in the late nineteenth century had been matched by a massive demographic increase (Belich 2009), but since 1945 there has been a decline in the birth rate, which is now below replacement levels in many Western countries (Kaufmann 2010).

Multiculturalism is best seen as an attempt to manage this new cultural diversity, just as societies in the past, including Reformation Europe, attempted to manage its religious differences. The real issue has been what culture means within the framework of a nation-state and hence how much difference is to be allowed. Multiculturalism has also developed at a time when a hyper-rationalism has come to exist in most Western states such that cultural differences come to be expressed in intellectual terms. Such a development follows from the emergence of significant numbers of educated individuals with a vested interest in making stark intellectual distinctions. Such an outlook is not conducive to an older 'live and let live' attitude based on not pushing one's ideas to extremes. One expression of this tendency to push ideas to their logical conclusion has been the emergence of postmodernism which enshrines principles of moral relativism.

The nation-state is full of contradictory tendencies, as discussed earlier, which means that multiculturalism equally reflects those contradictions. The state seeks cultural homogeneity through its monopoly of what is taught to the young. It has a monopoly over the law. At the same time there are powerful tendencies within contemporary Western states to limit freedom of expression and to impose speech codes, again primarily by educated individuals who are the product of a hyper-rationalist culture. And yet it also wants to allow for a diversity of cultural expression without knowing what that actually means in practice. Moral relativism seemingly coexists with a powerful desire to impose a rigid moral code.

Multiculturalism partakes of the chaos of the contemporary nation-state created by its many contradictions. Once political and military power are fused with ideological power, it is very difficult to see how something approaching a genuine multiculturalism can be put into practice. However, the situation is complicated by the fact that the contemporary state is often committed to the practice of diversity, in part because of the impact of moral relativism, and seeks to impose 'diversity' as a moral imperative.

Whatever else may be happening, it would be difficult to consider the current situation, especially as it exists within a nation-state, as a 'clash of civilisations'. There are some tensions between people of different cultural backgrounds in a country such as Australia, but they are not as severe or violent as was often the case in Europe after the Reformation. There are also tendencies for individuals holding unfashionable views to be denounced as heretics. But there is no contemporary equivalent of the Inquisition.

The real 'clash of civilisations' in the contemporary world occurs when states are involved. For example, this can involve the intrusion of the Chinese government into Australian politics and universities, as recently argued by Clive Hamilton (2018). A similar case can be seen when young Muslim Australians went off to fight for ISIS in the Middle East. In both examples politics intruded into culture and sought to manipulate it for political purposes.

Cultures change, people change. The problem with the idea of the 'clash of civilisations' is that it assumes that civilisations have an essential nature, a core which is hard and fixed. Yet the history of any civilisation indicates that beliefs which were once central to it have waxed and waned over time. The problem of our age is the development of a mentality which I have termed hyper-rationalist and which tends to view sets of beliefs as something which can be reduced to a formula. That which is by nature fluid becomes fixed in the shape of fundamentalism. The drawing of definite lines and boundaries can be a prelude to conflict.

Such boundaries can be worn down by time. The sectarian boundaries of Australia, like those generated by the Reformation in Europe, became softer over time and less relevant to the people which they divided. One precondition for such softening is the prevention of the formation of ghettos. Over time new cultures form as peoples intermingle and have descendants who come from a variety of cultures.

In this sense, the best antidote to 'clashes of civilisation' is to prevent ideas and ideologies from getting in the way of human beings getting on with each other at a personal level. The real problem is not the ideas and beliefs which provide comfort for individuals, but the 'ideas professionals' who seek to accentuate the boundaries between peoples. The 'rage of civilisations' is best overcome by ideals of civility and a willingness not to take one's ideas to extremes, just as the English understood in their response to the 'rage of party'.

Bibliography

Ames, C. 2015. *Medieval Heresies: Christianity, Judaism and Islam*. Cambridge: Cambridge University Press.

Beckwith, C. 2012. *Warriors of the Cloisters: The Central Asian Origins of Science in the Medieval World*. Princeton: Princeton University Press.

Belich, J. 2009. *Replenishing the Earth: The Settler Revolution and the rise of the Anglo World, 1783–1939*. Oxford: Oxford University Press.

Berman, H. 1983. *Law and Revolution: The Formation of the Western Legal Tradition*. Cambridge, MA: Harvard University Press.

Braddick, M. 2000. *State Formation in Early Modern England c. 1550–1700*. Cambridge: Cambridge University Press.

Ferguson, N. 2018. *The Square and the Tower*. New York: Penguin.

Fukuyama, F. 2011. *The Origins of Political Order: From Prehuman Times to the French Revolution*. New York: Farrar, Straus and Giroux.

Goffman, D. 2007. *The Ottoman Empire and Early Modern Europe*. Cambridge: Cambridge University Press.

Goodman, M. 2017. *Rome and Jerusalem: The Clash of Ancient Civilizations*. London: Penguin.

Hamilton, C. 2018. *Silent Invasion: China's Influence in Australia*. Melbourne: Hardie Grant.

Huntington, S. 1997. *The Clash of Civilizations and the Remaking of World Order*. New York: Touchstone.

Israel, J. 2014. *Revolutionary Ideas: An Intellectual History of the French Revolution from the Rights of Man to Robespierre*. Princeton: Princeton University Press.

Jenkins, P. 2008. *The Lost History of Christianity*. New York: HarperCollins.

Kaplan, B. 2007. *Divided by Faith: Religious Conflicts and the Practice of Toleration in Early Modern Europe*. Cambridge, MA: Harvard University Press.

Kaufmann, E. 2010. *Shall the Religious Inherit the Earth? Demography and Politics in the Twenty First Century*. London: Profile.

Keeley, L. 1996. *War Before Civilization*. Oxford: Oxford University Press.

Knights, B. 2005. *Representation and Misrepresentation in Later Stuart Britain: Partisanship and Political Culture*. Oxford: Oxford University Press.

Mann, M. 1987. *The Sources of Social Power*. Vol. 1. Cambridge: Cambridge University Press.

Maroney, E. 2006. *Religious Syncretism*. London: SCM Press.

Marshall, G. S. H. 1993. *Rethinking World History: Essay on Europe, Islam, and World History*. Ed. Edmund Burke. Cambridge: Cambridge University Press, 111.

Melleuish, G. 2009. 'The West, the Anglo-Sphere and the Ideal of Commonwealth,' *Australian Journal of Politics and History*, 55 (2): 233–247.

Métin, A. 1977. *Socialism Without Doctrines*. Trans. Russel Ward. Chippendale: Alternative Publishing Co-operative.

Moore, R. I. 1987. *The Formation of a Persecuting Society: Power and Deviance in Western Europe 950–1250*. Oxford: Blackwell.

Moss, C. 2013. *The Myth of Persecution: How Early Christians Invented a Story of Martyrdom*. San Francisco: HarperCollins.

Parkes, H. 12 September 1873. 'New South Wales Parliament, Legislative Assembly', *Sydney Morning Herald*.

Rae, H. 2002. *State Identities and the Homogenisation of Peoples*. Cambridge: Cambridge University Press.

Russell, G. 2014. *Heirs to Forgotten Kingdoms: Journeys into the Disappearing Religions of the Middle East*. London: Simon & Schuster.

Scheckter, J. 2014. ' "Modern in Every Respect": The 1914 Conference of the British Association for the Advancement of Science,' *The Journal of the European Association for Studies of Australia*, 5 (1): 4–20.

Strassler, R. B. (Ed.) 1996. *The Landmark Thucydides*. New York: Free Press.

Weber, M. 1970. 'Politics as a Vocation', in *From Max Weber: Essays in Sociology*, H. H. Gerth and C. Wright Mills (Eds.). London: Max Weber.

2 Creating and sustaining multicultural societies in the 'Anglosphere'

James Jupp

The experience of different states in controlling or modifying multiethnic communities varies internationally and takes many forms, from total acceptance of variety to totalitarian rejection of it. At present there are almost 200 independent or self-governing societies in the world, all with differing policies and histories. Very few of them have overwhelming majorities formed historically from one ethnic origin like Japan or the two Koreas. Even states deliberately constructed in favour of a single ethnicity, like Israel, allow minorities to survive and even flourish.

This chapter will examine the experience of the so-called 'Anglosphere' in managing ethnic diversity. Focus on the five countries involved is because they illustrate very well the range of approaches that have been adopted in this policy area. Even where societies share common features or family resemblances, as in the hypothesised Anglosphere, there may be significant differences in terms of both immigration and multicultural policy, as well as some commonalities with countries outside the group. Attention will also be paid in this chapter to the rapidly changing nature of both immigrant societies and emigrant and refugee nations, often due to warfare.

The Anglosphere

Since 1945 the concept of the Anglosphere has been promoted in the United States through books such as *The Diamond Age* by Neal Stephenson (1995) and *The Anglosphere Challenge* by James C. Bennett (Maryland, 2004). It has been mainly promoted by conservatives to emphasise the common inheritance of five interrelated societies – the UK, Australia, New Zealand, Canada and the United States. These societies claim to have a common inheritance of the Enlightenment and the Judeo-Christian ethic. The term has been taken up by some of the media in the five states, all of which have recent experience with multicultural immigration. It has also influenced British debate after the decision to leave the European Union.

Despite their common origins in the British Isles, however, there are many differences between these societies. Overemphasis on common origin can lead to serious misunderstanding of differences. Borrowing from widely differing societies is often futile. This has been especially problematic in the former colonies liberated from the British, French, Dutch, Spanish, Portuguese, Ottoman, and other empires. Models are copied but often work quite differently or do not work at all.

Things that the English-speaking states have inherited from their previous 'home country' include religions, political ideologies, administrative systems and even prejudices against others. However, the status of the English language, the defining characteristic of the Anglosphere, has changed over time. In some cases, such as Canada, it is shared with another. In the United States Spanish is widely used, while in New Zealand Māori is one of the official languages. Even in the UK, the old Celtic languages now have an official status regionally.

The UK dates back to the union of England with Scotland in 1707, but England dates back at least to 1066 with laws and traditions traceable from the Norman conquest. Many of these, such as Magna Carta, have been passed down as part of the constitutional inheritance of the United States and Australia.

While originating in the UK, these new English-speaking societies developed differently over the following three centuries. One important difference has been changes to their ethnic character due to international migration. There was considerable interchange between the Anglophone countries in the Victorian era due to a common language and connected history, related economies and connecting transport routes. Later one binding factor between the five was their participation in both world wars and continuing 'five eyes' security arrangements.

But their histories were also different in many ways. Australia, Canada and New Zealand kept the British connection well into the twenty-first century, while the United States had rejected it by 1780. A major change was in their attraction for immigrants and their ways of dealing with the consequent influences on their national populations. Their experience of and treatment of ethnic variety was far from uniform.

After the First World War (1914–1918) an attempt was made by the newly created League of Nations to rationalise the European political system. The old empires – Turkey, Russia, Germany, Austria/Hungary – had all been defeated and lost control of many minority populations, including the Poles, Arabs, Czechs, Croatians, Romanians and others. President Woodrow Wilson used the League of Nations to introduce the idea of self-determination. This meant that any recognisable minority community had the right to independence if formerly held by a defeated enemy power. Ethnicity would be judged predominantly by language, but also by earlier history. Requests that Ireland also be treated like this were ignored by the victorious British. The end result was the creation of many new states from the dismemberment of the defeated empires.

Self-determination

The principle of self-determination was thus introduced into Europe following the First World War and also in the Middle Eastern provinces of the former Ottoman Empire. It included the principle, revived in 1945 after the Second World War, that empires did not have the right to rule over defined 'nations' who sought to be free. This was not accepted in full by the British Empire, then the largest in the world, until well after the Second World War. The major urge for self-determination came from the United States, which did not have an empire in the usual sense, except for one in the Philippines won from Spain. The Philippines did not become independent until after the war with Japan in 1945. Ireland did not become independent until the 1920s and then in a divided condition. It is not usually included in the Anglosphere and was neutral in the Second World War. So even the concept of self-determination was viewed differently according to local interests.

Common identities?

The five nations of the Anglosphere are assumed to have a common cultural, ideological, and linguistic identity. However, this has been the case neither in their histories nor in their treatment of other ethnicities. They cannot, therefore, be taken as providing a single guide in the present. Edward III made the English language the official tongue of England, in which all laws were written, as early as 1362, when none of the other four states existed. English replaced French and Latin. However, the resident majority often spoke variants of Anglo-Saxon. The use of the term 'Anglo-Saxon' to refer to all five is quite misleading but still sometimes used as a racial descriptor based on colour. All five accept modern English as their official language, but local circumstances have increasingly allowed or even encouraged other languages. French has equal status in Canada because of its prior control by the French and its predominance in Québec, the second largest province. This bilingualism covers the whole of Canada and not just the French-speaking areas. The notion of equality for languages has more recently been widely accepted through the Anglosphere. In the United States great efforts were made in the education systems to teach English to the vast number of immigrants in the nineteenth century. But Spanish remains in the Southwest and is widely taught. In California this principle is extended to the use of minority languages, including Chinese, on election ballots.

Language

In the other 'Anglo' states liberalisation of language policy towards non-English speakers has been on two levels – first to provide information to new immigrants and second to sustain Indigenous languages which are in danger of declining. The former is central to policies of multiculturalism adopted especially in Australia and Canada. The latter can be seen in UK policy regarding Irish, Welsh and Scottish Gaelic, but no longer Manx and Cornish, which died out a century or more ago. In New Zealand Māori has equal status officially with English, along with New Zealand Sign Language, which is New Zealand's third official language. In Australia, a wide range of Aboriginal languages is used for relevant local purposes by government agencies. Most of these policies are of recent adoption. In Ireland the use of Irish was not encouraged in the Protestant North, which remained part of the UK.

In developing societies that are former colonies, language has become one of the major dividing marks between different ethnic groups, often with unfortunate results, as in Sri Lanka with the division between Sinhala and Tamil. Thus one of the freedoms implicit in self-determination may not always be beneficial, though now accepted in established democracies with old liberal traditions and institutions like the Anglosphere. Elsewhere language and religion are often divisive.

Religion

The original dividing line in historical Europe was between religions, with the rise of Protestantism in a Catholic world. This was resolved in Britain in the reign of Henry VIII (1509–1547). The Church of England took over all the communities, resources and legal basis of the preceding Catholic Church in England, later followed by the Church of Scotland. In Ireland the Church of Ireland, which was Protestant, was not disestablished until the mid-nineteenth century, and religion remained a serious dividing point up until very recently. In the rest of the Anglosphere forms of Protestantism were originally favoured over Catholicism.

However, Protestantism, unlike Catholicism, was not based on strict uniformity and obedience. Almost immediately objectors to the established Anglican Church arose. The Pilgrim Fathers, who emigrated from England to America in 1620, began the process whereby the future United States, with its constitutional protection of religious freedom, became one of the most varied Christian societies on earth. Much of this variety originated in Protestant England. But with the spread of mass immigration, Catholicism arrived from Ireland and Italy. African slavery brought new forms of Christianity. Later immigration brought Judaism from Russia and Poland.

America now has an almost unimaginable number of often quite fundamental Christian religions. This was not yet the case in the other 'Anglo' societies. Catholicism remained strong in French Canada and Ireland, Presbyterianism in Scotland and Wales and Anglicanism in Australia and New Zealand. Christianity remained central within a variety of interpretations, often widely different. Anglicanism continued to enjoy its association with the British royalty and aristocracy but had little following in the United States and has recently given way to Catholicism in Australia and Canada as the largest belief system.

The American experience of variety led to official support for religious freedom in the early nineteenth century, and this was also incorporated into constitutional law in Australia. Anglicanism remains the official established religion in England, but not anywhere else in the Anglosphere. In the nineteenth century there was continuing hostility between Protestants and Catholics, mainly because the latter were also regarded as Irish. As American immigration diversified, this hostility was sometimes extended to the Jews, who were slow to be accepted and given the same rights as Christians. Many of these prejudices came from descendants of British immigrants recruited as manual workers and holding existing attitudes from 'home'. Prejudice against Afro-American former slaves continued after the American Civil War of 1860, and its legacy continues into the present.

Early English influence

The dominance of the English language, English law, Protestantism and Catholicism and notions of self-determination, shaped the overall character of the five Anglosphere nations even before that term was invented. However, uniformity stemming from remote common origins did not completely shape their politics, their attitudes, policies, trade, international links and attitudes to minorities and migrants within their borders. They cooperated against common enemies in warfare and intelligence work, but did not maintain similar relationships, cultures or understandings of foreigners. They did, however, inherit some attitudes from the British Empire, of which racism towards coloured people was one. This was doubly relevant for the United States while it preserved slavery and later in relation to the Afro-American population, and for the British in their domination over vast subject populations in India and Africa. It was less significant in New Zealand and Canada, in both of which the Indigenous minority had waged effective military campaigns in the early days of colonisation. These Indigenous minorities still suffer a lower level of wellbeing, but have more freedom to maintain their culture than do Indigenous peoples in many other societies. Some Māori have risen to the highest positions in New Zealand society, including governor-general and acting prime minister. Canadian First Nations, both Indian and Inuit, have their own language rights and control over their local communities to a greater extent than Australian Aborigines.

The Anglosphere, then, has bequeathed a series of valuable experiences to its members, much of which has also been transferred with varying success to other nations. These include the English language, which is still the most widely used in the world for most purposes. It may be outnumbered by Chinese and Arabic, but it is also based on the alphabet bequeathed to Britain by the Romans, which is used by states of European origin or influence.

Through that language most modern inventions have been disseminated worldwide. Unfortunately, they include the atom bomb dropped on Japanese civilians from Anglosphere planes. The Anglosphere was also responsible for many of the intercontinental empires of recent years, although in accordance with the principle of self-determination they left them behind, often with limited training and resources for their futures. Many have prospered, but the smaller and weaker ones have not. Often they have failed through rejecting many aspects of the Anglosphere inheritance without having appropriate political and legal experience to replace it.

Moving the debate further on from the Anglosphere to other developed European and Asian nations, many also share the notions of religious and political freedom, personal liberty, economic and technical advance and respect for cultural variety. These are not necessarily based on British traditions. Many do not accept the Christian inheritance but have managed well without it. In terms only of economic success these include the rich Gulf states of the Muslim world, Japan and Korea, the European Union, Scandinavia, some post-communist societies some of the more stable Latin American republics, India, China, Israel, Taiwan, Malta and Cyprus. Many have had difficulties but have overcome them. Some are better than they once were, notably Russia.

How then do the Anglosphere and these other states deal with such issues as ethnic, religious and political variety; internal and external threats; democracy; poor resources and economies; conflicting ideologies' and other threats to 'peace, order and good government' in the old British colonial mantra? What is the escape route from the continuous wars, revolutions, massacres, refugee hordes and overall disasters which have marked the years of 'peace' since the end of the two massive 'wars to end all wars' in 1914–1918 and 1939–1945? A major problem has been massive refugee flows from these disasters and oppressive leaders.

'Values'

One approach to these dilemmas has been favoured in Australia and the United States in recent years. This is to argue that common 'values', principles, laws and practices are the 'glue' that holds nations together and should be taught to newcomers and neighbours where necessary. The idea that a nation should be based on these agreed principles and practices was already developed in Europe and Asia centuries ago as a theory of government by Aristotle, Confucius and many religious leaders. Unfortunately, it proved too vague in practice to prevent the consistent waging of wars, as well as persecutions and massacres by societies with apparently similar cultures. Christians, Muslims, even Buddhists, have fought and killed each other over the centuries from ancient times up until the First and Second World Wars and beyond and are still doing so, as have dictatorships and democracies. With the increasing number of nation-states in recent years created by the principle of self-determination, things have only become worse. Civil wars within the new states became as common as international wars, especially in the Middle East, Africa and the Balkans. These produced many refugees seeking to settle in more stable societies like the United States, Australia, the UK or Canada. These, in their turn, have been faced with large influxes of unfamiliar and alien newcomers seeking to settle in conformity with undertakings made to the United Nations (UN) or humanitarian expectations. This changes the internal politics and beliefs of these countries in ways which create tensions and even hostility against the newcomers and may revive previous prejudices against minorities Most stable modern societies are now subject to claims for recognition requiring new thinking about how to deal with new arrivals or existing disadvantaged minorities such as Aborigines or Afro-Americans. This often disturbs local politics by challenging previous beliefs held to be essential to stability and progress. The first response is simply to suggest that these new demands be modified through assimilation – the request to accept things as they are already.

Australia in particular, being remote and secure and part of the British Empire, spent many years asking 'why can't they be like us?' Jupp (2018). The United States had asked the same after they broke away from that empire and when they became the greatest attraction for immigrants in the nineteenth century. Canada was less concerned, being already a bicultural society of British and French descent, while New Zealand had learned to live with the Indigenous Māori after wars which neither side really won. Starting in 1900 Australia solved the problem by limiting itself essentially to British and Irish immigration through assistance programmes and by excluding all others outside Europe from settling under the White Australia policy. White Europeans were allowed in from similar and preferably Protestant countries, but those from southern Europe and Catholic countries were often limited by landing permits based on their ability to pay. Only the Irish (who were British subjects) were encouraged to arrive but continued to face widespread prejudices from the majority. The strongest prejudices were against the Chinese and Pacific Islanders. This set the official and public attitudes between the First and Second World Wars and immigration law until the 1970s. Canada, New Zealand and the United States had similar policies and obstacles, especially erected against Chinese and other Asians.

Assimilation to the resident majority thus became the normal rule in terms of the English language (with French exceptions in Quebec); understanding of British laws and traditions (including cricket especially for Australia); and admiration of the independence, wealth and constitution of the United States. In other European countries assimilation was just as urgently applied, France and Germany being outstanding examples. Eventually this regrettably led to the spread of nationalist and eventually fascist politics leading to the Second World War. Less drastically it meant that Australia and New Zealand remained loyal and British. As the Australian national anthem says of England – 'with all her faults we love her still' – although not all Australians actually sing this anymore. When massive numbers of post-war refugees arrived from Europe in 1945, the government and most of the residents advocated rapid assimilation, and this remained public policy for the next twenty years and a popular belief of many for longer. In the United States there was a greater understanding of the issues, as immigration from many sources was well understood. However, prejudice and exclusion continued against Afro-Americans. And while a large number of Americans of Irish or German descent did not love England, greater prejudice against Chinese and Jews remained. Assimilation to American culture was strongly pursued through public schools and commercial media, and still is, under the more recent slogan 'America – Love it or Leave it'.

Assimilation

Thus, since 1945 all five of the Anglosphere countries have faced massive population shifts with assimilationist policies, which, in turn, became increasingly dysfunctional. All had some experience of large-scale immigration, but this had alarmed them in the past. White Australia and White Canada and White New Zealand all had exclusion policies directed mainly against Chinese, but also including other non-Europeans. The United States had been wide open but also raised obstacles to Chinese and later to southern Europeans. Britain did not have an immigration policy before 1912 but then accepted a law directed mainly against an influx of Jewish refugees from Tsarist Russia. World War I brought more refugees, but also an increase in self-governing former colonies of the defeated empires. The United States remained the recipient of the largest number of foreign entrants, now including many from Latin America and southern Europe (as previously from Germany and Ireland). British immigration continued into all these states and did not arouse much hostility, but little enthusiasm either.

Britain itself allowed entry to all British Empire subjects until the arrival of many West Indians, Indians and Pakistanis from the 1940s, after which the policy was reversed and progressively tightened. Canada had an exclusion policy directed against Chinese and Indians. Regardless of regulations, all the Anglosphere states welcomed new arrivals of British origin and ancestry. Race was not directly a ground for exclusion except in Australia. The British government was anxious not to offend India and other British colonies until after they became independent. Australia lifted its White Australia prohibition on non-whites only after accepting the UN protocol on refugees, which inhibited such discrimination.

So the upheavals of the years after 1945 presented the old imperial powers with the dilemma that their populations were starting to vary from the original intentions of creating an assimilated, cohesive and uniform people. They were also faced with the reality that many of the self-determined new states from their respective empires were unstable and producing their own refugees.

The Americans faced two further dilemmas. First, the Afro-American population of slave origin was beginning to expect all the liberties described in the constitution and not always available to them in either former southern slave states or even farther north. This was a contradiction which took many years to resolve and then not without violence from some states and politicians. The problem was enhanced by the movement of many up from the south into the great cities of the north and industrial belts, thus raising discrimination as a national issue eventually settled uncertainly by presidential involvement. The equality of all Americans was eventually incorporated into law, but not always in local practice (Portes and Rumbaut, 1996).

The second dilemma, which still awaits satisfactory solution, has been the movement of Latin Americans and especially Mexicans into the United States across a lightly controlled border and away from poverty and political instability. Thus, the United States has witnessed a struggle for many years between those who seriously support the principles in its revered constitution and those who reject them. The most obvious current problems include the original provision allowing all citizens to bear arms, which dates back to the early escape from the British Empire more than two centuries ago.

The other problem always facing the United States from the nineteenth century on has been its great attraction for the poor of Europe and even from Britain and now from China and other Asian and Pacific countries. Even with restrictions, the United States still takes more refugees than any other state, with the arguable exception of India. The massive immigration between the 1860s and 1900s aroused considerable alarm among the urban public and media. Whole cities changed their character with expansion into the local countryside. Crime increased in city slum areas where living conditions were as bad as those in Britain or Europe. Above all, there was debate over the fact that these people were obviously not like many American ancestors from Britain. Most did not speak English. Many could neither read nor write and could not expect to rise up in society. They were a potential threat to law-abiding citizens. Those from Ireland, Italy and Poland were seen as a threat to what was still essentially a Protestant country. Even more of a threat were the Jews who began to dominate the vast clothing trade of New York and to compete with publicans and shopkeepers.

The answer to all this was for the US federal government to take the initiative in 1892 and to open a huge immigration control unit at Ellis Island in New York Harbor. This was controlled by the federal government, tested immigrants for health and disease and made judgements on their ability to find work in America. Sixty years later, new immigrants were also tested with the question 'Are you now or have you ever been, a member of the Communist Party?' Once inside the United States newcomers came within the powers of the local states and cities, which had varying ideas of how to cope with them. Many of these outside the major cities had basic prejudices against all minorities and foreigners, often including American-born Hispanics and Afro-Americans. This made race relations a continuing political issue up until the present. A whole variety of racial prejudices were unleashed, threatening peace and security. Not until the 1960s was this effectively tackled by national governments.

American migration

It was this American history which haunted Australia for many years as a reason for maintaining a 'whites only' immigration policy. Another worrying factor was that many immigrants appeared to be taking jobs from local Americans in a society where trade unions were very weak. Australia was only superficially like the United States but was determined not to follow its problems. Until 1945 non-British immigration to Australia was controlled and forbidden for non-Europeans, while European immigration was often tightly restricted. The central state took a more active role than in the United States, and the numbers arriving were much smaller and more carefully selected before arrival. America was also a vastly greater industrial power than Australia and had consequently much greater need for new workers, while Australia was slumbering under British Empire trade protection. But the fear of 'ghettoes' in particular was always present, despite the fact that ethnic concentrations were very small in the 1940s and European refugees were distributed out of the major cities for their first two years (Lieberson, 1980).

Post-1945 planning was also better in the United States than a century before, and negative references to the US experience were often to a different era. Australian immigration was always planned by the central government from federation in 1901, and a responsibility was similarly taken in Canada and New Zealand. But non-British communities were almost unknown in Australia and New Zealand, and what little might be known was largely based on American films and was very unattractive. Canada had more experience not only with European immigration but also with biculturalism. Britain, on the other hand, was quite surprised by the size of the post-war arrival of British subjects from the West Indies, India and Pakistan and began reluctantly to apply restrictions in the face of resentment and locally based problems. Settlement services were provided locally, as in the United States, and ethnic enclaves developed in major cities such as London, Birmingham and Bradford with resulting reactions, although less serious violence, than in the United States. In both countries assimilation was expected but not always attained. But neither was it in Australia or Canada because they consciously pursued a different path of multiculturalism, followed eventually by New Zealand – all with central government involvement.

Each member of the Anglosphere shared different policies and experiences at different times. Other major states such as Germany, Italy and

France have also experienced conflict between national traditions and modern ethnic changes.

Even greater variety exists within the almost 200 sovereign states in the modern world. Some, like Japan, have not welcomed or experienced ethnically varied immigration. Some, like Saudi Arabia, have not welcomed immigration at all. Others, like India, have extended it particularly to fellow Hindus, while Malaysia and the Gulf States have large immigrant populations of workers drawn from Muslim and other Asian states but not given the right to settle permanently. There is little point in detailing the infinite variety of trying to benefit from immigration while avoiding its undesired effects. Refugee migration in particular is different from planned or accepted labour and resettlement migration. It is caused by emergencies and creates unpredictable reactions, often hostile. It is also governed by UN rules, but these are often overlooked or frustrated even by democratic states like Australia that have ratified relevant international law such as the Refugee Convention.

What remains here is to look at differing attempts to resettle immigrants and to satisfy local ethnic minorities within the Anglosphere, given the common inheritances from Britain over the centuries and the alleged, if often imaginary, resemblances which are shared within the five cooperating societies. Each has its own politics and history and its own prejudices and favourites. These may be broadly divided between assimilationist approaches and planned settlement systems. Both are aimed at security for new arrivals who have been invited and, to a lesser degree, uninvited arrivals who qualify as refugees or students and temporary workers. The state usually plays an active role, but not always the same one. Some restrictions are usually imposed, such as visas or limitations on stay. These were usually instituted after the early 1900s, although a few states like Tsarist Russia had similar systems before that. Admission policies are quite varied and need to take account of the tourist industry, which is much bigger than ever before; the needs of education and manufacturing interests; the ability of the smaller or poorer societies to cater to newcomers; and (often the most important of all) the judgement of politicians and governments as to the likely reaction of the public to ethnic change.

There are also many labour recruitment schemes for particular projects which bring in newcomers, but without any desire or need to settle them permanently. These include construction, oil and mining. Impermanent labour is often used by the rich Arab Gulf states but is also favoured widely from Australia to the United States. These workers do not have a right to settle permanently, although this may vary. They are subject to exploitation by employers and are often resented by trade unions.

Two different but not always distinct approaches are assimilationist and population enhancement. Assimilationism is often favoured by public opinion. The expectation is that thanks to the education system, demands of employment and general satisfaction, newcomers will voluntarily abandon their previous loyalties and practices to become satisfied citizens of their new country. They will then raise their children to be loyal citizens without dual allegiances.

This has often been the hope of the United States, Australia, France and the UK. Canada and New Zealand would prefer this as well, but are aware that they are bicultural societies and therefore give a legitimate choice. The problem with the assimilationist approach is that many newcomers are very reluctant to give up the languages, religions and beliefs on which they have been brought up. This may apply to refugees who have unwillingly been forced from their birth places, as with those escaping the Nazi and Soviet regimes. Assimilation is very difficult for Catholics or Muslims in a Protestant or secular society. There is also the problem that governments may impose incentives to assimilate, such as insistence on language ability or religious conversion, which offends newcomers and even their descendants. Many refugees from totalitarian regimes have previously had to suffer from such coercion.

Another problem is that adults above a certain age find it hard to change, while their children are happy to do so, creating family disharmony. This has become especially a problem with the relatively recent arrival of Muslims in Christian countries. Parents often lose control of their children, and women seek the rights extended locally to women. Assimilation may be a slow process. Being forced by government, however carefully, may upset the very people they are seeking to assist. One example in Australia was the Citizenship and Welcome Conventions, which were mainly run by Anglo Australians. Many of the refugees newly arrived from the communist world resented suggestions that the culture they had defended was in some way inferior to the rather loose Australian way of life. Instead, they began the process of forming ethnic councils which preserved their languages, religions and, in some cases, politics. Many of these still exist years after the refugee arrivals of the 1940s. The ones which have withered a bit are from populations like the British and Dutch who were deemed assimilable. The ones which have survived are the Greeks, Italians, Croatians, Vietnamese and Chinese. More recent arrivals, such as Africans or Middle Eastern Christians, have also been keen to preserve their minority cultures, as they were often persecuted in their homelands.

A number of societies not confined to the Anglosphere have adopted the policy of multiculturalism, which allows and even encourages the maintenance of such organisations and practices within legal limits. These include not only Australia, New Zealand and Canada but also Sweden, Holland and Britain. France, in contrast, has taken the opposite path of insisting on assimilation and has experienced serious objections especially from its Muslim population. Within Australia there has been continuing criticism from conservatives, who have undermined policies when in government. In the UK there has been a similar tendency. However, multiculturalism is very useful for ensuring access to welfare through enhancing special services delivered by ethnic minorities, as well as promoting events like cultural festivals. It also allows different religions more freedom to express themselves than many would like, especially critics of Islam.

The great benefit of effective multicultural approaches is to alleviate alienation by settlers from widely different backgrounds. Although there can be some conflict between historic enemies, there is also much cooperation between a variety of different backgrounds in working for satisfactory public provision. Some of the strongest opposition has come from reactionary and racist elements in the United States, and this has influenced Britain and Australia to a limited extent. Multiculturalism cannot solve all problems, but it makes life more comfortable for immigrants from many different backgrounds. It has been especially attractive to refugees.

The most serious problems of adoption and acceptance stem from the great surge of refugees from former imperial possessions and wars. This has applied to the UK, France, Belgium and the Netherlands but also affects the United States, who allowed in many refugees from Vietnam and other wars in which Americans and Australians had engaged.

Having welcomed arrivals in the early days, many former masters were surprised by the escalation of arrivals over the years. In the case of the British Empire, as we have seen, arrivals from India, Pakistan and the West Indies became so large that the principle of free entry was abandoned by the UK government. Australia had also welcomed very large numbers of refugees from communism after 1945 but was less willing to take in similar numbers from Vietnam, a war they had lost. Although they did so, in later years increasingly restrictive policies were adopted, making it almost impossible for refugees arriving by boat without a visa to settle in Australia, as earlier Vietnamese had done. A policy of returning them or interning them in remote islands replaced previous benevolent responses.

Refugees

UN conventions protect refugees, and Australia, Canada and the United States have continued to accept them. But as the problem escalates, public sympathy has declined and international law is sometimes flouted. Difference from their potential hosts is much likelier than it was after 1945. Many refugees are from Africa, and others are Christians or Muslims on the wrong side of the Sunni/Shia divide, escaping from Muslim societies or from Arabic civil wars. They seem much less likely to assimilate or to conform with the expectations of their hosts than did previous refugees. However, their needs are great and their numbers are greater than ever before. Arguments about values, multiculturalism or assimilation are less relevant than their basic needs to save themselves and their families from destruction.

Challenges

In conclusion, the problems of receiving immigrants and settling refugees have grown increasingly serious, not only for the states of the Anglosphere but also for most of Europe and much of Asia and Africa. The liberal scheme of multiculturalism has been under fire from radical right populist movements in a number of European countries. Even the possibility of assimilation is often rejected for refugees from non-European societies.

However, the non-European populations of many European societies have continued to grow despite local objections. In the Anglosphere the need for immigrant labour, in the form of professional and expert entrants, continues to be recognised by the United States, Australia, Canada, and, rather reluctantly, by the UK. And New Zealand remains a magnet for South Pacific migration. Hence, the Anglosphere countries illustrate some of the broader challenges posed by refugee and immigration flows and the diversity of political and policy responses.

References

Bennett, J. C. *The Anglosphere Challenge*. Lanham, Maryland, MD, Rowman & Little, 2004.

Jupp, J. *An Immigrant Nation Seeks Cohesion*. London, Anthem Press, 2018.

Lieberson, S. *From Many Strands*. New York, Russell Sage Foundation, 1980.

Portes, A. and Rumbaut, R. *Immigrant America*. San Francisco, University of California Press, 1996.

Stephenson, N. *The Diamond Age*. London, Penguin, 1995.

3   The return of Australian values in the Australian citizenship test

Maria Chisari

In recent years, there has been growing debate about the importance of migrants and refugees embracing Australian values in order to become model Australian citizens. Australian values are generally understood as a set of core civic principles that are believed to be representative of Australia's national character. They include notions of freedom, equality and democracy and are promoted as originating from a Western, Judeo-Christian heritage. In popular terms, they are referred to as mateship and a fair go. Their strongest supporter, former Prime Minister John Howard, introduced Australian values into legislation as part of the Australian Values Statement and the Australian citizenship test, declaring that migrants should learn to embrace these core principles in order to integrate into the mainstream community and ensure social cohesion. Today, the Turnbull Coalition government has extended the meaning of Australian values in citizenship legislation to include notions of allegiance to Australia and as a way to combat terrorism. Yet despite their association with current securitization discourses, the concept of Australian values has a more checkered and complex past. Since the emergence of neoliberal politics in Australia, versions of Australian values have in fact featured in discourses about multiculturalism and social cohesion, as well as debates about what constitutes the model Australian citizen.

This chapter explores how the concept of Australian values has been transformed in key government policies that span more than thirty years of neoliberal governing. It consists of a historical analysis which examines the FitzGerald Report released in 1988, the Australian Compact drafted in 2000 and the Australian Values Statement introduced in 2007. All these three texts have included the recommendation of a values pledge, which acts as a form of affective citizenship, that is, as a mechanism of government which aims to appease national unease about migrant differences. Desiring that migrants officially commit to Australian values in their everyday lives also has the effect of reassuring the "mainstream" population, those that are considered to be "real Australians" because of their Anglo-Christian heritage, that national governments are working towards maintaining the security, well-being and prosperity of the Australian nation.

Neoliberal citizenship

The current legislative requirement that all newly naturalized Australian citizens formally embrace Australian values by successfully passing the citizenship test and signing the Australian Values Statement should be understood as processes born out of neoliberal governing. In this contemporary mode of governing, the traditional view that governments are responsible for all the people living within Australia's borders is challenged. Instead, migrants and refugees are expected to engage in a "reciprocal relationship" or a "personal contract" with the state by agreeing to commit to Australian values in order to be granted the status of Australian citizen (Perera 2007). This relationship is understood as a mutual obligation whereby the nation provides privileges to citizens, and in return they perform certain obligations and responsibilities, which include living by a prescribed set of "core" values (Chisari 2018, 37). In this new order, citizenship becomes "privatized" (Perera 2007), as migrants and refugees must take on the personal responsibility to become model Australian citizens.

This official promotion of Australian values is based on the popular view that in any national community there exists a dominant and homogenous cultural group who possess an innate core value system where the "host society is consolidated and represented through settled and essentialized cultural traditions and distinguishable set of values" and in many liberal-democratic nations in particular, these values are put at risk by differences (Bhandar 2010, 332) from non-Western migrants and their incompatible or deficient values systems. The values included in the Australian Values Statement include freedom of the individual and religion, commitment to the rule of law, parliamentary democracy and equality of men and women. In this way, Australian values become a normalizing discourse about what is constitutive of a good Australian citizen, as well as what is constitutive of Australian identity.

The emergence of Australian values in political discourse can also be theorized as a form of emotional or "affective citizenship" (Johnson 2010, 496) Citizenship becomes affective and "performative" (Perera 2009, 655) because it has as its main objective the eradication of "white unease" and the procurement of security and the well-being of the population. Furthermore, Australian values are affective and performative, because as migrants adopt Australian values in their everyday lives, they become familiar, knowable (Perera 2007) and reassuring to the mainstream through the elimination of their differences.

This form of affective citizenship can also be theorized as a form of governmental reassurance (Chisari 2009, 2015), as "the production of the nation involves . . . the everyday negotiations of what it means 'to be' that nation(ality)" (Ahmed 2000, 98). In this process of "self-identification," Australia "comes to be realized as belonging to the individual" who utters the "we" (Ahmed 2000, 98). Therefore, this notion of nation-hood also requires that the mainstream population receives constant reassurance and legitimization of its dominant position from the ruling government.

Defined as the way to restore or "give confidence, peace and a sense of security to a population" (Chisari 2018, 32), the term reassurance offers a productive way of theorizing the emergence of Australian values in contemporary Australian politics (Chisari 2009). Evidence of this desire to reassure can be found in the many media reports and government documents detailing immigration and the conferral of Australian citizenship, where reference is frequently made to what the "Australian people," the "general public" and "old Australia" want (Howard 2006; ACRC 2008; Whyte 2015), while the opinion of aspiring citizens is rarely sought. Rather, these "new" Australians are demonized and presented as either victim or villain while they are dictated to on how they should live according to Australian values. Successive governments, in turn, act as "providers of protection and security" (Bigo 2002, 65) and by constantly reminding the "mainstream" that they need reassurance, they in turn create the population's anxious need for reassurance.

The institutions and principles of the FitzGerald Report

This desire to promote Australian values as a way to educate migrants on how to be model Australian citizens first appeared in the government report, *Immigration: A Commitment to Australia*. More commonly known as the FitzGerald Report, this report was prepared under the Labor Hawke government by the Committee to Advise on Australia's Immigration Policies (CAAIP 1988) and was released in 1988, a year dominated by fervent nationalism when the nation celebrated two hundred years of white colonization. The FitzGerald Report also came at a time soon after comments had been made by eminent historian Geoffrey Blainey, who sparked the "race debate" by commenting that too many Asians were being allowed to migrate to Australia, which he believed the Australian population could not integrate because of their differences (Stratton 1998). This sentiment was reflected in the FitzGerald Report, which stated that "most Australians" were concerned about "change to their own society and often to their personal worlds" (CAAIP 1988, 2).

Today, the FitzGerald Report is more popularly remembered for its attack on the policy of multiculturalism (Stratton 1998). At that time, multiculturalism as the official policy that promoted cultural diversity had been enacted fifteen years earlier and commanded bipartisan support by the major political parties under the federal governments of Whitlam, Fraser and Hawke. Yet for the authors of the FitzGerald Report, multiculturalism and its focus on group membership were considered to be a threat to national social cohesion. The committee of authors dedicated considerable space and time to debating the relevance of multiculturalism in Australian society, as the report stated:

> There is disquiet about the way immigration is thought to be chang-
> ing Australia. Immigration policy is held by many to be a grab bag of
> favours.

Many Australian-born see government as protecting all interests but theirs. Multiculturalism, which is associated in the public mind with immigration, is seen by many as social engineering which actually invites injustice, inequality and divisiveness (CAAIP 1988, 3).

While the FitzGerald Report focused on attacking the policy of multiculturalism, it was also concerned with citizenship issues affecting migrants and refugees, and it defined Australian identity and the citizenship process through a set of core national values. These values were not labeled as "values" per se, but they were described specifically as the "institutions and principles" of the Australian way of life. The report stated:

> In inviting people to immigrate to Australia, we need to make it very
> clear that the unacceptable and repugnant are not to be transplanted,
> that the commitment we require to our society includes, fundamentally,
> a commitment to accept and respect basic institutions and principles.
>   These include parliamentary democracy, the rule of law and equality
> before the law.
>
> (CAAIP 1988, 4)

The principles and institutions outlined in the FitzGerald Report are almost identical to the principles that today have been officially defined as Australian values in the Australian Values Statement. The message that the report aimed to convey was that Australia has an established culture framed by core values and that these needed to be protected from the "repugnant" and "unacceptable" values of others. Hence migrant-cum-citizens needed to adopt Australian values, that is, the principles and institutions, in order to reassure the community and safeguard the social well-being of the Australian population.

The FitzGerald Report continued in its cautionary tone, warning that:

> Intending immigrants must be made aware that these (institutions and
> principles) are fundamental, and before departure be given the text of a
> declaration they will be asked to make at the time of taking citizenship,
> in which they will have to make a commitment to accept and respect
> these institutions and principles.
>
> (CAAIP 1988, 5)

This recommendation represents the first official demand for a values declaration and emphasized the responsibility that individuals had to take in order to ensure their sense of belonging in the Australian community. The committee provided a model of the "possible citizenship declaration" that should be made by new citizens at the citizenship ceremony, and this, too, included the same principles and institutions that today are included in the Australian Values Statement.

The proposed declaration included in the FitzGerald Report required that immigrants "endeavor to inform themselves" about the principles and related institutions which Australian laws are based on (CAAIP 1988, 68). They should "accept," "respect" and "fulfill" their duties as new Australian citizens, suggesting a form of affective citizenship that pre-dated the values discourse's current preoccupation with the securitiza-tion of immigration and citizenship. Hence, in this neoliberal climate, migrants become reconceptualized as individuals who have to self-regulate their conduct in order to demonstrate their commitment to Australia in exchange for the privilege of being granted migrant/worker status. It highlights how aspiring citizens fit into certain "games of truth" about Australian identity, and in the process, these aspiring citizens participate in practices of self-formation and practices of freedom in the hope of developing and transforming themselves to attain a certain mode of being (Foucault 1997, 282), in this case, in order to become model and knowl-edgeable Australian citizens.

Interestingly, at the time, the FitzGerald Report did not consider that the recommendation of a values pledge should be used as a way of defin-ing a set of core national values. The committee emphasized that there should not be "a prescription of core values," as it considered that "the core is too disputed and the values are too much in flux" (CAAIP 1988, 5). Hence, while there are similarities and continuities between the values, institutions and principles that the migrant needed to understand in the FitzGerald Report and Howard's Australian Values Statement of 2007, there was also the recognition during that "celebratory bicentennial year" in 1988 under a Labor Hawke government that values were contested and prone to changes.

The Hawke government rejected many of the FitzGerald Report's rec-ommendations, including the proposed values declaration, and in 1989 it released the National Agenda for a Multicultural Australia (NMAC 1999), reiterating its continued support for the policy of multiculturalism. In par-ticular, the National Agenda defined "the fundamental principles of mul-ticulturalism" as the right to express one's cultural identity and heritage, equality of treatment and opportunity and for individuals "to accept the basic structures and principles of Australia" (CAAIP 1988, 10). Once more, some of these listed obligations are very familiar to the Australian values that are current today. Hence, we see not only the articulation of multicul-turalism and Australian identity being conflated here but also the emergence of the notion of mutual obligation between the individual and the state.

The shared values of the Australian Compact

The next official attempt to introduce a civics values declaration in Australia appeared in 2000 in the report, *Australian Citizenship for a New Century*. This report was prepared by the Australian Citizenship Council under the Howard government. In his opening letter to the minister for citizenship, the council chair, Sir Ninian Stephen, a former High Court judge and governor-general of Australia, articulated the council's belief that Australian citizenship was a "major success story" and a "unifying concept" that needed to focus on continuity rather than change (ACC 2000, 1–2). One of the most important recommendations made in the report was the promotion of the "Australian Compact," a declaration detailing core civic values. Stephen informed Immigration Minister Ruddock that:

> with that Centenary (of Federation) in view we believe that the primary focus should be on Australian citizenship as involving certain widely held but often unexpressed civic values rather than simply on the legal status of Citizenship. These civic values, having evolved over time, already form the foundation of Australia's democratic society. We believe that they can be stated as a set of seven shared values in the nature of an Australian Compact.
>
> (ACC 2000, 1)

Values here were expressed in both positive and productive terms. Stephen made claims of the "widely held but often unexpressed civic values" that reflected community attitudes towards citizenship in Australia, reflecting the council's belief that these articulated civic values underpinned Australian citizenship. While stressing that these values were the "foundation of Australia's democratic society," Stephen also acknowledged that they have "evolved over time," suggesting a notion of progress and improvement in this "success story." The Australian Citizenship Council defined the meaning of citizenship as encompassing "ideals of civic life that can be seen as the public core values in a society whose people follow many different beliefs and ways of life, are of many different national and ethnic origins" (ACC 2000, 6). Australian values were thus conflated with civic life, and the council recognized, unlike in the FitzGerald Report, that the notion of public civic values was inclusive of differences. Furthermore, in stating that there should be no "nationalistic boasting or self-regard" (ACC 2000, 14–5), the Australian Citizenship Council offered the Australian Compact as an alternative way of conceptualizing national identity (Holland 2005, 2010). As the meaning of compact suggests, the council's objective was one of commonality and mutuality, that is, a tool for reassurance that infers the two-way process between the individual and the population that underpins neoliberal ways of governing.

Examining the Australian Citizenship Council's 2000 report reveals both the continuities and discontinuities that feature in Australian citizenship discourses in recent time. Again in a celebratory year, this time, the Centenary of Federation, there was continuity with the idea of defining core civic values as a mechanism to manage the Australian population. There were also discontinuities. For instance, "valuing the unique status of the Aboriginal and Torres Strait Islander peoples" and respecting and caring for "the land we share" (ACC 2000, 16–7), which were included as part of the values of the Australian Compact, had disappeared from the Australian Values Statement by the time it was introduced in 2007, reflecting the Howard government's conservative views on policies relating to Indigenous reconciliation and climate change. Different, too, was the significance granted to the relationship between multiculturalism and Australian values, as the council recommended that:

> the principles of the 'Australian Compact' should play an essential part in discussion on the civic values involved in 'Australian multiculturalism'.
> An emphasis of this kind can underline the differences between the idea of social cohesion (different social forces holding together) and the idea of social conformity (everyone being the same). Council believes that to speak of social cohesion is not to say 'you must all become like us', 'us' being an imagined 'typical Australian' who does not exist. It is to say that what we have in common, what holds us together, are the core civic values which, as Australian multiculturalism implies, include strong acceptance and respect for cultural diversity.
>
> (ACC 2000, 19)

The council's report continued that core civic values should be seen as part of the multiculturalism "package," and those Australian values "proclaim that Australians can live together in peace and have a strong sense of community with their country even though they are different from each other in many ways" (ACC 2000, 13). The council also emphasized that "the ideas about what is peculiar to the Australian experience change over time" (ACC 2000, 14). Hence, one of the main messages from the Australian Citizenship Council's report, *Australian Citizenship for a New Century,* was that differences could coexist and lead to social harmony. The council's notion of social cohesion differed significantly from what it would become by 2007, when social cohesion was sought to guard against differences and preserve the notion of a "typical Australian," with a core culture based on a British and Judeo-Christian heritage (Howard 2006).

The recommendation for the Australian Compact was not endorsed by the Howard government. Clearly, there was to be no need for government intervention in the year 2000 in ensuring that the concept of civic values was promoted as part of Australian multiculturalism because as the government's response stated, there was "no strong community demand"

(Commonwealth of Australia 2001, 9), highlighting the government's objective of wanting to reassure the mainstream foremost. Perhaps, too, it was the council's recommendation that shared values be understood as part of Australian multiculturalism which had discouraged the prime minister from approving it, for it must be remembered that Howard was a strong critic of multiculturalism (Chisari 2012). The council's report was shelved for the time being.

Australian values make a comeback in the Australian Citizenship Test

Seven years later, the Howard Coalition government had a change of mind and introduced the Australian Values Statement as one of its final legislative changes before its electoral defeat in November 2007. Also known as Form 1281, the Australian Values Statement is the current official declaration of core civic values that all long-term Australian residency visa holders must agree to respect and sign before being granted permission to enter Australia. As previously mentioned, this declaration was accompanied by the Australian citizenship test, a computerized multiple-choice test that all eligible migrants and refugees must sit and pass in order to become Australian citizens. The primary objective of these mechanisms was to ensure that all aspiring citizens learn and understand Australian values, the set of core civic principles officially defined by government.

At the second reading of the Australian Citizenship Amendment (Citizenship Testing) Bill 2007, Minister for Immigration and Citizenship Kevin Andrews stated that "while people are not expected to leave their own traditions behind, we do expect them to embrace our values and integrate into the Australian society" (Commonwealth of Australia 2007, 4). The prime minister, too, made similar comments during the lead-up to the launch of the Australian citizenship test. At a press conference in December 2006, Howard summed up his rationale for introducing a test to determine suitability for the conferral of Australian citizenship:

> This is a test that affirms the desirability of more fully integrating newcomers into the mainstream of Australian society. . . . It's about bringing people together after they've come here and that's what the country wants. The country wants a unifying commitment to the values and the future of this society.
>
> (Howard and Robb 2006, 3)

For the prime minister, a test that promoted Australian values would have the effect of reassuring "the country" that migrants could integrate and that this would in turn ensure social cohesion. And it was a mechanism of government that, unlike the Australian Compact, rejected the promotion of differences. Instead, it was integration, which has the meaning of making something whole, "as one," and complete, that was the desired outcome. Howard further suggested that "the country" wants this, where the country could be understood to be the "native-born" Australians he defined as "the mainstream." A values test, therefore, could demonstrate to the country that migrants want to make a significant commitment to the nation's present and future well-being. Hence, the federal government's discourse on Australian values was made technical through the implementation of the citizenship test, which draws on neoliberal forms of governing that place the impetus on the individual to acquire these values, rather than focusing on citizenship as a status that can deal with inequalities and other social problems faced by migrants in their everyday lives.

What is particularly interesting about the introduction of the Australian Values Statement and its accompanying Australian citizenship test is that both coincided with the dismantling of official policy on multiculturalism. And this was no accident. Ever since his days in opposition, John Howard had echoed the sentiments of the FitzGerald Report in opposing the policy of multiculturalism (Howard 1995). By 2006, Howard ensured that the national multicultural statement was not renewed, while talk on Australian values escalated (Chisari 2012, 139). Therefore, by the end of his government's fourth term in office, the focus on celebrating the population's cultural diversity that had been enshrined in the policies and services of multiculturalism had now become unacceptable to Howard's national vision and were replaced with a focus on emphasizing the individual responsibility of those seeking to become naturalized Australian citizens. Today, the word multiculturalism no longer features in government rhetoric and, when expressed publicly, it is merely done so in the context of folklore and spectacle (Chisari 2012). It has been conclusively replaced by the demand that migrants commit to Australian values.

Securing our Western values

It is clear then that since the introduction of the Australian citizenship test in October 2007, public debate about Australian values has greatly intensified. Today, Australian values are not only called upon to define national identity, but they have also been implicated in securitization discourses and are offered as the solution to combat youth radicalization and terrorism (Chisari 2018). Under the current Turnbull Coalition government, the concept of Australian values has also been incorporated as part of counter-terrorism processes in citizenship legislation (Allegiance Act 2015) that demands that certain dual nationals demonstrate allegiance to Australia through their support of Australian values. This is particularly astonishing since Turnbull, who had initially criticized the proposed legislation as "unconstitutional" (Kenny 2015), has modified his views upon becoming prime minister (Turnbull 2015a). During his first national security speech in November 2015 that immediately followed the fatal shooting of police civilian employee Curtis Cheng by a fifteen-year-old radicalized youth, Turnbull adopted the language of Australian values, stating that "the strongest weapons we bring to this battle are ourselves, our values, our way of life" (Turnbull 2015b). Turnbull continued:

> This is an important step as we all unite to ensure that we keep Australia safe and ensure that we make it utterly clear to everybody, those who love us and those who seek to harm us too, that we will never walk away from our Australian values.
>
> (Turnbull 2015b)

The promotion of national values as a mechanism of security is not uniquely Australian. It has also been taken up by other leaders in many liberal democratic nations who want to reassure their populations that they are taking measures to protect their national identities, their Western values and their way of life. For example, soon after the Paris terrorist attacks in November 2015, prominent political leaders condemned them as attacks against Western values. French President Francois Hollande spoke most passionately, declaring that "these attacks were war. It was an attack against our values, against our youth and our way of life" (Henn 2015). British Prime Minister David Cameron soon followed, evoking unity and harmony with France and consoling the French people that "your values are our values, your pain is our pain, your fight is our fight" (Crossley 2015). Pointedly, too, Barack Obama, president of the United States, summed up the tragic events with the declaration that "this is an attack not just on Paris. It's an attack not just on the people of France. But this is an attack on all of humanity and the universal values we share" (Rosenfeld and Pramuk 2015).

Clearly then, the call for nations to protect their national values is a phenomenon that is here to stay. Yet this does not mean that national values are fixed and stable concepts. As this historical analysis has illustrated, the concept of Australian values is an invention used by governments at particular times to serve particular purposes in an uncertain world affected by the processes of globalization. By highlighting their transformation over the past thirty years from principles and institutions linked to multiculturalism to their present-day use as mechanisms of securitization, we reveal the ever-changing, evolving and multiple functions of values. In doing so, we open up the possibility of new and multiples ways of defining national identities and national values and new and multiple ways of being Australian. In this way, Australian values will continue to serve as a neoliberal mechanism of affective citizenship that reassures the mainstream population and self-regulates the conduct of migrants, ensuring that the Australian population will remain protected and prosperous.

Bibliography

Ahmed, Sara. 2000. *Strange Encounters: Embodied Others in Post-Coloniality.* London and New York: Routledge.

Australian Citizenship Amendment (Allegiance to Australia) Act 2015 (Cth) (Austl.). www.legislation.gov.au/Details/C2015A00166.

Australian Citizenship Council (ACC). 2000. *Australian Citizenship for a New Century: A Report by the Australian Citizenship Council.* Canberra: Commonwealth of Australia. http://pandora.nla.gov.au/pan/53892/20070509-0000/www.citizenship.gov.au/law-and-policy/legislation/report.html.

Australian Citizenship Review Committee (ACRC). 2008. *Moving Forward . . . Improving Pathways to Citizenship: A Report by the Australian Citizenship Test Review Committee.* Canberra: Department of Immigration and Citizenship.

Bhandar, Davina. 2010. "Cultural Politics: Disciplining Citizenship." *Citizenship Studies* 14, no. 3: 331–43.

Bigo, Didier. 2002. "Security and Immigration: Toward a Critique of the Governmentality of Unease." *Alternatives: Global, Local, Political* 27: 63–92. https://doi.org/10.1177/03043754020270S105.

Chisari, Maria. 2009. "Critical Constructions of a National Australian Identity." In *Studies in Applied Linguistics and Language Learning*, edited by Ahmar Mahboob and Caroline Lipovsky, 14–28. Newcastle upon Tyne: Cambridge Scholars Publishing.

Chisari, Maria. 2012. "The History and Values of Australian Citizenship Testing." In *New Voices, New Visions: Challenging Australian Identities and Legacies*, edited by Catriona Elder and Keith Moore, 137–51. Newcastle, UK: Cambridge Scholars Publishing.

Chisari, Maria. 2015. "Testing Citizen Identities: Australian Migrants and the Australian Values Debate." *Social Identities* 21, no. 6: 573–89. https://doi.org/10.1080/13504630.2015.1013931.

Chisari, Maria. 2018. "Re-Imagining Australian Citizenship: Australian Values and Allegiance to Australia." *Coollabah* 24–25: 30–44. http://dx.doi.org/10.1344/co201824&2530-44.

Committee to Advise on Australia's Immigration Policies (CAAIP). 1988. *Immigration: A Commitment to Australia.* Canberra: Australian Government Publishing Services.

Commonwealth of Australia. 1999. *A New Agenda for Multicultural Australia* [Online]. Canberra. Viewed 11 May 2012, www.immi.gov.au/media/. . ./multicultural/pdf_doc/agenda/agenda.pdf.

Commonwealth of Australia. 2001. *Australian Citizenship . . . A Common Bond – Government Response to the Report of the Australian Citizenship Council.* Canberra: Commonwealth of Australia.

Commonwealth of Australia. 2007. "House of Representatives: Australian Citizenship Amendment (Citizenship Testing) Bill." Second Reading: Speech, Department of Immigration and Citizenship. Canberra. http://parlinfo.aph.gov.au/parlInfo/genpdf/chamber/hansardr/2007-05-30/0010/hansard_frag.pdf;fileType=application%2Fpdf.

Crossley, Lucy. 2015. "David Cameron Warns There May Be British Casualties in the Paris Terror Attack and Tells France: 'We Will Do Whatever We Can to Help'." *Daily Mail Australia*, 14 November. www.dailymail.co.uk/news/article-3318273/

We-help-David-Cameron-chair-emergency-Cobra-meeting-Paris-attacks-British-nationals-France-warned-stay-indoors.html#ixzz3y6zK8cUy.

Elder, Catriona. 2007. *Being Australian: Narratives of National Identity*. Sydney: Allen & Unwin.

Foucault, Michel. 1997. "The Ethics of the Concern for Self as a Practice of Freedom." In *Ethics: Subjectivity and Truth: Michel Foucault*, edited by Paul Rabinow, 281–301. New York: The New Press.

Henn, Peter. 2015. "Francois Hollande Declares France Is Now at War with Isis with Second Night of Bombings." *Express*, 17 November. www.express.co.uk/news/world/619784/Hollande-France-war-ISIS-Paris-attacks.

Holland, Alison. 2005. "The Common Bond? Australian Citizenship." In *Australia's History: Themes and Debates*, edited by Martyn Lyons and Penny Russell, 152–71. Sydney: UNSW Press.

Holland, Alison. 2010. "Australian Citizenship in the Twenty-First Century: Historical Perspectives." In *From Migrant to Citizen: Testing Language, Testing Culture*, edited by Christina Slade and Martina Mollering, 39–59. Basingstoke, Hampshire and New York: Palgrave Macmillan.

Howard, John. 1995. "Politics and Patriotism: A Reflection on the National Identity Debate: Speech," Commonwealth Parliamentary Library, Melbourne. http://parlinfo.aph.gov.au/parlInfo/search/display/display.w3p;orderBy=customrank;page=0;query=politics%20and%20patriotism;rec=8;resCount=Default.

Howard, John. 2006. "A Sense of Balance: The Australian Achievement." John Howard's Australia Day Address to the National Press Club. http://australianpolitics.com/2006/01/25/john-howard-australia-day-address.html.

Howard, John, and Andrew Robb. 2006. "Transcript of the Prime Minister the Hon John Howard MP Joint Press Conference with Mr Andrew Robb, Parliamentary Secretary to the Minister for Immigration and Multicultural Affairs, Phillip Street, Sydney." Media Release, 11 December. Viewed 16 May 2012, http://parlinfo.aph.gov.au/parlInfo/search/display/display.w3p;query=Source%3A%22PRIME%20MINISTER%22%20Author_Phrase%3A%22robb,%20andrew,%20mp%22;rec=0.

Johnson, Carol. 2010. "The Politics of Affective Citizenship: From Blair to Obama." *Citizenship Studies* 14, no. 5: 495–509.

Kenny, Mark. 2015. "Malcolm Turnbull Breaks Ranks on Citizenship, Declaring Constitution Cannot Be Compromised." *Sydney Morning Herald*, 16 June. www.smh.com.au/federal-politics/political-news/malcolm-turnbull-breaks-ranks-on-citizenship-declaring-constitution-cannot-be-compromised-20150616-ghpkl0.html.

National Multicultural Advisory Council (NMAC). 1999. *Australian Multiculturalism for a New Century: Towards Inclusiveness*. www.dss.gov.au/sites/default/files/documents/11_2013/australian_multiculturalism_for_a_new_century_towards_inclusiveness.pdf.

Perera, Suvendrini. 2007. "'Aussie Luck': The Border Politics of Citizenship Post Cronulla Beach." *Australian Critical Race and Whiteness Studies Association e-journal* 3, no. 1: 1–16. https://acrawsa.org.au/wp-content/uploads/2017/12/CRAWS-Vol-3-No-1-2007.pdf.

Perera, Suvendrini. 2009. "White Shores of Longing: 'Impossible Subjects' and the Frontiers of Citizenship." *Continuum: Journal of Media and Cultural Studies* 23, no. 5: 647–62.

Rosenfeld, Everett, and Jacob Pramuk. 2015. "French President Announces State of Emergency." *CNBC*, 13 November. www.cnbc.com/2015/11/13/obama-france-attack-is-on-all-of-humanity-and-universal-values-we-share.html.

Stratton, Jon. 1998. *Race Daze: Australia in Identity Crisis*. Sydney: Pluto Press.

Stratton, Jon. 2011. *Uncertain Lives: Culture, Race and Neoliberalism in Australia*. Newcastle upon Tyne, UK: Cambridge Scholars.

The Parliament Commonwealth of Australia, Australian Citizenship Amendment (Allegiance to Australia) Bill 2015.

Turnbull, Malcolm. 2015a. *Statement – Paris Terrorist Attack*. 14 November. www.malcolmturnbull.com.au/media/statement-paris-terrorist-attack.

Turnbull, Malcolm. 2015b. *Transcript – Prime Minister Malcolm Turnbull Addresses Summit*. 15 October. www.malcolmturnbull.com.au/media/prime-minister-malcolm-turnbull.

Whyte, Sarah. 2015. "People Killing, Raping and Pillaging in Syria Should Lose Citizenship: Dutton." *Sydney Morning Herald*, 25 May.

4 The effect of media on public perceptions of Muslims in the United States

Andreas Miles-Novelo and Craig A. Anderson

Media are omnipresent. In modern societies they pervade almost every moment. As we move further into the age of the internet and as smart phones have become prolific, it has become more and more difficult to escape the ever-encompassing aspects of media in our lives. Dystopic science fiction films of the second half of the twentieth century frequently displayed a world in which video screens are everywhere, and even going to a restaurant failed to provide relief from their constant exposure. Such over-the-top depictions have become the reality of early twenty-first-century life. Although there certainly are benefits to having instant access to digital information, there are costs as well. One of those costs is that the information presented is often inaccurate. This is particularly true of portrayals of minority groups. The main goal of this chapter is to examine the effects of exposure to media stereotypes of Muslims and the psychological processes underlying them.

When it comes to stereotypes portrayed in media, a psychological study shows us that it can be immensely powerful and persuasive. In fact, we may base most of our beliefs and attitudes about specific groups of people not from real-world experience with members of that group, but from what we see in the media. We know that this is especially true for most Americans when it comes to stereotypes about Muslims (Nisbet, Ostman, & Shanahan, 2009). We also know that minorities are underrepresented and are often shown in a negative light in American media news and entertainment media (Behm-Morawitz & Ortiz, 2013; Tukachinsky, Mastro, & Yarchi, 2015). In short, the effect that screen media can have on public discourse and political policies is powerful, especially for minority groups with which most Americans have little direct contact.

The media represent Muslims as violent and draw immediate links with terrorism (Saleem, Prot, Anderson, & Lemieux, 2015). This is true across all forms of media, whether it's cable news (Dixon & Williams, 2015), movies and television (Alsultany, 2012; Shaheen, 2009), print news (Nacos & Torres-Reyna, 2007; Powell, 2011), or even video games (Dill, Gentile, Richter, & Dill, 2005; Šisler, 2008). In light of this, research has found that screen media play a significant role in creating attitudes towards Muslims and that most negative attitudes towards Muslims stem from exposure to negative media portrayals (Das, Bushman, Bezemer, Kerkhof, & Vermeulen, 2009; Kalkan, Layman, & Uslaner, 2009; Nisbet et al., 2009; Saleem & Anderson, 2013).

Media effects on attitudes towards Muslims

A significant shift in portrayals of Muslims in media occurred after the September 11, 2001, attacks in the United States. The shift was felt not only in the United States but globally (Akbarzadeh & Smith, 2005; Saeed, 2007). What this shift represented was a consistent and persistent portrayal of Muslims as terrorists and violent and was meant to dehumanize them (presenting them as an "other"). What this led to is a public mind-set about Muslims that is largely negative (Alsultany, 2012; Dill et al., 2005; Dixon & Williams, 2015; Nacos & Torres-Reyna, 2007; Powell, 2011; Shaheen, 2009). Worldwide public opinion survey data show us that Islam and Muslims are commonly associated with violence by those who are non-Muslim (Pew Research Center, 2013; Sides & Gross, 2013). This stereotype of Muslim people, groups, and nations increases support for harsh policies against Muslims (Nisbet et al., 2009).

To compound this, research has shown that the media is the most formative tool when one creates attitudes towards Muslims. Attitudes towards (i.e., positive or negative affective reactions) and stereotypes about (i.e., beliefs and expectations) particular groups of people (e.g., Muslims, Republicans, Sherpas, men) are shaped by direct personal experiences and by indirect mediated experiences with members of the groups. People who have many positive experiences with a particular outgroup (a group of which one is not a member), either directly (e.g., working or playing with members of the outgroup) or indirectly (hearing and viewing positive stories about them), tend to develop generally positive attitudes and stereotypes about the group. But people who have many negative experiences, either directly and/or indirectly, naturally tend to develop negative attitudes and stereotypes. Thus, people who have little or no direct contact with a particular outgroup and who are frequently exposed to extremely negative stories and images of that group are particularly likely to develop extremely negative attitudes and stereotypes about that outgroup. Furthermore, people use their attitudes and stereotypes to guide their own behavior towards outgroup members, both on the occasions when they directly interact with members of that group and when they make more abstract decisions about that group, such as voting behavior on public policy issues. Indeed, once negative attitudes and beliefs develop about a group, other contradictory sources of information are often ignored (Kalkan et al., 2009). Thus, because most Americans have little direct experience with Muslims, exposure to media stereotypes about Muslims strongly influences the creation of negative attitudes towards them (Das et al., 2009; Kalkan et al., 2009; Nisbet et al., 2009; Saleem & Anderson, 2013). For Americans, the mental link between terrorism and Muslims is in fact so strong that studies have shown that cues about terrorism, with no reference to Arabs/Muslims in the report at all, actually increase an implicit bias against Muslims (Park, Felix, & Lee, 2007; Saleem & Anderson, 2013).

We also know that the type of media Americans consume plays a big role in political knowledge. This is important to note because some media outlets put more of an emphasis on certain kinds of stories and "scripts" than do other sources – often to meet ratings standards (Gilliam & Iyengar, 2000). Research has indicated that people who consume news media only from opinion-based cable-news sources score just as poorly, if not worse, on current events questionnaires than people who listen to NPR or Sunday morning talk shows (Cassino, Woolley, & Jenkins, 2012). The type of news that we consume, and its accuracy, has a lasting impact on our schemas of outgroups, especially if that news is our main source of information on them.

It is well known among attitudes scholars that people tend to have an implicit bias against members of typically disadvantaged groups and that this bias is unconscious (Jolls & Sunstein, 2006; Greenwald, McGhee, & Schwartz, 1998). Furthermore, most of our daily behaviors, and schemas, work implicitly, so we don't even recognize these biases that we hold. It has been noted that "the identifying feature of implicit cognition is that past experience influences judgment in a fashion not introspectively known by the actor" (Greenwald & Banaji, 1995). From what we now understand about media and its effects on cognition, we know that some of these biases and schemas are created by whichever media sources we consume, especially if the same message is consistently repeated.

This association between Muslims and violence is not new or entirely unique to them as an outgroup. We see similar biases and associations made in America about African Americans (Gilens, 1996; Valentino, 1999). Watching news of crime automatically primes negative stereotypes of African Americans (Dixon & Azocar, 2007; Gilliam & Iyengar, 2000; Valentino, 1999). This extends to support of harsh policies as well. Seeing African American suspects as opposed to white ones increases people's support of the death penalty and three-strike legislation (Gilliam & Iyengar, 2000; Gilliam, Valentino, & Beckmann, 2002). This association between crime and African Americans has become so readily available in memory, largely because of its prevalence in media, that it is hard to overcome (Saleem et al., 2015). The question now becomes, does this implicit negative association lead to actual policy support? If so, what are the psychological processes that underlie these effects?

Psychological processes

There are a couple of key social-cognitive theories that can help us understand the media's influence on our attitudes and behaviors (Anderson &

Bushman, 2018; Bandura, 1977; Huesmann, 1998). Things like memory, thought, and decision-making are reliant on these complex associative memory networks that represent our cognitions and emotions. Your experiences (in real life and in media) directly influence the development of the different links that create associations between different concepts. If you have particular concepts that are frequently simultaneously activated over a long period of time, they become interconnected and form what we call "highly accessible schemas." In other words, these well-practiced schemas become easily retrievable and readily available sets of thoughts, feelings, and beliefs. Schemas are what inform our interpretations, guide our perceptions, and inform our behaviors (Saleem, Prot, Anderson, & Lemieux, 2017).

Media influences these associations by, as briefly referenced before, constantly showing and affirming differing stereotypes and associations. This happens through priming processes in the short term (showing you the stereotype). This constant priming in the short term can then lead to long-term changes in our schemas (beliefs and attitudes) of those groups through learning processes. We know these sorts of effects happen with presentations of media stereotypes in both long-term and short-term changes in schemas (e.g., Dixon, 2006; Dixon & Azocar, 2007; Ramasubramanian, 2011).

The inverse is also true. When media display outgroups in a positive way, support and positive attitudes towards that group increase (Bodenhausen, Schwarz, Bless, & Wänke, 1995; Mastro & Tukachinsky, 2012; Power, Murphy, & Coover, 1996; Ramasubramanian, 2007, 2011, 2015; Saleem et al., 2015). When shown counter-stereotypical examples of an outgroup, people experience increased sympathy toward them and reductions of attribution of causal responsibility to the outgroup members for bad events (Bodenhausen et al., 1995; Power et al., 1996). These counter-stereotypical examples (especially ones that are purposefully "constructive") can also build positive attitudes about the outgroup and is the most effect way to reduce negative attitudes and beliefs about them (Mastro & Tukachinsky, 2012; Saleem et al., 2015).

Some correlational evidence suggests that in Caucasians, there is a recollection of negative media portrayals of African Americans that works in tandem with holding negative stereotypes of African Americans (Saleem et al., 2015). This also is attributed to support of harmful policies and agendas against them (Mastro & Kopacz, 2006; Tan, Fujioka, & Tan, 2000). To add to this, Ramasubramanian (2011) designed an experiment where they found that participants primed with stereotypical images of celebrities were less supportive of affirmative action legislation and showed more prejudicial feelings (Saleem et al., 2017).

Saleem et al. (2017) found that "exposure to news portraying Muslims as terrorists is significantly associated with support for military action in Muslim countries." They also controlled for exposure to media violence in general and found that this effect was independent of one's exposure to violent media. As they noted, the effect "was specific to media portrayals of

Muslims as terrorists." They also looked at the effects of exposure to Muslims as terrorists on Americans' support for civil restrictions for Muslim Americans.

What they found was that people who perceived Muslims as terrorists and also supported civil restrictions were mediated by perceptions as Muslims as aggressive. They also found that short-term exposure to news that posited Muslims as terrorists increased support for international and domestic policies that would actively harm Muslims (Saleem et al., 2015). They also found the inverse. Seeing counter-stereotypical portrayals of Muslims decreased support for the same policies. In addition to manipulating these short-term effects, the team looked at long-term exposure to terrorism news and found that those who were more exposed supported more of these harmful policies. They also found that you could predict how much these shifts would occur based upon political orientation. So the effect of showing someone counter-stereotypical examples is strongest if that person is a political conservative, as they generally go from being very favorable of harmful policies to finding them unfavorable (Saleem et al., 2015).

This work clearly shows a direct relationship between media portrayals of stereotypes and support for political policies. While there was always a fundamental theoretical underpinning of this in psychological research, only recently has it been manipulated in a laboratory setting and confirming those beliefs, especially for and against Muslims. Due to the harsh uptick in negative stereotypes portrayed of Muslims in media, we should expect this to be a cause of support, or even apathy, for policies harming Muslims.

What Saleem et al. (2015) did was ask participants about their support for policies exclusively and explicitly harming Muslims. This shows us that these aggressive responses were due to viewing Muslims as a threatening outgroup, and these were predicted by whether or not people saw Muslims as aggressive. Their study shows us how media coverage can get us to buy into a stereotype and then how belief in that stereotype leads to support for certain political policies. While much research had been done on how media can shape people's support for policies (welfare, the death penalty, three strikes laws) that may implicitly harm an outgroup, it hasn't been until now that we've been able to attribute it to aggressive action explicitly targeted at the group.

Discussion

As hinted at earlier, these underpinnings can be expanded into broader contexts of race-related media portrayals and subsequent policy support. Someone can claim a majority of Mexican immigrants are "rapists and murderers," and while there may no factual basis for this claim, simply having that stereotype out in the media will increase support for policies that would harm Mexican immigrants. Media are dominant and so important that they drive a majority of political discourse and should be treated as such.

We know that the inverse is true too. We can use media to help create empathy and to change perceptions of stereotypes, even if they are long-held beliefs. By having fair and balanced representation of outgroups, as well as showing counter-stereotypical examples, we can lead to less hostile feelings towards them (Bodenhausen et al., 1995; Mastro & Tukachinsky, 2012; Power et al., 1996; Ramasubramanian, 2007, 2011, 2015).

As noted before, while these studies are mostly focused on short-term changes, the psychological research shows us that repeated exposure leads to long-term changes in people's schemas. So beginning to implement these changes in our media now will lead to long-term support for more constructive and positive policies. However, these approaches should come hand in hand with other trainings, such as media literacy, since we know there is a prevalence of "fake news" perpetrating many of these topics.

In sum, psychological research shows that there is a negative portrayal of Muslims in media and constant exposure to these stereotypes leads to support of harmful policies against them. However, the inverse is true, and we can reverse these feelings and support for harmful policies by showing counter-stereotypical examples of Muslims. We should take this knowledge and apply it to other outgroups and policies as well; that way we can help mitigate the potentially harmful effects media may play on our perceptions of outgroups.

References

Akbarzadeh, S., & Smith, B. *The Representation of Islam and Muslims in the Media (The Age and Herald Sun Newspapers)*. Clayton, VIC: School of Political and Social Inquiry, Monash University, 2005.

Alsultany, E. *Arabs and Muslims in the Media Race and Representation After 9/11*. New York: New York University Press, 2012.

Anderson, C. A., & Bushman, B. "Media Violence and the General Aggression Model." *Journal of Social Issues* 74 (2018): 386–413.

Bandura, A. "Self-Efficacy: Toward a Unifying Theory of Behavioral Change." *Psychological Review* 84 (1977): 191–215.

Behm-Morawitz, E., & Ortiz, M. "Race, Ethnicity, and the Media." In K. Dill (Ed.), *The Oxford Handbook of Media Psychology* (pp. 252–264). New York, NY: Oxford University Press, 2013.

Bodenhausen, G. V., Schwarz, N., Bless, H., & Wänke, M. "Effects of Atypical Exemplars on Racial Beliefs: Enlightened Racism or Generalized Appraisals." *Journal of Experimental Social Psychology* 31 (1995): 48–63.

Cassino, D., Woolley, P., & Jenkins, K. "What You Know Depends on What You Watch: Current Events Knowledge across Popular News Sources." MS, Public Mind Poll, Fairleigh Dickinson University, 2012.

Das, E., Bushman, B. J., Bezemer, M. D., Kerkhof, P., & Vermeulen, I. E. "How Terrorism News Reports Increase Prejudice Against Outgroups: A Terror Management Account." *Journal of Experimental Social Psychology* 45 (2009): 453–459.

Dill, K. E., Gentile, D. A., Richter, W. A., & Dill, J. C. "Violence, Sex, Race and Age in Popular Video Games: A Content Analysis." In E. Cole & J. Henderson Daniel

(Eds.), *Featuring Females: Feminist Analyses of the Media* (pp. 115–130). Washington, DC: American Psychological Association, 2005.

Dixon, T. L. "Psychological Reactions to Crime News Portrayals of Black Criminals: Understanding the Moderating Roles of Prior News Viewing and Stereotype Endorsement." *Communication Monographs* 73 (2006): 162–187.

Dixon, T. L., & Azocar, C. L. "Priming Crime and Activating Blackness: Understanding the Psychological Impact of the Overrepresentation of Blacks as Lawbreakers on Television News." *Journal of Communication* 57 (2007): 229–253.

Dixon, T. L., & Williams, C. L. "The Changing Misrepresentation of Race and Crime on Network and Cable News." *Journal of Communication* 65 (2015): 24–39.

Gilens, M. "'Race Coding' and White Opposition to Welfare." *American Political Science Review* 90 (1996): 593–604.

Gilliam, F. D., & Iyengar, S. "Prime Suspects: The Influence of Local Television News on the Viewing Public." *American Journal of Political Science* 44 (2000): 560–573.

Gilliam, F. D., Valentino, N. A., & Beckmann, M. N. "Where You Live and What You Watch: The Impact of Racial Proximity and Local Television News on Attitudes About Race and Crime." *Political Research Quarterly* 55 (2002): 755–780.

Greenwald, A. G., & Banaji, M. "Implicit Social Cognition: Attitudes, Self-Esteem, and Stereotypes." *Psychological Review* 102 (1995): 4–27.

Greenwald, A. G., McGhee, D., & Schwartz, J. "Measuring Individual Differences in Implicit Cognition: The Implicit Association Test." *Journal of Personality and Social Psychology* 74 (1998): 1464–1480.

Huesmann, L. R. "The Role of Social Information Processing and Cognitive Schema in the Acquisition and Maintenance of Habitual aggressive Behavior." In R. G. Geen & E. Donnerstein (Eds.), *Human Aggression: Theories, Research, and Implications for Policy* (pp. 73–109). New York, NY: Academic Press, 1998.

Jolls, C., & Sunstein, C. R. "The Law of Implicit Bias." *California Law Review* 94 (July 2006): 969–996.

Kalkan, K. O., Layman, G. C., & Uslaner, E. M. "Bands of Others? Attitudes Toward Muslims in Contemporary American Society." *Journal of Politics* 71 (2009): 847–862.

Mastro, D. E., & Kopacz, M. A. "Media Representations of Race, Prototypicality, and Policy Reasoning: An Application of Self-Categorization Theory." *Journal of Broadcasting & Electronic Media* 50 (2006): 305–322.

Mastro, D. E., & Tukachinsky, R. "The Influence of Media Exposure on the Formation, Activation, and Application of Racial/Ethnic Stereotypes." In E. Scharrer (Ed.), *The International Encyclopedia of Media Studies, Media Effects/Media Psychology* (Vol. 5, pp. 295–315, A. Valdivia, Gen. Ed.). Boston, MA: Wiley-Blackwell, 2012.

Nacos, B. L., & Torres-Reyna, O. *Fueling Our Fears: Stereotyping, Media Coverage, and Public Opinion of Muslim Americans*. New York: Rowman & Littlefield, 2007.

Nisbet, E. C., Ostman, R., & Shanahan, J. "Public Opinion Toward Muslim Americans: Civil Liberties and the Role of Religiosity, Ideology, and Media Use." In A. Sinno (Ed.), *Muslims in Western Politics* (pp. 161–199). Bloomington, IN: Indiana University Press, 2009.

Park, J., Felix, K., & Lee, G. "Implicit Attitudes Toward Arab-Muslims and the Moderating Effects of Social Information." *Basic and Applied Social Psychology* 29 (2007): 35–45.

Pew Research Center. "After Boston, Little Change in Views of Islam and Violence." 2013. Retrieved from www.people-press.org/files/legacy-pdf/5-7-13%20Islam%20Release.pdf

Plutzer, E. "Becoming a Habitual Voter: Inertia, Resources, and Growth in Young Adulthood." *American Political Science Review* 96 (2002): 41–56.

Powell, K. A. "Framing Islam: An Analysis of U.S. Media Coverage of Terrorism Since 9/11." *Communication Studies* 62 (2011): 90–112.

Power, J. G., Murphy, S. T., & Coover, G. "Priming Prejudice: How Stereotypes and Counter-Stereotypes Influence Attribution of Responsibility and Credibility Among Ingroups and Outgroups." *Human Communication Research* 23 (1996): 36–58.

Ramasubramanian, S. "The Impact of Stereotypical Versus Counterstereotypical Media Exemplars on Racial Attitudes, Causal Attributions, and Support for Affirmative Action." *Communication Research* 38 (2011): 497–516.

Ramasubramanian, S. "Media-Based Strategies to Reduce Racial Stereotypes Activated by News Stories." *Journalism & Mass Communication Quarterly* 84 (2007): 249–264.

Ramasubramanian, S. "Using Celebrity News Stories to Effectively Reduce Racial/Ethnic Prejudice." *Journal of Social Issues* 71 (2015): 123–138.

Saeed, A. "Media, Racism and Islamophobia: The Representation of Islam and Muslims in the Media." *Sociology Compass* 1 (2007): 443–462.

Saleem, M., & Anderson, C. A. "Arabs as Terrorists: Effects of Stereotypes Within Violent Contexts on Attitudes, Perceptions, and Affect." *Psychology of Violence* 3 (2013): 84–99.

Saleem, M., Prot, S., Anderson, C. A., & Lemieux, A. "Exposure to Muslims in Media and Support for Public Policies Harming Muslims." *Communication Research* 44, no. 6 (2017): 841–869.

Shaheen, J. *Reel Bad Arabs: How Hollywood Vilifies a People.* Northampton, MA: Olive Branch Press, 2009.

Sides, J., & Gross, K. "Stereotypes of Muslims and Support for the War on Terror." *Journal of Politics* 75 (2013): 583–598.

Šisler, V. "Digital Arabs: Representation in Video Games." *European Journal of Cultural Studies* 11 (2008): 203–220.

Tan, A. S., Fujioka, Y., & Tan, G. "Television Use, Stereotypes of African Americans and Opinions on Affirmative Action: An Affective Model of Policy Reasoning." *Communication Monographs* 67 (2000): 362–371.

Tukachinsky, R., Mastro, D., & Yarchi, M. "Documenting Portrayals of Race/Ethnicity on Primetime Television Over a 20-Year Span and Their Association with National-Level Racial/Ethnic Attitudes." *Journal of Social Issues* 71 (2015): 17–38.

Valentino, N. A. "Crime News and the Priming of Racial Attitudes During Evaluations of the President." *Public Opinion Quarterly* 63 (1999): 293–320.

Part II
Education, citizenship, and cultural diversity
Introductory remarks

Abe W. Ata

The essays in this section provide an overview of select literature on the vicissitudes of multiculturalism, otherwise articulated as cultural diversity. An argument on the link between the growth in migration and redefinition of citizens through access to welfare, ignoring the inclusion of neo-nationals, is clearly elaborated.

Daneshpour (Chapter 5) examines our gendered identity and its role in shaping perceptions about social groups and the inequities that trouble our nation, their root causes and potential solutions. We are reminded at the outset that human experience has always been a gender-based story of diversity and evolving identity – from the roots planted many generations ago by Native Americans, immigrants and enslaved peoples to the fresh traditions brought by those arriving from all over the world. In order to have a solid understanding of our gendered identity and the history of our immigration and diversity, we must have an awareness of our enmeshed histories. Together these provide a vision of how to examine our experiences fairly and fully. Another main theme this part addresses relates to issues and implications of cultural diversity, cosmopolitan citizenship and education for Australia. Jakubowicz (Chapter 6) directs his attention to education which, he points out, has been at the centre of debates and struggles over the meaning and direction of Australia's ideologies and practices of nationalism. Two fundamental elements, cosmopolitanism and nationalism, offer competing visions and programmes for education in terms of curriculum, learning processes or performance outcomes. This chapter traces the major axes of tension in Australian education between religious and secular, private and state and developmental and functional. It takes a number of key events that reveal how the contradictions, and challenges, in Australian history are being expressed in the real worlds of educational discourse, such as the education ministers' statements on diversity, the place of language education, the struggle over religious definitions of the good life and the online attacks on an Indigenous poet in the aftermath of a senior high school exam that contained one of her poems. The analysis is extended by Miller and Amorsen in Chapter 7. This chapter examines intersections, opportunities and implications for social justice in relation to the three cross-curriculum priority areas in the Australian Curriculum for Foundation – Year 6, identified as Aboriginal and Torres Strait Islander histories and cultures, as Australia and Australia's engagement with Asia, and as sustainability. The three cross-curriculum priorities are designed to inform a "relevant, contemporary and engaging curriculum" that builds on the educational goals of the Melbourne Declaration on Educational Goals for Young Australians (Australian Curriculum, Assessment and Reporting Authority [ACARA], 2016). Underpinned by two goals, the Melbourne Declaration values the role of education in building a democratic, equitable and just society. How the social citizenship rights integral to being complete citizens have gradually diminished is a subject that Sealey addresses in focusing on Britishness and British values (Chapter 8). The chapter argues that net migration resulting in a 54% increase in post–World War II Britain, a growth that is higher than the EU average, triggered enormous policy changes. The two key foci of these policies have been reducing net migration and limiting entitlement to benefits for migrants vis-à-vis benefit tourism. The latter is the main focus of this analysis; how these policy changes are underpinned by a retreat from multiculturalism towards assimilation, consequences of the diminution of social citizenship rights integral to being complete citizens; the depth of their impact on the rights of new migrants; and its limitation on the citizenship rights of the wider non-migrant population.

Reference

Australian Curriculum, Assessment and Reporting Authority (ACARA). 2016. *National Education Evidence Base Inquiry* (pp. 1–8).

5   Gender, race, and identity in the United States

Manijeh Daneshpour

Many major political powers in the United States have used phrases like an "empire of liberty," "a shining city on a hill," "last best hope on earth," "the leader of the free world," and "the indispensable nation" to describe the United States (Walt 2011). These descriptions are based on the "American exceptionalism" idea, which suggests that American political structure, value system, and history are distinctive and unique and deserve global respect and appreciation. These statements also suggest that the United States is both predestined and entitled to be the sole superpower in the world.

While the United States possesses several unique qualities which mostly center around being a highly religious society and allowing individuals to have freedom of expression, the U.S. foreign policy follows the global politics and is responsible for many atrocities committed across the globe. Thus, it is highly critical for Americans to not focus on the country's "exceptional" qualities because by doing so, it prevents us from working to improve on areas where we act very much the same as any other country. For example, the United States has been one of the biggest colonial powers in modern history. It started with 13 small colonies on the eastern side of America, but ultimately took over Texas, Arizona, New Mexico, and California after a war with Mexico in 1846 and expanded across North America. In this process, it eradicated most of the Native Americans and constricted those who survived to impecunious and impoverished reservations. However, conversations about these atrocities rarely happen except for these constant reminders that America has always been and will be the land of the free and the home of the brave.

However, those of us who have lived in this country for many years and have witnessed lack of equality and social justice for many have come to realize that there are many areas of disparity and discrimination which continue to evolve and become worse. In other words, while in the United States our diversity is one of our great strengths, it poses a number of questions. Thus, many of us have been asking some fundamental questions: What does it mean to be American? Is it possible for us to have a collective sense of identity, regardless of our cultural and ethnic background? What are the standards and doctrines that strengthen our American society? How do we hold on to our multiple identities while being part of the broader community? And most importantly, why are gender and race two primary unresolved issues in our collective sense of identity?

This chapter brings together current thinking about our cultural identity, gender and minority status, immigration, and citizenship in America based on my academic and personal experience living in the United States. Though I am an Iranian native, I have lived in the West for the entirety of my adult life and have received all of my academic education in the United States. At the same time, I have been very closely and deeply connected to Eastern cultural dynamics and have grown to appreciate the remarkably diverse richness of the Eastern backdrop, particularly as it is juxtaposed with my Western way of life on a daily basis. Further, even though I served as somewhat of an ambassador between the Western and Eastern therapy mind-set, much of my research efforts and publications have been centered on examining challenges of immigrants and their evolving sense of identity (Daneshpour and Dadras 2018; Dadras and Daneshpour 2018; Daneshpour 2016, 2012, 2009a, 2009b, 2009c). Further, as a Muslim woman who wears a hijab as a symbol of modesty and has a high position in Western academia, I am always in battle with myself and others to hold on to my own gendered identity (Daneshpour 2009a). Thus, the discussion in this chapter is meant to be challenging, thought-provoking, and intentional in order to contribute to our ongoing examination of race, gender, and immigration issues. I hope we dedicate ourselves to our continuing discussion of race and gender issues in the context of the human rights and equality framework.

Cultural identity

For many of us, our non-European immigrant cultural identity serves as an excellent source of individuality and distinctiveness. Many ethnic identity approaches have centralized around understanding more recent immigrants of color from Africa, Latin America, and the Caribbean (Britto and Amer 2007), since for majority of these newcomers the color of their skin is the primary source of their distinctiveness and has been utilized as a tool for both theoretical and instrumental models of ethnic identity (Britto and Amer 2007). It is important to note that cultural identity here is defined as a multidimensional concept signifying an evolving sense of self when we see ourselves affiliated with a distinct group or two and when there is an interaction between religion, culture, ethnicity, and national identities (Raman 2006). In a sense, our cultural identity affects us more than our ethnic identity, which only signifies our connection to a specific group with a shared heritage, history, and cultural backgrounds. We also form our cultural identity over time, which evolves from a subtle and not very refined sense of identity to a more sophisticated sense of self. Thus, different aspects of our identity like our religious, cultural, and national identities may get reinforced at different rates autonomously and get altered unconventionally.

Minority women and gender-based inequality

The U.S. history of immigration for women of color begins with slavery for blacks; invasion of the country for Latinas, Puerto Ricans, Native Americans, and the Philippines; or involuntary and semi-involuntary immigration for Japanese and Chinese. Furthermore, compared to European settlers who were integrated into mainstream American society both culturally and linguistically within one or two generations, women of color continued to remain racially and culturally distinct groups with the pattern of marginalization starting at an early age. Not many of these women can earn a high school degree, a smaller group can afford to graduate from college, and only a few can continue their education and get a graduate degree (Patten 2016). The majority of ethnic minority women must provide for their families, and even when they do get a degree or become economically independent or even become a professional in a field, it is more about financial survival than advancement in a career (Patten 2016). Further, ethnic minority women's survival requires them to develop an informal community to support; finding ways to take care of their health care needs; and trying to effect organizational, political, and social change (Patten 2016).

The problem with separating race and gender inequality

Our mainstream American public policy somehow still assumes that even though there may be various forms of discrimination, racial disparity and the exclusion of minorities are gender-neutral experiences. However, research reveals that women of color experience inexplicably more discrimination in the workplace; they are marginalized economically, suffer from poorer health, and have fewer educational prospects (Mirza 2008). However, their prodigious "invisibility" in the discussion about race and gender equality is beyond imagination even though public policy should be based on and informed by these issues. And yet, they are highly "visible" in so many negative ways, like Muslim women wearing a hijab being constantly in the media spotlight. It seems like gender-related struggles of women of color are not recognized as a way to affect political issues or public policy to have a positive impact on their lives. In fact, many argue that in studies about women of color, these women are characterized by a "normalized absence/pathologized presence" approach (Mirza 2008: 6). This indicates that even in their inclusion they are either described as problematic or most are not included in the majority of discussions about race and gender, and unfortunately, gender continues to be perceived as a white women's issue, the same way that race is perceived as a black male issue (Mirza 2008).

The only possible way to change this pattern is by realizing the intersectionality of patriarchy and power that controls and preserves the gender hierarchy and conceals white privilege. Only then we can comprehend why women of color continue to suffer and pay higher consequences for gender and racial inequalities. It is impressive that against all the odds and increasing equality gaps, women of color continue to be social activists and change the face of their communities with hard work and self-sacrifice.

Intersectionality of gender, identity, immigration, and diversity

A lot of anti-discrimination and public policy legislation is trying to address the assiduous disparities and forms of social segregation and marginalization among people of color (Lester and Clapinska 2005). There are written laws about direct and indirect bias associated with age, sexual orientation, racial background, skin color, language, religious orientation, political views, national origin, place of birth, and disability. However, as much as these encompassing protections exist, they are not as obtainable as is needed for those who are mostly marginalized and excluded in society. Furthermore, the hidden way that women of color get excluded shows that these policies and measurements have not been successful in helping women of color effectively deal with many of these challenges. The intersectionality of women of color is never reflected in the equality discourses because women are still classified in unmeaningful ways when it comes to the application of much of the legislation (Mirza 2008). Women of color are often described universally and simplistically, utilizing biased political and social classifications that reinforce the status quo. For example, women's experiences of destitution, mistreatment, abandonment, ostracism, and discrimination are often dismissed in formal equality documentation and data because they get categorized as either women's issues and therefore "gendered," or women of color issues and therefore "raced." Further, other formal equality jargon gets distributed throughout various identities with regard to the intersection of social class, sexual orientation, age, disability, religious ideology, and cultural differences. Thus, in societal discourses about gender equalities, these women's lived experiences are not honored, and their multiple identities get falsely divided without realizing that all of these identities are highly intertwined. As Maynard explains, "racism and sexism are interlocking systems of domination that uphold each other. It does not make sense to analyze 'race' and 'gender' as if they constitute discrete systems of power" (Maynard 1994: 21). Further, Crenshaw states: "racism, patriarchy, social class and other systems of oppression simultaneously structure the relative position of these women at any one time creating specific, and varied, patterns of inequality and discrimination" (1991: 1245).

African American, postmodern, and feminists of color have repeatedly challenged the analysis of the lived experiences of women of color and are asking for a deeper level of understanding of the intersectionality of women's lives. Understanding this intersectionality will help us see the powerful interactions between power, ideology, and identity that sustain a system of inequality and discrimination affecting the complex multiple social positions of minority women's lived experiences. However, because there is no intersectional examination, women of color do not get included in legislation when there are separate provisions for race, sex, and disability discrimination. They often experience double discrimination with race and gender, or even triple discrimination, if, for example, disability, sexuality, age, or religion is also a contradictory aspect. Women of color cannot readily challenge accusations of discrimination based on racial or sexual discrimination without proving the multiple layers of discrimination based on power, privilege, and patriarchy. One group of women of color that has suffered the consequences of the intersectionality of their multiple identities are Muslim women.

Muslim women and their identity as other

Contrary to popular belief, Muslims have immigrated to the United States for decades (Zahedi 2011). Amber Haque states that "the first Muslims may have arrived in the Americas as early as 1178 when Chinese Muslim sailors landed on the West Coast." She also claims that "out of the estimated 6 to 10 million African slaves who came to the United States in later centuries, about 30 percent of them were Muslims" (Haque 2004: 4). Further, Suleiman (1999) reveals that "Arab Muslims migrated to America between 1870 and World War II. They came from Greater Syria (Syria, Lebanon, the Palestinians, Israel, Jordan and possibly Iraq), which was under Ottoman rule" (p. 2). Additionally, after World War II, and specifically after the abolishment of the national origin quota and the passing of the Immigration Act of 1965, Muslim immigration to the United States dramatically increased and became more diverse As a group, Muslims seem to have higher levels of education compared to average Americans, have higher salaries, and mostly enjoy integrated professional and personal lives (CAIR 2006: 3). Even though Muslims have been living in the United States for a long time and come from many different backgrounds, socioeconomic status, and social groups, mainstream Americans perceive them as a religious community without allowing for any diversity within the group (Daneshpour 2016) and view them as "different and as the perpetual 'Other'" (Afridi 2001: 2). It is important to note that even though other marginalized groups like Japanese, Chinese, Italians, Polish, Irish and African descent have also experienced discrimination historically, "Muslims remain the other – the outsiders, the enemy, and the threat" (Afridi

2001: 2). Europeans and Americans have continued to view the "Muslim Other" (Zahedi 2011) based on the belief in the Crusades Wars, which supported the dominance and supremacy of Christianity. Christian missionaries worked very hard to create this perception by postulating "the lens through which people of the West saw Muslims" (in way that they may be viewed as uncultured with lower standards and regard for their social life. (Haddad, Smith and Moore, 2006: 24). These popular paradigms have always been the main justification for Europeans' "civilizing mission" (Zahedi 2011).

Edward Said, in his book, *Orientalism* (1979), states that the expansionist and colonial powers of the West trying to dominate and control the colonized people of the East had to create a persona about the Easterners that was vastly different from the people of the West. This fabricated contrast was very much needed to justify the conquest of their lands and their oppression. The sad part of the story is that this legacy intensely and vigorously continues today, but, of course, using different moral and political justifications (Daneshpour 2016).

The more significant challenge is that Muslim women have to deal with the burden of this Otherization more than even Muslim men based on their gender, because many Muslim women use the hijab as a sign of modesty. The Western view of the hijab as a sign of female oppression has concealed the multidimensional issues Muslim women have had with many other forms of oppression. Interestingly enough, even though the veil overwhelmingly gets associated with the religion of Islam, in Persia and Byzantine dynasties, veiling was a sign of status and class. According to Esposito (1992), the practice of veiling as a form of modesty was also used by Jews and Christians, and in fact, veiling was adopted by early Muslims after their exposure to Western colonialist cultures (Nashat 2003: 38). It is important to note that today the practice of veiling for Muslim women is limited to covering their head and wearing loose clothing, and other than Iran and Saudi Arabia, which have made wearing the hijab mandatory for mostly political gains, the rest of the Muslim world does not even require women to wear a hijab. However, Westerners have always intertwined their perceptions of Muslim woman with the hijab, which perpetuates the essentialized view of Muslim women. In this view, Muslim women are submissive, dependent, oppressed, and in constant subjugation to the male power in the family. Muslim women in the United States, along with many Muslims around the globe, challenge this perception. Even though many years have passed since 9/11, the U.S.-led wars in Afghanistan and Iraq keep the American popular view of Muslims extremely harmful. Still, Muslim women continue to challenge this static and monolithic view by attending interfaith programs; doing radio and TV interviews; and providing training for companies, health care professionals, and police forces. Muslim American women hope that this alliance connects them with those men and women in all communities with more progressive views in order to change the gender dynamics oppressing women in all communities.

Sociopolitical implications of honoring diversity

Honoring and glorifying democracy in America has vacillated significantly at different points in history, given the struggles we have experienced with racism and ethnic diversity. For the most part, throughout history, the United States has not honored the arrival of newcomers to this country if they have not been from European nations and has endorsed a deliberate system of prejudice and discrimination against many ethnic minorities. However, there have been many advances since the Civil Rights Movement and the affirmative action policies to level the playing field in many ways. Some believe that Americans have shifted their perspectives and that blatant prejudice is no longer tolerable (Wolsko, Park, and Judd 2006), even though the election of Donald Trump in 2016 may have proven this theory wrong. In its place, the prevalent sociopolitical discussion about multiculturalism is about how to honor equality and serve the needs of a diverse population but also to preserve a unified and stable nation. This discussion brings up several essential questions: Does a democratic society operate better when we act as a unified society, ignoring differences, or when we honor differences and cultural diversity? How should we relate to each other to reinforce equality, interconnectedness, congruence, and open-mindedness versus reinforcing divisiveness, prejudice, and discrimination?

In the United States, these challenging questions have been discussed and answered in so many ways based on different sets of ideologies. The most prominent strains occur between those who support assimilation and those who support cultural diversity and multiculturalism. There are considerable differences regarding these two camps' perceptions of politics, education, and law that continue to drive them apart. For those to whom the idea of assimilation makes sense, they advocate for the traditional melting pot ideal, in which people put aside their cultural backgrounds and become part of the nation of individuals in harmony with each other (Wolsko, Park, and Judd 2006), utilizing a European intellectual tradition as the core for the educational system (Bauzon 2012). In this system, everyone continues to be loyal to the constitutional agreement about equal rights, eliminating affirmative action and any other race- and class-based solutions that are opposing a color-blind society. On the other hand, for those who promote the ideals of multiculturalism, unity, and harmony, the American melting pot is not possible (Wolsko, Park, and Judd 2006). Thus, they advocate for an educational system that can integrate the historical experiences of many diverse groups (Bauzon 2012), and the best way to move forward is to examine and question how the institutional racism has drenched the political and legal system of the United States (Crenshaw 1991).

It is apparent that there have been many disputes about how to address issues of inequality and diversity in America, and there continues to be an intense discussion related to politics, education, and law among supporters of both assimilation and multiculturalism. The supporters of assimilation discuss the critical values associated with following the conventional American culture (honoring cultural values and traditions defined directly or indirectly by the white mainstream power structure) and deemphasizing historical roots to an individual's ethnic values and cultural traditions. On the other hand, supporters of cultural diversity and honoring historical roots stress the significance of welcoming cultural diversity. These two opposing ideologies have a significant consequence in influencing relationships among different ethnic groups in the United States. A research study done by Wolsko, Park, and Judd in 2006 reveals that political views and public policies cause voting behavior to move in precisely opposite directions for those supporting assimilation versus multiculturalism. Those in support of honoring cultural diversity endorsed the continuation of policies related to affirmative action, much more merciful and compassionate immigration policy, and more humane principles for those who do not speak English. It seems like both groups valuing multiculturalism and honoring assimilation supported policies that matched their own political ideals.

It is important to note that ideals related to multicultural diversity and assimilation are based on individuals' ethnic backgrounds, with whites being the supporter of assimilation and ethnic minorities the supporter of honoring cultural differences. Basically, those who support assimilation greatly benefit from it because it upholds traditional white European perspectives and worldviews. Therefore, whites who support assimilation honor their European heritage and have much more positive feelings toward their own backgrounds and traditions compared to those of ethnic minorities. However, if ethnic minorities endorse and support assimilation, they need to abandon and relinquish their own cultural background and show loyalty to white European cultural heritage. Consequently, compared to whites, when ethnic minorities support assimilation, they do not assign positive meanings to their own cultural heritage and convey a less favorable connection to it.

A paradigm shift in race, gender, citizenship, and diversity in America

There has to be a new way of thinking that is independent of the conservative and liberal way of understanding race, gender, and ethnic minority relationships in this country. It is evident that conservatives have maintained their position on "blaming the victim" syndrome and continue to ascribe lack of conscientiousness and proper morality for all the pains and sufferings African American and other people of color have had to endure regardless of gender. It is also obvious that the liberals have kept their presumptuous perspective assuming that the answer to racism, classism, and sexism is more integration and dialogue about these issues regardless of gender. According to Cornel West, "both [perspectives] fail to see that the presence and predicaments of black people [and, by extension, other communities of color] are neither additions to nor defections from American life, but rather constitutive elements of that life" (1993: 3).

In theorizing about the significance of racial experiences in America, this paradigm shift in thinking and changing public policy should be based on how American foreign policy affects the constant flow of immigrants to this country. In essence, American international relations have always been organized based on the relic of colonialism and Cold War rationalizations, which have been the vital forces for the continuation of immigrants and people of color arriving in this country (Massey and Denton 1994).

One remarkable quality of this paradigm shift should be the progression of consciousness about the importance of gender inequality and include it in discourses about the struggles people of color face in terms of equal treatment and social justice. We need to keep the shift in our thinking by continuing an alliance with progressive forces representing immigrants and refugee communities, as well as human rights activists, third wave feminists, gay and lesbian advocates, and indigenous people all across the nation.

We should make ourselves familiar with the detrimental impact of globalization, including the increase in the wage gap and failure to provide important social services affecting the most vulnerable groups, such as immigrants, impoverished blacks, Native Americans, women, children, and the elderly. Even creating a model minority category has only been used as a weapon in the war against African Americans and Latin Americans, but it has also been used against the so-called "model" Asian immigrants themselves. It seems like race is the central theme in many of our experiences. According to San Juan Jr.: "Race, not ethnicity, articulates with class and gender to generate the effects of power in all its multiple protean forms" (Bauzon 2012: 16).

Conclusions

This chapter attempted to analytically review the struggles and challenges of ethnic minority women with their sense of identity as Americans and describe the nature and origins of contemporary race, gender, and ethnic relations in this country. It is apparent that the conservatives in the United States continue to disregard the significance of race and gender and believe that anyone can achieve the American dream if they only work hard enough. On the other hand, the liberal camp believes that there are racial inequalities and advocates programs to aid minorities if needed and believes that disadvantaged individuals need to be supported by the government. However, there has to be a paradigm shift in thinking about the intersection of race, class, gender, immigration patterns, and American foreign policy. Moreover, the United States destabilizes and starts wars with many countries across the globe, and when despite all odds immigrants can make this country their new home, there are clear and explicit structural obstacles preventing many from achieving economic success regardless of their work ethic. Further, the essence of multicultural diversity and gender-based sensitivity and inclusiveness is, at best, very trivial and does not even look at the central issues related to social justice and globalization policies of the American government. It seems like both conservatives and liberals choose to perceive these issues through the lens of American exceptionalism, patriarchal, and hierarchical standpoints and not even consider social justice and equality paradigms. They consciously and deliberately choose to forget the systemic and painful historical events that are mostly responsible for racism, as well as sexism, to function appropriately.

There must be grassroots public support and open and just political processes for racial minorities who have been traditionally marginalized to have equal access to resources. Marginalized groups, especially women of color, can play a significant role in creating a paradigm shift. In the long run, we have a lot to gain from shaping public policy and advocating for social justice. We cannot afford to be regarded as "invisible" in a society where conservatives and liberals claim that everyone can achieve his or her dreams while institutionally crushing those dreams. Further, ethnic minorities have so much to share from their past experiences in their own countries. Many people of color have immigrated to the United States from colonized countries by Western powers and have had direct and painful experiences with the way colonialism disregarded their rights in their own countries. They can stress the need for challenging the status quo and valuing justice, fairness, dignity, and mutual respect.

While much of what women of color encounter, as either immigrants or citizens in the United States, may also be common to their male counterparts, gender has always had real consequences for ethnic minority women. We have to consider how public policy and social services affect women differently based on our unique histories, beliefs, and resources in order to move toward developing strong identities, being recognized for our talents, and becoming economically independent in gendered ways. We have to realize that there are multiple and complex ways in which women of color participate in the paid workforce, simultaneously renegotiate their gender identities, and support their families.

For women of color, gender is formed, negotiated, and contested and is part of our everyday adaptation and social integration. There must be more efforts for transforming foreign and national policies that take gender into account more explicitly. There have to be more significant time investments in minority women's education, much more extensive workforce preparation and coaching, and fewer conventional gender-based career fields that can bring more significant social and economic parity and a higher level of integration in society.

Furthermore, this society can no longer disregard the tenacity of racial and gender repression and discrimination in political, economic, and social aspects for people of color. It is time to lift the burden of racial and gender inequality from the shoulder of minority men and women and take a much closer look at the institutional and structural perpetuation of racism and sexism together. The truth is that race and gender have always been an identity shaped by economic and human relations and not by biological sex and genetics. It is time to critically integrate racial inequalities and gendered identities into our discourses about the structural and institutional changes this country needs before we can think that Americans are genuinely "exceptional."

References

Afridi, Mehnaz. 2001. *Muslims in America: Identity, Diversity and the Challenge of Understanding.* Carnegie Corporation of New York. www.carnegie.org/pdf/muslims.pdf

Bauzon, Kenneth E. 2012. "Situating Communities of Color in The United States: Critical Reflections on The Paradigms of Multiculturalism and Diversity." www.academia.edu/8209807/Situating_Communities_of_Color_in_the_United_States_Critical_Reflections_on_the_Paradigms_of_Multiculturalism_and_Diversity

Britto, Pia Rebello, and Amer, Mona M. 2007. "An Exploration of Cultural Identity Patterns and the Family Context Among Arab Muslim Young Adults in America." *Applied Development Science* 11 (3): 137–150. Lawrence Erlbaum Associates, Inc. doi:10.1080/10888690701454633

Council on American-Islamic Relations (CAIR). 2006. "Western Muslim Minorities: Integration and Disenfranchisement." *Policy Bulletin*, 26 April. www.cair.com/Portals/0/pdf/policy_bulletin_integration_in_the_West.pdf

Crenshaw, Kimberlé Williams. 1991. "Mapping the Margins: Intersectionality, Identity Politics, and Violence Against Women of Color." *Stanford Law Review* 43 (6): 1241–1299.

Dadras, Iman, and Daneshpour, Manijeh. 2018. "Social Justice Implications for MFT: The Need for Cross-Cultural Responsiveness." In *Cross-Cultural Issues and Family Therapy*, edited by Shruti Poulsen and Robert Allan, 1–22. New York: Springer Publication.

Daneshpour, Manijeh. 2016. *Muslim Family and Family Therapy.* New York: Routledge, Taylor & Francis Group.

Daneshpour, Manijeh. 2013. "A 'Mini-Narrative' About My Praxis as a Muslim Feminist." *National Council of Family Relations Report* 54 (4): 1–3.

Daneshpour, Manijeh. 2012. "Family Systems Therapy and Postmodern Approaches." In *Handbook of Counseling with Muslim*, edited by Samira Ahmed and Mona Amer, 119–135. New York and London: Taylor & Francis Group.

Daneshpour, Manijeh. 2009a. "Steadying the Tectonic Plates: On Being Muslim, Feminist Academic, and Family Therapist." In *Handbook of Feminist family Studies*, edited by Sally A. Lloyd, April L. Few, and Katherine R. Allen, 340–351. Newbury Park, California: Sage Publications, Inc.

Daneshpour, Manijeh. 2009b. "Couple Therapy with Muslims: Challenges and Opportunities." In *Multicultural Couple Therapy*, edited by Mudita Rastogi and Volker Thomas, 100–121. Thousand Oaks, Ca: Sage Publication, Inc.

Daneshpour, Manijeh. 2009c. "Bridged Crossed, Paths Traveled: Muslim Intercultural Couples." In *Intercultural Couples: Exploring Diversity in Intimate Relationships*, edited by Terry Karis and Kyle Killian, 207–229. New York and London: Routledge, Taylor & Francis Group.

Daneshpour, Manijeh, and Dadras, Iman. 2018. "Muslim Families and Contemporary Challenges." In *Handbook of Contemporary Islam and Muslim Lives*, edited by Gabriele Marranci. Springer Netherlands: Springer Publication.

Esposito, John. 1992. *The Oxford Encyclopedia of the Modern Islamic World*. New York: University Press.

Haddad, Yonne Y., Smith, Jane, and Moore, Kathleen. 2006. *Muslim Women in America: The Challenge of Islamic Identity Today*. Oxford: Oxford University Press.

Haque, Amber. 2004. "Islamophobia in North America: Confronting the Menace," In *Confronting Islamophobia in Educational Practice*, edited by Barry van Dreil, 1–18. Oakhill, VA: Trentham Books.

Lester, Anthony, and Clapinska, Lydia. 2005. "An Equality and Human Rights Commission Worthy of the Name." *Journal of Law and Society* 32 (1): 169–186. doi:10.1111/j.1467-6478.2005.320_1.x

Massey, Douglas S., and Denton, Nancy A. 1994. *American Apartheid: Segregation and the Making of the Underclass*. Cambridge, MA: Harvard University Press.

Maynard, Mary. 1994. "Race, Gender and the Concept of Difference." In *The Dynamics of Race and Gender: Some Feminist Interventions*, edited by Afshar Haleh and Maynard Mary, 21. London: Taylor and Francis.

Mirza, Heidi Safia. 2008. "Ethnic Minority Women: A Prospectus for the Future." In *Seeing Double: Race, and Gender in Ethnic Minority Women's Lives*, edited by Zohra Moosa, 6–30. London: Lloyd TSB Foundation for England & Wales.

Nashat, Guitty. 2003. "Women in Pre-Islamic and Early Islamic Iran." In *Women in Iran from the Rise of Islam to 1800*, edited by Nashat Guitty and Beck Lois, 11–47. Chicago, IL: University of Illinois Press.

Patten, Eileen. 2016. "Racial, Gender Wage Gaps Persist in the U.S. Despite Some Progress." *Fact Tank*. http://pewrsr.ch/29gNnNA

Raman, Shanti. 2006. "Cultural Identity and Child Health." *Journal of Tropical Pediatrics* 52 (4): 231–234. doi:10.1093/tropej/fml034

Said, E. 1979. *Orientalism*. New York: Vintage Books.

Suleiman, Michael W. 1999. *Arabs in America Building a New Future*. Philadelphia, PA: Temple University.

Symington, Alison. 2004. "Intersectionality: A Tool for Gender and Economic Justice." *Women's Rights and Economic Change* 9. The Association for Women's Rights in Development (AWID).

Walt, Stephen M. 2011. "The Myth of American Exceptionalism." October 11. https://foreignpolicy.com/2011/10/11/the-myth-of-american-exceptionalism/

West, Cornell. 1993. *Race Matters*. Boston, MA: Beacon Press.

Wolsko, Christopher, Park, Bernadette, and Judd, Charles M. 2006. "Considering the Tower of Babel: Correlates of Assimilation and Multiculturalism Among Ethnic Minority and Majority Groups in the United States." *Social Justice Research* 19 (3). doi:10.1007/s11211-006-0014-8

Yuval-Davis, Nira. 2006. "Intersectionality and Feminist Politics." *Journal of International Women's Studies* 13 (3): 193–209.

Zahedi, Ashraf. 2011. "Muslim American Women in the Post-11 September Era: Challenges and Opportunities." *International Feminist Journal of Politics* 13 (2): 183–203. doi:10.1080/14616742.2011.56003

6 Education and national identity in Australia

Issues, options, and implications

Andrew Jakubowicz

Australia increasingly faces the contradictions of national citizenship in a globalizing world. A very high proportion of its population was born outside the country (about 25% in 2016), and many Australia-born also have nationality or citizenship links to other countries through parental or even grandparental heritage (Jakubowicz, 2011a). Questions of nationality, citizenship, loyalty, and identity have come to the fore, tempered by fierce debates over refugees, alleged foreign manipulation of diasporic communities, and religious diversity and conflict (Tsiolkas, 2013).

Recent years have seen a heightened flurry of legislative action to allow for the "denationalization" of people who have forsaken the privilege of citizenship. As Pillai and Williams note, "The Australian denationalisation laws may have greater utility as a symbolic statement that disloyalty or lack of allegiance will be met with exclusion from the Australian citizenry. This casts Australian citizenship as a conditional status, contingent upon good behaviour" (Pillai and Williams, 2018: 881).

During the period after the 2016 Australian federal election a number of parliamentarians were forced to resign due to High Court findings that they were still foreign citizens despite their claimed ignorance of this fact. In Australia foreign citizens cannot be candidates for the federal parliament (Orr, 2018). So despite its roots in immigration and its globalizing reach into the world, the country has yet to resolve what it means to be a multicultural society and how such a self-ascribed label affects its sense of nationhood.

The British invaded the Australian continent in the late eighteenth century, with the land seized by the invaders coming under British Crown control by an apparent right of conquest, even though few, if any, Indigenous nations "surrendered" to the invader (Jupp, 2007). Earlier White arguments that it was a Terra Nullius, occupied but not owned or controlled by the native peoples, were rejected by the High Court in the Mabo Case of 1992 (Cunliffe, 2007). However, unlike many other territories the Indigenous owners of which were defeated by the British Crown and its successor political entities, Australia never saw the signing of any peace treaties. Thus, even under British and now Australian law Native Title persists where it has not been extinguished. Australia is thus a patchwork of legal 'agreements' overlaid by colonial and national/state legislation designed to control the relations between European and other immigrants and the Indigenous 'Other'. The Indigenous population has for decades sought to regularize the relationship, pursuing "treaty" without making much headway against the opposition of the Commonwealth government (Jakubowicz and Icduygu, 2015).

Built on generations of immigration, the contemporary population is drawn from over 200 foreign nationalities, speaking many more languages, and following over 100 religions. The underlying tensions are those of a polyglot and multiethnic immigrant nation, compounded by the unresolved situation of the Indigenous peoples, defined by a hierarchical power structure that acknowledges the Charter British people, their mores, and institutions (Jupp, 2018). Historically education has been the key institution in melding this diversity into a broadly integrated national community through the sharing of language (English), history (British and empire), religion (primarily Christian), and cultural institutions (primarily sport, imperial ceremony, and broadcast TV) (Jupp, 2002; Swetnam, 2003). With increasing globalization, the political removal of cultural barriers to immigration, and the emergence of policies associated with multiculturalism, each of these integrative realms has become less coherent and more reflective of the diversity of the population. Education provides a specific arena where the fragmentation and new coalescences can be understood, where values are being tested, and where social cohesion is being placed under pressure (Smolicz and Secombe, 2009; Jakubowicz, 2010b).

Competition for identities and cultural diversity in education

Education forms the most important investment a society can make in its future in terms of its economy, its culture, and its social order. Education to a large extent determines personal well-being, health, income and social mobility, flexibility, and innovation. Education is thus both a personal and a social good; indeed, it demonstrates more than any other area of our lives how dependent we are on each other to fulfill our needs and contribute to the wider community benefit.

Over the past generation or so, Australians have come to see the value of the cultural diversity of its population, as well as its resilience and vitality. Cultural diversity, especially in its policy frame of "multiculturalism", carries three key implications – heritage culture preservation and survival, intercultural engagement and synergies, and capacity to operate as global citizens. Cultural diversity, the focus of a 2005 international convention through United Nations Educational, Scientific and Cultural Organization (UNESCO) (Australia acceded to the convention in 2009), has forced these issues onto the policy table of governments across the world.

Perhaps because of its difficulty as a concept in public policy, multiculturalism remains a point of division (Jakubowicz and Ho, 2013). This division is based on two totally different interpretations of the nature of the social world and the role of culture in sustaining social cohesion. One approach to "multiculturalism" recognizes that a plurality of cultural groupings can coexist and interact in complex modern societies – indeed, recognition of difference and the resolution of differential power between groups becomes the essence of public policy. The other approach portrays a society as unitary, as though it requires a single shared culture, with diversity an aberration that passes in time through processes of assimilation, to which end public policy should be directed. At the heart of these debates over cultural diversity lies the role of education (Jakubowicz, 2013).

Australia's cultural diversity has played an integral role in the formulation and implementation of Australia's education system, both in terms of those it sought to include and how it would do this and those it effectively did not include. Despite the intention of the early public education proponents, the public system did not lead to a unitary framework for education (Mayrl, 2016). The withdrawal of state aid did not ensure universal free and secular education. Rather, it created a three-sector system made up of wealthy, primarily Protestant private schools (joined by some elite Catholic colleges), an underfunded but doggedly non-secular diocesan Catholic sector, and an always less than fully funded state sector. It ensured that a religious orientation would necessarily underpin the non-state sector, embedding the division in the imagination of Australian public political culture, of a religious and value-saturated non-state sector in contrast to a secular and therefore supposedly value-free or relativist state sector. This distinction created the basis for a long-term and embittered divide that thwarted secularism as the hallmark of modern rational education.

One consequence of the development of Australian education arrangements was that most working-class children in the post-war waves of European (and later Asian) immigration were funneled either (by a large majority) into a state system that was assimilationist, rationalist, and nationalist or a Catholic diocesan system that preached religious singularity while being slightly less concerned about the catholicity of cultures that the children's parents brought. Neither version of 1960s modernity survived the end of White Australia, while both were transformed by the emerging debates about multicultural education (Australia Department of Education Employment and Workplace Relations, n.d.; Tsolidis, 2008; Victoria Department of Education and Early Childhood Development, 2009).

The advent of multicultural education in both systems during the 1970s was part of the more widespread acceptance of cultural diversity as a continuing and welcome element in the increasingly complex and cosmopolitan social fabric of the nation. That transformation paralleled the rapid expansion of Commonwealth involvement in and funding of both state and Catholic systems and the initially slow expansion of ethno-cultural private education.

In 1960 Justice Dovey, chair of a Commonwealth inquiry into the education of immigrant children, condemned those immigrant parents who sought to keep their cultures and pass them on to their children, viewing them as recalcitrant subversives undermining Australia's social homogeneity (Dovey, 1960). A decade later government policy had already been relabeled as "integration", and a decade further on it had become "multicultural" (Australia Review of Post-arrival Programs and Services to Migrants, 1978). These changes came from the recognition that Australia needed to retain its immigrants, which it would only do successfully, it was argued, if they felt their own histories and cultures were respected and their languages retained in the community. Some immigrants welcomed this recognition and its license to selectively nurture their own pasts; others sought only to escape their pasts and be accepted as undifferentiated Australians.

The multicultural context

The 1978 Galbally Report into migrant and refugee settlement services codified multiculturalism and laid out its key institutions. Forty years after the paradigm shift that it marked, there is considerable dissent about the policy and its implications. At the national level the anxiety about policies that accept cultural diversity, infamously labeled by conservative historian Geoffrey Blainey as generating "a nation of tribes", has resulted in significant withdrawal from proactive multiculturalism (Gobbo, 1995). National and state policies have moved in different directions, not necessarily related to the political bent of the government, but rather to the underlying sense of what might best hold Australian society together (Lewins, 1987).

While government policies broadly accept that there will be a constant inflow of people with differing histories, values, and experiences who will be physically and culturally differentiated by regions of origin, there is less agreement about what to do with this diversity. Will it naturally dissipate over generations, leaving only a surface multicolored aesthetic beneath which everyone loves cricket? Do immigrants want to remember their pasts within a frame of nostalgia, but get on with their lives so that they can enter a mainstream Australian future? How important is cultural transmission through the generations – should it be a private matter for families, a communal matter for those interested in cultural preservation, a national policy supported by governments at all levels, or alternatively, an outcome that governments should seek to prevent? What priority should be placed on learning languages, including English, Indigenous, and immigrant community languages, as well as the major world trading cultural and business languages? Are the dominant society's values partial or universal (Costello, 2006)? If universal, is any deviation from them (such as accepting there is cultural pluralism and value diversity) a surrender to prejudice and archaic self-interest (Fear, 2007; Betts, 2008b)?

Which of the dominant society's various values are truly shared among the native-born and reared, and which are partial, avoided, or regularly breached? If the dominant society's values are partial in that they express the ethno-cultural priorities of the charter peoples, what implications are carried for minority groups? How reciprocal and truly multidirectional are the relations between communities in a multicultural society (Colebatch, 2010)? These questions do not generate simple answers – however, they do serve to nuance a debate that has too often been brutish and simplistic.

Under the impact of political ideology, renascent nationalism, and neo-liberal economic ideas, the vision of public education as the beachhead for intercultural engagement appeared to be eroding. In the wake of 9/11 and the campaigns within Australia against violence-extolling extremism, public conversations about education have become heavily inflected by new intercultural tensions. As the population has become more diverse with the arrival of African refugees and the growth in families from the Pacific Islands joining those from Middle East sources, the public culture became increasingly infected by racialism. In September 2007 then Immigration Minister Kevin Andrews halted the movement of refugees from Africa, claiming they had shown themselves unable to integrate into Australian society (Jakubowicz, 2010a). Popular support for immigration among Victorian voters, Andrews's home ground, fell significantly at the 2007 federal election (Betts, 2008a). African migration has been marked out as another potentially threatening pressure on social cohesion, one that intensified until a parliamentary inquiry into crime was launched in 2017 that once more targeted African migrants (Jakubowicz, 2016).

Social cohesion, social inclusion, and social justice

A conservative national government sought to rewrite the national policy on multiculturalism at the turn of the millennium. The multicultural lobby had been highly effective under the previous Hawke Labor government, stymieing the push by Labor's right wing to throw out the multicultural model and its vocabulary. Prior to his election in 1996, Howard had been strongly critical of the concept of multiculturalism, deriding and denying its potential as "a national cement for all Australians" (Jakubowicz, 2011b).

A report to the Australian Labor Party (ALP) government in 1988 recommending the end of multiculturalism was sidetracked by the prime minister's Office of Multicultural Affairs. In return it prepared the 1989 Agenda for a Multicultural Australia. Essentially the 1989 Multicultural Agenda report and its modifications in 1992 mark the last proactive articulation of cultural diversity as an underpinning of Australia's national development (Jakubowicz, 2009). The report on multicultural Australia that Prime Minister Howard later approved in 1999 stressed the nationalism of a unitary and hierarchical Australia, where British (Judaeo) Christian values crown the apex of a pyramid of power and privilege, though cloaked in the language of egalitarian populism. The one term that Howard would not accept in the revised document, even if he had to give in on "multiculturalism", was "social justice". Whatever the neo-liberal market economy would produce, however cohesive a neo-conservative society might seek to be, neither competition nor cohesion would be concerned with equity and justice.

In Australia therefore "cohesion" has a particular set of connotations. howard as opposition leader in 1988 used "social cohesion" to articulate his and his party's increasing opposition to multiculturalism as public policy and to demand a major reduction in Asian immigration (Jakubowicz, 2009). His concern, fed by Professor Blainey's worrying at the danger of multicultural policy creating "a nation of tribes", reflected a sense that one could not both promote multiculturalism with its implicit acceptance of cultural relativism and argue for a set of unitary values based on Anglo-Australian institutions and traditions (Gobbo, 1995). Howard concluded that multicultural readings of Australian society represented the antithesis of social cohesion, so much so that in 1988 the Liberal and National parties formally abandoned any commitment to multiculturalism (John Howard at www.multiculturalaustralia.edu.au/library/media/Video/id/358). While the use of the term "multicultural" was somewhat recovered for the 1996 federal election, it could not find a secure base. A socially cohesive society, Howard posited, needed agreed-upon core values, a shared sense of its common history based on its charter members, and a unified orientation to the world. The role of government would be to shepherd such legal and policy processes into existence as might be necessary to put these practices firmly into place. Whatever arrangements people in private or communally sought to make in this multicultural society should be a matter for them, not government (Betts, 2008b).

Labor after Howard almost let multicultural policy slip away altogether, only reactivating it in a minor key to support the government being able to submit positive narratives to the UN Human Rights Committee in 2011 (Jakubowicz, 2011a). Thereafter a parliamentary inquiry in 2013 advocated more strongly for an institutional underpinning, but refused to discuss the possibility of legislative support (a multicultural act as in Canada) (Joint Standing Committee on Migration (Ch: Maria Vamvakinou, 2013). With the return of the conservative coalition to government in 2013 multicultural policies were once more placed in low gear, with strong pushback on key anti-vilification legislation proposed by conservative lobby groups. The government tried in 2014 and 2017 to remove Section 18C (racial vilification) from the Racial Discrimination Act, only to have the moves defeated by coalitions of lobby groups across ethnic and Indigenous communities.

The resurgence of an interest in social cohesion in the late 2000s reflected the increasing pressure from immigrant communities on the social structure and services of European societies. These pressures dramatically expanded with the so-called Arab Spring when states throughout North Africa and the Middle East collapsed and millions of refugees sought safety in Europe. Alexander Vladychenko, director general of social cohesion for the Council of Europe, noted in 2006 at the onset of the crisis that "a question which is currently fuelling political debate in all our societies [is] 'How can we achieve social cohesion in a multicultural Europe?'" (Council of Europe, 2006). The Europeans were trying to deal with an emergent paradox of social cohesion as a consequence of an "alleged 'excessive level of diversity'". The council proposed that governments should be calling on strategic interventions geared towards human rights, participation, and active citizenship. The problem then might not lie in an incompatibility of cultures, but rather in the incapacity of the receiving societies to recognize and modify their own structures of exclusion.

The European community faced three distinct though ultimately related problems relevant to Australia and marked by Australian conservatives in 2018 as a danger to the Australian vision of cohesion. First there is the question of European identity and how it should be articulated in relation to the national identities of the member states in ways which accord with the widespread desire to see the new expanding Europe as a secular federation based on common values. Second, social marginalization and alienation characterize parts of Europe, typically accompanied by economic distress and occupational disadvantage. These issues particularly affect the Roma and Sinti, whose history of survival against the extermination attempts of the Nazis adds poignancy to their current intimidation by governments such as those of Hungary and Italy. Finally the consequences of generations of immigration from outside Europe – for example, of Turkish guest workers; ex-Commonwealth citizens from the sub-continent and Africa; and Africans, Americans, and Asians with some former colonial relation with the European powers, overlaid by the movement west of citizens of former Soviet bloc nations – generated further concerns about the porosity of borders and the perceived social distance of immigrant cultures from the assumed European heartland. These already embedded worries were heightened after the eruptions of the Arab Spring, the collapse of state institutions throughout the Middle East and Maghreb, and the flight of refugees from around the Mediterranean to Europe.

The European model of economic integration and citizenship might have offered the most secure foundations on which to underpin social cohesion, with employment and education serving as the drivers for intergenerational mobility and a longer-term social order. In the Australian context the language of social cohesion has been further complicated, again by using European discourses around social inclusion. However, where social cohesion foregrounded cultural difference as a central problem in both thought and action to be dealt with through accommodation, social inclusion effectively ignores the issue. Whereas "cohesion" implies a set of negotiating relationships between disparate but interacting parties (albeit of unequal power), "inclusion" reinforces a hierarchy of power where dominant groups essentially set the parameters under which minorities will be expected to behave in order that they gain access to the benefits associated with inclusion without disrupting unduly the benefits already taken for granted by the host majorities.

Education and social cohesion

There is of course a close relationship between economic disadvantage and social background, as well as social background and educational performance. Australia does quite well in international comparisons using the key test frameworks such as the Organisation for Economic Co-operation and Development (OECD) Programme for International Student Assessment (PISA). However, performance is closely correlated with social background, in which income, migrant status, and linguistic capacity in English are included (McGaw, 2004, 2006).

Despite broadly common curricula, different schools, as McGaw notes, "clearly divide, and do so increasingly". He stresses the following:

> Schools frequently divide on the basis of gender, faith, social background, wealth, geography and so on. Schools are, therefore, well placed to build bonding social capital within their constituencies but the important question is whether they can build bridging social capital. From an Australian perspective, we can note that our schools clearly divide each cohort of students on all of the dimensions just mentioned. We need to ask whether their practices reinforce the divisions or whether they work in any way effectively to bridge them. Given the growth of the non-government sector, we need specifically to consider whether that development, in the name of choice and, with government funding, in the name of fiscal fairness, has positive or negative effects on education outcomes and on bridging social capital and, ultimately, social cohesion.
>
> (McGaw, 2006: 30)

Students who are corralled in privileged environments tend to do well, while students corralled in disadvantaged environments have their problems reinforced. Advantaged students who mix with more disadvantaged students do not appear to suffer, and the disadvantaged students gain a great deal. So socioeconomic and cultural mixing in general improves the overall level of social and human capital in a society; on the other hand, socioeconomic and cultural segregation reduce the productivity of the society and intensify social stratification.

Antiracism approaches

One project that links all the states, though it is driven out of New South Wales, remains the "Racism No Way!" website. Begun by the Conference of Education Systems Chief Executive Officers in 2000, it carries a foreword by then Governor General Sir William Deane. Deane's perspective is personal and tough: "Knowledge of the history and impact of racism is essential for understanding and change. It can be the spark that ignites action against racism by individuals and local communities. And education is the key to that process" (Deane, 2000).

Anti-racism as an educational practice has had a difficult history. While it was strenuously advanced by lobby groups and teachers during the 1990s, especially after the 1991 Human Rights and Equal Opportunity Commission (HREOC) Racist Violence report (Moss and Castan, 1991), Keating government proposals to criminalize hate speech and activate the relevant sections of the 1966 International Convention on the Elimination of All Forms of Racial Discrimination were defeated in the Senate in the mid-1990s by a coalition of free-speech advocates and reactionary conservatives. The new Howard government after 1996 was dedicated to an "educational" approach on racism, a view underpinned by market research carried out by Eureka Strategic Research in 1997 (Eureka Research, 1998), that created the "Living in Harmony" brand. A Labor government review of Living in Harmony summarized the dominant perspective thus:

> The Eureka Strategic Research indicated that strong anti-racism messages tended to produce negative results by alienating a broad range of the audience. 'Anti-racism' was found to be too negative and too explicit for the title of a mass media or community education campaign as it was likely to exclude both extreme racists and those who hold racist views but do not see themselves as racist.
>
> (Jakubowicz, 2011c)

The review also noted that "all sets of research concluded that the most effective approach to an anti-racism campaign was to engage people through activities and messages that are subtle, non threatening, positive, apolitical, engaging, encouraging, warm, optimistic and non dictatorial." Such strategies have not been widely implemented or evaluated.

Even so in the context of the time the government proposed that "the program objectives be revised to provide a stronger focus on addressing issues of cultural, racial and religious intolerance, while promoting respect, fairness, inclusion and a sense of belonging for everyone". In the decade since that review, the growth of social media and the increasing apprehension about Islamist terror, Chinese alleged subversion, and supposedly African gang violence in Australia has increased intercommunal tension, with many of the key social cohesion parameters falling after some years of initial improvement (Markus, 2014, 2018).

Cosmopolitan citizenship

Australia can be thought of as an empire project, a continuing political and cultural process through which a nation is being formed, reformed, and transformed within a global setting. The imperial desire that created the Commonwealth as that "better Britain" in 1900 has been permeated since with many more nations and cultures than the defensive exclusionary rhetoric of the late Victorian age would allow. The underlying dynamic remains – to suppress and halt any claims to autonomy from the original Indigenous peoples and their descendants, to defend the nation against claims and sallies from competing empires, and, most importantly, to transform populations into a people. The creation of a national imaginary, which proves to be inclusive and equitable, remains a central challenge for the modern state (Jakubowicz and Icduygu, 2015).

While governments appear aware of the critical importance of a globally oriented consciousness for the emerging generation of Australians, they seem less than willing to make the decisions necessary to implement such an awareness. Difficult principles remain to be adopted, many of which directly conflict with strongly held views in some communities, governments, and civil society organizations.

A first principle would be that in Australia, government and public institutions are secular and that any organization seeking public support must accept the underpinnings of secularism. By this I mean that religion can be accepted as a personal, familial, and communal area of emotion and belief, but the state must assert the primary role of reason and science as the underpinning of society and only then allow that all religions should be allowed to practice subject to public safety, accepting thereby the importance of peoples' spiritual identities (Jupp, 2009). Over recent years the growth of faith-based schools teaching religious alternatives to evolution and theological explanations for social issues have compounded anti-science social movements associated with global warming and climate change.

The second principle resides in the mutuality of recognition, where acceptance of cultural difference does not necessitate the acceptance of the truth claims of different cultures (Healy, 2006). It requires an ethnographic consciousness, so that one is able to view one's own and other cultures as contingent and historical, rather than unique and universal.

Third, there should be an emphasis on the creative synergies that are generated in interaction and dialogue, such that priority is given to multicultural rather than monocultural engagement (Jakubowicz, 2011a).

For a multicultural society like Australia, ensuring commitment from and thus cohesion among the diversity of populations depends on ensuring that equity and justice are also achieved, so that diverse identities are built around a sense that rights are realizable for all and reciprocity sits at the heart of the recognition of difference. Our most important resources will be those that emerge from the interaction of our cultures, from what used to be described as productive diversity. Australia as yet does not have a sophisticated and careful plan to ensure this occurs. So many of our educational settings – from ethno-cultural separation to monolingual and monocultural historical narratives – have the country pointed somewhere else altogether.

References

Australia Department of Education Employment and Workplace Relations (n.d.) 'Civics and Citizenship Education'. www.civicsandcitizenship.edu.au/cce/ (Accessed: 15 April 2009).

Australia Review of Post-arrival Programs and Services to Migrants, C. F. G. (1978) 'Migrant Services and Programs', Report of the Review of Post-arrival Programs and Services for Migrants, A.G.P.S., Canberra.

Australian Human Rights Commission (n.d.) 'Racism', Quick Guide, AHRC. www.humanrights.gov.au/quick-guide/12083.

Betts, K. (2008a) 'The 2007 Australian Election: Blue-Collar Voters, Migrants and the Environment', *People and Place*, 16(2), pp. 71–85.

Betts, K. (2008b) 'Dissatisfaction with Immigration Grows', *People and Place*, 16(3), pp. 19–35.

Colebatch, H. (2010) 'The Left Rewrites Its History on Refugees', *Quadrant*, October.

Costello, P. (2006) 'Worth Promoting, Worth Defending: Australian Citizenship, What It Means and How to Nurture It', Speech to the Sydney Institute. www.treasurer.gov.au/DisplayDocs.aspx?doc=speeches/2006/004.htm&pageID=005&min=phc&Year=2006&DocType=1 (Accessed: 10 October 2012).

Council of Europe (2006) *Achieving Social Cohesion in a Multicultural Europe – Concepts, Situation and Developments*. Trends in Social Cohesion, No. 18. Strasbourg: Council of Europe Publishing.

Cunliffe, E. (2007) 'Anywhere but Here: Race and Empire in the Mabo Decision', *Social Identities*, pp. 751–768. doi:10.1080/13504630701696435.

Deane, W. (2000) 'A message from the Former Governor-General, Sir William Deane', RacismNoWay: About Us. www.racismnoway.com.au/site-info/about/.

Dovey, W. R. (1960) *First Report on the Progress and Assimilation of Migrant Children in Australia*. Canberra: Commonwealth of Australia.

Eureka Research (1998) *The Anti-Racism Campaign: Quantitative Market Research to Guide Campaign Development*. Canberra: Multicultural Affairs Branch, Anti-Racism Campaign Unit, Department of Immigration and Multicultural Affairs. https://andrewjakubowicz.files.wordpress.com/2011/11/dimiaantiracismreport-quant1998.pdf (Accessed: 28 November 2016).

Fear, J. (2007) 'Under the Radar: Dog-Whistle Politics in Australia', The Australia Institute Discussion Paper, 96.

Gerrard, J., Savage, G. and O'Connor, K. (2017) 'Searching for the Public: School Funding and Shifting Meanings of 'the Public' in Australian Education', *Journal of Education Policy* 32(4), pp. 503–519. www.tandfonline.com/doi/abs/10.1080/02680939.2016.1274787.

Gobbo, J. (1995) 'Criticisms of Multiculturalism', 1995 Global Cultural Diversity Conference Proceedings, Department of Immigration and Citizenship, Sydney, Australia. www.immi.gov.au/media/publications/multicultural/confer/06/speech30a.htm (Accessed: 4 July 2009).

Goodman, J. (2006) *Regionalization, Marketization and Political Change in the Pacific Rim*. Guadalajara, Jalisco, Mexico and Sydney, Australia: Universidad de Guadalajara and University of Technology Sydney.

Healy, S. (2006) 'Cultural Resilience, Identity and the Restructuring of Political Power in Bolivia', Paper Submitted for the 11th Biennial Conference of the

International Association for the Study of Common Property. www.indiana.edu/~iascp/bali/papers/Healey_susan.pdf.

Ho, C. (2015) ' "People Like Us": School Choice, Multiculturalism and Segregation in Sydney', *Australian Review of Public Affairs*. www.nswtf.org.au/files/people_like_us_-_school_choice_multiculturalism_segregation_in_sydney_-_christin_ho.pdf.

Jakubowicz, A. (2009) 'New Groups and Social Cohesion in Australia', in *Nations of Immigrants: Australia and the USA Compared* [Online Version]. www.elgaronline.com/view/9781848446366.00014.xml.

Jakubowicz, A. (2010a) 'Australia's Migration Policies: African Dimensions', Background paper for African Australians: A Review of Human Rights and Social Inclusion Issues. Australian Human Rights Commission. www.humanrights.gov.au/publications/african-australians-project-australia-s-migration-policies-african-dimensionsaustralia.

Jakubowicz, A. (2010b) 'Making Multicultural Australia'. http://multiculturalaustralia.edu.au.

Jakubowicz, A. (2011a) 'Empires of the Sun: Towards a Post-multicultural Australian Politics', *Cosmopolitan Civil Societies: An Interdisciplinary Journal*, 3(1), pp. 65–86.

Jakubowicz, A. (2011b) 'Playing the Triangle: Cosmopolitanism, Cultural Capital and Social Capital as Intersecting Scholarly Discourses About Social Inclusion and Marginalisation in Australian Public Policy Debates', *Cosmopolitan Civil Societies: An Interdisciplinary Journal*, 3(3). http://epress.lib.uts.edu.au/journals/index.php/mcs/article/view/2215 (Accessed: 3 May 2016).

Jakubowicz, A. (2011c) 'Racism, Anti-racism Campaigns and Australian Social Research: A Case Study in Recovering Socially-Useful Knowledge', andrewjakubowicz.com. https://andrewjakubowicz.com/publications/antiracism1998/.

Jakubowicz, A. (2013) 'Comparing Australian Multiculturalism: The International Dimension', in Jakubowicz, A. and Ho, C. (eds.) *For Those Who've Come Across the Seas. . . ': Australian Multicultural Theory Policy and Practice*. Melbourne: Australian Scholarly Press, pp. 15–30.

Jakubowicz, A. (2016) 'Once Upon a Time in . . . Ethnocratic Australia: Migration, Refugees, Diversity and Contested Discourses of Inclusion', *Cosmopolitan Civil Societies: An Interdisciplinary Journal*. http://epress.lib.uts.edu.au/journals/index.php/mcs/article/view/5239/5772.

Jakubowicz, A. (2017) 'Alt_Right White Lite: Trolling, Hate Speech and Cyberracism on Social Media', *Cosmopolitan Civil Societies: An Interdisciplinary Journal*, 9(3).

Jakubowicz, A. and Ho, C. (eds.) (2013) *For Those Who Have Come Across the Seas . . .': Australian Multicultural Theory Policy and Practice*. Melbourne: Australian Scholarly Press.

Jakubowicz, A. and Icduygu, A. (2015) 'After Gallipoli: Empire, Nation and Diversity in Multicultural Turkey and Australia', in Michael, M. (ed.) *Reconciling Cultural and Political Identities in a Globalized World*. Houndmills: Palgrave Macmillan.

Joint Standing Committee on Migration and Maria Vamvakinou, M. (2013) *Inquiry into Migration and Multiculturalism in Australia*. Canberra: Commonwealth of Australia.

Jupp, J. (2002) 'Ethnicity and Immigration', in Warhurst, J. and Simms, M. (eds.) *The Centenary Election*. Brisbane, St. Lucia: University of Queensland Press.

Jupp, James. 2007. *From White Australia to Woomera: the Story of Australian Immigration*. 2nd ed. Melbourne: Cambridge University Press.

Jupp, J. (2009) *The Encyclopedia of Religion in Australia*. Port Melbourne, VIC: Cambridge University Press.

Jupp, J. (2018) *An Immigrant Nation Seeks Cohesion: Australia from 1788*. London: Anthem Press.

Lewins, F. (1987) ' "The Blainey Debate" in Hindsight', *Journal of Sociology*, 23(2), pp. 261–273.

Markus, A. (2014) 'Mapping Social Cohesion: The Scanlon Foundation Surveys 2014', Scanlon Foundation, Australian Multicultural Foundation, and Monash University. http://scanlonfoundation.org.au/wp-content/uploads/2014/10/2014-Mapping-Social-Cohesion-Report.pdf.

Markus, A. (2018) 'Mapping Social Cohesion 2017', Scanlon National Survey. http://scanlonfoundation.org.au/socialcohesion2017/.

Mayrl, D. (2016) *Secular Conversions: Political Institutions and Religious Education in the United States and Australia, 1800–2000*. New York: Cambridge University Press.

McGaw, B. (2004) 'Quality Education: Is the Sky the Limit? Education Systems Are Being Examined. And Individual Countries Are Finding They Can Improve Their Performances by Learning from Others. What Are the Key Lessons?' *OECD Observer*, p. 242. www.oecdobserver.org/news/printpage.php/aid/1217/Quality_education:_Is_the_sky_the_limit_.html.

McGaw, B. (2006) *Education and Social Cohesion*. Dean's Lecture Series. Melbourne: University of Melbourne.

Moss, I. and Castan, R. (1991) *Racist Violence: Report of the National Inquiry into Racist Violence*. Canberra: Human Rights and Equal Opportunity Commission. https://view.officeapps.live.com/op/view.aspx?src=www.humanrights.gov.au/sites/default/files/document/publication/NIRV.doc (Accessed: 6 September 2016).

Murdoch, R. (2008) 'The Boyer Lectures', ABC Radio National, Australian Broadcasting Corporation. www.abc.net.au/radionational/programs/boyerlectures/a-golden-age-of-freedom/3192214.

Neill, R. (2016) 'Schools in Many Parts of Australia Are Study in Self-segregation', *The Australian, Inquirer*. www.theaustralian.com.au/news/inquirer/schools-in-many-parts-of-australia-are-study-in-selfsegregation/news-story/a45dcd94be5cbabe8f95fabec45ca3b5.

Organisation for Economic Co-operation and Development (OECD) (2008) 'Enhancing Educational Performance 2008', Economic Survey of Australia: OECD. www.oecd.org/document/35/0,3343,en_33873108_33873229_41441891_1_1_1_1,00.html (Accessed: 15 April 2009).

Orr, G. (2018) 'Fertilising a Thicket: Section 44, MP Qualifications and the High Court', *Public Law Review (PLR)*, 29. https://espace.library.uq.edu.au/data/UQ_728429/gorr_plr_v29_pt1.pdf?

Pillai, S. and Williams, G. (2018) 'The Utility of Citizenship Stripping Laws in the UK, Canada, and Australia', *Melbourne University Law Review*, 41, pp. 845–889.

Smolicz, J. and Secombe, M. (2005) 'Globalisation Cultural Diversity and Multiculturalism: Australia', in *International Handbook on Globalisation, Education and Policy Research*, Zajda, Joseph (ed). Dordrecht, Netherlands: Springer, pp. 207–220.

Smolicz, J. and Secombe, M. (2009) 'Globalisation, Identity, and Cultural Dynamics in a Multiethnic State: Multiculturalism in Australia', in Joseph Zajda, Daun, H. and Saha, L.J. (eds.) *Nation-Building, Identity and Citizenship Education*. The Netherlands: Springer, pp. 83–96.

Swetnam, L. A. (2003) 'Lessons on Multicultural Education from Australia and the United States', *Clearing House*, 76(4), p. 208.

Tsiolkas, C. (2013) 'Why Australia Hates Asylum Seekers', *The Monthly*. www.themonthly.com.au/issue/2013/september/1377957600/christos-tsiolkas/why-australia-hates-asylum-seekers.

Tsolidis, G. (2008) 'Australian Multicultural Education: Revisiting and Resuscitating', in *The Education of Diverse Student Populations*, Wan.G (ed.). Dordrecht, Netherlands: Springer, pp. 209–225.

UNESCO (2010) 'Teaching and Learning for a Sustainable Future: Globalisation'. www.unesco.org/education/tlsf/mods/theme_c/mod18.html.

Victoria Department of Education and Early Childhood Development (2009) 'About Multicultural Education', Melbourne. www.education.vic.gov.au/studentlearning/programs/multicultural/about.htm.

7 Teaching citizenship against conflicting cross-cultural priorities in the Australian primary curriculum

Implications for social justice

Melinda G. Miller and Adele Amorsen

This chapter examines intersections, opportunities and implications for social justice in relation to the three cross-curriculum priority (CCP) areas in the Australian Curriculum for Foundation – Year 6. Identified as (1) Aboriginal and Torres Strait Islander histories and cultures, (2) Australia and Australia's engagement with Asia and (3) sustainability, the three CCPs are designed to inform a "relevant, contemporary and engaging curriculum" that builds on the educational goals of the Melbourne Declaration on Educational Goals for Young Australians (Australian Curriculum, Assessment and Reporting Authority [ACARA], 2016). Underpinned by two goals, the Melbourne Declaration values the role of education in building a democratic, equitable and just society. Goal 1 relates specifically to the role of schooling in contributing to a "socially cohesive society that respects and appreciates cultural, social and religious diversity", with Goal 2 referring to outcomes for students such as becoming "active and informed citizens" (MCEETYA, 2008, p. 7).

For teachers, the three CCPs are identified in content descriptor elaborations for learning areas (e.g., English, mathematics, science, the arts) in the Foundation – Year 6 curriculum, using a specific icon, as shown in extracts of elaborations later in this chapter. The content descriptor elaborations provide teachers with ideas about how content could be taught. The inclusion of the CCPs in the content elaborations affords teachers opportunities to add depth and richness to student learning. Each of the three CCPs will have "a strong but varying presence depending on their relevance to the learning area" (ACARA, 2016). A set of organising ideas for each CCP reflects the essential knowledge, understandings and skills for the priority. The organising ideas are set out in a separate table as part of the introduction to each CCP and are then embedded in the content descriptions and elaborations of each learning area, as appropriate (ACARA, 2016). Icons for general capabilities (e.g., critical and creative thinking, intercultural understanding, literacy, numeracy, ICT) are also located within the learning areas to highlight capabilities that align with a specific learning task.

To this point, commentary about the potential for the CCPs to enable depth and richness in student engagement with socio-political content and related social justice issues has outlined a mixture of hope, scepticism and concern. For example, Hill and Dyment (2016) expressed hope around the imperative of societal change around sustainability and ACARA's intent to prioritise sustainability in school curriculum, but have concern about CCPs not having "the same place as a learning area" (p. 226) in curriculum development and design. In a state-wide analysis of the implementation of the sustainability CCP undertaken in kindergarten to year 12 schools in Tasmania, Hill and Dyment (2016) found that while reasonable support for sustainability was evident in some schools, variables, including teacher understanding and capability, a distinct lack of professional learning and development and the framing of sustainability as an optional extra to learning areas, prevented effective integration of sustainability into the curriculum. Similarly, in an analysis of the inclusion of Aboriginal and Torres Strait Islander content in the Australian Curriculum (Foundation to Year 10), Lowe and Yunkaporta (2013) argued that the curriculum has failed "to provide students with learning opportunities to explore the notion of social justice within the construct of social policy making in Australia vis-à-vis Aboriginal and Torres Strait Islander peoples" (p. 11). Further, ACARA has shifted the responsibility "to the often-ill-resourced classroom teacher", resulting in "curriculum serendipity" (p. 12) rather than explicit shared meaning for both teachers and students.

Intersections with social justice issues

While not explicitly stated by ACARA, the three CCPs in the Australian curriculum intersect prevailing social justice issues on the Australian landscape, including but not limited to colonisation, assimilation, multiculturalism, racism and reconciliation. The CCPs also intersect each other in ways that have been silenced or mispresented throughout Australian history through colonisation processes and discourses of multiculturalism. A primary aim of this chapter is to explore some of the concealed yet critical intersections between the three CCPs, including:

- Indigenous dispossession and socio-political aspects of sustainability concerned with relationships between groups of people and reparation between people and place;
- Shared characteristics of sustainability education and multicultural education, through which teachers can regain pedagogical traction for early ideologies of multiculturalism that promoted diversity and difference as a social resource; and
- The geographic, human and social diversity of the Asia-Pacific that parallels the continuing contribution of rich and distinct Indigenous

knowledges, practices and perspectives that benefit both Indigenous and non-Indigenous populations in Australia.

Of interest in the discussion is the ways in which these intersections are reflected (or not) in the examples of practice provided by ACARA in the Foundation – Year 6 curriculum documents whereby "a single learning area content description or elaboration may cover one or more organising ideas, across one or more of the priorities" (ACARA, 2016). For both teachers and students, the ways in which socio-political intersections and matters of social justice are made explicit in curriculum content matters for a common framework and shared meaning around historical and contemporary circumstances and policies that continue to affect different groups of people in Australian society. Shared meaning contributes to depth and richness in student learning.

The role of the individual teacher in embedding and building shared meaning around the CPPs, being (1) Aboriginal and Torres Strait Islander histories and cultures, (2) Australia and Australia's engagement with Asia and (3) sustainability, is recognised as both critical and problematic. Most of the teaching force in Australian classrooms identify as Anglo-Celtic (white), monolingual and middle class (McKenzie, Rowley, Weldon & Murphy, 2011). Despite the emergence of some exemplars of practice around engagement with socio-political concepts in the curriculum in recent years, grave issues remain around a lack of cultural awareness and cultural integrity among a majority white teaching service (Rose, 2012). Inconsistent approaches to responding to Aboriginal and Torres Strait Islander perspectives and knowledges in curriculum (Price, 2012b; Rose, 2012) and experiences of racism in schooling for Aboriginal and Torres Strait Islander children and families (Price, 2012a) also prevail. Variables including school leadership, access to professional development, resourcing, and the capability to question one's own assumptions and biases affect the extent to which teachers think critically about curriculum. This is particularly concerning for CCPs that underpin but sit outside of learning area content which informs curriculum design and implementation.

Cross-curricula priorities: intersections and opportunities

In returning to explore some of the concealed yet critical intersections between the three CCPs, we draw attention first to definitions of sustainability that identify interrelated social, cultural, political, economic and environmental dimensions and areas of concern (UNESCO, 2006). Attention to socio-political dimensions of sustainability promotes attention to context, including historical circumstances, government agendas and priorities over time and related social impacts for different groups of people within a society (Miller, 2015). In Australia, socio-political dimensions of sustainability encompass a shared history between Indigenous and non-Indigenous peoples, stemming from the colonial doctrine of terra nullius and the result-ing dispossession of Aboriginal and Torres Strait Islander peoples from lands and territories. Dispossession is an act founded on western notions of occupation; ownership; and (ab)use of lands for economic, social and politi-cal gain (Behrendt, 2003). In the Australian context, conversations around sustainability should address reconciliation as one of the most pressing issues on the national landscape, as "sustainability and reconciliation are both concerned with relationships between groups of people, and repara-tion between people and place" (Miller, 2015, p. 128).

In recent years, numerous authors have drawn attention to the ways envi-ronmental and socio-political dimensions of sustainability interrelate and affect each other. For example, Nordström (2008) identifies shared charac-teristics including respect, belonging and goals for individual, institutional and social reform within both environmental and multicultural education. Burnett and McArdle (2011) view education for sustainability as offering "new discursive nodes around which educators can regain pedagogical trac-tion for many of the original tenets of multiculturalism" (p. 51). Here, Bur-nett and McArdle respond to teachers' tendencies to marginalise the goals of multicultural education and sustainability, including cultural diversity, peace and human security, when curriculum content centres solely on envi-ronmental concerns. The organising ideas for the sustainability CCP address intersections between sustainability and the goals of multicultural education in the key curriculum concept of . . . enabling a diversity of world views on ecosystems, values and social justice to be discussed and recognised when determining individual and community actions for sustainability (ACARA, 2016).

Distinct waves of multiculturalism have been evident in Australia in line with post-war migration marked first by multiculturalism and more recently by political intolerance. In the early 1970s, multiculturalism was an ideology that encouraged the maintenance of arrivals' cultural identities rather than assimilation into the mainstream. The positioning of diversity and difference as a social resource contrasted with later approaches to multiculturalism from the 1990s. In this later period, a cohesive and unified nationhood was projected as the national ideal under a conservative government policy shift (Gozdecka, Ercan & Kmak, 2014). Influential public discourse substituted a more isolationist, intolerant and xenophobic position on arrivals at the expense of the early goals and ideals of multiculturalism. State apparatus which had given support to multiculturalism and Indigenous peoples' rights were also dismantled under conservative government agendas (Every & Augoustinos, 2007). In current times, conservative government policy con-tinues to avoid direct engagement with racism in Australia and contributes to a moral panic and deficit narratives around arrivals (Gozdecka, Ercan & Kmak, 2014).

Throughout Australian history, Indigenous peoples, non-white migrants and refugees have been positioned in proximity to whiteness, as a homogenous category of the non-white 'other' (Moreton-Robinson, 2003). Positioned at the margins rather than at the centre, Indigenous groups, non-white migrants and refugees have been classified as a homogenous minority that is distanced from the category white. Applying racial labels to a homogenous 'other' reserves "extra value for whiteness" (Lipsitz, 2006, p. 3) at the centre. The racial diversity of the Australian population has meant that investments in whiteness have not related simply to black–white binaries. For example, in the post-war period, the situatedness of some migrants (e.g., Vietnamese, Greek) as different from other migrants (e.g., Irish, English, Scottish) showed a relation to whiteness as a legal power and status and differences in proximity to British imperialism (Moreton-Robinson, 2003). During this time frame, whiteness enforced distance for non-white migrants between 'real' whites and those not white enough (Lipsitz, 2006). In the CCP Aboriginal and Torres Strait Islander histories and cultures, there is recognition of the sovereignty of Aboriginal peoples which supports a de-centring of whiteness at the centre. Recognition of continuing impacts of colonisation is also evident, as seen in the organising idea: Aboriginal and Torres Strait Islander Peoples live in Australia as first peoples of country or place and demonstrate resilience in responding to historic and contemporary impacts of colonisation (ACARA, 2016).

In drawing further threads between the CCPs, the Asia-Pacific region is home to two-thirds of the world's Indigenous peoples. The human and social dimensions of the Asia-Pacific account for much of the world's linguistic and cultural diversity, with approximately 280 million Indigenous peoples the custodians of diverse lands and territories within the region (United Nations Development Programme, 2012). The geographic, human and social diversity of the Asia-Pacific is equal to the continuing contribution of rich and distinct Indigenous knowledges, practices and perspectives that benefit both Indigenous and non-Indigenous populations in Australia and elsewhere. The organising ideas for CCP 1 reflect this point in relation to Indigenous Australian populations: [this priority is] . . . designed for all students to engage in reconciliation, respect and recognition of the world's oldest continuous living cultures (ACARA, 2016).

Historically, Australia has had a distinctly negative relationship with Asia. Prior to federation, white opposition to Asian migration incited race riots across the mid to late 1800s, followed closely by the White Australia policy from 1901 where British settlers were bought out to ensure Australia remained white (Fozdar, 2016). These polices stemmed from concerns over the cheaper labour Asian market and a resulting Asian 'invasion'. Over time, Australia developed an anxiety-based fear stemming from China's economic and military power. This perceived threat supported the persistent negative attitude toward the Asia region (Philpott, 2001). In the 1980s to 1990s, a re-thinking of political, economic and military relations with Asia occurred. Increased military engagement, improved economic ties and a more liberal approach to immigration policy supported a shift in thinking about Australia's engagement with Asia during this period, despite re-ignited debates about the place of Asians in Australia from conservative politician Pauline Hanson. The 2013 white paper, *Australia in the Asia Century*, saw the beginning of influence on Australian curriculum priorities and content (Fozdar, 2016). The organising ideas in the Asia CCP are generally futures-focussed – perhaps a reflection of the current interests of the nation-state in advancing in the 'Asia Century'. Salter and Maxwell (2016) suggest that this orientation "reveals a colonialist imagery where the Asian economy is exploited for Australian economic advancement; Australia is the 'colonial power' and Asian economies the 'colonised' entity" (p. 304). Recognition of a distinctly negative relationship with Asia is not acknowledged in the organising ideas for the Asia CCP. Rather, historical relations are positioned as the basis for future engagement.

The third concept addresses the nature of past and ongoing links between Australia and Asia and develops the knowledge, understanding and skills that make it possible to engage actively and effectively with peoples of the Asia region.

- Australians of Asian heritage have influenced Australia's history and continue to influence its dynamic culture and society;
- Australia is part of the Asia region and our histories from ancient times to the present are linked (ACARA, 2016).

How the often concealed yet critical intersections between the CCP areas outlined earlier are reflected in the Foundation – Year 6 curriculum documents forms the basis for analysis in this chapter. Next, we outline the approach to analysis and present extracts from the content descriptor elaborations. Implications for social justice as they relate to the Australian context are outlined.

References to cross-curriculum priority areas in the Australian curriculum

To examine references to the CCPs in the Foundation – Year 6 curriculum documents, we began by analysing the number of references to each priority area within seven key learning areas – English; Mathematics; Science, Humanities and Social Sciences (HASS); The Arts; Technologies; and Health and Physical Education (HPE) – followed by the number of cross-references to two or more priority areas in any combination. The results of the initial analysis are outlined here. The analysis focused on version 8.3 of the Australian curriculum and was undertaken during the period January 9–21, 2018, in the two weeks prior to the commencement of the school year when most teachers are engaged in curriculum planning.

In total, reference to any of the three CCPs occurred 437 times across seven learning areas, from a potential 2751 content descriptors. The learning areas

HASS (n = 241), Technologies (n = 57), English (n = 39) and Science (n = 37) had a higher number of references to any one of the three CCPs, with fewer references in Mathematics (n = 26), The Arts (n = 24) and HPE (n = 13). Of the 437 references to any one of the three CCPs, there were 45 occurrences of two CCPs referenced under one elaboration in a content descriptor and only 1 occurrence of all three CCPs referenced together. Specifically, there were 25 occurrences of (1) Aboriginal and Torres Strait Islander histories and cultures and (2) Australia and Australia's engagement with Asia referenced together, 15 occurrences of (3) sustainability and (1) Aboriginal and Torres Strait Islander histories and cultures referenced together, and 5 occurrences of (3) sustainability and (2) Australia and Australia's engagement with Asia referenced together under a content descriptor. The one occurrence of all three CCPs referenced together was in the Technologies learning area, in the sub-strand Design and Technologies for Years 5–6.

Of interest in the initial layer of analysis was missed opportunities for learning areas, including The Arts, to support explorations of social justice matters relevant to the Australian context. Engagement with The Arts creates spaces to learn in different ways and to learn about life matters beyond the constructs of traditional forms of schooling (Piscitelli, 2011). McArdle, Knight and Stratigos (2013) describe The Arts as a "crucial methodological and intellectual tool" (p. 357) for exploring matters of social justice. Numerous studies focused on Arts strands, including drama, storytelling and music (see Downey, 2005; Phillips, 2011), have shown the potential of The Arts to be a tool and catalyst to provoke primary-aged students' critical awareness and thinking and to create lasting impressions of social justice over time. The Arts provide accessible entry points for children's critical inquiry and open possibilities for exploring and enacting forms of active citizenship.

The optional nature of the CCPs is also of concern, given they appear in the curriculum at teachers' discretion. Locating intersecting CCPs on the ACARA website (via the icons ⚘ ᴀᴀ ✦) requires numerous click-downs through content, with the icons for the general capabilities appearing directly under the content descriptors in place of the CCP icons. The content descriptors rarely provide an indication of where the CCPs are included in elaborations, with the CCP icons only becoming visible after opening one or more elaborations (a minimum of two to three drill-downs in online content). In this sense, the CCPs are the final layer, hidden beneath the content descriptor and elaboration link.

For further analysis, we collated the elaborations from the 46 occurrences of cross-referencing to analyse how the individual and collective CCPs were represented and to identify some of the concealed yet critical intersections that have potential to contribute depth and richness to student learning. Layered analysis focused on the influence of grammatical structure which positions cultures, peoples and regions in particular ways and how critical intersections between the CCPs were reflected. How the CCP organising ideas were translated in the elaboration to guide teachers' pedagogy frames discussion around implications for social justice.

While the content descriptors in the Australian curriculum specify what teachers are expected to teach, the Elaborations illustrate the content descriptions to provide teachers with further guidance and pedagogical ideas about how content could be taught. Analysis of the 46 occurrences of CCP cross-referencing in the elaborations revealed limitations in representation of cultures, peoples and regions, including themes of othering, and silences around a history of dispossession, colonial impacts and contemporary urban existences. Here, we present extracts from the Elaborations to provide further analysis and commentary, beginning with the influence of grammatical structure.

Influence of grammatical structure

Attention to grammatical structure enables analysis of the subtle influence in how sentences position subjects as central or not (Hung Ng & James, 1993). In analysing the positioning of peoples, cultures and practices related to CCPs 1 and 2, it was apparent that the grammatical structure of the elaborations has the potential to influence understanding about the positioning of cultural groups within and outside Australia and shows how power relations become codified in language. In the examples that follow, Aboriginal, Torres Strait Islander and Asian populations are located on the periphery, or as afterthoughts in relation to subject positions and the function of pedagogical intent. As readers place more importance on concepts at the beginning of the sentence (Hung Ng & James, 1993), the contributions of Aboriginal, Torres Strait Islander and Asian peoples as a basis for exploring curriculum content is secondary.

ACTDEP014 (CCP 1, 2): exploring the different uses of materials in a range of products, including those from Aboriginal and Torres Strait Islander communities and countries of Asia. ⚐ ₳₳

ACTDIP006 (CCP 1, 2): planning and creating text, drawings and sound files to share online, for example jointly creating a photo story to illustrate a fable or fairy-tale from the Asia region or a local Aboriginal and Torres Strait Islander community story. ⚐ ₳₳

ACADAR012 (CCP 1, 2): identifying and discussing meanings and significance intended by the choreographer's use of movement, space and energy, referring to their knowledge of the context in which the dance was created, for example, an Aboriginal or Torres Strait Islander dance, a Chinese ribbon dance, or a Sumatran tambourine dance. ⚐ ₳₳

ACTDEK019 (CCP, 1, 2, 3): Considering the impact designed products, services or environments have in relation to sustainability and also on local, regional and global communities, including Aboriginal and Torres Strait Islander communities and countries in the Asia region. ⚐ ₳₳ ⚐

Here, the readers' attention is distracted from the contributions of Aboriginal, Torres Strait Islander and Asian populations as a basis for exploring concepts related to technology, design and drama. The subject positioning at the end of each elaboration suggests that peoples, and cultural practices and symbols are removable and replaceable. Within the elaborations, grammatical structures of tense also frequently position the focus cultures as historic and static, as seen in the elaboration . . . [Aboriginal and Torres Strait Islander communities] altered the environment and sustained ways of living (ACHASSK112). Reader focus can be re-directed with simple re-structuring of the sentence to ensure the contributions of Aboriginal, Torres Strait Islander and Asian peoples are prioritised and central to pedagogical intent.

Representations of peoples, cultures and regions

The visibility or specific mention of Aboriginal, Torres Strait Islander and Asian populations within the CCPs suggest a shift away from Eurocentric curricula. However, the mere appearance of priority and inclusion requires further analysis to consider how peoples and cultures are represented in the content descriptor elaborations, as seen next.

ACHASSK086 (CCP 1, 2): examining paintings and accounts (by observers such as Watkin Tench and David Collins) to determine the impact of early British colonisation on Aboriginal Peoples' Country.

ACHASSK049 (CCP 1, 3): describing the connections of the local Aboriginal and Torres Strait Islander Peoples with the land, sea, waterways, sky and animals of their Country/Place, and how this influences their views on the use of environmental resources.

Indigenous peoples have endured a long history of representation by non-Indigenous peoples. In the first elaboration, teachers are encouraged to draw on western accounts and interpretations of the impacts of colonisation on Aboriginal peoples' country. Paintings and accounts presented as facts become products of colonial narratives that filter representations and the visibility and voices of Aboriginal peoples who continue to experience impacts of colonisation on a country first-hand (Nakata, 2007). Here, colonial representations are given primacy in curriculum content and have the potential to reproduce racialised and simplistic notions of the effects of colonisation amid stories of a developing Australia (Moreton-Robinson, 2003). Whose voices are represented and whose are absent or spoken for by others has implications for representations of peoples and cultures.

Connections between Aboriginal and Torres Strait Islander peoples and sustainability are evident in the second elaboration. Aboriginal and Torres Strait Islander peoples are positioned as central to sustainable environmental practices, but only in terms of benefits for members of the in-group culture. Here, the contributions of Aboriginal and Torres Strait Islander peoples are not positioned as being of value to all Australians to learn about and through environmentally sustainable practices, despite a key organising idea for the sustainability CCP stating that . . . the significant contributions of Aboriginal Peoples and Torres Strait Islander Peoples in the present and past are acknowledged locally, nationally and globally (ACARA, 2016). In the elaboration, there are silences around dispossession and Aboriginal and Torres Strait Islander peoples' independent access to and control over environmentally viable lands and territories. The elaboration also suggests that Aboriginal peoples' cultural practices are recognised and valued within all local communities despite ongoing acts of dispossession, marginalisation and experiences of racism.

Representations of cultures as historic and static are seen in the following two elaborations which point to misrepresentations around temporality.

ACAVAM106 (CCP 1, 2): identifying and using visual conventions in their artworks after investigating different art, craft and design styles from other cultures and times, for example, Expressionism, Fauvism, Aboriginal and Torres Strait Islander Peoples, and Asia. ⚐ ᴀᴀ

ACHASSK088 (CCP 1, 3): explaining the significance of vegetation endemic in the local area to survival of Aboriginal and/or Torres Strait Islander Peoples (for example, as a source of food, shelter, medicine, tools and weapons). ⚐ ✦

The first elaboration juxtaposes cultures and times statically, equating only early twentieth-century art movements (beginning around 1905) with the art, craft and design styles of Aboriginal, Torres Strait Islander and Asian peoples. These three cultural groups are othered within the elaboration, first by way of distancing from a supposed mainstream group [from other cultures], and secondly by way of distancing from contemporary art movements and practices [from other . . . times]. Within the elaboration, there is an imbalance in historical and contemporary representations which mobilises colonial discourses by way of positioning cultural groups as historical figures. The second elaboration also suggests a historical positioning, with missed opportunity for counter-narratives that draw attention to the resilience, ingenuity and advanced technologies of Aboriginal and Torres Strait Islander peoples. The term survival is an example of a singular word with loaded connotations (Hung Ng & James, 1993), which in this case has power to reproduce primitivist colonial narratives, often synonymous with suffering (Elder, 2009). Hence, there is potential to influence readers' thinking away from the certainty of Aboriginal and Torres Strait Islander cultures as continually evolving and thriving in contemporary times.

Reader discretion is central to the following two elaborations in terms of tenuous links to the CCPs. In the first elaboration below, icons on the website indicate links with CPPs 1 and 3, but without clarity around how these CCPs are connected to curriculum content and pedagogical intent. In thinking about Aboriginal and Torres Strait Islander histories and cultures (CCP 1), the choices available in the elaboration include Order of Australia medals or conflicting parties in a planning or environmental dispute, both of which are positioned as "issues". For teachers, an appropriate pedagogical response relies on their capacity to locate meaning around Aboriginal and Torres Strait Islander histories and cultures within a tenuous and adverse framing.

ACHASSI095 (CCP 1, 3): conducting surveys to gather primary data and summarising the key points or particular points of view relating to an issue (for example, interviewing recipients of awards such as Order of Australia medals; surveying the views of conflicting parties in a planning or environmental dispute).☙ ⟡

ACTDEK010 (CCP 2, 3): critiquing designed products, services and environments to establish the factors that influence the design and use of common technologies, for example the characteristics that contribute to energy-efficient cooking such as wok cooking; the suitability and sustainable use of particular timbers.▲▲ ⟡

Similarly, the second elaboration provides a tenuous link to Australia's engagement with Asia (CCP 2) via explicit mention of wok cooking. This link is a form of selectivity (Phillips, 2005), whereby elements of cultures are cherry-picked and presented as robust cultural representations. Selectivity is usually based on cultural elements considered palatable within the mainstream (Phillips, 2005), thus enabling an impression of cultural acceptance within a multicultural society. Of note across all elaborations linked with the Asia CCP is representations of a homogenous group, with rare acknowledgement of the historical, cultural, linguistic and religious diversity of the 48 countries which comprise the Asia region.

Themes of universal 'knowing' and othering also featured in elaborations across several key learning areas. Western constructions of knowing about another peoples' culture are reflected by way of extracting "bits of histories and cultures [drawing on literature; exploring stories; songs . . . about Indigenous peoples] in an attempt to make them knowable to others" (Salter & Maxwell, 2016, p. 303). Imposing a conceptual framework to know an 'other' from outside a culture (Moreton-Robinson, 2000) is also seen in the suggestion to investigate contemporary protest songs about Indigenous peoples. This is also a form of politicising Indigenous peoples by way of association to dissent and by positioning students to engage with Aboriginal 'politics'. An example of othering presents itself in the final elaboration below, whereby unknown or unnamed groups attach value to exploring stories about cultural groups [such as groups that value Aboriginal, Torres Strait Islander or Asian heritage]. There is a suggestion that unnamed groups are separate from the Australian mainstream, thus value in exploring stories is not applied to the Australian population as a whole. This form of othering denies the contribution of rich and distinct Indigenous knowledges, practices and perspectives from Australia and the Asia-Pacific region that benefit both Indigenous and non-Indigenous populations.

ACELTI611 (CCP 1, 3): investigating the qualities of contemporary protest songs, for example those about Indigenous peoples and those about the environment.☙ ⟡

ACELT1596 (CCP 1, 2): drawing on literature from Aboriginal, Torres Strait Islander or Asian cultures, to explore commonalities of experience and ideas as well as recognising difference in lifestyle and world view.🌿 ᴬᴬ

ACHASSI074 (CCP 1, 2): exploring stories about the groups people belong to, for example, about cultural groups (such as groups that value Aboriginal, Torres Strait Islander or Asian heritage), from interest and community groups (such as recreational and volunteering organisations) and from gender or religious groups.🌿 ᴬᴬ

Implications for social justice

The purpose of the content descriptor elaborations is to provide teachers with specific pedagogical guidance. However, the transference of key concepts from the organising ideas for each CCP is often tenuous and limited. The analysis earlier revealed limitations in the representation of peoples, cultures and regions, including themes of othering and silences around a history of dispossession, colonial impacts and contemporary urban existences. As stated by ACARA (2016), the CCPs have "become priorities that give students the tools and language to engage with and better understand their world at a range of levels". Gauci and Curwood (2017) add that the cross-curricula priorities are reflective of the current social context of Australian students, with the potential to make use of the priorities to examine cultural and power structures to enable depth in student learning. We suggest that the very structure of the elaborations affects the extent to which individual teachers can draw deep meaning, locate intersections and design and implement an appropriate pedagogical response. Thus, the potential to address social justice matters relevant to the Australian context within the CCPs focus primarily on the actions of individual teachers rather than the structure of the curriculum itself. Issues with the structure of the elaborations sit alongside existing variables, including teacher capability and access to professional learning.

While the CCPs have great intrinsic value, missteps in transference to the elaborations and, potentially, classroom practice have implications beyond local school grounds. As explained by Salter and Maxwell (2016), implications of social justice identified in policy "should not be thought of as being removed from people – as simply abstracted concerns with no practical impact" (p. 303). Poorly implemented educational initiatives have real and prevailing consequences for particular groups in Australian society, but the detriment is shared across the population and across generations. From a practitioner perspective, Kindler (2015) writes "curriculum holds a mirror to each successive generation, and asks what is and what is not being managed well" (p. 35). To limit the potentiality of the CCPs in policy and reduce students' exposure in practice is to avoid engagement with prevailing social justice issues on the Australian landscape in current times.

In concluding this chapter, we call for a more cohesive application of the CCPs within the content descriptor elaborations that guide teachers' practice. It is the role of policy to support teachers to identify and respond to the interconnected nature of the CCPs, with the potential to improve pedagogical intent and depth and rigour in student understanding. The integration of the CCPs as a starting point for curriculum design could support the role of teachers and schooling in contributing to a more socially cohesive society.

References

Australian Curriculum, Assessment and Reporting Authority (ACARA). (2016). *Cross-curriculum priorities*. Accessed September 1, 2017, from: www.acara.edu.au/curriculum/cross-curriculum-priorities

Behrendt, L. (2003). *Achieving social justice: Indigenous rights and Australia's future*. Sydney, NSW: The Federation Press.

Burnett, B., & McArdle, F. A. (2011). Multiculturalism, education for sustainable development (ESD) and the shifting discursive landscape of social inclusion. *Discourse: Studies in the Cultural Politics of Education, 32*(1), 43–56.

Downey, A. L. (2005). The transformative power of drama: Bringing literature and social justice to life. *English Journal, 95*(1), 33–38.

Elder, C. (2009). *Dreams and nightmares of a white Australia. Representing Aboriginal assimilation in the mid-twentieth century*. Switzerland: Peter Lang.

Every, D., & Augoustinos, M. (2007). Constructions of racism in the Australian parliamentary debates on asylum seekers. *Discourse and Society, 18*(4), 411–436.

Fozdar, F. (2016). Asian invisibility/Asian threat: Australians talking about Asia. *Journal of Sociology, 52*(4), 789–805.

Gauci, R., & Curwood, J. S. (2017). Teaching Asia: English pedagogy and Asia literacy within the Australian curriculum. *Australian Journal of Language and Literacy, 40*(3), 163–173.

Gozdecka, D., Ercan, S. A., & Kmak, M. (2014). From multiculturalism to post-multiculturalism: Trends and paradoxes. *Journal of Sociology, 50*(1), 51–64.

Hill, A., & Dyment, J. E. (2016). Hopes and prospects for the sustainability cross-curriculum priority: Provocations from a state-wide case study. *Australian Journal of Environmental Education, 32*(3), 225–242.

Hung Ng, S., & James, J. B. (1993). *Power in language: Verbal communication and social influence*. Newbury Park, CA: Sage.

Kindler, M. (2015). Review of the Australian curriculum: A view from a school leader. *Curriculum Perspectives, 35*(1), 29–38.

Lipsitz, G. (2006). *The possessive investment in whiteness: How white people profit from identity politics*. Philadelphia, PA: Temple University Press.

Lowe, K., & Yunkaporta, T. (2013). The inclusion of Aboriginal and Torres Strait Islander content in the Australian National Curriculum: A cultural, cognitive and socio-political evaluation. *Curriculum Perspectives, 33*(1), 1–14.

McArdle, F., Knight, L., & Stratigos, T. (2013). Imagining social justice. *Contemporary Issues in Early Childhood, 14*(4), 357–369.

McKenzie, P., Rowley, G., Weldon, P., & Murphy, M. (2011). *Staff in Australia's schools 2010: Main report on the survey*. Australian Council for Educational Research.

Miller, M. G. (2015). Reconciliation and early childhood education for sustainability: Broadening the environmental paradigm. In J. Davis (Ed.), *Young children and the environment: Early education for sustainability* (2nd ed., pp. 124–144). Port Melbourne, VIC: Cambridge University Press.

Ministerial Council on Education, Employment, Training and Youth Affairs (MCEE-TYA). (2008). *Melbourne declaration on educational goals for young Australians.* Accessed from: www.curriculum.edu.au/verve/_resources/National_Declaration_on_the_Educational_Goals_for_Young_Australians.pdf

Moreton-Robinson, A. (2000). *Talkin' up to the white women: Aboriginal women and feminism.* St. Lucia, QLD: Queensland University Press.

Moreton-Robinson, A. (2003). I still call Australia home: Indigenous belonging and place in a white postcolonizing society. In S. Ahmed, C. Castañeda, A. Fortier & M. Sheller (Eds.), *Uprootings/regroundings: Questions for home and migration* (pp. 23–40). Oxford, UK: Berg.

Nakata, M. (2007). The cultural interface. *The Australian Journal of Indigenous Education*, 36, 7–14.

Nordström, H. K. (2008). Environmental education and multicultural education – Too close to be separate? *International Research in Geographical and Environmental Education*, 17(2), 131–145.

Phillips, J. (2005). Indigenous knowledge: Making space in the Australian centre. In J. Phillips & J. Lampert (Eds.), *Introductory Indigenous studies in education: The importance of knowing* (pp. 11–26). Frenchs Forest, NSW: Pearson.

Phillips, L. G. (2011). *Young children's active citizenship: Storytelling, stories, and social actions.* Unpublished Doctoral Thesis, Queensland University of Technology, Brisbane, Australia.

Philpott, S. (2001). Fear of the dark: Indonesia and the Australian national imagination. *Australian Journal of International Affairs*, 55(3), 371–388.

Piscitelli, B. (2011). Young children, the arts and learning: Outside of school, at home and in the community. In S. Wright (Ed.), *Children, meaning making and the arts* (2nd ed., pp. 158–176). Frenchs Forest, NSW: Pearson.

Price, K. (2012a). A brief history of Aboriginal and Torres Strait Islander education in Australia. In K. Price (Ed.), *Aboriginal and Torres Strait Islander Education: An introduction for the teaching profession* (pp. 1–20). Melbourne, VIC: Cambridge University Press.

Price, K. (2012b). Aboriginal and Torres Strait Islander studies in the classroom. In K. Price (Ed.), *Aboriginal and Torres Strait Islander Education: An introduction for the teaching profession* (pp. 151–163). Melbourne, VIC: Cambridge University Press.

Rose, M. (2012). The silent apartheid as the practitioner's blindspot. In K. Price (Ed.), *Aboriginal and Torres Strait Islander Education: An introduction for the teaching profession* (pp. 64–80). Melbourne, VIC: Cambridge University Press.

Salter, P., & Maxwell, J. (2016). The inherent vulnerability of the Australian curriculum's cross-curriculum priorities. *Critical Studies in Education*, 57(3), 296–312.

UNESCO. (2006). *The interlocking dimensions of sustainability.* Accessed from: www.eqa.edu.au/verve/_resources/MeetingTheNeeds1.gif

United Nations Development Programme. (2012). *Indigenous voices in Asia-Pacific: Identifying the information and communication needs of Indigenous peoples.* Bangkok, TH: UNDP.

8 Britishness and British values

The diminution of migrants' social citizenship rights

Clive Sealey

Increasing net migration has been the main driver for the increasing UK population over the last 20 years, and reducing immigration and limiting benefit tourism entitlement for migrants have been the two key policy foci to deal with this. This chapter focuses on the latter of these. It will analyse how such changes in welfare entitlements for migrants is also impacting in an exclusionary way on the citizenship rights of the wider native population.

One of the most outstanding demographic trends in the UK in the last 20 years or so is the growth of the population, a growth that is higher than the EU average and highest of the four most populous EU member states (Office for National Statistics [ONS], 2014). Increased net migration has been the main driver for this changing demographic profile, contributing 54 per cent of the increase to the UK population, although this trend has reversed slightly in more recent years (Cangiano, 2014). There have been a number of policy changes relevant to this trend. The two key foci of these policies have been reducing net migration and limiting entitlement to benefits for migrants vis-à-vis benefit tourism. This chapter focuses on the latter of these. The important point that this chapter makes is that these changes in welfare entitlement are not just impacting on the rights of new migrants but are also limiting in a parallel way the citizenship rights of the larger non-migrant native population.

How and why has the demographic nature of the UK been changing over the last 20 years?

The 2011 *Census of the Population* shows that while the vast majority of the population are of the White ethnic group (86%), 14% of the population are from other minority ethnic groups, ranging from African, Caribbean, Pakistani, Bangladeshi, Indian, Arab, Chinese, and Mixed, according to the 2011 census (Office for National Statistics, 2012). However, the key finding from the 2011 census was that over the last two decades, the UK has become more ethnically diverse, with the White ethnic population decreasing from

94.1 percent in 1991 to 86 percent in 2011. This means that conversely, the minority ethnic population increased from 5.9 percent to 14 percent, which is a more than doubling over a period of 20 years and is a trend that shows an increase in minority ethnic populations.

An important reason for this is increasing net migration, as shown in Figure 8.1.

As Figure 8.1 shows, since 1997, net long-term migration has increased significantly, never being close to the pre-1997 levels, and 2014 saw the highest net migration peak for the years shown. There have been a number of reasons for this growth since 1997, including increasing migration from Commonwealth countries, increasing migration from EU enlargement countries, less emigration from the UK by British people, increased asylum, and economic migration.

This increasing net migration has had an important effect on the multicultural nature of the UK and has led some to outline the UK as no longer being defined simply by diversity, but by 'super diversity', wherein the diversity of the UK has a level and kind of complexity surpassing anything it has previously experienced (Vervotec, 2007), and particularly characterised by a multi-ethnic society with high numbers of both white and non-white Britons from many different ethno-cultural backgrounds (Phillips and Webber, 2014). For example, in one region of Birmingham, which is the second largest city in the UK, 170 countries of origin have been identified as represented among the population (Walters, 2015)

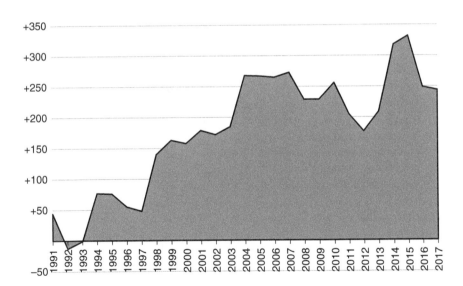

Figure 8.1 Net migration to the UK, 1991–2017

What has been the main policy response to this increased net migration?

These large increases in net migration in the UK over the last 20 years or so have led to extensive debates about their causes and consequences, and there have been two overarching and linked policy responses, focusing on restricting migration and restricting the benefits paid to migrants.

The focus on restricting such migration is best exemplified by the stance taken by David Cameron before becoming prime minister during the 2010 general election campaign, when he outlined reducing net migration to tens of thousands as part of a 'contract' with a proviso that 'If we don't deliver our side of the bargain, vote us out in five years' time' (Chorley, 2015). This was repeated and reinforced in 2011 after he subsequently became prime minister to a 'no if, no butts' a pledge to reduce migration; however, as shown in Figure 8.1, this has not been achieved. Subsequently, the 2010 Coalition government put in place a number of polices towards this pledge, including:

- Limiting the number of visas available to skilled workers with a job offer and introducing stricter criteria to determine who is eligible to stay permanently in the UK.
- Closing the visa allowing highly skilled workers to come to the UK without a job offer, but creating some more selective visa provisions for highly skilled/'high-value' migrants (such as investors, entrepreneurs, and those with 'exceptional talent').
- Amending student visa conditions in order to deter abuse, including by re-introducing visa interviews and limiting international students' rights to work and bring family members to the UK, and subjecting education providers to more demanding requirements.
- Closing the post-study work visa and replacing it with more limited provisions.
- Introducing new family visa eligibility criteria, such as the £18,600 'minimum income' requirement for partner visas, in order to encourage integration and protect public funds.
- Restricting new migrants' entitlements to certain welfare benefits in an attempt to address some of the perceived 'pull factors' for European immigration (Gower, 2015:1).

This last policy reflects the second overarching strand of policy responses, that of restricting the benefits paid to migrants to reduce the 'pull' factors of benefit tourism to the UK. Benefit tourism is the claim that large numbers of migrants from the poorest EU countries are attracted to the UK by the offer of more generous state welfare benefits; it is focussed on the perceived generosity of benefits paid to such new migrants, with a belief that such generosity is an encouragement to further migration or that migration is economically driven (Sealey, 2015). This was exemplified, according to Mayblin (2014), in the 1998 *Fairer, Faster and Firmer* white paper which led to the Immigration and Asylum Act 1999, wherein the then Labour government suggested that welfare benefits were acting as an incentive to economic migrants to use the asylum route to enter Britain. It also suggests that the vast majority of migrants come to the UK simply to claim benefits without having made any contribution to the system. Specifically, it presupposes such migrants are an economic drain to the UK welfare system, in that they are more likely to claim benefits than the native-born population and so be a drain on the economic system. Benefit tourism is described as occurring especially in the National Health Service (NHS), but also for income maintenance benefits (such as jobseekers allowance, housing benefit, and child benefit), and social housing.

A specific policy response to such benefit tourism has been the use of habitual residential status to restrict access to such benefits. For example, the Localism Act 2012 allowed local authorities to use local connections as a criterion for entitlement to social housing. This means that even when a migrant family might be more in need, such local connection means that priority can be given to those who are long-term residents (Oliver, 2013). As Jaywerra and Oliver (2013:56) observe, such notions are referenced to 'easing tensions arising from arising from public perceptions of migrants seen as taking resources away from long standing residents who have greater entitlement'.

In December 2013, in anticipation of the lifting of transitional restrictions on A2 Romanian and Bulgaria nationals, the government introduced several measures focussed on limiting the possibility of such benefit tourism. These included:

- a 'stronger, more robust' Habitual Residence Test for those claiming means-tested benefits.
- requiring people coming to the UK to have been living in the UK for three months before they can claim income-based Jobseeker's Allowance.
- EEA jobseekers or former workers having to show that they had a 'genuine prospect of finding work' to continue to get JSA after six months (and if applicable, Housing Benefit, Child Benefit and Child Tax Credit).
- a new minimum earnings threshold to help determine whether an EEA national is or was in 'genuine and effective' work, and so has a "right to reside" as a worker or self-employed person (and with it, entitlement to benefits).
- preventing new EEA jobseekers from accessing Housing Benefits even if they are in receipt of JSA.
- new jobseekers arriving in the UK needing to have lived in the UK for three months in order to claim Child Benefit and Child Tax Credit.
- EEA jobseekers not being able to claim Universal Credit (Kennedy, 2015:1).

Following the Conservative Party's victory in the 2015 general election, David Cameron proposed further measures to limit the impact of benefit tourism. These included in particular the proposal to ban new arrivals from the EU from claiming benefits such as tax credits and social housing for a period of four years (Cameron, 2015).

It should be noted, however, that the body of evidence that exists for the claim of benefit tourism is far from clear. This is because it is not something that is easy to prove (Bridgen et al., 2016). Tellingly, when the UK government was asked by the European Commission to substantiate its claim that benefit tourism is a real problem, its response was that the commission was placing too much emphasis on needing 'quantitative evidence', meaning too much reliance on facts and figures rather than evident 'common sense' intuition for its existence (Portes, 2014). This is supported by research which suggests that benefit tourism is not a priority for those who migrate to the UK. Rather, research by the Migration Advisory Committee (2014) has shown that the primary reason for EU-born migrants coming to the UK is to work, with just over three-quarters of migrants from EU2 and EU8 countries reporting that they came to the UK for employment reasons.

This compares with just over a third of other EU-born migrants stating that they came for the same reason. This suggests that the majority of migrants who come to the UK come to work and do find employment, as migrants are more likely to be in work than UK-born citizens (CEBR, 2013). More specifically, migrants are also less likely than those living in the UK to receive state benefits or tax credits, and similarly less likely to live in social housing than people in the same region (Dustmann and Frattini, 2013). Overall, between 2001 and 2011, it is estimated that migrants contributed £25 billion more in taxation than they received in benefits (Dustman and Frattini, 2013), highlighting that 'in particular, immigrants who arrived since 2000, especially those from EEA countries, have – through their positive net fiscal contributions – helped to reduce the fiscal burden for native workers' (Dustman and Frattini, 2014:4). Burgess (2014) has argued that significant observed improvements in the educational attainment of pupils in London in the last 10 years in comparison to the rest of the UK pupil progress is entirely accounted for in its increased ethnic composition, which has occurred from increased migration. More recent data from the government also show that high levels of net migration have been a key factor in present and future economic growth and that without such high net migration, the UK economy would still be suffering significantly from the economic crisis that remains in many EU countries (Office for Budgetary Responsibility, 2015). Overall, this suggests that benefit tourism is not as problematic as has been described recently.

The fact that policy has been built around the claim of extensive benefit tourism for which evidence is so sparse, even from the government, suggests a need to consider a more distinct rationale for such changes and the potential outcomes from this rationale. This is the focus of the rest of this chapter.

First, it should be noted that these policy responses have occurred within the context of increasing public anxiety about rising immigration. For example, prior to the 2015 general election, many opinion polls highlighted immigration as either the primary or secondary concern of British voters (Ipsos MORI 2014, 2015), which is an interesting point in the context of the high level of austerity which the UK has undergone. Additionally, analysis of reasons for people voting in the EU referendum of 2016, which resulted in a vote to leave the EU, highlighted immigration as the key concern for people who voted to leave (Prosser et al., 2016). An example of this is in relation to social housing, where the claim exists that in some areas, large numbers of mono-ethnic individuals and families have displaced UK-born social housing tenants to create mono-ethnic cultural enclaves, which serve to increase both the insularity of ethnic groups and ethnic division and community tensions with the displaced native population (Walters, 2015).

The specific consequence of the focus on residential status has been that it has made it harder for welfare professionals and organisations to justify working with such migrant groups Boccagni (2015). For example, as Walters (2015:9) observes in relation to social housing:

> Migration has been brought into the public understanding of the 'problem' of social housing, with Rutter and Latorre (2009) finding that media reporting of issues around migration and social housing is setting an unhelpful public agenda. Anti-migration messages are more prevalent than pro-migration messages and appeal to a mass media conception of 'common sense' – for example, that migrants (and by extension, superdiverse neighbourhoods) put pressure on social housing; that migrants receive preference in the allocation of social housing; that migrants commit tenancy fraud by 'borrowing' children from compatriots.

As Walters further observes, such problematising, particularly in the context of austerity, can and has become the basis for community tensions within super-diverse neighbourhoods, particularly from the perception that such migrants are displacing UK-born citizens from provisions. This is significant in the context of Mulvey's (2015:372) observation that immigrant integration into a new environment 'is clearly affected by the degree to which they feel welcomed within any particular spatial unit'. This means that those delivering services have increasingly had to actively and publicly challenge such misperceptions in order to justify the services they provide to such groups. Additionally, due to the complexity of rules and their constantly changing nature, most time is spent on learning and interpreting such rules, rather than frontline services delivery (Oliver, 2013). It is also relevant to note that this mirrors an observed wider 'hostile' shift to 'responsibilities rather than rights' for the general population, not just migrants (Oliver, 2013).

Phillimore (2011) defines such actions as the use of welfare as a tool of welfare 'restrictionalism' and identifies a whole range of different measures that have been enacted which exemplify such welfare restrictionalism. The key point about such welfare restrictionalism is that it *de facto* sanctifies poor welfare outcomes for migrants and immigrants through the experiences of high levels of unemployment, poor housing conditions, low levels of educational attainment and poor health outcomes that occur from such policies (Phillimore, 2011:11). For example, the policy of limiting subsidised English-language courses for non-native speakers also works against their integration, as the evidence from other countries suggests that 'this is the most fruitful for integration' (Oliver, 2013). This is because limiting language skills has a major impact on migrants' ability to access basic welfare provision such as healthcare, help their children with school work and that speaking English is one of the requirements for the Life in the UK citizenship test (Oliver, 2013).

One specific consequence of this is that when such migrants do work, because they lack the knowledge of basic welfare entitlements, they are often subject to experiences of labour market exploitation, such as in relation to low wages, poor conditions and precarious employment. Furthermore, such evident marginalised status can and often does lead to exploitation in further areas, such as the sexual exploitation of undocumented women migrant workers (Wilkinson, 2012). An example of this is the tied visa system introduced by the Coalition government in 2012, from which such tied workers are not allowed to leave their employer; if they do, they have to leave the country. According to Mantouvalou (2015:5), 'the effect of this has been conditions close to "slavery" for worker, wherein the effect of the visa appears to be the creation of an extremely vulnerable workforce that stays in the UK undocumented and fearful, trapped in ongoing cycles of exploitation'. What this highlights is that the Coalition government focus has been on tackling illegal immigrants, not migrant worker exploitation, such as worker rights (Wilkinson, 2012). This is significant because such negative experiences have impacts beyond the citizenship of such migrants, also affecting the citizenship of UK nationals, as for example:

> a lack of rights and knowledge, discrimination and exploitation . . . often reduce housing options and result in migrants living in overcrowded accommodation lacking basic facilities, furniture. . . . The poor state of migrant accommodation and overcrowding can lead to tensions with long-term residents who blame migrants, rather than neglectful landlords, for deteriorating housing stock.
>
> (Pemberton et al., 2014:11)

Another relevant example here is the experiences of low pay and the claim that such migrants, in being prepared to work for much lower wages than UK nationals, are dragging down wages for the native population. However, as Hill (2007) notes, it is not the migrants that are dragging down the wages, but the active creation of a 'reserve army of labour' by employers, wherein the lack of rights for newer migrants makes their lower cost and greater flexibility particularly attractive to employers, and this in turn is reflected in higher unemployment rates among earlier migrants. So here, we can see how the codified, limited citizenship rights of migrants is impacting negatively on the living standards of the native population, and therefore also their social rights as citizens, suggesting that as Craig (2015:16) argues, 'increasing diversity of itself does not undermine social cohesion but political and public responses to it do'.

Moreover, such policy ignores the contradictory barriers that exist in, for instance, the labour market, which work against the integration of both new and long-established migrants (Herbert et al., 2006). For example, as Anderson and Ruhs (2012) observe, a significant factor in the increase in the migrant labour force is the demand from employers for cheap labour, as reflected in employers' common claims that migrants have a superior 'work ethic' and 'attitude', especially when comparing relatively new arrivals to native foreign-born people more generally. This is a factor which works against not only the integration of the existing migrant population through the low wages that it provides but also against the integration of established migrants through their effective exclusion from the labour market. This suggests that rather than self-segregation, it is exclusion by others which works against the integration of established migrants.

The proposed abolishment of the Human Rights Act (HRA) 1998 (which is the enshrinement of the European Convention on Human Rights into British law) and its replacement with a Bill of Rights exemplifies how limiting migrants rights also impacts on non-migrants' rights. One of the main reasons given for such abolishment is from its claimed abuse by migrants, particularly Article 8, which is the right to family life. Various cases have been highlighted where such abuse has ostensibly taken place, most famously the claim by the home secretary that an asylum seeker's cat had enabled them to avoid deportation (Wagner, 2011). It is interesting to note that any abolishment of the HRA 1998 would not only affect migrants' human rights but also the native population, particularly those most vulnerable (Equalities and Human Rights Commission, 2011).

A relevant point to note in this respect is that the UK has no codified political constitution that guarantees citizenship rights. This means that the meaning of citizenship can and has been open to both political and legal change (Craig, 2015). Instead, T.H. Marshall's (1950) seminal analysis of the development of citizenship in the UK is very often the reference point to citizenship rights. Marshall's conceptualisation foregrounds civil, political and social rights as the three elements of citizenship, with the development of social rights as the last piece in the citizenship jigsaw; as Dwyer (2010:4) outlines 'social citizenship is a centrally important aspect of any wider notion on citizenship, are central to the idea of citizenship'.

This emphasis on citizenship from social rights was encapsulated for Marshall by the development of the UK welfare state in the late 1940, and particularly the emphasis on the principle of universalism to an extensive set of guaranteed social policy provisions in many welfare services, such as health, education and income maintenance provision. In particular, 'rights to welfare continue to be regarded as a central important aspect of "effective citizenship". . . . Rights and in particular social or welfare rights as they are often referred to, are central to the idea of citizenship' (Dwyer, 2010:4) and meant that some modicum equality became a basic principle of citizenship (Olssen, 2004). In this context, we can see that the use of residential status as a defining criterion for accessing such provision, particularly for income maintenance benefits, has limited this principle of universal rights, and hence the notion of citizenship. Thus, just as the access to such benefits delineates 'the right to share in the full heritage and to live the life of a civilised being according to the standards prevailing in the society' (Olssen, 2004:179), so the restriction of access to welfare benefits paid to migrants demarcates no such privileges, as these are reserved for those deemed to be full citizens. Rather, it means state-sanctioned welfare status diminution, and therefore status diminution to that of second class, of those legally entitled to be residing in the country.

Conclusion

The significant rises in net migration in the UK over the last 20 years has led to its transformation from mere diversity to super-diversity. However, it is the case that this has become an increasingly problematic political and public issue, as evident from the result of the EU referendum vote in 2016. This is apparent from the two main policy emphases of reducing immigration and limiting entitlement to benefits for migrants.

This changed policy emphasis has fundamentally redefined the notion of citizenship as it applies to migrants, as it means the state-sanctioned welfare status diminution to that of second-class citizens of those legally entitled to be residing in the country. This has made it harder for welfare professionals and organisations to justify working with such migrant groups, and so increased their already marginalised status. However, just as significant is that such negative experiences have impacts beyond the citizenship of such migrants, also affecting the citizenship of UK nationals, with *de facto* state-sanctioned persistent low pay being a good example of a factor which works not only against the integration of the existing migrant population through the low quality of life it enables but also against the integration of established migrants through their effective exclusion from the labour market.

This suggests that rather than self-segregation, it is exclusion by others which works against the integration of established migrants. The prominence given to the abuse of the HRA by migrants as a rationale for its prospective abolishment is a particularly good example of this. In a wider sense, it shows that a failure to defend the basic citizenship rights of the most vulnerable in society can and does lead to the coincidental loss of those social rights which define us as citizens.

References

Anderson, B, and Ruhs, M, 2012, Reliance on migrant labour: Inevitability or policy choice? *Journal of Poverty and Social Justice*, 20, 1, 23–30

Boccagni, P, 2015, (Super)diversity and the migration-social work nexus: A new lens on the field of access and inclusion? *Ethnic and Racial Studies*, 38, 4, 608–620

Bridgen, P, Meyer, T, and Moran, J, 2016, *Benefit tourism and Britain's new deal: Will the renegotiation stop EU migrants coming to the UK*, London: King's College London, http://ukandeu.ac.uk/benefit-tourism-and-britains-new-deal-will-the-renegotiation-stop-eu-migrants-coming-to-the-uk/

Burgess, S, 2014, Understanding the success of London's schools, *Working Paper No. 14/333*, University of Bristol, Centre for Market and Public Organisation

Cameron, D, 2014, *British values: Article by David Cameron*, www.gov.uk/government/news/british-values-article-by-david-cameron

Cameron, D, 2015, *A new settlement for the United Kingdom in a reformed European Union*, Letter by David Cameron to Donald Tusk, 10 Downing Street, London

Cangiano, A, 2014, The impact of migration on UK population growth, *Migration Observatory Briefing February 2014*, University of Oxford: Compass Group UK

Centre for Economics and Business Research (CEBR), 2013, *Impact of EU labour on the UK*, London: CEBR, www.cebr.com/reports/migration-benefits-to-the-uk

Chorley, M, 2015, 'I'll cut immigration or kick me out': What Cameron told voters at the LAST election before numbers arriving soared to 300,000', *Mail Online*, www.dailymail.co.uk/news/article-2979135/I-ll-cut-immigration-kick-Cameron-told-voters-election-numbers-arriving-soared-300-000.html

Craig, G, 2015, Migration and integration. A local and experiential perspective, *IRIS Working Paper Series, No. 7/2015*, Birmingham: Institute for Research into Superdiversity

Dustmann, C, and Frattini, T, 2013, The fiscal effects of immigration to the UK, *Discussion Paper Series CDP No. 22/13*, London: Centre for Research and Analysis of Migration, University College London

Dustmann, C, and Frattini, T, 2014, The fiscal effects of immigration to the UK, *The Economic Journal*, 124, 580, 593–643

Dwyer, P, 2010, *Understanding social citizenship. Themes and perspectives for policy and practice*, 2nd edition, Bristol: Policy Press

Equalities and Human Rights Commission, 2011, *The case for the Human Rights Act. Part 1 of 3 responses to the commission on a bill of rights: HRS plus not minus*, London: Equalities and Human Rights Commission, www.equalityhumanrights.com/sites/default/files/documents/humanrights/bor_full.pdf

Gower, M, 2015, Accommodation and financial support for asylum seekers, *House of Commons Note: SN/HA/1909*, London: House of Commons Library

Herbert, J, Datta, D, Evans, Y, May, J, McIlwaine, C, and Wills, J, 2006, *Multiculturalism at work: The experiences of Ghanaians in London*, London: Queen Mary University

Hill, M, 2007, Book review: Migration, citizenship and the European welfare state, *Social Policy and Administration*, 41, 7, 795–797.

Ipsos MORI, 2014, *Ipsos MORI issues index June 2014*, London: Ipsos MORI, www.ipsos.com/ipsos-mori/en-uk/economistipsos-mori-june-2014-issues-index

Ipsos MORI, 2015, *Ipsos MORI issues index April 2015*, London: Ipsos MORI, www.ipsos.com/ipsos-mori/en-uk/economistipsos-mori-april-2015-issues-index,

Jaywerra, H, and Oliver, C, 2013, *Mapping the conditions of stay and the rationale for entitlements and restrictions for family migrants in the United Kingdom*, University of Oxford: Compass Group UK

Kennedy, S, 2015, Measures to limit migrants' access to benefits, *House of Common Note: SN06889*, London: House of Commons Library

Mantouvalou, V, 2015, Overseas domestic workers: Britain's domestic slaves, *Socialist Lawyer*, March, no. 69, p. 44.

Marshall, TH, 1950, *Citizenship and social class*, Cambridge: Cambridge University Press

Mayblin, L, 2014, Asylum, welfare and work: Reflections on research in asylum and refugee studies, *International Journal of Sociology and Social Policy*, 34, 5–6, 375–391

Migration Advisory Committee, 2014, *Migrants in low-skilled work: The growth of EU and non-EU labour in low-skilled jobs and its impact on the UK*, London: Migration Advisory Committee, www.gov.uk/government/uploads/system/uploads/attachment_data/file/333084/MAC-_Migrants_in_low-skilled_work_Summary_2014.pdf

Mulvey, G, 2015, Refugee integration policy: The effects of UK policy-making on refugees in Scotland, *Journal of Social Policy*, 44, 2, 357–375

Office for Budgetary Responsibility, 2015, Economic and fiscal outlook, *Cm 9024*, March, London: Her Majesty's Stationery Office

Office for National Statistics, 2012, *Ethnicity and national identity in England and Wales 2011*, London: Office for National Statistics, www.ons.gov.uk/ons/dcp171776_290558.pdf

Office for National Statistics, 2014, *Annual mid-year population estimates*, London: Office for National Statistics, www.ons.gov.uk/ons/dcp171778_367167.pdf

Office for National Statistics, 2018, *Provisional long-term international migration estimates*, London: Office for National Statistics, www.ons.gov.uk/file?uri=/peoplepopulationandcommunity/populationandmigration/internationalmigration/datasets/migrationstatisticsquarterlyreportprovisionallongterminternationalmigrationltimestimates/current/provisionalestimatesoflongterminternationalmigrationyeseptember2017.xls

Oliver, C, 2013, *Country case study on the impacts of restrictions and entitlements on the integration of family migrants: Qualitative findings*, University of Oxford: Compass Group UK

Olssen, M, 2004, From the Crick report to the Parekh report: Multiculturalism, cultural difference and democracy – The revisioning of citizenship education, *British Journal of Sociology of Education*, 25, 2, 179–192.

Pemberton, S, Phillimore, J, and Robinson, D, 2014, Causes and experiences of poverty among economic migrants in the UK, *IRIS Working Paper Series, No. 4/2014*, University of Birmingham: Institute for Research into Superdiversity

Phillimore, J, 2011, Approaches to health provision in the age of super-diversity: Accessing the NHS in Britain's most diverse city, *Critical Social Policy*, 31, 1, 5–29

Phillips, T, and Webber, R, 2014, Superdiversity and the browning of labour, The *Political Quarterly*, 85, 3, 304–311.

Portes, J, 2014, Immigration: Could we – Should we – Stop migrants coming to Britain? *The Observer*, 19 October, www.theguardian.com/uk-news/2014/oct/19/immigration-policy-ukip-restrictions-european-union

Prosser, C, Mellon, J, and Green, J, 2016, *What mattered most to you when deciding to vote in the EU referendum*, www.britishelectionstudy.com/bes-findings/what-mattered-most-to-you-when-deciding-how-to-vote-in-the-eu-referendum/#.Ws9eeZdJncs

Rutter, J. and Latorre, M. 2009. *Migration, Migrants and Inequality*. In Towards a more Equal Society (ed.) Hill, J., Sefton, T and Stewart, K. (UK: University of Bristol).

Sealey, C, 2015, *Social policy simplified*, Basingstoke: Palgrave Macmillan

Vervotec, S, 2007, Super-diversity and its implications, *Ethnic and Racial Studies*, 30, 6, 1024–1054.

Wagner, A, 2011, Catgate: Another myth used to trash human rights, *The Guardian*, www.theguardian.com/law/2011/oct/04/theresa-may-wrong-cat-deportation

Walters, G, 2015, The challenges of superdiversity for social housing, *Iris Working Paper Series, No. 5/2015*, University of Birmingham: Institute for Research into Superdiversity

Wilkinson, M, 2012, 'Out of sight, out of mind': The exploitation of migrant workers in 21st century Britain, *Journal of Poverty and Social Justice*, 20, 1, 13–21

Part III

Civil liberties, multiculturalism and marginalisation

Introductory remarks

Abe W. Ata

Part III provides an overview of policies towards migration and multiculturalism, particularly the failures, achievements and implications of integrating minorities in select countries, including the Netherlands, Australia and Canada. In Chapter 9, Sunier builds on the themes outlined previously, stressing that diversity has not only risen to academic prominence but has also become an inherent part of policy reports on a wide range of issues, especially as demonstrated in the Netherlands. Diversity in Islam, for example, has recently become a core characteristic of modern Western society and a direct consequence of globalisation, digitalisation and social and cultural mobility. Side by side with this reality there is a gradual but clear tendency to be discerned in European countries towards a more cultural notion of citizenship. This not only results in a stronger emphasis on assimilation into the imagined core values of 'Western' society, it also reduces any reference to recognition of cultural and religious diversity into a merely symbolic principle. This paradoxical situation has resulted in a deterioration of the position of Muslims in many sectors of Dutch society.

The difficulties and challenges encountered by Germany, and Europe at large, as a result of recent arrivals of sudden waves of refuges and asylum seekers are examined by Grosu-Rădulescu (Chapter 10). This chapter provides a contextual background of the complexities and contradictions related to government policies and community attitudes to a newly emerged melting pot. A cutting-edge reference to Angela Merkel, the German chancellor, announcing that multiculturalism is "a sham" set the tone for further nuanced meanings arguably to the waves of immigration that had taken the whole of Europe by surprise. Other themes under examination include the genesis of multiculturalism in Europe, how it has acquired nuanced meanings and interpretation in the past few decades. To achieve this, Grosu-Rădulescu traces a brief history of the multiculturalist project and its success or limits in Canada and reviews the European efforts to implement multi-culturalist ideals on a national level and within the broader pluricultural EU policies. The concept of transculturalism or cultural diversity (a melting of cultural markers) is also examined and compared to multiculturalism (a gathering of multiple and distinct contributions to the mainstream culture).

A comparison of the trends, approaches and patterns of thee growing reality of multiculturalism between Canada and Australia is made by Ozdowski (Chapter 11). This chapter describes its social and political origins, as well as major policy and programme implementation shifts over the previous decades, outlining references to its aims, successes and challenges to national identity. Also discussed are key achievements of Australian multiculturalism and the emerging challenges resulting from globalisation, changing immigration patterns and redefinition of the Australian concepts of 'fair go' and democracy.

Ali (Chapter 12) broadens the analysis that was explored in the two previous chapters. He addresses the issue of compatibility between Islamic and Western core values. He observes that since the events of 9/11, the perception of Islam as the "internal other" and the "external enemy" has lent further weight to the debate that Islam and the West are incompatible. He argues that viewing Islam and the West as a dialectical paradigm is a politically expedient and socially false construct. Several fundamental values such as justice and compassion are shared by both cultures, albeit differences that are crucial to the preservation of cultural coexistence.

9 Diversity and Islam

The case of the Netherlands

Thijl Sunier

In the so-called 'civil integration' exam, mandatory for every new immigrant in the Netherlands, there are questions about their attitude towards LGTBQ communities and about the position of women in Dutch society. Instruction films for potential new residents always address these issues as core elements of Dutch civil culture. The new migrant should understand that 'the Dutch culture' considers all sexual identities equally valid and accepted and all women, irrespective of their background, equal to men. Equality and diversity are the key 'gate-keeping' concepts in the information for newcomers.

In many civil integration courses, the recognition of diverse sexual identities is pitted against the allegedly 'radical', 'conservative' and 'intolerant' core of Islamic culture (Mepschen et al. 2010). Embracing 'Dutch civil culture' is presented as the only viable integration route into Dutch society. In the public debate 'diverse but equal' has become the basis for a narrative in which Muslims are framed as the proverbial 'pre-modern' who do not accept this.

Similar cases can be found elsewhere in Europe. They mirror a similar problematic – namely how to make sense of the growing prominence of 'diversity' as a guiding principle of public administration, while at the same time witnessing the spread in recent decades of increasingly explicit nationalist 'identity politics' across the continent. Do these developments refer to different, even contradicting, phenomena? The prime goal of these identity politics is the call for one leading national civil culture to which all inhabitants should abide and often formulated as 'national core values'. Nationalist identity policies are instigated by neo-nationalist parties and movements, but have become part and parcel of mainstream political agendas and public debates.

By contrast, the growing prominence of 'diversity' as a basic device of public and private administration and management policies can hardly be overlooked. Training programs about how to deal with diverse backgrounds of employees and how to benefit from them are currently mushrooming. In the Netherlands all public institutions paid by tax money should have an elaborated diversity policy that reflects contemporary society.

Nationalist identity politics coincided with the demise of multicultural-ism (Sunier 2018). Already in the late 1990s a general consensus emerged that multiculturalist politics had failed. In recent years a considerable body of literature has been produced addressing various aspects and causes of this demise (see e.g. Silverstein 2005; Wacquant 2005; Modood 2007; Ver-tovec & Wessendorf 2010; Vertovec 2010; Lentin 2012; Alexander 2013). As one of the causes for the demise, a number of authors point at the consolidation of nationalist politics in the wake of globalization (see e.g. Wiborg 2000; Schiffauer et al. 2004; Brubaker 2016). Sassen has argued that migration and increasing human mobility due to globalization is one of the prime concerns of modern nation-states. She observed an intrigu-ing paradox. Where nation-states generally accepted the transfer of certain forms of legal and economic decision-making to higher levels of control, migration policies were more explicitly (re)claimed as an exclusive realm of national sovereignty (1996: XXIV). Others have built on this argument by emphasizing the role of the modern state as a significant cultural agent propagating a dominant civil culture (Rose & Miller 1992; Geschiere & Meyer 1998; Blom Hansen & Stepputat 2001; Schiffauer et al. 2004; Van Klinken & Barker 2009; Mepschen et al. 2010; Sunier et al. 2016).

The endorsement of a single dominant national civil culture abided by all citizens is shorthand for cultural assimilation and seems at odds with 'diver-sity' as a policy instrument. In recent years there has been a booming output of studies dealing with diversity policies and 'diversity governance' (Horsti et al. 2014). Largely based on the political language of anti-racism and anti-discrimination agendas, the 'diversity discourse' has turned into a powerful political paradigm in the organization of public and private institutions and in governmental policies (see Holvino & Kamp 2009). The question arises how to make sense of these seemingly opposing tendencies.

In this chapter I argue that nationalist and assimilationist policies and diversity discourses are not opposing trends, but are based on the same dis-cursive frame and the same political and cultural assumptions. This becomes clear when we analyse the genealogy of Islam as a policy category.

The genealogy of Islam as a policy category

Apart from the constitutional provisions granted to all religious denomina-tions, including Muslims, such as religious freedom and the principle that the state does not interfere in religious affairs, the equality of all religious denominations and the principle of 'non-recognition' are important con-stituting elements of Dutch state–religion relations (Rath et al. 2001). In addition to that, the Dutch history of religious 'pillarization' that shaped religious landscapes in the country in most of the first half of the twentieth century is still relevant. The decisive feature of this political system was the extensive cultural autonomy of religious communities. Towards the 1960s with the emergence of the central welfare state and the gradual process of deconfessionalisation, the system lost its function, but the juridical remnants of the system do still play a role in some crucial areas. The most important is the Dutch school system (Sunier 2004).

The vast majority of Muslims in the Netherlands have a migrant background. To understand how Islam became a policy category and the pivot in both neo-nationalist identity politics and the current diversity discourse, we have to include integration policies over the past thirty-five years in our analysis. It should be noted that the Netherlands developed the most elaborate integration policies in Europe. As such, it became an exclusive policy field with its own dynamics and agendas. Until the early 1980s, the religious background of migrants did not play any significant role in debates about their position in society. Migrants were primarily seen as members of a temporary labour force who would return to their countries of origin (Nielsen 1992; Sunier 1996; Rath et al. 2001).

However, the acknowledgment that most migrants would stay permanently resulted in a stronger emphasis on the cultural background of these new settlers. Migrants brought with them their cultural and religious backgrounds. This 'culturalization' process would intensify in the 1990s and 2000s (Duyvendak et al. 2010), but the foundations were laid in the early 1980s.

Further, it should be emphasized that integration policies in the 1980s were basically collective, in that migrants were treated as cultural or religious communities for which collective policies would work best. The rapidly increasing number of Islamic organizations in the 1980s was basically perceived as organizations of migrants. At the same time, the developments in the Islamic world, such as the revolution in Iran and the assassination of the Egyptian president Sadat, resulted in the 'Islamization' of migrants: the overemphasis of the religious background of migrants as an explanation for their outlooks and practices.

Migrants with completely different backgrounds were lumped together under the heading of 'Muslim culture'. Although the position of migrants was the result of a complex interplay of economic, social, political and ideological factors, the assumed nature of Islam became a dominant explanatory principle. Towards the end of the 1980s this discursive transformation was almost fully accomplished and would further develop in successive decades.

The late 1980s also marked a turning point in the status of cultural and religious diversity, with two important characteristics: the shift from a collective notion of integration to an individualized one and the introduction of the term 'allochtonous', denoting non-native Dutch, or 'having a different cultural background'. Cultural properties were located in the individual influencing someone's attitudes. The focus of integration policies shifted to the individual level. Over the years 'allochtonous' would acquire a degrading and exclusionary meaning (Vasta 2007; Geschiere 2009). Due to its vagueness and plasticity, the term is applied in a wide variety of situations.

It gradually made its way into the dominant discourse and in practical political matters in the early 1990s.

The beginning of the 1990s also marked a shift in integration policies to the emerging discussion about Islam and the character of the Dutch nation-state. Not only could we observe the gradual conflation of 'culture' with 'Islam' (Sunier 1996) but also the growing entanglement of integration trajectories with nation-building. The Rushdie affair in 1989 counted as catalytic in emphasizing this line of political thinking. Since the majority of Muslims were 'here to stay', it invigorated a debate about the place of Islam in Dutch ('secular') society. Integration is not just a matter of participation in society; it is also an issue that touches on the very roots of the Dutch nation. The right-wing influential Dutch political leader Frits Bolkestein, in a speech in 1991 at the International Liberal Conference in Lausanne, called on European societies to be aware of the presence of Muslims and to think about how 'we' should relate to Islam and to 'our' own liberal roots (1991). The Western nation, according to Bolkestein, has accomplished a higher civilizational stage than Islamic societies. With reference to the claimed universality of these accomplishments, Bolkestein urged European liberal politicians not to give in to some sort of multicultural idea of cultural equality.

Towards the end of the 1990s, the relation between culture and social status became more complicated. The assumption that 'Muslim equals underclass' did not anymore correspond with the statistical facts (SCP 1996, 2009). The awareness grew that especially young Muslims would demand their place in society more articulately. These young Muslims could not simply be discarded as 'not-yet-integrated' individuals. Many of them were born in the Netherlands and considered it their society. Their ability to articulate their demands not towards but within society brought about new challenges to the existing cultural hierarchy paradigm. Muslims were increasingly visible in those sectors of society that were long exclusively 'white'. This threw into relief the fundamental question as to how society relates to these 'new citizens'.

Now the debate took on a more alarming undertone. The self-confidence that characterized the discourse in the 1980s and 1990s was gradually replaced by the awareness that the 'cultural engineering' that dominated the 'integration apparatus' until then did not work out. The increasing articulacy among young Muslims, the demands addressed by them towards Dutch society and not least their increasing visibility in the public sphere prompted a reconsideration of the concept of 'Dutchness'. Many intellectuals argued for a deepening and dissemination of national awareness and protection of Dutch national identity, both in relation to the presence of ethnic minorities and European unification. Their plea for more attention to national roots fitted within a general change in the political climate that took place in the course of the 1990s. The main idea is that the Dutch seem to be at a loss when they have to define precisely what the Dutch nation is. What is Dutch about Dutch national culture? What does it consist of? Why is the nation (still) an important frame of reference (Van Ginkel 1999)? The cultural feeling of national belonging has become so 'natural' in the Netherlands that for a long time many thought it hardly needed contemplating. Some have mistaken this self-evidence for a lack of national consciousness, and even a denial of 'Dutchness'. This poses a dilemma for ethnic minorities: If they are willing to integrate into the nation, what is required of them? How can one become a member of Dutch society when it is unclear what this membership implies (Sunier & Van Ginkel 2006)?

Already prior to 9/11 a shift occurred in the thinking about the relation between culture and integration. The worries about the Dutch national core values and the critique of the 1980s integration policies provided a fruitful basis for the anti-multicultural discourse that emerged at the start of the new millennium. In a seminal opinion article in the daily Nieuwe Rotterdamsche Courant (NRC) by publicist Paul Scheffer 'The Multicultural Drama' (2000), the author remarked that the Dutch people in the mid-twentieth century integrated well with the mainstream society in a fairly smooth transition. This had been accomplished by a highly active struggle against poverty, an effective schooling and assimilation program and all kinds of other measures meant to improve their position. Scheffer blamed the government for a slack attitude in these matters, arguing that the cultural diversity we can observe in the public sphere, such as Islamic schools, all kinds of language programs, the strong ethnic cohesion among many migrants and their children, and not least the increasing cultural assertion and visibility, is the direct result of this laissez-faire attitude. This, according to Scheffer is multicultural policy in practice (see also Scheffer 2007). Scheffer invited all those protagonists of multiculturalism to look at what happens in the poor neighbourhoods of the big cities. He also refers to the fundamental differences between Islam and Christianity, and he accuses all those who argue that one hundred years ago Catholics and Protestants were no less adversaries than Muslims and Christians are today of being naive (Scheffer 2000, 2007).

Scheffer not only suggested a direct link between culture and backwardness, he also predicted that the problems will be even more difficult than those with 'our own underclasses'. He further argued that the cultural distance between 'us' and 'them' is much bigger than we seem to believe. Although Scheffer did not openly evaluate cultures, he implicitly assumed that it is in the best interest of migrants to assimilate into Dutch society. In other words, a lasting cultural diversity is the direct proof of a failed integration project and an open invitation for even bigger future problems. Such a 'multicultural neglect' endangers the very foundation on which our society rests. Increasing cultural diversity implies diminishing national cohesion. Multiculturalism, a term which Scheffer nowhere explicated, is a typical example of an ideology born out of the lack of capacity to define what binds together a nation. 'We boast of a national identity having no national identity', Scheffer (2000) argued, but this will certainly not invite immigrants to participate in that society. He then concluded by stating that cultural reciprocity in an 'open society' puts a limit on the extent of cultural diversity, that the only way to prevent a second Rushdie affair is to make clear what Dutch national identity implies and, above all, requires a strictly neutral public sphere.

The essay by Scheffer constituted another turning point in the relation between 'national civil culture' and 'diversity'. His moral call for a more assertive Dutch national identity went hand in hand with further dismantling of multiculturalism as a policy tool to emancipate newcomers that was set in motion a decade earlier. In that respect his essay constituted a transition stage between the 1990s and the 2000s. The attacks on the Twin Towers a year later would enhance this transition in a compelling way. The urgency according to a growing number of people to confront newcomers, especially those of 'non-Western' origin with a dominant civil culture, has only become stronger in subsequent years.

The new integration policies issued by the government in 2007 reflected this urgency. It implied a zero tolerance on cultural diversity and a strict and coercive program on citizenship trajectories. In subsequent years, a nation-wide consensus emerged about the importance of a so-called dominant 'Leitkultur'. Even leftists parties who were hitherto in favor of 'multicultural' policies are now hammering on the importance of shared cultural values. When Queen Maxima (Argentinian by origin) stated in 2007 that she had not yet met 'the' Dutch and that there is not just one Dutch identity, she was sharply criticized for her statement, but there was also a lot of support. In 2018 this support certainly diminished. And this makes the rise in the prominence of diversity all the more intriguing.

Diversity as a moral imperative

In this chapter I have addressed the question of how to make sense of the broad societal consensus about the necessity of committing to one dominant civil culture and at the same time the rise in prominence of diversity as a policy instrument and a civic virtue. The question is relevant because they are seemingly opposing developments and need to be unpacked. I have argued that this question can only addressed contextually in concrete cases of policymaking. The example with which I started this chapter cannot be fully grasped if we simply consider it as a 'clash' of legal principles or of different cultural frames. The case is illustrative of an intriguing development that unfolded over the last three decades. Diversity transformed from an empirical description of ethnic, religious and cultural plurality into a principle that represents the core characteristic of a 'modern', 'tolerant' and 'open' civil culture. Initially it referred to existing cultural, ethnic and religious differences, with Muslims as the obvious case in point. As the denominator of an existing societal reality, diversity was a precursor to the development of integration policies in the Netherlands in the 1980s that took this societal plurality as a point of departure because it was assumed that an acknowledgement of the ethnic and religious plurality of the immigrant population would facilitate a smooth integration process. However, this multiculturalism Dutch style should not be confused with the common definition as a political ideology that recognizes and facilitates cultural, ethnic and religious diversity and that is based on the principle of equality of cultures (see Vertovec 2010). The Dutch integration policies in those years were multicultural in a purely instrumental sense. The final goal of these policies would be complete assimilation (Sunier 2010).

When the Dutch government in the early 1990s shifted from a policy based on collective integration trajectories to one that took the individual migrant as the starting point, it also redefined ethnic and religious backgrounds. From a property of migrant communities, it became a quality attributed to individual migrants shaping his or her attitudes, outlooks and motivations. The 'burden of proof' to integrate became the responsibility of the individual migrant. Certain cultural or religious traits would hamper or retard integration, and it was up to the individual migrant to address that. Multiculturalism became the focus of a critical public debate, not least because the staggering integration and the persistent social inequality were said to be caused by earlier multiculturalist policies.

In the 1990s the demise of multicultural politics, Dutch-style, was invigorated by the growing worries about the alleged incompatibility of Islam with Dutch society. In the course of the 1990s and built on this notion of incompatibly, the contours of a Dutch civil culture emerged, but it was only in the 2000s that it took shape and that diversity made its way back into the debate.

One of the most observable developments that emerged from this unfolding Dutch civil culture was the so-called 'culturalization of citizenship' (Duyvendak & Scholten 2011). In the 1980s and 1990s the Dutch government used a notion of citizenship that was closer to the classical French idea of 'citizens equal before the law'. Immigrants would be granted rights from the start, and policies would be developed to eliminate structural inequalities. Cultural citizenship, by contrast, defines the citizen in cultural terms, denoting the process by which culture (emotions, feelings, cultural norms and values and cultural symbols and traditions, including religion) has come to play a central role in the debate on social integration. It is a process in which more meaning is attached to cultural participation (in terms of norms, values, practices, and traditions), either as an alternative or in addition to citizenship as rights and socioeconomic participation (ibid: 7).

Duyvendak and Scholten mention a number of relevant characteristics of this process. One important aspect is the depiction of Dutch civil culture as the result of a timeless consensus about liberal modernity; hence, the perfect citizen should be loyal to these ideals. In this way, it has become a powerful criterion for integration (ibid: 4).

As I have indicated, one crucial aspect of this 'universal' civil culture is the embrace and acceptance of diversity. Where ethnic and religious diversity, albeit under different assumptions, were put to work in the 1980s and 1990s with the aim to alleviate social and structural inequalities, diversity in its present disguise epitomizes modern Dutch society with strong moral imperatives and strong pedagogical underpinnings. Diversity has transformed from the recognition of the multiplicity of outlooks and value systems into a symbolic ideological device of modernity that should be taught to newcomers.

A crucial characteristic of diversity as a moral imperative is its vagueness in terms of aims and trajectories as to what should be achieved. It is precisely this vagueness that generates consensus. Indeed as Bell and Hartmann (2007) argue, as long as diversity remains vague and malleable with no reference to underlying assumptions, it works, but it leaves structural inequalities untouched. The outcome of their survey in the United States about the meaning of diversity shows that people have completely different understandings of what diversity entails. In most cases informants refer to 'harmless' apolitical aspects such as cooking, dress, entertainment and other expressions of difference. Assumptions behind 'diversity talk' remain vague or are not at all addressed. Thus, diversity refers to superficial and external expressions of difference and obscures deep structural inequalities in society.

Their findings resonate well in the Netherlands. Diversity in its present form is seen as a qualification denoting the multiplicity of identity markers of individuals, without any reference to societal position. Although the narrative of diversity refers to discrimination, exclusion and power inequality on the basis of biological, social and cultural differences, it remains remarkably vague about what sort of differences are included.

Diversity as a moral imperative is articulated with the power to define what the legitimate parameters of the diverse landscape are and which identity claims are deemed irrelevant or even undesirable and thus illegitimate. In some cases diversity claims are subject to heated debates. The recurring discussion in the Netherlands towards the beginning of December about 'Black Peter' is a case in point. Black Peter is the black assistant of Santa Claus who brings presents for children in the Netherlands on 5 December. Every year there are protests against the racist connotations of the figure of Black Peter. Protesters point at the colonial past and the history of slavery that is connected to the figure. Supporters deny the inbuilt racism and reject the claim that Black Peter is insulting to black people. Protesters want to show that skin colour still generates structural inequality. Supporters deem skin colour an irrelevant 'thing of the past' (see also Wekker 2016).

As Miles and Brown (2003) argue, biological or cultural difference between human beings only become signifying practices in political contexts. As such, diversity as an inherent aspect of liberal modernity has no consequences for power relations in society, because the basic question of who has the power to define which forms of diversity matters and which are irrelevant remains unanswered.

To conclude, diversity as an ideological prerequisite of modernity not only results in a stronger emphasis on assimilation into the imagined core values of 'Western' society, it also reduces any reference to recognition of cultural and religious diversity into a merely symbolic principle. A diversity policy in any public office must reflect the proportion of Muslims in society, but only nominally and only if they comply with the imagined core values of society. This paradoxical situation has resulted in a deterioration of the position of Muslims in many sectors of Dutch society in recent years, despite their remarkable socio-economic upward mobility.

References

Alexander, J.C. (2013) 'Struggling over the mode of incorporation: Backlash against multiculturalism in Europe', *Ethnic and Racial Studies*, Vol. 36/4: 531–556.

Bell, J. & D. Hartmann (2007) 'Diversity in everyday discourse: The cultural ambiguities and consequences of "happy talk"', *American Sociological Review*, Vol. 72: 895–914.

Blom Hansen, T. & F. Stepputat (eds.) (2001) *States of Imagination: Ethnographic Exploration of the Postcolonial State*. Durham: Duke University Press.

Bolkenstein, F. (1991) *Address to the Liberal International Conference at Luzern*. Den Haag: VVD.

Brubaker, R. (2016) 'The politics of national identity: A new "Christianist" secularism in Europe', *The Immanent Frame*.

Duyvendak, J.W. & P. Scholten (2011) 'Beyond the Dutch multicultural model', *International Migration and Integration*, Vol. 12: 331–348.

Duyvendak, J.W., E. Tonkens & M. Hurenkamp (2010) 'Culturalization of citizenship in the Netherlands', in: Chebel d'Appolonia, A. & S. Reich (eds.) *Managing Ethnic Diversity After 9/11: Integration, Security, and Civil Liberties in Transatlantic Perspective*. New Brunswick: Rutgers University Press: 233–252.

Geschiere, P. (2009) *The Perils of Belonging*. Chicago: University of Chicago Press.

Geschiere, P. & B. Meyer (1998) 'Globalization and identity: Dialectics of flow and closure', *Development and Change*, Vol. 29: 601–615.

Holvino, E. & A. Kamp (2009) 'Diversity management: Are we moving in the right direction? Reflections from both sides of the North Atlantic', *Scandinavian Journal of Management*, Vol. 25/4: 395–403.

Horsti, K., G. Titley & G. Hultén (2014) *National Conversations: Public Service Media and Cultural Diversity in Europe*, Bristol: Intellect ltd.

Lentin, A. & G. Titley (2012) 'The crisis of "multiculturalism" in Europe: Mediated minarets, intolerable subjects', *European Journal of Cultural Studies*, Vol. 15/2: 123–138.

Mepschen, P., J.W. Duyvendak & E.H. Tonkens (2010) 'Sexual politics, orientalism, and multicultural citizenship in the Netherlands', *Sociology*, Vol. 44: 962–979 (digital library).

Miles, R. & M. Brown (2003) *Racism*. London: Routledge.

Modood, T. (2007) *Multiculturalism*. Cambridge: Polity Press.

Nielsen, J.S. (1992) *Muslims in Western Europe*. Edinburgh: Edinburgh University Press.

Rath, J. & T. Sunier (1994) 'Angst voor de islam in Nederland?' in: *Kritiek: Jaarboek voor socialistische discussie en analyse.* Utrecht: Stichting Toestanden: 53–63, 93–94.

Rath, J. et al. (2001) *Western Europe and Its Islam.* Leiden: Brill.

Rose, N. & P. Miller (1992) 'Political power beyond the state: Problematics of government', *The British Journal of Sociology,* Vol. 43/2: 173–205.

Sassen, S. (1996) *Losing Control? Sovereignty in an Age of Globalization.* New York: Columbia University Press.

Scheffer, P. (2000) 'Het multiculturele drama', *NRC,* 29 January.

Scheffer, P. (2007) *Het Land van Aankomst.* Amsterdam: De Bezige Bij.

Schiffauer, W. et al. (2004) *Civil Enculturation.* Oxford: Berghahn.

SCP (1996) *Sociaal Cultureel Rapport.* Den Haag: SCP.

SCP (2009) *Jaarrapport Integratie 2009.* Den Haag: SCP.

Silverstein, P. (2005) 'Immigrant racialization and the new savage slot', *Annual Review of Anthropology,* Vol. 34: 363–384.

Sunier, T. (1996) *Islam in Beweging.* Amsterdam: Het Spinhuis.

Sunier, T. (2004) 'Naar een nieuwe schoolstrijd?' *BMGN,* Vol. 119/4: 552–576.

Sunier, T. (2010). 'Assimilation by conviction or by coercion? Integration policies in the Netherlands', in: Silj, A. (ed.) *European Multiculturalism Revisited.* London: Zed Press: 214–235.

Sunier, T. (2018) 'Between Islam as a generic category and Muslim exceptionalism', in: Valdamar Vinding, N., E. Racius & J. Thielmann (eds.) *Exploring the Multitude of Muslims in Europe: Essays in Honor of Jorgen N. Nielsen.* Leiden: Brill: 3–20.

Sunier, T., H. van der Linden & E. van de Bovenkamp (2016) 'Transnational Islam: Moroccan and Turkish State competing for the Ummah', *Contemporary Islam* (special issue on 'Citizenship in transition: Islamic actors and discourses in the public domain', Bergh, S., K. Willemse & A. Chhachhi, eds.), Vol. 10/3: 402–420.

Sunier, T. & R. Van Ginkel (2006) ' "At your service!" Reflections on the rise of neo-nationalism in the Netherlands', in: Gingrich, A. & M. Banks (eds.) *Neo-nationalism in Europe and Beyond.* Oxford: Berghahn: 107–125.

Van Ginkel, R. (1999) *Op zoek naar eigenheid. Denkbeelden en discussies over cultuur en identiteit in Nederland.* Den Haag: SDU.

Van Klinken, G. & J. Barker (eds.) (2009) *State of Authority: State in Society in Indonesia.* New York: Cornell University.

Vasta, E. (2007) 'From ethnic minorities to ethnic majority policy: Multiculturalism and the shift to assimilation in the Netherlands', *Ethnic and Racial Studies,* Vol. 30/5: 713–740.

Vertovec, S. (2010) 'Towards post-multiculturalism? Changing communities, conditions and contexts of diversity', *International Social Science Journal,* 83–95.

Vertovec, S. & S. Wessendorf (eds.) (2010) *The Multiculturalism Backlash: European Discourses, Policies, and Practices.* London: Routledge.

Wacquant, L. (2005) 'Enemies of the wholesome part of the nation', *Sociologie jrg,* Vol. 1/1: 31–51.

Wekker, G. (2016) *White Innocence: Paradoxes of Colonialism and Race.* Durham: Duke University Press.

Wiborg, S. (2000) 'Political and cultural nationalism in education', *Comparative Education,* Vol. 36/2: 235–243.

10 Multiculturalism under attack in Europe

Lucia-Mihaela Grosu-Rădulescu

Multiculturalism: where to next?

As the heading of this section implies, when it comes to discussing multiculturalism, there is a process, a progression, an evolution of the concept which needs to be addressed. In an interview offered to the BBC and broadcasted in 2011, Stuart Hall was talking about the multicultural society in terms of a "permanent revolution"[1]. Indeed, in his book *The Multicultural Question*, Hall had emphasized the uncertainty embedded in terminology, calling multiculturalism not only an "imprecise" discourse but also pointing to the amount of political tactics it usually refers to (Hall 2001, 3). Our decision to delve into an analysis of the debates surrounding multiculturalism was motivated by the noticeable attack on this concept in European political discourse. Controversies regarding multiculturalism are not new, but it is only recently that we have witnessed its use as a scapegoat for political and social action in Western Europe. A second, more personal, reason to approach this subject is rooted in a desire to show the importance of terminology and contextualization in social and political discourse, or rather the effects of not doing so.

According to Michel Wieviorka quoting Nathan Glazer, the term multiculturalism can be traced back to 1941 when it was used in a New York Times article (Wieviorka 1998). Since then, the term has been used and abused, glorified and discredited all around the world. The flexibility of a term which already denotes multiplicity (multi-) and is clearly bracketed by an ideological understanding (the term is an -ism) can cause misunderstandings if used in political contexts, as well as when devising social policies. In the following part we will try to trace a brief history of the multiculturalist project with a focus on its success or limits in Canada, the first country to have considered multiculturalism from a legal point of view.

To best grasp the evolution of Canadian multicultural policy, we will use a very recent study by Will Kymlicka, one of the most notorious proponents of multiculturalism. In his paper, "The Three Lives of Multiculturalism" (Kymlicka 2015), he explains that Canadian multiculturalism, though it has been part of Canada's official policies for almost 50 years, is not a concept that has lost its credibility. Moreover, Kymlicka believes that all polyethnic states (a term he used as early as 1996, see Kymlicka 1996) would benefit from the Canadian experience. The critic also claims that we have not yet reached a post-multicultural era, and he supports his statement by describing the three changes undergone by multiculturalism: the ethnic, the racial and the religious stages (Kymlicka 2015).

Following other critiques of multiculturalism (Brosseau and Dewing 2009; Malik 2015), we believe that the evolution of the multicultural state or of the multiculturalist project has been a reaction to external (social and political) pressures.

Canadian beginnings

Canada was the first country in the world to propose and pass a multiculturalism law. Canadian Prime Minister Pierre Trudeau initially supported the introduction of multiculturalism as an official policy in 1970. The fundamentals of this policy were summarized by Brosseau and Dewing in a 2009 study:

- to assist cultural groups to retain and foster their identity;
- to assist cultural groups to overcome barriers to their full participation in Canadian society [. . .];
- to promote creative exchanges among all Canadian cultural groups; and
- to assist immigrants in acquiring at least one of the official languages (Brosseau and Dewing 2009, 3).

The Canadian Multiculturalism Act, first recognized in 1982 in Section 27 of the Canadian Charter of Rights and Freedoms, was officially adopted in 1988. This policy has been acclaimed and accused ever since. It declared multiculturalism to be a "fundamental characteristic of the Canadian heritage and identity" (Trudeau qtd. in Kymlicka 1998, 185). According to Brosseau and Dewing, it included a "clearer sense of purpose" which meant reducing discrimination through the enhancement of cultural awareness and at the same time supporting "the preservation of culture and language" (2009, 4). In 1991, the Department of Multiculturalism and Citizenship was created. This newly shaped multiculturalism program was aiming to surpass the earlier "intercultural sharing through promotion of ethnic presses and festivals" (Brosseau and Dewing 2009, 5) and focus on "cross-cultural understanding and the attainment of social and economic integration through institutional change" (Brosseau and Dewing 2009, 5).

The overture to the official adoption of the Multiculturalism Act of 1988 is twofold. Due to Quebecois nationalism and secessionist movements in the 1960s, the Canadian government established the Royal Commission on Bilingualism and Biculturalism in 1963 in order to strengthen equality between the British and the French. This decision in its turn had an impact on long-settled ethnic communities (the Poles, the Ukrainians, the Italians) who expressed their worry at the government dividing funds only between the British and the French (Kymlicka 2015, 18–20). These groups demanded that their ethnic diversity be recognized along with their linguistic duality. Indeed, Kymlicka says that "the initial impetus for multiculturalism was a political bargain to help address the national unity crisis" (Kymlicka 2015, 19).

After Canada changed its immigration rules towards the end of 1960s, a large number of immigrants settled there, and by the end of 1970s these newer minority groups were becoming more politically engaged. Kymlicka points out that the original multicultural policy was not taking into account issues related to "settlement, integration and naturalization" (2015, 21) because it had been created for long-term settled groups and not newcomers. Furthermore, since most new immigrants were visible minorities, they were also facing "barriers of racism" (Kymlicka 2015, 21) which needed to be added to the multicultural policy.

An important aspect of Canadian multiculturalism rests on its avowed purposes to support human rights and liberties and to redefine Canadian citizenship. Thus, Canadian multiculturalism should be understood as "a way of understanding Canadian citizenship, a new way of understanding one's Canadianness, not an alternative to being (or becoming) a Canadian" (Kymlicka 2015, 23). The critic emphasizes that this connectedness to national unity, citizenship and human rights is what is missing from other countries' interpretation of multiculturalism (2015, 25).

Soon after the adoption of the Multiculturalism Act in 1988, Canada witnessed a rise of groups and communities on a religious basis. It was becoming apparent that especially second- and third-generation immigrants were moving towards religious identification more than their ethnic or racial identities. The reasons for this reorientation are multifold; the 9/11 attacks are only one such instant in recent history that has fueled Islamophobia and therefore a reactive response on the part of those identified as Muslims (no matter their ethnic or racial belonging).

Kymlicka believes the religious stage will be the third one in the evolution of Canadian multiculturalism, as it "is now under pressure to add a third track of religion, alongside ethnicity and race" (Kymlicka 2015, 27). It remains to be seen if the Canadian multiculturalism policy can accommodate the religious feature of Canadian diversity.

To be or not to be multicultural?

Thirty years have passed since the ground-breaking decision of the Canadian government to adopt the Canadian Multiculturalism Act, and although many voices were raised by its opponents, we cannot deny its importance either for Canada or the world.

Sociologists, cultural critics, politicians, literary critics and other voices have had a say in either supporting or rejecting the multiculturalism policy. Debates on integration vs. segregation have been the most frequent.

In 1994, Trinidad-born novelist, Neil Bissoondath talked in his book *Selling Illusions: The Cult of Multiculturalism in Canada* about the fact that an official recognition of ethnic groups can lead to a cultural rift. He argued that with this act, minorities will be clearly labeled as such, impeding on their attempts at embracing Canadian values and fully participating as citizens, beyond the us–them divide. Bissoondath's stance has been supported by other voices (Day 2000; Handa 2003; Thobani 2007) that revealed the inadequacies of the multicultural policy. Amita Handa highlights the racism hidden behind terminology and attacks the "cultural tolerance" promoted by the Multicultural Act. As pointed out in one of our previous research studies, Handa's standpoint needs to be understood from the perspective of the superior power position implied by the term "tolerance" and embodied by government officials (Grosu 2012): "part of the invisibility of white as norm has to do with a discourse of multiculturalism that emphasizes tolerance" (Handa 2003, 91).

Sunetra Thobani brought forth the issue regarding the inability of the Multicultural Act to solve the contradiction between the assumed bilingual and bicultural Canadian national identity and the "heterogeneous nature of the population" (Thobani 2007, 145). Thobani even saw the multicultural agenda as having helped "stabilize white supremacy" (Thobani 2007, 146).

Richard Day (2000) contends that the us–them divide cannot be transcended either through assimilation or through integration.[2] Day points out that neither the assimilationist project (usually ascribed to the United States' melting pot) nor the integrationist Canadian aims (through which minority groups participate in the political, economic, social and cultural life of the country—see Day 2000, 195) do justice to ethnic groups. Day views the two processes as being constructed "upon the transformation of a problematic Other into a nonproblematic – 'eliminated' or 'participating' – Self" (Day 2000, 195).

Interestingly, among the first to have reacted to the Multiculturalism Act were the Quebecers who felt that such legislation would immediately place them in a minority position versus the Anglo-Saxon component of Canada. Issues related to the recognition of Quebecer identity as well as the value of traditional culture, are discussed at length in a pivotal paper by Charles Taylor, "The Politics of Recognition" (1994). The previously mentioned Quebecer lack of "comfort" with the official Canadian Charter of Rights and Freedoms has been addressed by a study mandated by the Consultation Commission on Accommodation Practices Related to Cultural Differences established in 2007 by the government of Québec (Bouchard and Taylor 2008). One of its conclusions stated that "the Canadian multiculturalism model does not appear to be well suited to conditions in Québec" (Bouchard and Taylor 2008, 39) and that interculturalism is a much better-suited concept in the Quebecer context. As we will explore later in this chapter, the term interculturalism and its relative, intercultural dialogue, are currently adopted by the official EU documents.

Probably the most quoted supporter of the multiculturalism project, Will Kymlicka, has perfected his theories on Canadian multicultural policy over the years. In his earlier work, "Multicultural Citizenship: A Liberal Theory of Minority Rights" (1996), he constructed a theory which justified the Canadian Multicultural Act. For Kymlicka, minority rights are essential for the multicultural state. In order to support his thesis, he coins the term "societal culture" that is "a culture which provides its members with meaningful ways of life across the full range of human activities, including social, educational, religious, recreational, and economic life, encompassing both private and public spheres. These cultures tend to be territorially concentrated and based on a shared language" (76). Kymlicka admits that the term multicultural state can be misleading because of its vagueness, and he forwards a more detailed classification, namely the multinational state ("where cultural diversity arises from the incorporation of previously self-governing, territorially concentrated cultures into a larger state") as distinct from the polyethnic state ("where cultural diversity arises from individual and familial immigration") (6).

Will Kymlicka claims that this distinction is necessary to understand the case of Canada, which is both a multinational (the Aboriginal tribes were overrun by French settlers, who in their turn were conquered by the English) and polyethnic state (due to the fact that over the years Canada has received a large number of immigrants). Furthermore, he believes that the resistance of Quebecers to the Multiculturalism Act stemmed from the inherent ambiguity of the term multicultural, which might have entitled them to feel that their nationhood had been reduced to the status of immigrant ethnicity (Kymlicka 1998, 17).

Richard Day's analysis of Canadian multiculturalism (without disregarding Kymlicka's stress on terminology) calls for a revaluation of the term and policy. Day identifies three issues to be addressed (he calls them "symptoms"): multiculturalism must first admit its "impossibility of full identity", clearly "affirm the value of difference and the Other as such" and, lastly, it needs to negotiate "all universal horizons, including that of the nation(s)-state" (224).

Day's identification of multicultural symptomatology is a good start for future policy development worldwide. Paired with Kymlicka's classification of states (multinational vs. polyethnic), as well as with his recent explanation of the ethnic, racial and religious stages of Canadian multiculturalism, this might be seen as a basis on which the increasingly globalized cultures of the world could build their new social and political trajectories.

European views

In 1994, Christopher Husbands was voicing his concern regarding national identity visible in the UK, the Federal Republic of Germany and the Netherlands. Husbands was aware of an increasing anxiety about immigrants in Europe which was motivated by a fear of being outnumbered by foreigners. However, Husbands also pointed out that "such panics derive particular sustenance from the anxieties and uncertainties held by many indigenous people in western Europe about whether their own national identity does have sufficient resilience and adaptive capacity to survive intact when facing an economically inhospitable future and a geopolitical moral vacuum" (Husbands 1994).

Yet these anxieties are not a recent concept. In 1903, the Royal Commission on Alien Immigration was concerned with the fact that foreigners coming "to the United Kingdom would be inclined to live 'according to their traditions, usages and customs' " (Malik 2015). Fear of the unknown, of the exotic (both positively and negatively construed; see Huggan 2001) and the different has always influenced people's behaviours across the globe. It is this anxiety, along with external pressure from ethnic groups, that we believe has motivated the need to classify and label a multicultural approach.

Immigrant anxiety has not only increased with time in Europe, but it has reached new highs in recent years. Indeed, as mentioned in the introductory part of this chapter, it is the overt attack on multiculturalism happening in Western Europe that has mainly motivated this research. In political discourse, multiculturalism appears to have been constructed as a scapegoat for most problems derived from immigration. Three years ago, on the occasion of a speech[3] delivered in Karlsruhe, Angela Merkel, the German chancellor, announced that multiculturalism was "a sham". The context of her statement is complex, as it followed an overwhelming wave of immigration that had taken the whole of Europe by surprise. Germany had been viewed as a beacon of hope by tragedy-struck individuals fleeing the Middle East. Merkel herself had voiced Germany's willingness to harbor fugitives and support people in need, and many viewed her immigration policies as beneficial for Germany.[4] But as critic Gutiérrez Rodríguez pointed out in her work "Archipelago Europe: On Creolizing Conviviality" (2015), Merkel had already announced the failure of multiculturalism in a 2010 speech[5] (86). Gutiérrez Rodríguez draws attention to Merkel's use of the abbreviation Multikulti (which would stand for "happily living side by side") instead of multiculturalism, as she concludes this tactic has never worked in Germany. Her attitude is both interesting and paradoxical (Gutiérrez Rodríguez 2015, 86) if we take into account that Germany has never had an official governmental policy regarding multiculturalism. It appears that the German chancellor is justifying the current problems related to immigration by blaming a concept which had never been integrated into German state policy.

Merkel's opinion on multiculturalism should not be taken at face value (although the majority of people have already done exactly that). Merkel's claim refers to how multiculturalism and cultural and personal identities have been interpreted and lived in Germany.

In 2011, David Cameron, former UK prime minister, was blaming the multiculturalism state for homegrown terrorism.[6] Again, Cameron, like Merkel, used a construct which does not exist in the official policies of the UK. He actually coins state multiculturalism to stand for, on the one hand, the segregation of ethnic groups away from mainstream British culture and, on the other hand, for irresponsible funding of ethnic associations which appear not to prevent extremism. Cameron speaks of too much tolerance and too little integrative efforts. His stance could be perceived as discursively valid, yet in the absence of clearly defined official measures to ensure harmony through cultural diversity, his words remain purely declarative, and it was natural for ethnic groups to react.

As Kenan Malik announces, "[i]n both the United Kingdom and Germany, governments failed to recognize the complexity, elasticity, and sheer contrariness of identity" (Malik 2015). Malik stresses the fact that European multiculturalism has been (mis)used to serve political and/or social purposes which have varied greatly from one country to another. Like other critics of multiculturalism, Malik explains that "practicing" multiculturalism in different European countries has only deepened the gap between majority and minority groups, resulting in "fragmented societies, alienated minorities, and resentful citizenries" (Malik 2015).

Indeed, if we are to speculate, the "death" of multiculturalism in Europe was announced by official voices in the absence of a solid legislation on multiculturalism, one which was socially tested in time and which might after all be accused of having failed.

Transculturalism, creolization and the reality of European terrorist attacks

In 2002, Seyla Benhabib warned about the "use and abuse of culture" (the very title of her book's introductory chapter), stating that "culture has become a ubiquitous synonym for identity, an identity marker and differentiator" (Benhabib 2002, 1). The critic's argumentation points toward the danger of drawing states into "culture wars" (1). Benhabib builds a theoretical scaffolding which could help policy makers manage the ever-increasing diversity of nation-states. Benhabib supports a "universalist deliberative democracy model" (19), provided that three normative conditions are met, namely "egalitarian reciprocity", "voluntary self-ascription" and "freedom of exit and association" (19). Egalitarian reciprocity stands for the same rights (political, economic, civil, cultural) of minority groups (cultural, religious, linguistic, etc.) as those of the majority. Voluntary self-ascription, in Benhabib's view, refers to the resistance of individuals to be "automatically assigned to cultural, religious, or linguistic groups by virtue of his or her birth" (19). Self-identification must be made possible. The third condition, freedom of exit and association, represents the freedom of individuals to leave any ascriptive group, even at the expense of the loss of certain privileges. (19) According to Kraidy, "Benhabib's invitation to political theorists to consider identity groups as complex and dynamic movements whose political outlook is not predetermined by their ethnicity, religion, or race." (55). If Benhabib's three conditions are met, Kraidy believes we are heading toward a new understanding of relations between cultures, one which recognizes hybridity at its core, namely critical transculturalism, which "is at once an engagement with hybridity as a discursive formation, a framework for international communication theory, and an agenda for research" (Kraidy 2005, vi–vii).

In their efforts to cope with the permanent social shifts in Europe, official policy makers of the European institutions have come up with intercultural dialogue as an allegedly superior concept to multiculturalism: "Intercultural dialogue is, essentially, the exchange of views and opinions between different cultures. Unlike multiculturalism, where the focus is on the preservation of separate cultures, intercultural dialogue seeks to establish linkages and common ground between different cultures, communities, and people, promoting understanding and interaction" (European Commission website). In 2006, the Parliamentary Assembly of the Council of Europe issued the Recommendation 1740 in which it stated that all European citizens have the "right to education and the right to a cultural identity" and "the preservation of linguistic heritage, at both European and world levels [. . .] the promotion of dialogue and exchange through linguistic diversity" (Recommendation 1740, Parliamentary Assembly of the Council of Europe).

In 2014, The Resolution of the Council of 16 November 2007 on a European Agenda for Culture is reinforced, and it mentions among its strategic objectives "the promotion of cultural diversity and intercultural dialogue, the promotion of culture as a catalyst for creativity and the promotion of culture as a vital element in the Union's international relations" (Conclusions of the Council. . .).

In previous research (Grosu 2012), we have attempted to compare transculturalism and multiculturalism by focusing on how the two concepts differ, namely "the essential difference between them stem[ing] from the way we perceive their outcomes. Cultural diversity is seen either as a melting of cultural markers (transculturalism) or as a gathering of multiple and distinct contributions to the mainstream culture (multiculturalism)" (Grosu 2012, 107). However, today, given the volatile environment in Western Europe, which has been facing unprecedented terrorist attacks, can we still think in binaries anymore? Is the us–them divide clearly delineated in a European Union where European-born citizens suddenly radicalize and take to the streets stabbing people or blowing up airports? The egalitarian attitude of the transculturalist approach, one in which people no longer rely on politicians and political discourse but only on seeing beyond differences in the name of human rights and common citizenship, seems naïve, even utopian.

The most recent series of terror attacks in Europe,[7] the Charlie Hebdo killing of 12 people at the office of the French newspaper in January 2015, sent a shock wave in Europe and the world. Terrorism is not a new occurrence in European countries. There have been many violent incidents either political or religious in Spain – the Madrid train bombings; the UK and Ireland – the numerous Irish Republican Army (IRA) shootings and bombings; or in Germany – the National Socialist Underground terrorist attacks, to mention just a few and only after the year 2000. The difference between former violent outbreaks in Europe and the more recent ones appears to stand on the common denominator of the post–Charlie Hebdo terrorist attacks, which is their allegiance to Islamic radicalism.

To get a better understanding of the European context today, we need to highlight a few key points on the recent political timeline. In 2014, the Islamic State of Iraq and Syria (ISIS) slaughtered their way to take control of Iraq and Syria, forcing a huge emigration wave from the east to the west. In 2015, these refugees reached great numbers in Central European countries and then Western states in search of asylum. The first ISIS-claimed terror attacks in Europe occurred at the beginning of 2015[8] and multiplies with the passing of time. There is no doubt that the simultaneity of these two episodes has stirred European discontent and unprecedented fear.

However, as Peter O'Brien aptly points out in his work *The Muslim Question in Europe: Political Controversies and Public Philosophies* (2016), this seemingly causal relationship between the arrival of refugees in Europe and the terrorist attacks should be deemed superficial. O'Brien's thorough analysis of Islamophobia on the one hand and radical Islamism on the other sheds light on the current situation in Europe. One salient viewpoint to which the critic adheres is that for Muslim radicalization to develop, the respective subjects would have had to reside for a longer period of time in Europe (O'Brien 2016, 203). Another "ingredient" added to the radicalization recipe appears to be a feeling of alienation and mistreatment "by the very European societies in which they make their homes" (O'Brien 2016, 202). Returning to the refugee wave that overwhelmed European countries in recent years, it is important to stress the fact that these stranded populations were also fleeing unprecedented terrorist attacks in their homelands and are most probably abhorring violent acts (O'Brien 2016, 246).

The term Islamophobia represents today "dislike and prejudice against Islam or Muslims, especially as a political force" (Oxford Dictionaries), but etymologically the term includes the idea of fear (phobia). In 1954, Gordon Alport was stressing the importance of a broad outlook on how prejudice is born, and he includes fear among its triggers: "It would be a serious error to ascribe prejudice and discrimination to any single taproot, reaching into economic exploitation, social structure, the mores, fear, aggression, sex conflict, or any other favoured soil. Prejudice and discrimination [. . .] may draw nourishment from all these conditions, and many others" (xviii).

It is our belief that at least at a social level, Europeans have come to discriminate against Muslims out of a heightened feeling of fear. As Benhabib (2002) was warning, culture (in our case, religious identification) has become synonymous with identity and thus an element of alterity at the root of social conflict and ghettoization.

To what extent is it then plausible for theories of culture and cultural anthropology to make their way into or influence the development of social and political agendas? As we have mentioned earlier in this chapter, multiculturalist, transculturalist or interculturalist dialogue theories have merit as long as they are not (mis)used in political discourse just for the sake of rhetoric.

If we recall Kymlicka's construal of the non-Canadian multiethnic state's approach to multiculturalism, we need to point out his insistence on the tight relationship between national unity, citizenship and human rights (Kymlicka 2015, 25). The critic believes this to be the solution to peaceful cohabitation and prosperity of multiethnic states. If the third stage of Canadian multiculturalism (the religious track) will be successfully included in the Canadian multiculturalism policy (Kymlicka 2015, 27), we could hope for a future formula to be applied in other contexts as well. Still in the theoretical realm, we might mention Glissant's creolization theory (1997) that focuses on thinking "beyond mimesis or opposition" (Gutiérrez Rodríguez 2015, 83). Encarnación Gutiérrez Rodríguez builds on Glissant's theory to create an approach which goes beyond the British "communitarianism". In her view, creolization in Europe should path the way toward "ethics of conviviality" (Gutiérrez Rodríguez 2015, 84) which needs to stand on "the interrelational, interconnected and interdependent character of our Being" (Gutiérrez Rodríguez 2015, 84).

A question still remains: Is there any chance for people to go beyond fear either of terrorism (affecting Europeans) or of ghettoization (affecting immigrants)? Could a new theoretical strand offer the solution to this dilemma?

Postsecularism and the return to human rights

Manav Ratti, author of *The Postsecular Imagination – Postcolonialism, Religion, and Literature* (2013), seems to have perceived the change in discourse occurring in literary works from secularism to a postsecular era. He constructs a new paradigm called postsecular imagination that he applies to South Asian literature belonging to diasporic authors originating from India, Sri Lanka and Bangladesh.[9] His literary criticism stems from an avowed purpose to make use of literary analysis in order to support real social change. Ratti believes that literature can offer "insights into thinking through the limits of secularism and religion" (Ratti 2013, xix) and that fiction can serve as an instrument for the improvement of real-life social interaction. He views the literary world as an "experimental space" (Ratti 2013, 4) from where we might obtain solutions for conflicts and crises.

Ratti's theory is constructed on interpretations of diasporic authors' fiction, caught in the in-between space of homeland and hostland. The critic identifies a certain mechanism common to his authors of interest, one through which they appear to secularize religious values and "then translate them into thoroughly worldly, contingent situations, ones that emerge from a minority position" (Ratti 2013, 3). By embodying the dichotomies majority–minority and secularism–religion as diasporic creators, the authors Manav Ratti discusses construct their fiction by focusing on mediation of differences towards postsecularism. This concept is seen as a solution to "the violence, inequalities, and injustices pursued in the name of religion, nation, and secularism" (Ratti 2013, 31).

In a European context fraught with conflicts built, as we have previously shown, on fear of alterity the "search for values that can retain the best features of religion and secularism" (Ratti 2013, 209) might just be a valid way ahead. Ratti's conceptual solution which supports a mix of secular and religious values (based on fundamental human rights) seems to be in accordance with Kymlicka's understanding of Canadian multiculturalism, namely an emphasis placed on citizenship and human rights (Kymlicka 2015, 25). Both Ratti's postsecularism and Kymlicka's religious track of multiculturalism rely on the importance of combining cultural (religious) and social identities to the citizens' benefit. It remains to be seen to what extent and in how long a period people could internalize such theoretical concepts if they ever come to be put into practice.

By way of conclusion

We started this chapter with the stated purpose of analyzing how the concept of multiculturalism has been used and abused in recent political and social debates and the extent to which it is still a valuable policy in Europe. We have seen that multiculturalism has been misinterpreted and hence scapegoated in political discourse, even in countries where policies of multiculturalism per se have never been in place. Given the recent flux of immigrants coming to Europe and the numerous terrorist attacks, the clash of cultures appears more visible to Europeans nowadays. Racial, ethnic or religious differences have become daily topics of discussion in mass media, thus exacerbating a feeling of fear that crept into Europe.

In search of a possible discursive "redemption" of multiculturalism, we have reviewed important critical stances that might shed light on the reason why Europe is not welcoming Multikulti anymore. Transculturalism and creolization are worthy conceptual frameworks, but it is our belief that in terms of practical application in view of the recent European dread of immigrants and extremist Islamist terrorists, they are still too deeply rooted in a utopian perspective. On the other hand, we have also seen that both the religious track of multiculturalism (Kymlicka 2015) and postsecularism (Ratti 2013) could become useful tools in devising policies of representation and harmonization of interests around the essential values embedded both in the secular and in the religious.

It is our faith that social unrest and fear due to stereotyping and extremist agendas can be fought against not only discursively, through educational means, but also by adjusting political, economic and social instruments to realities beyond the us–them divide and by highlighting the normality of harmonious cohabitation beyond religious, ethnic or racial differences.

Notes

1 *Great Thinkers in Their Own Words*, broadcasted by BBC-Four, 2011. www.bbc.co.uk/programmes/b011r8p8/episodes/guide. Accessed 22 May 2018.
2 The two mechanisms had been described in Gus Mitges's official report of the Standing Committee on Multiculturalism, *Multiculturalism: Building the Canadian Mosaic*, of 1987. https://search.library.utoronto.ca/details?2230206&uuid=1fa7ea0f-e35c-4052-bc25-59327cfe63fd
3 Original post: www.spiegel.de/politik/deutschland/fluechtlinge-angela-merkel-spricht-von-historischer-bewaehrungsprobe-fuer-europa-a-1067685.html translated and commented on in an article signed Rick Noack, 14 December 2015 www.washingtonpost.com/news/worldviews/wp/2015/12/14/angela-merkel-multiculturalism-is-a-sham/?utm_term=.b606c613cf11
4 www.independent.co.uk/voices/how-angela-merkels-open-door-immigration-policy-protects-germany-from-terrorism-in-the-long-run-a7156756.html
5 www.spiegel.de/politik/deutschland/integration-merkel-erklaert-multikulti-fuer-gescheitert-a-723532.html.
6 www.bbc.com/news/uk-politics-12371994
7 Charlie Hebdo (Paris, France, January 2015), Paris attacks (France, November 2015), Brussels bombings (Belgium, March 2016), Nice terror attacks (France, July 2016), several attacks in Germany (July 2016), Normandy church attack (July 2016), Berlin Christmas market attack (Germany, December 2016), Louvre knife attack (Paris, February 2017), Westminster attack (London, March 2017), Stockholm attack (Sweden, April 2017), Paris shooting (France, April 2017), Manchester terror attack (UK, May 2017), London Bridge terror attack (UK, June 2017), Barcelona terror attack (Spain, August 2017).
8 Ibid.
9 Michael Ondaatje, Salman Rushdie, Allan Sealy, Shauna Singh Baldwin and Amitav Gosh.

References

Benhabib, Seyla. 2002. *The Claims of Culture: Equality and Diversity in the Global Era*. Princeton and Oxford: Princeton University Press.

Bissoondath, N. 1994. *Selling Illusions: The Cult of Multiculturalism in Canada*. Toronto: Penguin.

Bouchard, Gérard and Taylor, Charles. 2008. *Building the Future: A Time for Reconciliation*. Bibliothèque et Archives nationales du Québec. ISBN: 978-2-550-52769-5. Retrieved from https://web.archive.org/web/20120213083051/www.accommodements.qc.ca/documentation/rapports/rapport-final-abrege-en.pdf. Accessed on 9 February 2018.

Brosseau, Laurence and Dewing, Michael. 2009 (revised 2013). *Canadian Multiculturalism* (Background Paper). Library of Parliament. Retrieved from https://lop.parl.ca/content/lop/ResearchPublications/2009-20-e.pdf. Accessed on 9 February 2018.

Conclusions of the Council and of the Representatives of the Governments of the Member States, Meeting Within the Council, on a Work Plan for Culture, 2015–2018. Retrieved from http://eur-lex.europa.eu/legal-content/EN/TXT/?uri=celex:52014XG1223(02)#ntr1-C_2014463EN.01000401-E0001

Day, Richard J. F. 2000. *Multiculturalism and the History of Canadian Diversity*. Toronto: University of Toronto Press.

European Commission website. Retrieved from https://ec.europa.eu/culture/policy/strategic-framework/intercultural-dialogue_en. Accessed on 9 February 2018.

Glazer, Nathan. 1997. *We Are All Multiculturalists Now*. Cambridge, MA: Harvard University Press.

Glissant, Édouard. 1997. *Poetics of Relation*, trans. and ed. by Betsy Wing. Ann Arbor: University of Michigan Press.

Great Thinkers in Their Own Words, Broadcasted by BBC-Four, 2011. Retrieved from www.youtube.com/watch?v=RhK4nLuyeYM. Accessed on 9 February 2018.

Grosu, Lucia M. 2012. "Multiculturalism or Transculturalism? Views on Cultural Diversity". *Synergy* 8, No. 2: 102–111. Bucharest: ASE Publishing House.

Gutiérrez Rodríguez, Encarnación. 2015. "Archipelago Europe: On Creolizing Conviviality". In *Creolizing Europe – Legacies and Transformations*, 80–99. Edited by Encarnación Gutiérrez Rodríguez and Shirley Anne Tate. Liverpool: Liverpool University Press.

Hall, Stuart. 2001. *The Multicultural Question*. Milton Keynes, UK: Pavis Centre for Social and Cultural Research, The Open University.

Handa, Anita. 2003. *Of Silk Saris and Mini Skirts: South Asian Girls Walk the Tightrope of Culture*. Toronto: Women's Press.

Huggan, Graham. 2001. *The Postcolonial Exotic, Marketing the Margins*. London: Routledge.

Husbands, Christopher. 1994. "Crises of National Identity as the 'New Moral Panics': Political Agenda Setting About Definitions of Nationhood". *Journal of Ethnic and Migration Studies* 20, No. 2: 191–206. Retrieved from www.tandfonline.com/doi/abs/10.1080/1369183X.1994.9976419. Accessed on 10 February 2018.

Kraidy, Marwan M. 2005. *Hybridity or the Cultural Logic of Globalization*. Philadelphia: Temple University Press.

Kymlicka, Will. 1996. *Multicultural Citizenship: A Liberal Theory of Minority Rights*. Oxford: Oxford University Press.

Kymlicka, Will. 1998. *Finding Our Way: Rethinking Ethnocultural Relations in Canada*. Toronto: Oxford University Press.

Kymlicka, Will. 2015. "The Three Lives of Multiculturalism". In *Revisiting Multiculturalism in Canada*, 17–36. Edited by Shibao Guo and Lloyd Wong. Rotterdam, Boston and Taipei: Sense Publishers.

Malik, Kenan. 2015. "The Failure of Multiculturalism: Community Versus Society in Europe". *Foreign Affairs* 94, No. 2. New York. Retrieved from www.foreignaffairs.com/articles/western-europe/failure-multiculturalism. Accessed on 22 May 2018.

Mitges, Gus. 1987. *Multiculturalism: Building the Canadian Mosaic: Report of the Standing Committee on Multiculturalism*. Ottawa: The Committee.

O'Brien, Peter. 2016. *The Muslim Question in Europe: Political Controversies and Public Philosophies*. Philadelphia: Temple University Press.

Oxford Dictionaries. 2018. Retrieved from https://en.oxforddictionaries.com/defini
tion/islamophobia

Recommendation 1740. 2006. Parliamentary Assembly of the Council of Europe.
The Place of Mother Tongue in School Education. Retrieved from http://assembly.
coe.int/nw/xml/XRef/Xref-XML2HTML-en.asp?fileid=17421&lang=en

Taylor, Charles. 1994. "The Politics of Recognition". In *Multiculturalism – Exam-
ining the Politics of Recognition*, 25–73. Edited by Charles Taylor, K. Anthony
Appiah, Jürgen Habermas, Steven C. Rockefeller, Michal Walzer and Susan Wolf.
Princeton, NJ: Princeton University Press.

Thobani, Sunera. 2007. *Exalted Subjects: Studies in the Making of Race and Nation
in Canada*. Toronto: University of Toronto Press.

Wieviorka, Michel. 1998. "Is Multiculturalism the Solution?" *Ethnic and Racial Studies* 21, No. 5: 881–910. https://doi.org/10.1080/014198798329702. Routledge.

11 History of multiculturalism in Canada and Australia

Its aim, successes and challenges to national identity

Sev Ozdowski

Contemporary Australia, like Canada, is a relatively young and multicultural nation established on an Aboriginal heritage, with a mainly British foundation and through mass migration. Despite the similarities of European origins and institutions, the national identities of Australia and Canada differ from each other and from those of European countries. Close geographic proximity of world superpowers – to the United States in Canada's case and the People's Republic of China in Australia's case – impact on their historical experiences, worldviews, attitudes to border protection and immigration and national identities.

Both countries have experienced different waves of migration since the 1800s which resulted in the settlement of people from multiple racial, ethnic, religious and cultural backgrounds. The majority of Canadians are of British and French origin, while Australia's majority originate from the United Kingdom and Ireland. Canada is regarded as the first country to develop a policy of multiculturalism under Pierre Trudeau during the early 1970s; Australia followed suit soon after.

The development of Canadian multicultural policies and programmes was informed by their Royal Commission on Bilingualism and Biculturalism established in 1963 and its subsequent 1970 report. The report attempted to preserve Canada's status as a bilingual and bicultural society, but it was neither popular nor correct as, by the 1980s, almost 40 per cent of the population were of neither British nor French origins. The report was attacked by both English- and French-speaking nationalists, but most vociferously by the so-called 'Third Force', Canada's other minority population, who advocated for 'multiculturalism'. Faced with the very real possibility of their nation being torn apart, the formula was changed from 'bilingualism and biculturalism' to 'bilingualism and multiculturalism' (Knopff & Flanagan, 1989: 131).

Canadian multiculturalism is now enshrined in law through the Canadian Multiculturalism Act of 1988 and Section 27 of the Canadian Charter of Rights and Freedoms. Also, the Canadian 1991 Broadcasting Act asserts that the Canadian broadcasting system should reflect the diversity of cultures in the country. Canadian multiculturalism also addressed the under-representation of French-Canadians in positions of power and provided access to government services in the French language, with other linguistic groups assigned a minority status.

Australia has neither a federal Multiculturalism Act nor a Bill of Rights, but it has the Special Broadcasting Service Act 1991 'to provide multilingual and multicultural radio, television and digital media services that inform, educate and entertain all Australians, and, in doing so, reflect Australia's multicultural society'. English is the only Australian national language, and this perhaps constitutes a key distinguishing feature between the Canadian and Australian approaches to multiculturalism. The difference is most pronounced in Quebec's official approach to multiculturalism, which differs from that of the other provinces. Quebec prefers to use the concept of 'interculturalism', which approaches English and French cultures on a more equal footing and promotes dialogue and interaction between them.

Historical backdrop

To understand Australia's contemporary approach to the management of migration and settlement issues, one must go back to the early days of settlement. First, Australia, despite its 40,000 to 60,000 years of First Peoples history, is a relatively young country. The history of modern Australia began with Captain James Cook's arrival at Botany Bay in 1770 and with the establishment of a British penal colony in 1788. The original colonies evolved into individual states, each with their own legislature and government system, and were federated in 1901 under a commonwealth constitution. Initially a dominion, Australia finally emerged in the 1930s as a sovereign nation, with Australian citizenship created in 1949.

Second, Australia, like Canada, is a migrant country. Every person who lives in Australia, excepting Aboriginal and Torres Strait Australians, is either a migrant or a descendent of a migrant. In 1788, Australia's Aboriginal population was about 400,000; in 1901, the total population was close to 4 million, of whom one in four was born overseas. Now Australia's population is about 25 million people.

Third, migrant entry and migration into to Australia have always been tightly controlled and often financed by the relevant government authorities (Ozdowski, 2013). Such government controls were key in determining who could enter, when, where and under what conditions. The first free settlers arrived in 1793, but numerically significant free migration started in the 1820s. From 1856, the Australian colonies, excepting Western Australia, became self-governing and took over migration management, including controls over levels of immigration, selection of migrants and management of various forms of assistance.

The need for a common immigration policy was one of the key factors driving the federation movement of the 1890s. The first act of the federal parliament was the Immigration Restriction Act 1901 which established the

'White Australia' policy nationally and introduced the infamous dictation test to be taken in any European language at the discretion of immigration officials. Two years later, Parliament legislated for The Naturalization Act 1903, which referenced British subjects but did not mention Australian citizenship. It specified that Asians and other non-Europeans would be denied the right to apply for naturalization

Post–World War II migration also required significant changes to the immigration system. Australian citizenship had to be created by the Nationality and Citizenship Act in 1948, as many new arrivals were not 'British subjects'.

Fourth, respective government authorities have often attempted to manage community relations. The management of relationships between Aboriginal and European communities has been of significance. The frontier clashes between the First Peoples and white settlers were cruel and left long-lasting consequences. Aboriginal resistance against the settlers was widespread and led to the deaths of at least 20,000 Aboriginal and Torres Strait Islander peoples and 2,000 and 2,500 Europeans between 1788 and the 1920s.

Also significant was the conflict which developed between European and Chinese miners in the gold fields of Victoria during the 1850s, despite the Chinese accounting for only about 20% of the mining population in Victoria.

In Canada (mainly British Columbia), anti-Chinese sentiments developed in the 1870–80s. This resulted in the 'head tax' of the early 1880s being so effective that it eventually ended Chinese migration. During the late nineteenth and early twentieth centuries, additional measures were introduced to keep non-Europeans out. The 'White Canada' policy was abandoned in the 1960s. Similarly, during World War I and World War II, both Australia and Canada saw strong anti-German sentiment, which resulted in the establishment of internment camps for 'enemy aliens' in both countries.

Fifth, egalitarianism was established as a defining characteristic of Australian society from early on. One of the first decisions taken by Captain Arthur Phillip was to distribute food equally amongst convicts and freemen and to apply the same penalties to anybody who stole from the stores. Governor Phillip was also quick to set up an emancipation system whereby convicts could earn their freedom and take land grants in the new colony and be appointed to high government office (Ozdowski, 2012).

The notion of a 'fair go' and equality of all men continued post federation. However, the initial concept of 'fair go' included only male British subjects. In particular, the concept of Terra Nullius – that Australia was 'empty, unoccupied land' – was the antithesis of a 'fair go' to Aboriginal and Torres Strait Islander peoples. However, with the passage of time, this initially limited egalitarianism has been significantly extended to include other social groups, including women, non-British minorities, people with disabilities and, most recently, LGBTIQ people. Further, 'fair go' has become the towering concept of Australian human rights culture, often overshadowing civil liberties and freedoms.

Finally, it needs to be recognised that migration policies have long been highly sensitive to the Australian electorate. Any perceived loss of migration border control by the government has always had significant electoral consequences and has often resulted in significant policy and legislative changes.

The temporary lost control over immigration between 1851 and 1860 resulted in the Victorian government legislating to restrict Chinese migration. The waves of unauthorized arrivals in the early 1990s, mainly from Iran, Iraq, Afghanistan and Sri Lanka, resulted in the Pauline Hanson–led challenge to Australia's non-discriminatory immigration policy and multiculturalism. The 'stop-the-boats' policy contributed to the re-election of the Coalition government in November 2001 and to Labor losing power in 2013 after it reversed the policy.

Current migration and resulting diversity

Government-controlled overseas migration continues to be a dominant factor in contemporary Australia's population growth. Since 1945, some 8 million people have settled in Australia; annual intake rates often exceed 1% of Australia's population. In the last 15 years, Australia's overseas-born population has increased from 23% to over 28% of the total population. Almost 50% of Australians are either migrants or have at least one parent who is a migrant. This means that Australia now has the largest overseas-born population of all large Organisation for Economic Co-operation and Development (OECD) nations, while Canada has 22% of people born overseas.

The recent Australian Migration Programme (AMP) annual intake varied between approximately 180,000 and 230,000 people until it was cut to 163,000 this year after the introduction of stricter vetting controls. The majority of places under AMP are given to skilled migrants (about 68%), with remaining places held for relatives sponsored by immediate family members.

The second component of Australia's immigration intake is the Australian Humanitarian Programme (AHP), designed for refugees and others in refugee-like situations. Since 1945, more than 800,000 refugees have settled in Australia, which has consistently ranked as one of the top three resettlement countries globally. By comparison, Canada has also recorded high migration intake levels since 2010 with 296,346 settlers admitted in 2016.

As Australian programmes are non-discriminatory regarding national origin, race, religion, gender or ethnicity, they significantly contribute to the increased ethnic diversity of Australia's population. In 2010–11, China surpassed the UK as Australia's primary source of permanent migrants. Since then, most migrants arrived from India (21%) and China (14%), followed by the UK (12%). The refugee intake adds to the diversity with 15,552 humanitarian visas granted in 2015–16 to Iraqis (4358), Syrians (4261), Burmese (1951), Afghanis (1714) and Congolese (657), among others.

According to the Australian Bureau of Statistics 2016 Census, over 300 cultural and ethnic ancestries were separately identified. The top five most common were English (36.1%), Australian (33.5%), Irish (11.0%), Scottish (9.3%) and Chinese (5.6%). More than one-fifth (21%) of Australians spoke a language other than English at home, with the top five languages spoken at home being English only (72.7%), Chinese (Mandarin 2.5% and Cantonese 1.2%), Arabic (1.4%) and Vietnamese (1.2%). The census also indicated that usage of non-English languages is not equally distributed across Australia. For example, nearly 23% of the New South Wales population speak a non-English language at home, while English-language usage dominates rural regions.

Finally, the religious makeup of Australia has shifted over the past 50 years. In 1966, Christianity was the main religion (88%). According to the 2016 census, Christianity is still the most common religion, with 52.1% following, while nearly 30% reported no religion. Followings for some other religions are Islam: 604,200 (2.6%), Buddhism: 563,700 (2.4%) and Hinduism: 440,300 (1.9%).

To conclude, contemporary Australia is clearly a multicultural society in the descriptive use of this word. Such diversity requires a government response to deliver economic opportunities, integration and social cohesion. Australian multiculturalism is also described as a system of policies and programmes delivering such a response.

Australian multiculturalism: evolution of policies and programmes

The emergence of ideas associated with what we today call multiculturalism can be traced back to the Menzies Coalition government who embraced an ambitious programme of non-British migration after World War II. In 1960, the term 'White Australia' was removed from the Liberal Party's Federal Policy Platform; in 1965, a similar change was made in the Australian Labor Party platform. In 1966, the Holt Coalition government allowed migration of non-Europeans.

Initially, the expectation of the post-WWII immigration policy was that non-British migrants would, in a short time, melt seamlessly into Australian society and adopt the Australian lifestyle quickly, become local patriots and abandon their past national allegiances and cultural 'baggage'. However, upon their arrival, European migrants did not dissolve easily into the Anglo-Celtic melting pot, but established their own lively communities with churches, sporting, youth and cultural clubs, associations, language schools, media, welfare and financial institutions.

The process of moving away from an assimilation policy and towards multiculturalism gained momentum in the late 1960s. With non-British settlers' concentration in certain localities and their growing wealth and political influence, the so-called ethnic vote started to make a difference. In addition, the policy of assimilation started losing the high moral ground and public support, including amongst the Anglo-Celtic majority. The ideals of racial equality were gaining acceptance.

By the early 1970s, it had become obvious that cultures brought to Australia by migrants were not going to fade away and that the nation would be better served by accepting diversity and working with it. Australian multiculturalism has developed incrementally over the years as successive national governments have created architecture, policies and programmes acknowledging and responding to cultural diversity. It is usually seen as a bipartisan undertaking, with Labor focussing more on social justice and racial discrimination, and the Coalition on social cohesion, fundamental values, citizenship and integration. All post-1975 federal governments have issued major policy statements defining and endorsing multiculturalism. In addition, some states, including New South Wales, Queensland, Victoria and South Australia, have specific multicultural legislation in place.

Early multiculturalism: Whitlam's Labor government (1972–75)

In 1972, Whitlam's Labor government was elected to power. Minister for Immigration Al Grassby discovered the term 'multicultural' on a 1973 trip to Canada and brought it back to Australia.

Although Grassby never proposed a precise definition of multiculturalism, his speeches suggest that, for him, multiculturalism was a combination of different ideas, concepts and policies associated with equality, cultural identity and social cohesion in application to non-British migrant settlement. His concept of 'the family of the nation' (Grassby, 1973) is the closest to the first official definition of multiculturalism: 'In a family the overall attachment to the common good need not impose sameness on the outlook or activity of each member, nor need these members deny their individuality and distinctiveness. . . . The important thing is that all are committed to the good of all.'

The Whitlam government's key achievement was to outlaw racial discrimination and to remove the discriminatory provisions from the immigration legislation. The Racial Discrimination Act was enacted in 1975, and an office of Commissioner for Community Relations was established.

Ethno-specific services: Fraser Coalition government (1975–83)

When Malcolm Fraser's conservative Coalition government came to power in late 1975, it significantly extended Australian multiculturalism both as a concept and as a practical government response to cultural diversity.

A major initiative under the Fraser government was the 1977–78 Review of Migrant Programs and Services by Frank Galbally.

The resulting 1978 report provided a well-articulated concept of multicultural policy, incorporating principles of social cohesion, equality of opportunity and cultural identity that was endorsed by the government. The report also identified a range of ethno-specific services and programs to ensure that non-British migrants had equal opportunity of access to government-funded programmes and services. It recommended the creation of the Special Broadcasting Service (SBS), the Australian Institute of Multicultural Affairs (AIMA) and the Multicultural Education Program, among others.

Fraser also created several advisory and consultative bodies, including the Australian Ethnic Affairs Council, the Australian Population and Immigration Council and the Australian Refugee Advisory Council. Ethnic communities and their leaders gained access to government and were regularly consulted on issues of relevance to them.

The mainstreaming of services under Hawke/Keating (1983–96)

Labor was returned to government under the leadership of Bob Hawke in 1983 and initially started dismantling some of the multicultural institutions and programmes established by the Fraser government. This included a review of AIMA that resulted in its closure and an idea to merge SBS with ABC that resulted in protests.

In December 1985, a Committee of Review of Migrant and Multicultural Programs and Services was created to advise on the federal government's role in assisting migrants to achieve their equitable participation in Australian society. The committee recommended moving away from an ethno-specific service delivery model to provision of government services through mainstream agencies. Another key outcome was the establishment of the Office of Multicultural Affairs (OMA) in the Department of Prime Minister and Cabinet and also of an advisory body, the Australian Council of Multicultural Affairs. Further, the government established the Bureau of Immigration, Multicultural and Population Research in 1989 (to fill the vacuum created by closure of AIMA).

The establishment of OMA as a central coordinating agency for multicultural policy and programmes created a golden era in Australian multiculturalism. Throughout the Australian bicentenary in 1988 and afterwards, efforts were made to 'place multiculturalism within a national narrative where cultural diversity and tolerance were part of Australian national identity' (Koleth, 2010).

The Hawke government issued the 'National Agenda for a Multicultural Australia. Sharing Our Future' in 1989. The agenda advanced the concept of multiculturalism by defining its limits. Multiculturalism was described as requiring an overriding and unifying commitment to Australia, an acceptance of the rule of law, freedom of speech and religion, English as the national language and the equality of the sexes. It also stated that the right to express your own culture carried the responsibly to afford others the same right to express theirs. Economic efficiency was made an integral part of the concept.

Hawke's era was also characterised by consultations with ethnic communities and by the establishment of strong links between ethnic leadership and the Commonwealth and state Labor governments. Teaching of non-English languages was enhanced and interpreting and translating services re-engineered. When Paul Keating replaced Bob Hawke as prime minister at the end of 1991, this approach to multiculturalism continued.

The high profile of multiculturalism under Hawke/Keating governments brought about a populist backlash. In this context, the government created an ad-hoc 1988 Committee to Advise on Australia's Immigration Policies; the committee warned of a 'clear and present need for immigration reform' and found that, as the philosophy of multiculturalism was not widely understood, the 'ensuing uninformed debate was damaging the cause it seeks to serve' (FitzGerald, 1988).

Citizenship and cohesion under the Howard government (1996–2007)

In 1996, the Coalition leader John Howard was swept into power. Also, Pauline Hanson was elected on an anti-multiculturalism and anti-Asian platform. In her maiden speech to parliament Hanson said, 'I and most Australians want our immigration policy radically reviewed and that of multiculturalism abolished. I believe we are in danger of being swamped by Asians' (Hanson, 1996).

John Howard had been a known critic of aspects of multiculturalism while in opposition. Howard had advocated instead the idea of a 'shared national identity', grounded in concepts of 'mateship' and a 'fair go'. It was unsurprising when Howard closed the Office of Multicultural Affairs and transferred the responsibility for multicultural issues to the Department of Immigration and Multicultural Affairs. The Bureau of Immigration, Multicultural and Population Research was also closed, and funding to ethnic organisations was reduced. However, funding was increased to the Adult Migrant English Programme (AMEP) responsible for training in English language and settlement skills.

Howard was initially reluctant to criticize Hanson, claiming free speech as her right. However, after she formed the One Nation Party, which split the conservative and blue-collar vote, and her assertions began to affect international relations, Howard acted. In December of 1996, just two months after Hanson's maiden speech, Howard said 'that there is no place in the Australia that we love for any semblance of racial or ethnic intolerance. There is no place within our community for those who would traffic . . .

in the business of trying to cause division based on a person's religion, a person's place of birth, the colour of the person's skin, the person's values, ethnic make-up or beliefs' (Howard, 1996).

The National Multicultural Advisory Council was established and delivered 'Australian Multiculturalism for a New Century: Towards Inclusiveness' statement in April 1999. Soon after, in December 1999, the government launched a new policy statement called A New Agenda for Multicultural Australia with an added focus on citizenship and promoting a community of harmony through the Living in Harmony grants and the establishment of Harmony Day.

The Howard government also placed the value of Australian citizenship into the foreground, with those applying for citizenship required to undertake an Australian history and culture test in English and to pledge 'loyalty to Australia and its people . . . whose democratic beliefs I share . . . whose rights and liberties I respect . . . and whose laws I will uphold and obey'. Surprisingly, Howard also introduced the right to hold dual citizenship.

Surprisingly, the terrorist attack in New York on 11 September 2001 gave Australian multiculturalism an additional lease on life. In 2003, the government issued a new policy statement, 'Multicultural Australia: United in Diversity: Updating the 1999 New Agenda for Multicultural Australia: Strategic Directions for 2003–2006'. This further shifted the focus of multiculturalism to unity and social cohesion. It also meant a return to old practices of community consultation and of opening government access to community leaders. In 2005, after the Prime Minister's Summit with Muslim Community Leaders, a Muslim Community Reference Group was created to advance Muslim integration with the wider community.

Equality and justice under the Rudd/Gillard governments (2007–13)

The Labor government was returned in 2007 with Kevin Rudd as prime minister. Upon election, Labor's initial approach to multiculturalism disappointed many. The electoral platform to re-establish OMA was not implemented after the election. Then, in the 2010 election, for the first time since the Whitlam government in 1972, Labor did not put forward a multicultural policy proposal. During Rudd's first period in government (2/12/07–24/06/10) multicultural issues were not given much prominence. The focus of attention (and resources) further shifted toward the needs of 'boat people' and away from other migrant groups.

The Gillard government gave a temporally higher profile to multiculturalism. The finally released policy 'The People of Australia' focused primarily on fairness and inclusion, equality and anti-discrimination issues. It also reaffirmed the well-established concepts of multiculturalism, including rights and responsibilities, non-negotiable respect for Australian foundational values of democracy and the rule of law, reaffirmation of equality between men and women and the concept of a shared identity based on the common ground of 'mateship' and a 'fair go'. The new Australian Multicultural Council was subsequently launched to advise government on implementing the policy and advocate on multicultural issues.

In February 2015, Kevin Rudd, re-appointed as prime minister, announced Labor's new hard-line approach to boat arrivals. It reinstated the earlier 'Pacific solution' denying settlement in Australia to asylum seekers who paid people smugglers for unauthorised passage.

Integration and values under the Abbott/Turnbull governments (2013–present)

The coalition was returned to power in 2013. Prime Minister Tony Abbott gave priority to border protection, Islamic terrorism and social cohesion issues, and these coloured Australia's approach to multicultural policies and programmes. A range of new measures were put in place to 'stop the boats' and to communicate better with Muslim community leadership and specially to stop the radicalization of Muslim youth.

The Australian Multicultural Council was appointed in 2015 and then reappointed for a further three years in June 2018, with Dr Sev Ozdowski as its new chair, to advise the government on multicultural affairs, but without an advocacy role. Minister for Social Services Kevin Andrews requested that

> the Council will advise the Government on ways to sustain and support socially cohesive communities, to ensure all Australians have the opportunity to participate, engage and contribute to Australian life. It will examine ways to further harness the economic and social benefits of our Nation's cultural and linguistic diversity and advise on how we can promote social cohesion by fostering the successful integration of migrants into the broad Australian community.

Malcolm Turnbull replaced Tony Abbott as prime minister in September 2015. During the 2016 federal election campaign, the prime minister asserted that tough border protection is essential to guarantee and sustain Australia as the most successful multicultural nation on earth. The re-emergence of the One Nation Party under Pauline Hanson in Australian politics presented additional challenges.

On 21 March 2017, Prime Minister Turnbull released a new multicultural statement, 'Multicultural Australia: United, Strong, Successful', reaffirming the government's commitment to a culturally diverse and harmonious society. The statement declared multiculturalism as a 'success' and emphasised that Australians are bonded by the 'shared values' of respect, freedom and equality and the 'fundamental rights of every individual'.

The Multicultural Statement also placed emphasis on national security and addressed the growing concerns about the threat of global terrorism and the need for social cohesion. It declared that every Australian is expected to obey the nation's laws and support its democratic processes. It promoted the principle of mutual respect and mutual obligations and stated that the government 'continues denouncing racial hatred and discrimination as incompatible with Australian society.' In addition, the statement recognized the need to support economic and social integration by new migrants and their families, so they could feel connected to their new home, while also contributing to Australia's prosperity.

In July 2018, in a speech to an Australia/UK Leadership Forum in London, Minister for Citizenship and Multicultural Affairs Alan Tudge expressed a concern that Australia is veering towards a 'European separatist multicultural model' and stated the government's wish to the return to the integration path. He flagged a change to immigration settings that would require new migrants to be assessed against Australian values such as freedom of speech and worship, democracy and the rule of law, a fair go for all, equality of sexes and on English-language skills before being granted permanent residency. Mr Tudge stressed that diversity and tolerance can only flourish within an agreed-upon set of collective values.

Australian multiculturalism: success or otherwise

Most Australians regard both Australia's immigration outcomes and its multicultural policy as a success and take pride in them. Some would go as far as to claim that multiculturalism is an inherent part of Australian DNA.

The 2015 Scanlon Foundation National Survey Report, Mapping Social Cohesion (Markus, 2015), revealed that public concern over migration to Australia is at its lowest level since 2007, with some 41% agreeing that the number of immigrants accepted to Australia is 'about right' and 19% that it is 'too low'. It suggests that Australia is a country with one of the highest levels of positive sentiment towards migration in the Western world. The Scanlon Foundation findings are supported by the results of the Western Sydney University–led Challenging Racism Project which reported that 'about 87 percent of Australians say that they see cultural diversity as a good thing for society' (Dunn, 2016).

Similarly, most Australians support multiculturalism. The 2015 Scanlon Survey found high levels of agreement to the following statements: 'multiculturalism has been good for Australia' (86%); 'multiculturalism contributes to our economic development' (75%); 'multiculturalism encourages migrants to integrate' (71%); and 'diversity strengthens the Australian way of life' (60%) (Markus, 2015).

There is also a range of other social indicators that the multiculturalism policy is working well in Australia. According to the Australian Bureau of

Statistics (2015) data, the average employee income of a skilled visa holder was approximately $5,000 higher than the national average. Also, unemployment rates are lower for second-generation migrant youth than they are for children of Australian-born parents.

There is also enormous economic upward intergenerational mobility amongst the new settlers. Children with overseas-born parents perform relatively better in education compared to those with Australian-born parents. Additional social indicators of successful multiculturalism include interethnic marriages and participation in mainstream political processes and civic undertakings.

However, there are some emerging issues with the potential to undermine social cohesion. The 2016 census indicated that some migrants concentrate in suburbs of large cities. They are highly likely to live in areas where a 30% or higher proportion of the population shares their identity.

Another issue of concern is the increase in people who do not speak English well or at all. Almost 10% of the overseas-born migrants cannot speak English well or at all after 17 years of residence. The 2016 census recorded almost 820,000 with poor English-language skills, a significant increase from 655,000 in 2006.

Social researchers also report the existence of a feeling of discrimination and injustice is reported to exist amongst some visibly different migrant groups, for example, South Sudanese youth, young Australian Muslims and youths of Middle Eastern extraction, among others. The Scanlon Foundation surveys found that respondents who reported experiencing discrimination based on skin colour, ethnicity or religion increased from 9% in 2007 to 15% in 2015 and to 20% in 2016 (Markus, 2017).

To conclude, Australian multiculturalism is unquestionably a success story. It reflects a demographic reality, it is supported by national policy and institutions and it is centred on a social compact that is built on mutual respect and shared rights and responsibilities. The current policy of multiculturalism, with its stress on core values of democracy, equality, social justice and English as a national language, is likely to continue as government-endorsed social policy.

References

Australian Bureau of Statistics (2015). *ABS Releases Data on Personal Income of Migrants in Australia.* Australian Bureau of Statistics, Canberra. www.abs.gov.au/ausstats/abs@.nsf/mediareleasesbyCatalogue/C86AC9580113E534CA257EB400 142C72?OpenDocument, viewed 10 July 2018.

Australian Government (2017). *Multicultural Australia – United, Strong, Successful.* Department of Home Affairs, Canberra. www.homeaffairs.gov.au/LifeinAustralia/Documents/MulticulturalAffairs/english-multicultural-statement.pdf, viewed 13 July 2018.

Dunn, K. (2016). *Challenging Racism: The Anti-Racism Research Project.* Western Sydney University.

FitzGerald, S. (1988). *Immigration: A Commitment to Australia Report*. Multicultural Australia. AGPS, Canberra.

Grassby, A. (1973). *A Multi-Cultural Society for the Future*. Multicultural Australia, 11 August. AGPS, Canberra.

Hanson, P. (1996). *Pauline Hanson – Party Leader – Maiden Speech*. www.onenation.com.au/paulinehanson#maiden, viewed 10 March 2016.

Howard, J. (1996). *John Howard on Multiculturalism*. Multicultural Australia, 3 December. AGPS, Canberra.

Knopff, R. & Flanagan, T. (1989). *Human Rights and Social Technology: The New War on Discrimination*. Carlton University Press, Canada.

Koleth, E. (2010). *Multiculturalism: A Review of Australian Policy Statements and Recent Debates in Australia and Overseas*. Research Paper No. 6, 2010–11, Parliament of Australia, Canberra.

Markus, A. (2015). *Mapping Social Cohesion – The Scanlon Foundation Surveys 2015*. http://scanlonfoundation.org.au/wp-content/uploads/2015/10/2015-Mapping-Social-Cohesion-Report.pdf, viewed 10 March 2016.

Markus, A. (2017). *Mapping Social Cohesion: The Scanlon Foundation Surveys 2017*. Monash University, Melbourne.

Ozdowski, S. (2012). Australia – Emergence of a Modern Nation Build on Diversity and 'Fair Go'. *Political Crossroads*, 19(1), 25–46.

Ozdowski, S. (2013). Australian Multiculturalism: The Roots of Its Success. In Mazur, K., Musiewicz, P., & Szlachta, B. (Eds.), *Promoting Changes in Times of Transition and Crisis: Reflections on Human Rights Education*. Ksiegarnia Akademicka, Kraków. www.akademicka.pl.

12 Muslims as second-class citizens

Jan A. Ali

The Muslim population in the West

Although Muslims have been linked with Europe since the early days of Islam, the twentieth century, particularly since decolonisation, witnessed a unique type of Islamic movement westward. This movement involved two specific factors: a push factor and a pull factor. The push factor was that the *dar al-Islam* (abode of Islam), once self-sufficient, self-ruling, and a powerful world, gradually declined in the face of European imperialism and colonialism, causing large-scale disruptions, dislocation, and malaise in all spheres of life. The pull factor was that the European civilisation in the second half of the twentieth century made unprecedented social and economic advances. The catastrophes in Europe between 1914 and 1945, for instance, the First World War, the communist revolutions in Russia and certain parts of Europe, the Great Depression, the Nazi and fascist dictatorships, the Second World War, the Holocaust, and class conflict, were all over. Finally, order was restored and major advancements ensued in different areas of living for which workers were needed.

The places in which European nations could find workers were their former colonies or dependent territories. According to Ballard (1996), these former colonies were targets because their subjects already had the experience of working under European rule. In fact, they were eager immigrants. This is why, for example, Britain has received large numbers of immigrants, particularly from India, Pakistan, and Yemen; France particularly from Algeria, Morocco, Tunisia, and the former French West Africa; and Germany particularly from Turkey (Hansen, 2003).

Muslims left their homes in large numbers searching for employment, refuge, and in some instances, religious freedom (Hansen, 2003). Muslim immigration to the West, therefore, on the one hand, was a manifestation of the lands of Islam in crisis, and on the other hand, the West, particularly Europe, in need of workers. Ballard (1996) suggests that though the history of Muslim immigrant communities in the West varies in terms of population size, social and economic composition, and colonial connection to the host society, they share similar experiences. One important similarity, according to Smith (2002: 4), is their "shared . . . understanding that their reasons for entry into a new country were primarily if not exclusively economic and that soon they would be returning to their home countries".

Since decolonisation, the immigration of millions of Muslims has gradually altered the demography of the Western societies and their social and economic landscape. Today, after Christianity, Islam, although still a small percentage compared to the mainstream Christian population, is the next largest religion in almost every Western country (Pew Research Center, 2017). Despite this, Islam is seen as a foreign religion and presents a unique set of challenges for the Muslims who have opted for the West as their new home, as well as to the Western host societies that are facing mounting pressures in an attempt to accommodate new recruits and the locally born Muslim population (Smith, 2002).

Figure 12.1 depicts a demographic picture of Muslims in Europe in greater detail. By looking at Europe's growing Muslim population, we are able to gain an important understanding about Muslims in the West more generally. The Pew Research Center's Religion and Public Life Demographic Report (2017) offers some figures of Muslims living in Europe. Although the figures here are for only some key European countries, given the fact that most of the countries of the West are in Europe, and considering its past historical significance regarding the relationship between Islam and the West, the focus on Europe here is justified. It reveals that Muslims constituted 4.9% of Europe's population in 2016, and a combined total of Muslims in just six main European countries – France, Germany, United Kingdom, Italy, Netherlands, and Spain was 20.06 million. This is not an insignificant demographic reality and as Muslim populations continue to grow (the Pew Research Center predicts a growth from 4.9% to 7.4% by the year 2050), Muslims will become a significant socio-cultural, economic, and political force not only in Europe but in many the countries of the West.

Integration and assimilation

Muslims in the countries of the West are minority communities and, therefore, as some scholars (Sander, 1996; Cesari, 2002) argue, are expected by the host societies or dominant cultures to conform to the essential values and institutions. The recent calls for 'schools for imams' in Europe and in Australia to educate them in the values and traditions of the host society are expressions of such an expectation (Albayrak, 2012). However, conformity is neither a simple process nor is necessarily desired by immigrants.

For Muslim immigrants, integration into the culture of Western societies is clearly problematic. Van Den Berghe suggests that immigrants in general are "Subordinate minorities, . . . are under constant pressure to acculturate, because becoming like the dominant group almost invariably confers social advantages" (1981: 215). Sander (1996), whose work focuses on Muslims in Sweden and yet has relevance to the Muslim situation in general in the

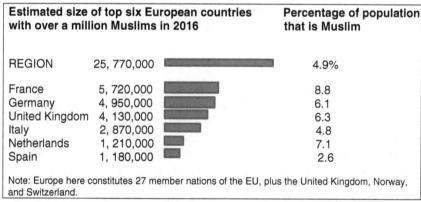

Figure 12.1 European Muslim population in 2016.

Source: Pew Research Center (November 29, 2017), Religion and Public Life, Europe's Growing Muslim Population Muslims Are Projected to Increase as a Share of Europe's Population – Even with No Future Migration

West, sees the integration of Muslim immigrants as a big problem. He claims that it is not that Muslims resist integration, but that, as in many Western countries, the Swedish structures are largely unfavourable to them. Sander notes that as part of Western monolith, Sweden sees itself being built on the idea of "One nation, One people, One religion" (1996: 272). He connects the separation of Muslims in Sweden to this notion of "a common culture and religion, including common manners, norms and value system, as well as a common way of thinking in general" (1996: 273). Sander further argues that the state's officially declared 'multiculturalism', where equality, freedom of choice, partnership, and citizenship are important features, is understood in different ways by the Swedish non-Muslim population and by the Swedish Muslim population. Swedes, in general, understand multiculturalism basically through the principle of equality, denoting "equality between universal individuals regardless of culture, ethnicity, race, religion and gender" (1996: 274). Muslims, however, are likely to see multiculturalism in terms of equal citizenship right to freedom of choice. Sander argues that for Swedish authorities the idyllic 'multiculturalism' is one in which the public life is characterised by equality, denoting similarity, while religious and cultural expressions should be restricted to the private sphere. Hence, while officially an integrationist model is promoted, in reality, the expectation is for an elevated degree of assimilation. Muhammad Anwar (2007), a sociologist from Great Britain, presents a similar argument for the case of Muslims in Britain when he suggests that integration in Britain means one thing to the majority of Britons and another to immigrant Muslims. Anwar claims that immigrant Muslims conceive of 'integration' as "acceptance by the majority of their separate ethnic and cultural identity" (2007: 110). However, from the majority perspective, 'integration' reproduces the "ideology of the dominant group", which implies that "any group which remains unabsorbed, or unassimilated, is usually considered as upsetting the equalisation of social relations in the society" (2007: 10).

Islamophobia

Immigrants have always faced different forms of treatment and by extension discrimination based on factors such as race and ethnicity, an inability to speak the national language of the host country, dress, mores, and religion. This has been described as Muslim unwillingness to integrate and assimilate in the wider structure of the societies in the West. For Muslims, this discrimination has been made worse as a result of increasing opposition towards Islam in the West, sometimes referred to as 'Islamophobia' (Haddad and Smith, 2002; Vertovec, 2002; Werbner, 2002). Werbner asserts that "Islamophobia targets the Muslim community as fanatical and violent, a legitimising veneer which at its most virulent covers over deep-seated racialisms" (Werbner, 2002: 258). Importantly, it "results from the religion being depicted as violent, and the attribute of violence then stigmatises minority Muslims" (Haddad and Smith, 2002: xii).

In recent times, the religion factor has been particularly vital. The stereo-typing that has emerged from media coverage of international events, such as the Iranian Revolution; the 'Rushdie Affair'; the Gulf crisis; the events of September 11, 2001; and the Bali, Madrid, and London bombings, "have had a deep impact in shaping perceptions of Islam on the part of European citizens", as Ramadan (2002: 158) has expressed it. Muslims have become the focus of attention in a highly negative way. In Ramadan's words:

> It is difficult to estimate the degree to which these events have helped foster a negative perception of Islam among Europeans, but what we do know is that such a negative perspective is currently a widespread phenomenon that transcends particular national European borders. We also know that the scandals and events in the Middle East have fed the tensions stemming from the social crisis that has gripped much of Europe, manifested in its high levels of unemployment, exclusionary reactions, and recurring violence.
>
> (2002: 159)

Echoing Ramadan's sentiments, Vertovec (2002) asserts that in Britain in the last decade or so, Muslims have come under intense public scrutiny. He says that such widespread attention has generated a highly negative attitude towards Muslims. The source of this, Vertovec argues, is the media which has portrayed Muslims "in very derogatory and vilifying way". He further adds that such a media portrayal of Muslims has affected Muslims in very real ways and "among the effects of such depiction, which has contributed to what is now widely referred to as 'Islamophobia,' Muslims in Britain have been subject to considerable discrimination and even violence" (Vertovec, 2002: 19).

Discrimination and violence against Muslims vary in nature and from place to place in the West. However, some common forms of discrimination against which Muslims have complained, and even have gone to the courts, are men not being permitted to wear beards in the police force, Muslims not allowed to offer prayer at work, the refusal to grant Muslims time off to attend Friday congregational prayer, being refused employment, women stopped from wearing the *hijāb* (veil) at work and in public schools, and the lack of alternative food items when pork is offered in school lunches (Nimer, 2002). With regard to violence, Vertovec (2002) notes that Muslims in the West have been subjected to verbal abuse and spat upon, and mosques have been burnt. This has been echoed by Haddad and Smith, who claim that there have been "violent attacks on the Muslim community (such as mosque burning, bombing, and trashing)" (2002: xii). Of course, just as extremist groups in Islam hardly reflect the whole tradition, violent extremists in the West form cultural renegades. Part of the problem in analysing negativities of 'the West' in a reified way, also, is that Western countries now play host to other immigrant minorities, who may have memories of suffering marginalization in Muslim-majority countries and yet who now cluster in the same ethnic urban context as Muslim migrants. But generally speaking, Muslims have experienced discrimination in essentially every facet of life and in some instances even violence across the Western world.

The point Islamophobia underscores is that Muslim presence in the West (despite Muslims being there, in some cases, for three generations and the West's claim of a tolerant culture) continues to be a problem for both Muslims and the dominant cultures in the countries of the Western world. It raises the issues of "the prevailing position of deprivation of Muslim minorities in Europe" (Shadid and Van Koningsveld, 1996: 2–3), "race relations . . . throughout Europe" (Van der Veer 1997: 102), and "Muslim attempts to achieve full religious equality. . . . [and Muslims'] sense of alienation" (Werbner, 2002: 258). Furthermore, Islamophobic framing of average Muslim in the West as disloyal and threatening 'other' despite their formal citizenship status further marginalises Muslims and clears the path for the large-scale encroachment on civil liberties and citizenship rights.

Muslim marginalisation

In the West, being Muslim means being located in the 'immigrant working class' and labelled as religiously 'conservative'.[1] This class description of Muslims has developed from the origins of Muslim immigrants and their real experience with the labour force in the countries of the West (Humphrey, 2000). A vast majority of Muslim immigrants have arrived in the West from rural and poor urban backgrounds from mostly underdeveloped and developing countries. After arriving, they largely engage in unskilled or semi-skilled jobs within the manufacturing and service industries. Muslim immigrants with academic qualifications and professional experience are usually forced by the processes of immigration to take up non-professional menial jobs. Many Western countries consider some qualifications from underdeveloped and developing countries comparatively sub-standard and thus refuses to recognise them and in some instances it is the perception of the employers that qualifications from underdeveloped and developing countries are inferior and thus unacceptable.

In the case of Australia, Lowenstein and Loh note that "often Australia does not recognise the overseas trade and professional qualifications of migrants, so skilled people are forced to work either at unskilled jobs or to carry out skilled work at unskilled rates of pay" (1977: 10). As in the context of immigrants in general, the demand by Western societies for cultural accommodation of Muslim immigrants entails a slow transition. They are required to initiate social and cultural adjustments to their daily social and vocational endeavours by accepting the routines of the manufacturing industry where they work and take more than one job to maintain a family or depend on limited welfare benefits with some income derived from working in the 'black economy'. The whole process of cultural accommodation imposes upon Muslim immigrants a modification of the undertakings of their daily life in accordance with the practices of the broader Western society. In so doing it impacts on the entire basis of their social existence. For example, the impact is felt on all aspects of social life such as marriage, social networks, residency, gender relations, housing, and consumption patterns. This makes the reconciliation between ethnic culture and customs and new social and work patterns problematic.

These are the demands of the class culture (Humphrey, 2001), and when Muslim immigrants fail to fulfil them, they also fail to meet, as a group, their expected economic contribution and are consequently censured for not making a fair contribution to the national economic growth and development of the whole society. Their statistical over-representation in the records of welfare benefits, workers' compensation claims, and unemployment demonises them, gives them a negative image, and pushes them to the lowest strata of the social hierarchy (Humphrey, 2001). This highlights their peripheralness in urban structures, their marginalisation and disenfranchisement, and their second-class citizenship status in the West.

Western citizenship

According to Richard Bellamy, there are three linked components of citizenship where

> membership of a democratic political community, the collective benefits and rights associated with membership, and participation in the community's political, economic and social processes – all of which combine in different ways to establish a condition of civic equality.
>
> (2008: 12)

For Linda Bosniak, "citizenship" can be understood in relation to a variety of conceptualisations more broadly, "depending on whether we are addressing citizenship as a legal status, as a system of rights, as a form of political activity, or as a form of identity and solidarity" (2000: 542).

Different sets of individuals stress the importance of citizenship, ranging from politicians, to church leaders, to leaders of industry, to campaigning parites – from those struggling for global causes, such as combating international refugee crisis, to others with a more local focus, such as combating child labour. Types of citizenship abound, for example, dual and transnational citizenship or corporate citizenship or international citizenship. Whenever there are certain problems in the society such as child abuse, rise in migrant unemployment level or terrorism, "citizenship" is proposed as a remedy. For instance, recently allegations were levelled against some Western-born Muslims for fighting with ISIS against a coalition forces, and upon their return home from Syria some politicians suggested revoking their citizenships. The sheer variety and range of "citizenship" definitions, models, and uses can prove to be very challenging and even perplexing, and what constitutes political membership within the broader structure of the state remains, in almost all instances, unresolved Nevertheless, citizenship has important social, cultural, legal, and political functions.

Minimally, citizenship can be understood as a legal relationship to the state. Limited by space, I do not intend to enter into a comprehensive discussion about citizenship broadly, but for our purposes, will pay attention to the welfaristic construction of citizenship in relation to Muslims in the West. Welfaristic construction conceptualizes citizens as different to each other based on difference in social needs. In this construction, according to Edwards, "those with similar needs ought to get similar resources and those with different needs, different resources, or – more succinctly – treatment as equals rather than equal treatment" (Edwards, 1988: 135). In this construction, social welfare rights are about the fulfilment of social needs of the citizens, particularly the working classes, so that improvement in the quality of their lives can be achieved (Beveridge, 1942).

The citizenship rights for racial and ethnic minorities are closely linked with their social rights. In Western multiculturalism this is a cause for major concern for immigrants because Western multiculturalism tends to homogenize racial and ethnic minorities and at the same time claims to be pluralistic society in which every citizen is equal. The homogenization of racial and ethnic minorities in the Western multiculturalism is problematic, in which the heavy emphasis is placed on the treatment of immigrants as equal rather than equal treatment of immigrants (Lister, 1990). "However, such a model does not take into account potential conflicts of interest among the different groupings of citizens, nor does it consider the collective, rather than the individual, character of the special provisions given to members of groupings defined as ethnic minorities" (Jayasuriya, 1990: 23). For example, in Australia, Lebanese immigrants constitute one ethnic clustering, but within this clustering there are Christian Lebanese and Muslim Lebanese, who have sharp and distinct cultural and even social needs, and a collective provision reflective of policies of positive action to meet their needs does not necessarily avoid conflicts of interest but instead fuels them. The multicultural policy becomes even more problematic when it is implemented to render collective provisions to different cultural needs in the same ethnic group or different ethnic groups. They can vary from something like the appropriateness of Meals on Wheels service to the allocation of funds to religious organizations. Matters can be exacerbated in a unique or extreme situation such as the debates around Christians in Pakistan or Muslim minorities around the Rushdie affair in Britain. In either situation, efforts have been mobilized towards obtaining autonomy and self-determination.

For Muslims in the West full citizenship rights mean the capacity and choice to practise Islam as a complete way of life. In matters of birth rites; daily prayers; Islamic education; burial and dietary requirements; and marriage, divorce, and inheritance rules, all can be practiced freely and without penalty. In other words, the implementation of the *shari'ah* (Islamic law) is at the very heart of the question of full citizenship rights. Under the current systems in place in Western societies, this is problematic for Muslims. Whilst the majority group is able to carry on with its everyday rituals without having to undergo any level of change and have its demands fulfilled by the system because it is an inalienable part of it, the minority groups such as Muslim immigrants have to campaign hard and overcome all sorts of obstacles to gain recognition both as a part of the social fabric and as an individual with social and civil rights. Unlike the members of the mainstream society, Muslims in the West have to struggle to become equal part of the society and maintain their Islamic identity.

It will not be an exaggeration or deceptive to postulate that after the events of 9/11 Muslims in many countries of the West lost their citizenship in terms of identity. In other words, they have been seen as not representing the nation and are described as outsiders and an unwanted 'other'. I want to posit that in post-9/11 era Muslims in many Western countries as a minority community are not only further deprived of citizenship as identity, they are also divested of citizenship regarding rights and political participation. Perhaps the only continuing citizenship discourse for Muslim group is formal legal status, though what value lies in it if one is not given the rights associated with that status remains hazy.

Citizenship as legal status denotes the formal legal recognition that an individual is a member of a polity (Stewart, 1995). Linda Bosniak (2000) notes that citizenship as a status is generally viewed as exclusively connected to the nation-state. "As a practical matter, citizenship is almost always conferred by the nation-state, and as a matter of international law, it is nation-state citizenship that is recognized and honoured" (Bosniak, 2000: 456). In this understanding of citizenship where citizenship is tied to a nation-state, a citizen has the right to belong to an organized political community because he or she has the "right to have rights" (Arendt, 1948). Minority communities, who are often seen as foreigners then, remain outside of this community, and although they do take part in many socio-cultural and economic activities and enjoy benefits provided by the state, they do so only at the mercy of the host state. Even when the foreigners take up the formal legal status as citizens and are actively involved in a variety of ways of community building, they still are continually viewed as outsiders, and Muslims are the main targets these days of this view.

With respect to Muslims living in certain Western countries such as Australia, Britain, Canada, and France who have formal legal citizenship status today, there have been calls for or proposals made to formally denationalize them via revocation (Joppke, 2016). Muslims are treated as naturalized citizens, meaning that there is always a risk that their citizenship can be revoked in light of their continuing perceived disloyalty. This has been based on some isolated but real cases. For example, in Australian the Islamic State fighter Khaled Sharrouf, who had dual nationality, was stripped of his citizenship under the federal government's anti-terror laws (Norman and Gribbin, 2017). In the United States in the Holy Land Foundation case, the government attempted to denaturalize the defendants against whom allegations were made for providing material support to Hamas, a designated foreign terrorist organization (Department of Justice, 2009). In Canada, Zakaria Amara, who was imprisoned for his role in the plot to bomb Toronto's downtown in 2006, was stripped off his citizenship (Winter and Previsic, 2017). These are only a few examples of citizenship revocations, but citizenship revocation law also exists in many other Western countries, as Travina notes:

> Several states, including the United Kingdom, Canada and Austria, to name a few, have amended their legislation to allow for the easier revocation of the citizenship by introducing new causes. The UK in particular appears to be setting a trend in remodeling citizenship deprivation powers while many other states are considering similar measures as the phenomenon captures global attention.
>
> (2016: 1–2)

In the wake of 9/11 and other international incidents, such as the bombings in the London subway in July 2005 that followed bombings in Bali in 2002, among other incidents, debates have intensified in the West about the place of Islam and Muslims in Western societies and how to manage the Muslim-minority population. These have aided in questioning Muslim national identity and their citizenship rights, as well as in amplifying suspicions about Muslims in the West and made them the target of intensified material implementation of remarkable 'counter-terrorism' and 'countering violent extremism' strategies. In an attempt to combat this, governments have institutionalized various civil liberties violations and bolstered the surveillance. Key to these counterterrorism and countering violent extremism strategies has been new strict anti-terror laws purportedly designed and targeted at iconoclastic threats posed by terrorists, but in fact are cryptogrammic instruments for the management of the risky, dangerous Muslim enemy 'other'.

> They Muslims have become a shared "security" concern for Western governments and been made the object of suspicion and the focus of state intervention and political management. Their citizenship has become increasingly conditional on their "performance" as citizens

measured by active efforts to integrate on the one hand and their rejection of radical Islam on the other.

(Humphrey, 2009: 136)

Muslims are equated with terrorism, religious and cultural difference, extremism, and 'high risk', resulting in them being pushed to the social margins and the limits of citizenship in the West, where constant demands are placed on them to prove their political loyalty, demonstrate integration into the mainstream society, and justify the claims over their citizenship through an 'attitude test', language competency, and knowledge of national civic values (Kaya, 2009). With some exceptions where some Muslims may not feel excluded, the general outcome of this is the demonisation of Islam and Muslims. This weakens the Muslim sense of belonging and citizenship in the West, relegating them to a second-class citizens.

Conclusion

Muslims as second-class citizens in the West is a feeling not only experienced by immigrants but also locally born Muslims of Western countries. Second-, third-, fourth-, and fifth-generation Muslims feel a sense of non-belongingness to the country in which they were born. These Muslims are being socialised in the same world as their non-Muslim counterparts but with different outcomes. For these Muslims, the socialisation and participation in the mainstream society have not necessarily helped them overcome their social and economic problems, such as unemployment, ghettoisation, racism, and securitisation, and many still suffer from these on an on-going basis. Seeing themselves as nationals and citizens, they have come to realise their marginality within the state and their second-class citizenship status and even non-citizenship status.

Thus the fundamental problem of Muslims' second-class citizenship status in the West is to a degree rooted in the relationship between Islam and the West – the so-called 'clash of cultures' – and specific colonial and imperial legacies, partly in assimilation and integration policies and partly in social, economic, and political marginalisation and consequent alienation of Muslims. Although Muslims have been living in the West, particularly in Europe, for centuries, they have always had to live in the shadows of the dominant West living as an ethnic and cultural 'other'.

Note

1 Conservative signifies a proclivity towards a traditional or customary lifestyle.

References

Albayrak, Ismail 2012. "Friday Sermons and the Question of Home-Trained Imams in Australia", *Australian eJournal of Theology*, 19 (1): 29–42.

Anwar, Muhammad 2007. "Religious Identity in Plural Societies: The Case of Britain", *Journal of Institute of Muslim Minority Affairs*, 2 (2): 110–121.

Arendt, Hannah 1948. *Origins of Totalitarianism*, New York: Harcourt Brace Jovanovich.

Ballard, Roger 1996. "Islam and the Construction of Europe", in *Muslims in the Margin: Political Responses to the Presence of Islam in Western Europe*, ed. W. Shadid and P. Van Koningsveld, Kampen: Kok Pharos Publishing House, pp. 15–51.

Bellamy, Richard 2008. *Citizenship: A Very Short Introduction*, Oxford: Oxford University Press.

Beveridge, William 1942. *Report on Social Insurance and Allied Services*, London: HMSO.

Bosniak, Linda 2000. "Citizenship Denationalized (The State of Citizenship Symposium)", *Indiana Journal of Global Legal Studies*, 7 (2): 447–509.

Cesari, Jocelyne 2002. "Islam in France: The Shaping of a Religious Minority", in *Muslims in the West: From Sojourners to Citizens*, ed. Y. Haddad, Oxford: Oxford University Press, pp. 36–51.

Conrad, Hackett 29 November 2017. "5 Facts About the Muslim Population in Europe", Pew Research Center, www.pewresearch.org/fact-tank/2017/11/29/5-facts-about-the-muslim-population-in-europe/ (Accessed 27 July 2018).

Department of Justice 27 May 2009. "Federal Judge Hands Downs Sentences in Holy Land Foundation Case: Holy Land Foundation and Leaders Convicted on Providing Material Support to Hamas Terrorist Organization", www.justice.gov/opa/pr/federal-judge-hands-downs-sentences-holy-land-foundation-case (Accessed 4 August 2018).

Edwards, John 1988. "Justice and the Bounds of Welfare", *Journal of Social Policy*, 17 (2): 127–152.

Haddad, Yvonne and Smith, Jane 2002. "Introduction", in *Muslim Minorities in the West: Visible and Invisible*, ed. Y. Haddad and J. Smith, Walnut Creek: Altamira Press, pp. v–xviii.

Hansen, Randall 2003. "Migration to Europe Since 1945: Its History and Its Lessons", *The Political Quarterly*, 74 (1): 25–38.

Humphrey, Michael 2009. "Securitisation and Domestication of Diaspora Muslims and Islam: Turkish Immigrants in Germany and Australia", *International Journal on Multicultural Societies*, 11 (2): 136–154.

———— 2001. "Muslim Communities in Australia", in *Muslim Communities in Australia*, ed. Abdullah Saeed and Shahram Akbarzadeh, Sydney: University of New South Wales Press, pp. 33–52.

———— 2000. "Globalisation and Arab Diasporic Identities: The Australian Arab Case", *Bulletin of the Royal Institute for Inter-Faith Studies*, 2 (1): 1–18.

Jayasuriya, Laksiri 1990. "Multiculturalism, Citizenship and Welfare: New Directions for the 1990's", A Paper Presented at the 50th Anniversary Lecture Series, Department of Social Work and Social Policy, University of Sydney, Sydney.

Joppke, Christian 2016. "Terror and the Loss of Citizenship", *Citizenship Studies*, 20 (6–7): 728–748.

Kaya, Ayhan 2009. *Islam, Migration and Integration: The Age of Securitization*, London: Palgrave Macmillan.

Lister, R. 1990. *The Exclusion Society: Citizenship and the Poor*, London: Child Poverty Action Group.

Lowenstein, Wendy and Loh, Mora 1977. *The Immigrants*, Melbourne: Hyland House Publishing.

Nielsen, Jorgen 1992. *Muslims in Western Europe*, Edinburgh: Edinburgh University Press.

Nimer, Mohamed 2002. "Muslims in American Public Life", in *Muslims in the West: From Sojourners to Citizens*, ed. Y. Haddad, Oxford: Oxford University Press, pp. 169–186.

Norman, Jane and Gribbin, Caitlyn 17 February 2017. "Islamic State Fighter Khaled Sharrouf Becomes First to Lose Citizenship Under Anti-Terror Laws", *ABC News*, www.abc.net.au/news/2017-02-11/islamic-state-fighter-khaled-sharrouf-stripped-of-citizenship/8262268 (Accessed 4 August 2018).

Peucker, Mario 2016. *Muslim Citizenship in Liberal Democracies: Civic and Political Participation in the West*, London: Palgrave Macmillan.

Peucker, Mario and Akbarzadeh, Shahram 2014. *Muslim Active Citizenship in the West*, London: Routledge.

Pew Research Center 29 November 2017. "Religion and Public Life, Europe's Growing Muslim Population Muslims Are Projected to Increase as a Share of Europe's Population – Even with No Future Migration", www.pewforum.org/2017/11/29/europes-growing-muslim-population/ (Accessed 27 July 2018).

Ramadan, Tariq 2002. "Islam and Muslims in Europe: A Silent Revolution Toward Rediscovery", in *Muslims in the West: From Sojourners to Citizens*, ed. Y. Haddad, Oxford: Oxford University Press, pp. 158–166.

Roy, Olivier 2003. "EuroIslam: The Jihad Within?" *The National Interest*, 65 (2): 63–73.

Sander, A. 1996. "The Status of Muslim Communities in Sweden", in *Muslim Communities in the New Europe*, ed. G. Nonneman, T. Niblock and B. Szajkowski, London: Ithaca Press, pp. 269–289.

Shadid, W. and Van Koningsveld, S. 1996. "Politics and Islam in Western Europe: An Introduction", in *Muslims in the Margin: Political Responses to the Presence of Islam in Western Europe*, ed. W. Shadid and P. Van Koningsveld, Kampen: Kok Pharos Publishing House, pp. 1–14.

Smith, Jane 2002. "Introduction", in *Muslims in the West: From Sojourners to Citizens*, ed. Y. Haddad, Oxford: Oxford University Press, pp. 3–16.

Stewart, Angus 1995. "Two Conceptions of Citizenship", *British Journal of Sociology*, 46 (1): 63–78.

Travina, Maria 2016. "Citizenship Revocation in Response to the Foreign Fighter Threat," Master Thesis, University of Oslo, Oslo.

Van Den Berghe, Pierre 1981. *The Ethnic Phenomenon*, Westport: Elsevier.

Van der Veer, Peter 1997. "'The Enigma of Arrival': Hybridity and Multiplicity in the Global Space", in *Debating Cultural Hybridity: Multi-Cultural Identities and the Politics of Anti-Racism*, ed. P. Werbner and T. Modood, London: Zed Books, pp. 90–105.

Vertovec, Steven 2002. "Islamophobia and Muslim Recognition in Britain", in *Muslims in the West: From Sojourners to Citizens*, ed. Y. Haddad, Oxford: Oxford University Press, pp. 19–35.

Werbner, Pnina 2002. *Imagined Diasporas Among Manchester Muslims: The Public Performance of Pakistani Transnational Identity Politics*, Oxford: James Currey.

Winter, Elke and Previsic, Ivana 2017. "Citizenship Revocation in the Mainstream Press: A Case of Re-Ethnicization?" *Canadian Journal of Sociology/Cahiers Canadiens de Sociologie*, 42 (1): 55–82.

Part IV
Western values, Muslim migrants and compatibility of identity

Introductory remarks

Abe W. Ata

This section is of the greatest current relevance and covers several areas of investigation. Three of these are national surveys that explore what constitutes compatible and incompatible values of Western cultures and the Muslim community. These are of great interest because the 'objects' of the study are allowed to speak for themselves. It examines the scale and nature of the problem, the issues challenging the two communities and their struggle against apathy, misunderstanding and changing identity. Millns and Dustin (Chapter 13) successfully incorporate an examination of Brexit by situating it within British debates on migration and multi-culturalism. They undertook to reinterpret citizenship and identity in the United Kingdom and Europe following Brexit in mid-2016 when the people of the United Kingdom voted in a referendum narrowly in favour of leaving the European Union. This chapter examines the extent to which people living in the United Kingdom risk being marginalised or discriminated against on the basis of their identity – including their gender, religion, ethnicity and sexual orientation. The contribution critically evaluates the UK's changing 'diversity' agenda since the 1960s – through tolerance, multiculturalism, cohesion and now integration – and discuss how this path has been similar or distinct from other EU member states, as well as the impact of the changing agenda on minorities, their beliefs and values.

In Chapter 14 Ata reports on the sense of compatibility of dual Muslim and Australian identities as perceived by mainstream Australian students. The results are based on a large-scale national survey of attitudes of senior secondary students in private and government schools towards Islam and Muslims. Widespread negative stereotypes and the relatively new presence of the Muslim community in Australia tend to interfere with reconciling the Muslim and 'Australian' identities. Variation in responses between boys and girls, as well as religious and non-religious affiliates also revealed a high level of significance. The findings show Australian non-Muslim students agree that acceptance of Muslims does not come easily in Australia, nor do the school emerge as a site for change.

In another national survey (Chapter 15) Ata assesses how compatible Muslim students perceive of dual Islamic and 'Australian' identities. The results of this five-year-long investigation are based on a field research questionnaire involving 430 students in 10 Muslim high schools. The primary aim of the study was to examine how compatible these students viewed their dual identities as Muslims and Australians. A major finding revealed that the percentage of female participants (57%) recognised that the two identities were harmonious. This was slightly higher than male students (43%). Combined, however, the two groups (93%) declared themselves to be first and foremost Muslim. The findings also reflect a wide spectrum of nuanced responses, with room for further analysis regarding their ultimate adjustment, wellbeing and ease of living in both cultures. Crucially, the survey found that students were equally divided on statements related to the degree to which Muslim students feel integrated in various aspects of the host society in which they have grown.

Postelnicescu (Chapter 16) examines the European Commission's policy on immigration and asylum and the way Germany and France address the issues of integration, tensions, sources of conflict, justice and identity within an emerging diverse society. Comparative remarks are drawn out between these two societies as appropriate. Two main points are specifically addressed within its pages: whether the term 'integration', mandatory or otherwise, infringes on any fundamental rights embraced in these two countries and the legitimacy of the host states to mandate rules of the immigrants' self-identity and perpetuation their cultural and ethnic core values

Moulettes positions her work (Chapter 17) in the realm of immigration, and in particular the discourse of labour market integration. It takes its point of departure in Swedish labour market policy and politicians concerned with how to come to terms with unemployment and how to integrate immigrants into the labour market. With an overall aim to discuss the current labour market policy and how it contributes to transforming unemployed immigrants into commodities, the analysis draws on ideas from critical theory. In doing so, it brings to the surface epistemological misinterpretations and power asymmetries between labour market intermediaries and unemployed immigrants.

In Chapter 18 Ata and Baumann outline selected results of a six-month pilot study leading to a national survey in Germany. The study focused primarily focused on the attitudes, knowledge and perceptions of mainstream university students in Germany towards Islam and Muslims. Over 400 tertiary non-Muslim German students in six universities participated in the survey. Attitudes of Muslim German students to Germany are to be surveyed in a follow-up study for comparative analysis. Widespread negative stereotypes and the relatively new presence of the Muslim refugee community tended to skew the results away from a fairly positive image reserved for the Turkish Muslim community. Variations in responses between male and female students revealed a high level of significance regarding the degree of knowledge and level of tolerance towards German Muslims – less so towards their contribution, acceptance and integration. The findings show German students are generally ignorant about Muslims and Islam, and few believe that schools are filling the gaps in their knowledge. While the majority agree that acceptance of Muslims does not come easily in Germany, the university does not emerge as a site for change.

13 Reinterpretation of citizenship and identity in Britain following Brexit

Susan Millns and Moira Dustin

On 23 June 2016 the people of the United Kingdom voted in a referendum narrowly in favour of leaving the European Union. This historic decision, which will end the UK's more than four-decade-long membership of the EU in 2020, has important consequences for all European citizens, consequences that will be felt far into the future. While some citizens will have the resources to meet the challenges that lie ahead with resilience and will be able to take full advantage of the opportunities that the promised return of national sovereignty and a new form of politics offer, other citizens may be less fortunate and may see the rights and protections offered by the EU starkly withdrawn, leaving them more vulnerable and with diminished horizons and fewer prospects than previously.

This chapter will explore the effects of the Brexit vote in the United Kingdom in the context of citizenship in its multiple forms – national (UK), European and non-European. It will examine the extent to which people living in the United Kingdom risk being marginalised or discriminated against on the basis of their identity – including their gender, religion, ethnicity and sexual orientation. The contribution will critically evaluate the UK's changing 'diversity' agenda since the 1950s – through tolerance, integration, multiculturalism, cohesion and now integration (again). The chapter will examine what this changing agenda has meant for minorities living in the UK. The chapter will further explore the implications of the loss of the protections of EU citizenship to UK nationals and their families post-Brexit and the prospect of the UK closing the doors to EU rules as well as people. The alternative scenario – of the UK being free post Brexit to better promote inclusivity – will also be imagined. Above all, however, Brexit has shown how fractured and un-integrated the UK currently is, with divides crossing fault lines that extend well beyond ethnicity. It is this fracturing of society, and its consequences for post-Brexit Britain, that will be investigated for their implications regarding respect for alternative cultures, beliefs and values.

Background to Brexit

The UK was not a founding member of the European Union (EU). When the European Economic Community (EEC) – the previous incarnation of what is now the EU – was established in 1957, the UK was not one of the original six members. The UK tried to join in the following decade, but its application was twice blocked by then French President Charles de Gaulle before it was finally accepted as a member in 1973 (Mile End Institute 2016; Jones 2007; Armstrong 2017, 9–20). However, UK membership of what became the EU with the signing of the Maastricht Treaty in 1992 has never been uncontested. The UK did not sign up to the EU's common currency of the Euro and join the Euro Zone (Giurlando 2015, chap. 7) and also opted out of the Schengen agreement abolishing border controls between member states (Peers 2015). In UK public discourse, EU membership has long been a political football, with those opposed to membership griping about EU bureaucracy and the Brussels 'gravy train' (Express 2018). A first referendum on EU membership in 1975 resulted in a healthy majority in favour of membership; however, hostility to the EU continued to bubble under, particularly in the Conservative Party where there were strong pro- and anti-EU constituencies (Diamond 2016). In an attempt to resolve the debate once and for all and strengthen his own position, the Conservative Prime Minister David Cameron called a second referendum in 2016, not doubting that the result would be anything other than a vote in favour of remaining.

That result did not happen. After an unconvincing campaign by 'remainers' and a strong campaign that many argued was based on falsehoods by the 'Brexiteers', on 23 June 2016, the UK electorate voted narrowly in favour of leaving the EU (Clarke, Goodwin, and Whiteley 2017, 146–74). In the months following the referendum it became clear that the new Conservative government led by Theresa May had no strategy for exiting the EU and also that the ramifications of EU membership were more extensive than many people had realised, continuing funding of and engagement with the EU's Galileo satellite programme being only one example of many disputed areas (The Guardian 2018; BBC 2018).

Like EU membership, multiculturalism in the UK has never been universally welcomed, as we discuss further later in the chapter. However, while the full impact that Brexit will have for minorities and marginalised communities and individuals has yet to be felt, a lack of representation was visible in the debate leading up to the referendum, with little recognition of the specific concerns of women and sexual and gender minorities (Dustin, Ferreira, and Millns Forthcoming). And what many argued were myths about migration dominated the political campaign, with a notable low point being the UK Independence Party's (UKIP) poster with the words 'Breaking point' and 'We must break free of the EU and take back control' superimposed over a picture of a crowd of young non-European men lining up, presumably to enter the EU. Equally, there were few women's voices and little discussion of women's interests in the run-up to the referendum; after the vote, concerns were raised about the gender imbalance of the UK's negotiating team (BBC 2017).

The voting breakdown is widely accepted as putting cleavages across the UK's population into sharp relief. Put in crudely simplistic terms, older people, men, people in rural areas and people in the North of England and Wales were more likely or certainly perceived as being more likely to have voted for Brexit than the young, women, voters in metropolitan areas and Scottish and Northern Irish voters (Clarke, Goodwin, and Whiteley 2017; European Institute 2017; Becker, Fetzer, and Novy 2017). The majority support in Scotland and Northern Ireland for remaining in the EU is particularly problematic (Hughes and Hayward 2018). Scotland had its own referendum on independence in 2014, and while a majority favoured remaining part of the UK, Scottish politics are very different from those of Westminster in key areas where devolution has occurred: the Scottish government is far more committed to human rights and also to the rights of refugees and migrants, and Scotland has a refugee integration strategy (Scottish Government, COSLA, and Scottish Refugee Council 2018) and an action plan on human rights that sets it apart from the rest of Great Britain (Scottish Human Rights Commission 2013). The politics of Northern Ireland are even more critical for the process of disengaging from the EU. Following many years of violence and political upheaval, peace was achieved in 1998 through the Good Friday Agreement and the establishment of a power-sharing assembly. The threat that a hard border between Northern Ireland and (Southern) Ireland – a separate EU member state – will be reintroduced through Brexit is seen as a particularly insurmountable problem in the Brexit negotiations (Gormley-Heenan and Aughey 2017; Boffey 2018).

While superficial, this overview of the history and context for the EU referendum provides the basis for more detailed consideration of the implications for UK citizenship.

Developing multiculturalism in the UK

The birth of the EU (although not UK membership of it) broadly coincides with the period when immigration because politicised in UK politics and the start of a series of policy and public discourse centred on how to manage relations between majority and minority communities. In the immediate period after the Second World War, there was no discussion of multiculturalism or diversity; it was through policies concerning 'race' and immigration that black and Asian people were problematised, either as victims of racism or as the perpetrators of unwelcome immigration. And it is here we see the beginning of two policy paths – immigration controls concerned with restricting the number of black, Asian and minority ethnic (BAME) people entering the UK and what were originally called race relations policies that set out to improve community relations. While the terminology has gone through a number of changes since the 1950s, the imperatives of keeping (specific) people out and controlling the behaviour of (specific) people here remains.

Legislation on immigration and race is a relatively recent phenomenon, most of it dating back only as far as the period after the Second World War, when people from the Caribbean were encouraged to come to the UK to meet the need for labour by filling low-paid positions in the health service, transport system and manufacturing (Modood et al. 1997; Anwar and Bakhsh 2003). Up to the early 1960s, the entry right of the UK's colonial and Commonwealth subjects was accepted, but the 1960s saw the beginning of immigration controls, with the 1962 and 1968 Commonwealth Immigrants Act placing restrictions on primary migration (Hansen 2000, 251; Alibhai-Brown 1999). The 1971 Immigration Act contained further measures denying black members of the Commonwealth the right to settle in the UK. In 1972, the Ugandan government announced the expulsion of 50,000 Asians, most of whom had British passports. Sections of the British press and some local authorities put pressure on the British government to prevent a 'flood' of Ugandan refugees: in Leicester and Ealing, local authorities placed adverts in the media discouraging Ugandan Asians from moving to their areas(Alibhai-Brown 1999). The UK government accepted the exiles, after first asking other countries to share the 'burden'. It was subsequently recognised that this was a group of people with a great deal to contribute to British society and the economy, but the initial portrayal of the 'crisis' suggested that the UK must protect itself from 'swamping' by immigrants, setting a pattern for similar 'crises' in the future.

In the 1980s and 1990s, restrictive immigration controls increasingly focused on asylum seekers and refugees, and partners and relatives of people already resident in the UK. Despite opposing Conservative measures when in opposition, on its election in 1997, New Labour also stressed the need for a 'strong' immigration policy. Legislation continued the trend of viewing asylum as an illegitimate means of entry to the UK, rather than an ethical and legal obligation under international law. A new preoccupation with combating terrorism was reflected in a series of laws that many perceived as stigmatising Muslim communities and undermining civil liberties, including the Prevention of Terrorism Act (2005) and the Terrorism Act (2006).

The impact of European treaties and regulations should also be recognised. On the one hand, the UK's membership in the EU meant engagement with the movement towards 'fortress Europe' even while the UK opted out of full integration with member states in the area of free movement through the Schengen Agreement, which still requires border checks of EU nationals passing into the UK. Yet European law, along with the European Convention on Human Rights, has also acted as the catalyst for some of the key progressive anti-discrimination and human rights measures in the UK, including the Human Rights Act 1998 and new equality laws such as the Equality Act 2010 (Dustin, Ferreira, and Millns Forthcoming).

In the early years of mass immigration, it was assumed that new arrivals would be 'tolerated' because they would be easily assimilated into mainstream society. Immigrants would give up the distinctive aspects of their culture in favour of British values and traditions. They would be absorbed into the mainstream to the point where they no longer stood out. Assimilation was believed to be in everyone's interests: it meant that black and white Britons would be treated equally – in a 'colour-blind' sense – under the law, and by losing the characteristics that differentiated them, the new immigrants would find it easier to fit in and find work and housing. The erosion of cultural differences was also seen as necessary for social cohesion. Assimilation was also politically uncontroversial in that it made little or no demands on the majority population in terms of a change in attitudes or values (Poulter 1998).

While the first wave of immigrants from the Caribbean shared a language and often a religion with white British society, from the mid-1960s there were an increasing number of immigrants from the Indian subcontinent – Muslims, Hindus and Sikhs – whose lifestyle was more visibly different from that of white Britons (Poulter 1998). It was from this date that there was a shift towards a more pluralist – initially called integrationist – position, marked by the then Home Secretary Roy Jenkins's rejection of the US idea of a cultural melting pot: 'I define integration, therefore, not as a flattening process of assimilation, but as equal opportunity, coupled with cultural diversity in an atmosphere of mutual tolerance' (Jenkins 1970, 267).

Cultural pluralism or integration involved more initiative on the part of the state or the host community than assimilation but remained a reactive position. The two Race Relations Acts of the 1960s and 1970s contained measures against direct and indirect discrimination, but it was not until the 1980s that equal opportunities policies and training became the norm in local authority and voluntary organisations. It was only with the Race Relations (Amendment) Act of 2000 that a positive duty to promote equality was established. In the meantime, recognition of minority identity was limited to matters of food and dress, with legislation exempting Jews and Muslims from general requirements on slaughtering animals and exempting Sikhs from the requirement to wear a crash helmet (to accommodate their turbans).

As a description of policy, multiculturalism first emerged in relation to education. In the 1970s, assimilationist language was replaced by an emphasis on 'integration' and then on 'multiculturalism' or what was known as 'multi-racial education'(Tomlinson 2008; Tierney 1982; Modood and May 2001; "Education for All. Report of the Committee of Enquiry into the Education of Children from Ethnic Minority Groups (The Swann Report)" 1985). This phase marked a move from equality of treatment to equality based on need. The multicultural approach, as expressed in educational policy in the 1980s, was seen as soft and ineffectual by many, assuming that children should be taught about these different and discrete cultures and that knowledge of differences would lead to racial harmony. It was a version of the 'cultural supermarket' school of multicultural politics still evident today, in which difference equates to exotic food and dress and is the cause for endless celebration.

However, black and Asian feminists criticised multiculturalism from a different perspective, seeing it as privileging patriarchal leaders of minority communities and empowering them in certain areas – specifically relating to the family – in ways that disadvantaged women:

> Multiculturalism . . . is based on an assumption – not always explicit – that minorities can be given limited autonomy over internal 'community' affairs, such as religious observance, dress, food, and other supposedly 'non-political' matters, including the social control of women, without their presence offering any major challenge to the basic framework of social, economic and political relations in society.
>
> (Ali 1998; see also Sahgal 2004)

Under the Conservative governments of Margaret Thatcher and John Major between 1979 and 1997, multiculturalism had a low profile and was most evident in the development of equal opportunities policies on race and gender in local government and the voluntary sector (Hesse 2000). Multiculturalism remained the unchallenged description of British society in the early years of New Labour, although still with little theoretical underpinning. However, following unrest in the northern English towns of Bradford, Burnley and Oldham in the summer of 2001, in which white and Asian communities clashed, the government-commissioned Cantle Report suggested that segregated communities were undermining social cohesion (Home Office 2001). The report was highly influential in the development of a community cohesion agenda and the creation of a Community Cohesion Unit in the Home Office. Under David Blunkett, home secretary from 2001 to 2004, cohesion concerns took the form of focusing on citizenship and how to engender a sense of 'Britishness' in minorities as well as majorities. Proficiency in English language and citizenship classes and ceremonies were the concrete means of doing this. In terms of the values or principles that might be binding for British citizens, it proved more difficult to find something uniquely British.

In the early twenty-first century, the view that multiculturalism as a policy model was not working took hold across western European countries (Dustin 2006, 3). In the UK, it was – perhaps surprisingly – the chair of the Commission for Racial Equality who questioned the concept in a speech widely interpreted as arguing for the end of multiculturalism (The Guardian 2004). The speech and his further comments suggested that multiculturalism could mean different communities sharing the same space but leading entirely separate lives.

Several phenomena contributed to this questioning of multiculturalism: the fallout of American's 'war on terrorism' in terms of increasing Islamophobia and the 'disturbances' in the north of England during the summer of 2001 are two of the more obvious, leading to a perceived need to make Britain's Muslim community feel part of wider British society, while at the same time stamping out 'rogue' fundamentalist or terrorist elements within that community threatening the project. there was also recognition that, after forty years of equality legislation, racism and racial violence persisted and statistics showed continuing inequality in terms of employment, housing, health and education according to ethnic origin (Anwar and Bakhsh 2003; Runnymede Trust 2008).

After the red herring of Prime Minister David Cameron's promise of a shared spirit of national identity through the concept of 'Big Society'(BBC News 2010) – which unfortunately coincided with swinging public sector cuts and the perception that the rich were retreating into their citadels in response to recession, cohesion in turn lost favour with a return to the language of integration under the coalition and Conservative governments of the early twenty-first century. In a green paper for an Integrated Communities Strategy published in 2018, the prime minister claimed that 'Britain is one of the world's most successful multiethnic, multi-faith societies' and that on leaving the EU, we will 'seize the opportunity to create the kind of country we want to be: a global, outward-looking, connected nation, at ease with itself and others, built on the backbone of strong, integrated communities' (Ministry of Housing, Communities and Local Government 2018).

European citizenship

UK membership in the European Union, however, brought with it different issues around the migration and integration of people from different European states and with different cultural backgrounds. The status of European Union citizenship was introduced with the Treaty on European Union, which entered into force in 1993 with the aim of moving from a purely economic union to one that had a more political dimension. The status of EU citizen is conferred on all nationals of the EU member states and brings with it a number of key rights. These include the right to stand and to vote in municipal elections and in the European Parliament elections while resident in any member state in the same way as nationals of that member state. The most useful of the citizenship rights though is the right of citizens to move and freely reside in the territory of any of the member states.

While initially the idea of EU citizenship tended to reflect the economic parameters of the Union facilitating the possibility for economically active migrants to move and freely reside in other member states, mirroring provisions on the free movement of workers and those who sought to establish a business or provide services in another member state, through the interventions of the Court of Justice of the EU, we have begun to see a more expansive interpretation of citizenship rights broadening into a larger European commitment to social solidarity and social citizenship across the member states (Ross and Borgmann-Prebil 2010).

The Court of Justice was particularly active in expanding the entitlements of EU free movers. For example, there was the early case of Martinez Sala[1] in which a Spanish national resident in Germany, who had not worked there for many years because of her childcare responsibilities, was able to rely upon a combination of the prohibition on nationality discrimination contained in Article 18 of the Treaty on the Functioning of the EU and the citizenship provisions in Article 20 in the same treaty to gain equal access to a German child-raising benefit. Hence, as an EU citizen (and for the first time), she was able to claim equality of treatment even though she was not economically active and solely dependent on welfare. Commentators suggested that the application of the non-discrimination principle and citizenship provisions in the treaty 'gives something close to a universal right of access to all manner of welfare benefits to all those who are Union citizens and who are lawfully resident in a member state' (Shaw 2000, 222) and decoupled economic activity from citizenship entitlements which had previously been required in order for the principle of non-discrimination to apply (O'Leary 1999, 77–78).

The development of case law in this direction began to trouble national governments and evidently some (UK) citizens. Notably, public discourse turned to accusations of welfare tourism and the suspicion that EU nationals from some members states were moving to other states where welfare provision was better than at home (see Thym 2015). The development of this anxiety was linked also to the relatively generous (compared to domestic UK law) interpretation of EU law around the concept of family members and those entitled to move and reside with the EU citizen free mover. Thus ascendants and descendants would benefit from the possibility of moving with an EU citizen even if the family members were themselves so-called third country nationals (i.e. from a state outside of the European Union). A further development which unsteadied national governments came with the case of Zambrano in which the third country national parents of two EU citizen children born in Belgium were also accorded a right to stay in the EU despite in this case there being no question of movement.[2] The court found that without their primary carers, the rights of the children as EU citizens would be meaningless and thus third country nationals gained residency rights on the back of the citizenship rights of their children.

The increase in migration from both inside and outside the EU (based legitimately on the EU's free movement provisions) is one of the key factors behind the UK's decision to leave the EU. Migration was used in the Brexit campaign to prompt voters to express a decision to leave the EU based upon concerns about increased pressure on public services, including education, welfare, housing and health care services. Little attempt was made to distinguish between legal and illegal migration and between the position of EU nationals and those of non-EU member states.

With the Brexit vote, though, comes the loss of EU citizenship rights for all EU nationals, including British citizens living in other parts of the EU as well as non-UK nationals living in Britain. This loss of citizenship rights is just one of the most obvious consequences of Brexit. It is likely to be accompanied by the loss of the many other protections afforded by EU law which may disappear in areas such as employment law, environmental law and consumer law, as well as the loss of the human rights set out in the EU's Charter of Fundamental Rights. Minorities, women, children, the elderly and the vulnerable are the potential losers in this scenario since they often lack the means to provide for themselves and are dependent upon the protections of the law to sustain their daily lives (see Dustin, Ferreira, and Millns 2019, Forthcoming). With reports of a rise in hate crime after the Brexit vote, it is clear that anti-minority sentiments are running high and this, it is feared, will continue into 2020 when the UK actually leaves the EU with the inevitable surge of nationalism that this will bring (Justice Inspectorates 2018).

Conclusion

The vote to leave the EU takes the UK in a different direction from its European neighbours in terms of national identity, most obviously because on leaving the EU, Britons will no longer be both UK and EU citizens. From the perspective of minorities and marginalised individuals and communities, the framework of rights post Brexit looks vulnerable. While the EU began as an economic body, its remit extended to cover many areas of social policy – one of the reasons why Brexiters were so concerned to 'take back control' in the first place. EU regulations on equality and human rights in particular have enhanced the rights of women and minorities in areas from employment law to access to goods and services. While many of the protections for citizens that originally derived from the EU are now embedded in UK law, outside the EU framework, they will be dependent on the political will of whichever party happens to be in government. As we saw earlier in relation to multiculturalism, this results in policies and legislation in a state of flux. And while there may be opportunities for the UK to forge ahead with a new social justice agenda embracing women, ethnic and religious minorities, disabled people and others who experience discrimination, this seems unlikely. Those who have campaigned most strongly for leaving the EU have done so on the basis of the opportunities it will bring for restricting some people's rights – specifically the rights of people outside the UK to become British citizens and residents. Moreover, the reality is that the process of disengagement from the EU will occupy civil servants for years to come, and in fact one positive outcome of this is the current government has lost sight of its manifesto commitment to replace the UK's Human Rights Act which incorporates the European Convention on Human Rights (derived from the Council of Europe rather than the EU).

The concern from the perspective of citizenship and accompanying rights for both majorities and minorities is the removal of the building blocks of equality and rights. As we said earlier, policies on multiculturalism and integration have been used as political footballs, varying according to the whims of successive governments. The heavy bureaucracy associated with Brussels at least means that frameworks and regulations take longer to develop but have a degree of permanency once established. Social justice movements in the UK, working with and on behalf of people disadvantaged on diverse grounds, rightly fear that the individual and community rights associated with citizenship and European human rights law may very soon be in jeopardy.

Notes

1 Case C-85/96 *Martinez Sala* v *Freistaat Bayern* [1998] ECR I-2691.
2 Case C-34/09 *Ruiz Zambrano* [2011] ECR I-1177.

References

Ali, Yasmin. 1998. "Muslim Women and the Politics of Ethnicity and Culture in Northern England." Women Living Under Muslim Laws Dossier 20.

Alibhai-Brown, Yasmin. 1999. *True Colours: Attitudes to Multiculturalism and the Role of the Government*. London: Institute for Public Policy Research.

Anwar, Muhammad, and Qadir Bakhsh. 2003. *British Muslims and State Policies*. Warwick: Centre for Research in Ethnic Relations.

Armstrong, Kenneth A. 2017. *Brexit Time: Leaving the EU – Why, How and When?* Cambridge: Cambridge University Press. https://doi.org/10.1017/9781108233385.

BBC. 2010. "Cameron Launches 'Big Society'." *BBC News*, July 19, Sec. UK Politics. www.bbc.com/news/uk-10680062.

———. 2017. "Call for More Women in UK's Brexit Team." *BBC News*, July 18, Sec. UK Politics. www.bbc.com/news/40646586.

———. 2018. "UK Wants £1bn Galileo Costs Back from EU." *BBC News*, May 24, Sec. UK Politics. www.bbc.com/news/uk-politics-44232269.

Becker, Sascha O., Thiemo Fetzer, and Dennis Novy. 2017. "Who Voted for Brexit? A Comprehensive District-Level Analysis." *Economic Policy* 32 (92): 601–50. https://doi.org/10.1093/epolic/eix012.

Boffey, Daniel. 2018. "Northern Ireland Papers: No Simple Solution to Hard Border, Say UK Officials." *The Guardian*, April 25, Sec. UK News. www.theguardian.com/uk-news/2018/apr/25/northern-ireland-papers-no-simple-solution-to-hard-border.

Clarke, Harold D., Matthew Goodwin, and Paul Whiteley. 2017. *Brexit: Why Britain Voted to Leave the European Union*. Cambridge: Cambridge University Press. https://doi.org/10.1017/9781316584408.

Diamond, Patrick. 2016. "The Conservative Party and Brexit." UK in a Changing Europe (blog), October 4. http://ukandeu.ac.uk/the-conservative-party-and-brexit/.

Dustin, Moira. 2006. "Gender Equality, Cultural Diversity: European Comparisons and Lessons." London School of Economics/the Nuffield Foundation. http://sro.sussex.ac.uk/64051/1/NuffieldReport_final.pdf.

Dustin, Moira, Ferreira, Nuno and Millns, Susan, eds. (2019) *Gender and Queer Perspectives on Brexit*. Palgrave Macmillan.

Dustin, Moira, Nuno Ferreira, and Susan Millns, eds. Forthcoming. *Feminist and Queer Perspectives on Brexit*. Palgrave Macmillan.

"Education for All. Report of the Committee of Enquiry into the Education of Children from Ethnic Minority Groups (The Swann Report)." 1985. Department for Education and Science.

European Institute. 2017. "Mind the Gap. Brexit the Generational Divide." London School of Economics. www.lse.ac.uk/europeanInstitute/events/Images/Mind-the-Gap-Brexit-the-Generational-Divide.pdf.

Express. 2018. "EU News: Brussels Train to Strasbourg Breaks down Leaving MEPs Stranded." June 11. www.express.co.uk/news/world/972662/eu-european-union-parliament-meps-stranded-brussels-train-to-strasbourg-gravy-train.

Giurlando, Philip. 2015. *Eurozone Politics: Perception and Reality in Italy, the UK, and Germany*. New York and London: Routledge.

Gormley-Heenan, Cathy, and Arthur Aughey. 2017. "Northern Ireland and Brexit: Three Effects on 'the Border in the Mind', Northern Ireland and Brexit: Three Effects on 'the Border in the Mind'." *The British Journal of Politics and International Relations* 19 (3): 497–511. https://doi.org/10.1177/1369148117711060.

The Guardian. 2004. "Race Chief Blasts Homophobia." April 25. www.theguardian.com/society/2004/apr/25/gayrights.britishidentityandsociety.

———. 2018. "May's Plan 'Sticks in the Throat', Says Boris Johnson as He Resigns Over Brexit." July 9. www.theguardian.com/politics/2018/jul/09/boris-johnson-resigns-as-foreign-secretary-brexit.

Hansen, Randall. 2000. *Citizenship and Immigration in Post-War Britain: The Institutional Origins of a Multicultural Nation*. Oxford and New York: Oxford University Press.

Hesse, Barnor. 2000. *Un/Settled Multiculturalisms: Diasporas, Entanglements, "Transruptions."* London: Zed Books.

Home Office. 2001. "Community Cohesion: A Report of the Independent Review Team Chaired by Ted Cantle." www.researchgate.net/publication/239466847_Community_Cohesion_a_Report_of_the_Independent_Review_Team.

Hughes, Kirsty, and Katy Hayward. 2018. "Brexit, Northern Ireland and Scotland: Comparing Political Dynamics and Prospects in the Two 'Remain' Areas." Scottish Centre on European Relations (SCER). www.scer.scot/database/ident-6308.

Jenkins, Roy. 1970. *Essays and Speeches*. Edited by Anthony Lester. N. I. edition. Glasgow: HarperCollins Distribution Services.

Jones, Alistair. 2007. *Britain and the European Union: Politics Study Guides*. Edinburgh: Edinburgh University Press. www.jstor.org/stable/10.3366/j.ctt1bgzdn1.

Justice Inspectorates. 2018. "Understanding the Difference – The Initial Police Response to Hate Crime." www.justiceinspectorates.gov.uk/hmicfrs/wp-content/uploads/understanding-the-difference-the-initial-police-response-to-hate-crime.pdf.

Mile End Institute. 2016. "Britain and the European Union: Lessons from History." Mile End Institute, Queen Mary University of London. http://ukandeu.ac.uk/wp-content/uploads/2016/04/Mile-End-Institute-publication-from-UKEU-conference.pdf.

Ministry of Housing, Communities & Local Government. 2018. "Integrated Communities Strategy Green Paper." www.gov.uk/government/consultations/integrated-communities-strategy-green-paper.

Modood, Tariq, Richard Berthoud, Jane Lakey, James Nazroo, Patten Smith, Satnam Virdee, and Sharon Beishon. 1997. "Ethnic Minorities in Britain: Diversity and Disadvantage. The Fourth National Survey of Ethnic Minorities." Policy Studies Institute Publications. www.researchcatalogue.esrc.ac.uk/grants/R000234440/outputs/read/2d815477-8f39-4495-8fa5-65eb7400cf5a.

Modood, Tariq, and Stephen May. 2001. "Multiculturalism and Education in Britain: An Internally Contested Debate." *International Journal of Educational Research* 35 (3): 305–17. https://doi.org/10.1016/S0883-0355(01)00026-X.

O'Leary, Siofra. 1999. "Putting Flesh on the Bones of European Union Citizenship." *European Law Review* 24: 68.

Peers, Steve. 2015. "The UK and the Schengen System." UK in a Changing Europe, December 3. http://ukandeu.ac.uk/the-uk-and-the-schengen-system/.

Poulter, Sebastian. 1998. *Ethnicity, Law and Human Rights: The English Experience*. Oxford: Oxford University Press.

Ross, Malcolm, and Borgmann-Prebil, Yuri, eds. 2010. *Promoting Solidarity in the European Union*. Oxford: Oxford University Press.

Runnymede Trust. 2008. *The Future of Multi-Ethnic Britain: The Parekh Report*. Main edition. London: Profile Books Ltd.

Sahgal, Gita. 2004. "Two Cheers for Multiculturalism." Warning Signs of Fundamentalisms.

Scottish Government, COSLA, and Scottish Refugee Council. 2018. "New Scots Refugee Integration Strategy 2018–2022," 84.

Scottish Human Rights Commission. 2013. "Scotland's National Action Plan for Human Rights." ww.snaprights.info/.

Shaw, Jo. 2000. "The European Union and Gender Mainstreaming: Constitutionally Embedded or Comprehensively Marginalised?" *Feminist Legal Studies* 10: 213.

Thym, Daniel. 2015. "The Elusive Limits of Solidarity: Residence Rights of and Social Benefits for Economically Inactive Union Citizens." *Common Market Law Review* 52: 17.

Tierney, J. 1982. *Race, Migration and Schooling*. Eastbourne: Holt, Rinehart and Winston.

Tomlinson, Sally. 2008. *Race and Education: Policy and Politics in Britain*. Berkshire: McGraw-Hill Education (UK).

14 Compatibility of Muslim and Australian identities as viewed by non-Muslim Australian students

A national survey

Abe W. Ata

Since mass immigration to Australia began after the World War II, official policy has passed through several phases. In the 1950s the aim was 'assimilation' when migrants would become Australian as quickly as possible and to that end were dubbed 'New Australians'. By the 1960s native Australians were more accepting and 'integration' was officially the goal, but the authorities 'still sought social cohesion but more gently' (Hirst, 2016, p. 160). And by the 1970s a more socially relaxed Australia was ready to embrace difference, and 'multiculturalism' became the catchword.

Australia is now entering a new phase, but one for which there is no ready policy nostrum. Now the issue is not what 'Old Australians' demand of the New, but what New Australians (or, more likely, some of their descendants) demand of the Old Australia. And Australia is not alone in confronting this issue, of course; it is a global phenomenon.

Encounters on a large scale between the Christian and other sections of mainstream Australia and Muslims have become a reality only recently. Social media are abuzz with daily articles asking the same questions: Do Muslims find it harder than other migrants to integrate, or is it the bigotry of some that perpetuates it? Is Islamophobia the flipside of the inherent racism that some Australians released in stages against Aboriginals, Greeks, Italians, Chinese, Africans, and Middle Easterners – both Christian and Muslim? Or perhaps it is the cultural and historical (and religious) differences between the Christian and Muslim communities globally that are too wide to make a complete reconciliation? Why do religious minorities in Muslim countries have fewer rights than Muslims do in Western societies? Do Muslims need reform and reflection similar to those of Catholic priests? Are Muslim and Australian identities compatible with one another, or are they mutually exclusive? And lastly, are the schools doing enough in fostering goodwill and inter-communal relationships? (Bastian, Lusher and Ata, 2012; Ata and Batrouney, 1989)

That said, a recent grievance about the way mainstream Australians are being 'taken for a ride by the growing number of Muslim and other people who exploit the benefits and goodwill of the very country they might live in but refuse to join', was pointed out in a major headline 'Community turns a blind eye to changes in our culture: Biting the hand that feeds you'. The writer, Peta Credlin, remarks that

> things have got so bad in NSW that they passed a special law a year or so ago to deal with the growing numbers of Muslim men (and now women) refusing to acknowledge the jurisdiction of the court and show necessary respect to the bench. . . . Despite the concessions, Mrs Elzahed refused to remove her veil and also refused to stand when the judge entered the room, because, as her legal counsel explained, she stood only for 'Allah'.
>
> (The Heraldsun, Dec. 11th, 2016, p. 31)

The mainstream community at large may differ on the nature, causes, and consequences of vulnerability and volatility of such youngsters and on their implications for policy, but there remains much common ground, particularly on why 'unease' and potential radicalism happens and who is most at risk. What are some common elements in the experiences of most people who have become disenchanted in Australia, regardless of their beliefs or motivations? To the mainstream Australian society, composed of both Anglo and non-Anglo Australian born, expressions of opinion – acceptance, concerns, or criticism of their lifestyle – is often driven by patriotism, separation, in-group protection, lack of knowledge, cultural centricism, or a combination thereof. To them, an environment that separates the religious and secular identities is a cultural and political given. The mainstream community may have been influenced by Christian values, but unlike citizens of Muslim countries and broadly, including Christian minorities from the Middle East – Lebanese, Palestinians, Jordanians, Egyptians, Iraqis, and others – their identity is not exchangeable with a religious affiliation.

In two recent reports by the Pew Research Centre (2006, 2008) the opinions held in several European countries by the two communities – Muslim and Christian – were found to vary markedly except for a fundamental variable: Muslims were decidedly found to be more positive than the general public in their adopted country about the way things are going for them and their future, but many worried about the future of Muslims in their country of origin. Their greatest concern was unemployment. Islamic extremism emerged as the number two concern. The majority do not regard most non-Muslims as hostile towards Muslims (Ata, 2014, 2009).

Others, however, believe that the majority of European (and arguably by implication Australia) Muslims are neither well integrated nor radicalised (Rabasa and Benard, 2014). They point out that for the minority amongst the second generation who are disaffected, some find it difficult to live within either the traditional culture of their parents or the modern Western culture where they reside. Extremist ideologies offer a new identity that allows the individual to identify with an imagined worldwide community.

Benard (2015), who has written widely on political Islam, posits that the Islamic violence is on the rise. She points out with equivocation:

> What we lumped together as moderates includes what we might better have termed aggressive traditionalists, people who believe that Muslims living in the West must struggle to remain external to Western values and lifestyles, and should owe little or no loyalty to Western institutions and persons. They might be against violence, but they are also against integration. Divided loyalties can cause individuals to stay silent when they notice suspicious activity in their neighbourhood or family or social circle.
>
> (Rabasa and Benard, 2014, pp. 1–2)

The present study is concerned with understanding what may constitute compatible and incompatible values between mainstream Australians and the Muslim community as perceived by Australian students nationally. It is also aimed at exploring the scale and nature of the problem and how we are able predict the drivers behind it. Indeed, we will look behind those walls and explore the issues challenging the mainstream Australian community and their struggle against apathy, misunderstanding, and integrating the Muslim community with Western values and lifestyle mannerisms.

Survey method and sample characteristics

The participants are 1000 students in 20 secondary schools around Muslim Australians (excluding the Northern Territory and Western Australia[1]) who were administered a full-length survey[2] examining general attitudes towards Muslims and Islam. Participating students were from Years 10–12 (Ata, 2016b).

Table 14.1 Survey participant characteristics by gender (N = 1000)

			Female (n = 655)	*Male (n = 340)*	*TOTAL*
Language	English only		518	289	807
	Other/English and Other		136	50	186
Religion	Christian		490	259	749
	Non-religious		152	74	226
Do you have Muslim friends?		Yes	171	45	216
		No	482	293	775
School Type	Private		569	311	880
	State		86	29	115
	Coeducational		385	320	705
	Girls only		270	0	270
	Boys only		0	20	20
Year Level	10		21	11	33
	11		329	219	548
	12		295	107	402

The sample consisted of just under half boys (43 per cent) and over half girls (57 per cent). This may be because among single-sex schools, girls' schools were slightly more likely to agree to participate than were boys' schools. We found that the principals of boys' schools were more inclined than those of girls' schools to think the survey might disturb school harmony. About half the sample came from Catholic schools (53 per cent), and roughly a quarter each from other Christian schools (26 per cent) and non-denominational schools (21 per cent). The predominance of Catholic students was a consequence of the relative reluctance of state schools to participate.

Discussion

Favourable attitudes towards the Muslim community

When asked what they liked most about Muslim Australians, just under two-thirds offered a comment of some kind (Figure 14.1). Some 44% gave positive comments: 4% alluded to courage, often with a mention of the difficult time Muslims have in Australia; 10% saw Muslims as being just like other Australians; and 30% gave other positive comments. Some 17% of respondents

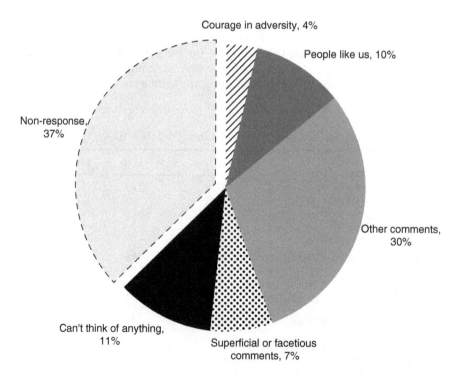

Figure 14.1 Responses to question 'What do you like most about Muslim Australians?'

Note: Apparent errors in addition are due to rounding N = 2023 *(inc. non-response)*

gave superficial or facetious comments (7%) or explicitly stated that they could not think of anything they 'liked most about Muslims' (not to be confused with non-response, which might signify simply lack of motivation to respond). Just over a third of respondents (37%) gave no response.

Box 14.1   Selected responses to the question 'What do you like most about Muslim Australians?'

Courage in adversity: Copping it both ways . . . they survive prejudice/racism in Australia and they suffer solemnly at their country home.

- **People like us:** . . . they are normal and we are all different. Most like Australia and respect other culture and religions. Isn't this multiculturalism.

  I like their bravery, courage, being honest about peace; they are friendly and give everything for being religious.

- **Superficial or facetious comment:** I don't know anything about them so how the hell will I know.

  I like their curry and kebabs. They have funny accent

- **Other comments:** I don't think Australians have close families who stick to each other like them. They can also be cool and very generous when you visit them. . . . even open the door to strangers.

  The innocent Muslims are OK. I have a Muslim friend, really generous, and cool, confident and well mannered. I like them and treat them just as I want to be treated.

  I am really not phased. I don't judge them by their looks or culture, that's my view.

  They have nice skin; their falafel; No one particular aspect; they are people; they don't speak to me; the way they say "Peace upon Him'; they don't underestimate themselves; I don't know anything about them so how the hell will I know; I like their curry and kebabs; They have funny accent.

Unfavourable attitudes towards the Muslim community

When asked what they liked least about Muslim Australians, just under two-thirds offered a comment of some kind (Figure 14.2). Some 27% mentioned terrorism: 8% alluded to the poor media image[3] of Muslims; 5% alluded to threats to the Australian way of life; and 9% stressed the strangeness of Muslims. Some 7% of respondents gave ambivalent comments of some kind

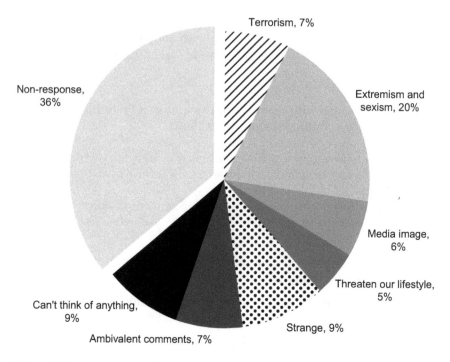

Figure 14.2 Responses to the question 'What do you like least about Muslim Australians?'

(7%), and 9% explicitly stated that they could not think of anything they 'liked least about Muslim Australians' (not to be confused with not to be confused with non-response, which might signify simply lack of motivation to respond). Just over a third of respondents (37%) gave no response.

Box 14.2   Selected responses to the question 'What do you like least about Muslim Australians?'

- **Terrorism:** They are all wrong. All this terrorism stuff happened because of Muslims. They just look really filthy.
- **Extremism and sexism:** The way they treat women, women's clothes, over the top, violence, ruthless, how they believe killing is a good thing.
- **Media image:** The way media portrays them, and the way all of us are sucked in bouncing off what we hear about them again and again. There is bad in every culture.

- **Threaten our lifestyle:** . . . frightening our culture and not wanting to assimilate cause they don't live by the rule lifestyle etc, riots and everything, they should go back home.
- **Strange:** The way they stare at you and their attitude to parties or school camps. They don't want to assimilate or be social like Italians or Greeks.
- **Ambivalent comments:** Because they . . . wear heavy clothes.
- I have not met any. I don't know them well enough to know and judge them badly. . . . There is bad in every culture. This questionnaire is racist. For one hundred years Australian schools used to play Xmas carols, this does not happen anymore. WHY? Next, will do Easter, then Sunday as a rest day.

So far we have explored the attitudes of the sample as a whole. But does this mask differences within the sample? For instance, do boys differ systematically from girls in their attitudes towards Islam and Muslims? To answer this and similar questions, participants were asked to rate their agreement with 23 statements (Figure 14.3) on a 5-point scale.[4]

On most questions between a third and a half of the sample was neutral, indicating that they neither agreed nor disagreed with the statement. This could signify honest ignorance of the issues or alternatively laziness. However, there was a significant overlap of respondents who gave 'Don't know' responses to the various knowledge questions and those who gave 'Neutral' responses to the attitude questions. This shows that 'Neutral' attitudes are statistically associated with ignorance of Islam and Muslims and could therefore be a consequence of it.

Significant differences were found between the responses of boys and girls. These findings show that boys were broadly less accepting of Muslims and Islam than were girls. Boys and girls differed significantly on the statements (Table 14.2). Interestingly, boys agreed more than girls with the statement *Most Muslims treat women with less respect than do other Australians* – clearly a view not founded in direct experience.

Similarly, significant differences were found between the respondents according to their religious affiliation (or lack of one). With many statements, there was a strong tendency for the two Christian groups – Catholics and other Christians – to resemble each other and to differ from the non-religious (Table 14.3).

On two statements, all three religious affiliations differed significantly from each other:

- On the statement *Muslims threaten the Australian way of life*, all disagreed, but to different degrees: non-religious most, Catholics next, other Christians least.

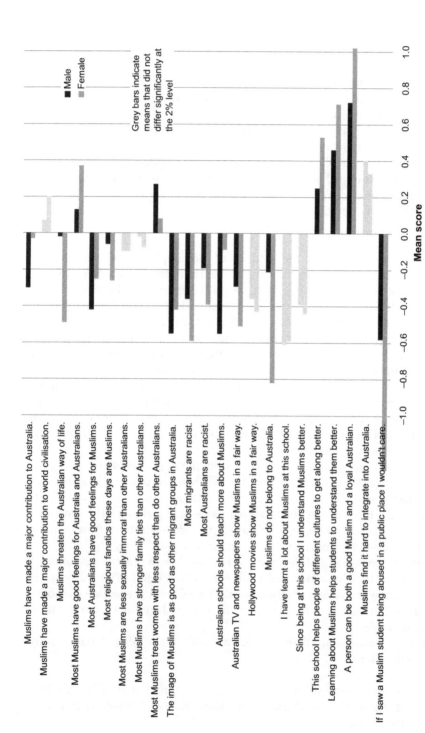

Figure 14.3 Mean attitude scores by gender

Table 14.2 Differences in attitudinal response concerning Muslims between male and female students

Girls agreed more than boys regarding:	Boys agreed more than girls regarding:
Most Muslims have good feelings for Australia and Australians.	Most Muslims treat women with less respect than do other Australians.
This school helps people of different cultures to get along better.	Muslims threaten the Australian way of life.
Learning about Muslims helps students to understand them better.	Most religious fanatics these days are Muslims.
A person can be both a good Muslim and a loyal Australian.	Most migrants are racist.
	Most Australians are racist.
Muslims have made a major contribution to Australia.	Australian TV and newspapers show Muslims in a fair way.
Most Australians have good feelings for Muslims.	Muslims do not belong to Australia.
The image of Muslims is as good as other migrant groups in Australia.	If I saw a Muslim student being abused in a public place I wouldn't care.

Table 14.3 Differences in attitudinal response concerning Muslims according to the religious affiliation of Australian students (or lack of one)

Non-religious agreed more than Christians regarding:	Christians agreed more non-religious regarding:
• Muslims have made a major contribution to world civilisation.	• Most religious fanatics these days are Muslims.
• Muslims have made a major contribution to Australia.	• Most migrants are racist.
• Most Muslims have good feelings for Australia and Australians.	• Muslims do not belong to Australia.
• Australian schools should teach more about Muslims.	

- On the statement *Most Muslims treat women with less respect than do other Australians*, they all agreed: other Christian most, Catholics next, non-religious least.
- On one statement: *Australian TV and newspapers show Muslims in a fair way*, other Christian and non-religious did not differ significantly, but did differ from Catholics: all groups disagreed, Catholics the least. These findings show that the two Christian groups were significantly less well-disposed towards Muslims and Islam than were the non-religious.

Attitudinal responses reflecting favourable images of Muslims

Making a contribution to Australia. Those who registered a neutral response account for the largest groupings. Finding it difficult to identify contributions by Muslims on a par with early migrants such as Italians, German, and

Jewish, 51% were unable to agree or otherwise with this statement. Other responses eliciting agreement or disagreement were almost equal. Presented with the follow-up statement *Most Australians have a good feeling to Muslims* (Figure 14.5), up to 42% (contrasted with 21%) agreed. Those who expressed neutrality (38%) may want to seek a wider occurrence or firmer evidence of this reality.

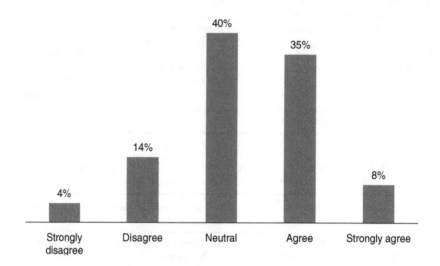

Figure 14.4 Responses to the statement 'Most Muslims have good feeling for Australia and Australians'

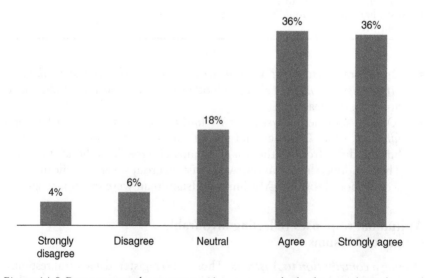

Figure 14.5 Responses to the statement 'A person can be both a good Muslim and loyal Australian'

Of all the other attitudinal statements, 'A person can be both a good Muslim and a loyal Australian' drew the second highest 'positive' response combing both percentages for Agree and Strongly agree (72%). This response would be of great interest o compare with the way Muslim-Australian students perceive themselves on this issue as presented in the next chapter 15. This response indicated here dispels much doubt from sections of the wider community about the ability of Muslims to accommodate the two identities in question.

The findings here would serve as much-needed evidence amidst the recent debate on one's ability to manage dual citizenships and dual identities that emerged in full force. The premier of Western Australia, for example, argued that people in Australia should choose only one identity – the two are incompatible and potentially dangerous. The new category on a national Australian, it was claimed, should supersede religion. Advocates of pure nationalism argue that hyphenated so-called Australians are not to be encouraged to display dual loyalty. The term hyphenated was arguably first used by Prime Minister Howard. They argue, for example, 'that British-Australians are unquestionably Australians. But for other more hyphenated nationals like Muslims they have to justify their existing loyalties' (Aly, 2006).

Most Muslims have stronger family ties than other Australians. The proportion of those who agreed with this statement is slightly higher (31%), but not significant, than those who disagreed (27%). The presence of a large proportion of students in Catholic schools from south European parentage is a possible explanation for that. Another may be the belief that the sexual roles between the sexes in Muslim families were unequal – a factor that would have impacted on the distribution of these responses (see Figure 14.6 and elsewhere with open-ended questions).

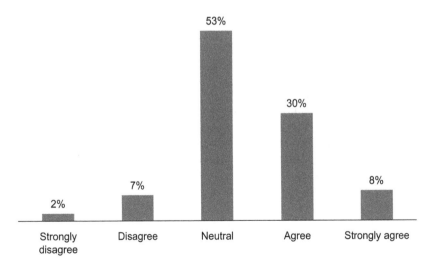

Figure 14.6 Responses to the statement 'Muslims find it hard to integrate into Australia'

This statement drew a smaller percentage (38%) of respondents who strongly agree/agree that Muslims find it hard to integrate into Australia than in the previous statement. One may simply explain this discrepancy in that integration involves a labour-intensive mutual recognition between Muslims and other Australians, whereas accommodating two identities is a personal matter. Interestingly there was no difference of significance (sig. = 0.21) between male and female students' perception on this statement. By contrast non-religious affiliates scored higher or agreed more than Catholics and other religions that Muslims do find it hard to integrate (sig. = 0.03).

Hollywood movies show Muslims in a fair way. The percentage of those who disagreed with this statement (43%) is large, though slightly smaller than that relating to Australian TV and newspapers (50%). The relative not-too-frequent releases of Hollywood showing negative Muslim images compared with the 1980s and 1990s may be a factor. This may coincide with a surge of incidents implicating the Muslim migrant community with violence and difficulties in integrating socially, as reported in local media outlets. The pattern of responses revealed here is of interest. Mindful of the negative image of Muslims in local and international media, the largest group of respondents (56%) strongly disagree/disagree with the statement 'Muslims do not belong to Australia'. Nevertheless the response by a minority (18%) who agree/strongly agree seems to conflict with the national agenda on multiculturalism and acceptance and has to be addressed.

Australian schools should teach more about Muslims. A larger proportion of respondents disagreed/strongly disagree (40%) this statement than those who agreed/strongly agreed (25%). Thirty-five per cent had no opinion or did not wish to express it. A variety of reasons may have triggered a response indicating disagreement. Nevertheless, a quarter of respondents have acknowledged the need that more teaching about Muslims needs to take place at Australian schools.

The literature on the link between knowledge and attitudes is fairly recent. Several researchers focusing on anti-prejudice education showed that participants believed that factual information about out-groups is crucial in challenging negative feelings and improving positivity towards them (Ata 2016a, 2016c; Pedersen, Walker and Wise, 2005; Dunn, 2004; Nelson, Dunn and Paradies, 2011; Hargreaves, 2016). Several researchers from Europe and Australia found that low- and high-prejudiced people share the same knowledge of cultural and ethnic stereotypes of a minority, thus signifying that the level of knowledge and depth of prejudice are independent of one another (Walton et al., 2015; Gordijn, Koomen and Stapel 2001; Lepore and Brown, 1997). This could, however, relate to the validity of the test itself. Gordijn, Koomen and Stapel (2001, p. 157) argue that the measuring instrument may be insensitive enough to detect finer 'differences in the knowledge of cultural stereotypes as a function of level of prejudice, namely due to providing an open-ended response option'.

Attitudinal responses reflecting unfavourable images of Muslims

The unfavourable attitudes reported towards Muslim were large and varied. On the statement that the Muslim community threatens the Australian way of life, half of the respondents (50%) do not agree with this (Figure 14.7). Factors that may have influenced those who agreed (14%) and strongly agreed (6%) with the statement are analysed in the body of the report. However, when asked for a response to *Muslims have a good feeling to Australia and Australians*, the largest grouping (40%) expressed neutrality, arguably wanting to draw their own conclusions in due course. This pattern clearly reinforces an expression of 'goodwill', with (35%) eliciting agreement and (31%) replying in the negative. The response, however, to the statement *Most religious fanatics these days are Muslims* was different A greater proportion disagreed with the statement (38%), 21% agreed, and 40% were neutral. (Follow-up interviews revealed that the gap between these groups would have reflected a more skewed response distribution had the statement been 'Most Muslims are religious fanatics').

Others, however, believe that the majority of European (and arguably by implication Australian) Muslims are neither well integrated nor radicalised (Rabasa and Benard, 2014). They point out that for the minority amongst the second generation who are disaffected, some find it difficult to live within either the traditional culture of their parents or the modern Western culture where they reside. Extremist ideologies offer a new identity that allows the individual to identify with an imagined worldwide community.

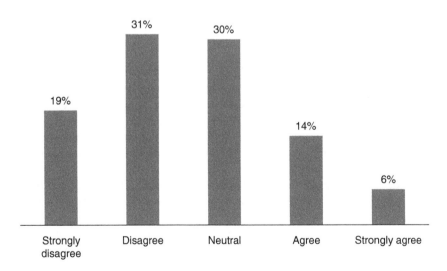

Figure 14.7 Responses to the statement 'Muslims threaten the Australian (Western) way of life'

The pattern of responses revealed towards the statement *Muslims do not belong to Australia* is of great interest. Mindful of the negative image of Muslims in the local and international media, the largest group of respondents (56%) strongly disagree/disagree with this statement. A minority (18%) agree/strongly agree – a view that arguably conflicts with the national agenda on multiculturalism and acceptance and has to be addressed. However, the statement *A person can be both a Muslim and loyal Australian* drew the second-highest 'positive' response (72%) of all other 18 statements. Nevertheless, the response by a minority (18%) who agree/strongly agree seems to conflict with the national agenda on multiculturalism and acceptance and has to be addressed. Undoubtedly, it dispels much doubt from sections of the wider community about the ability of Muslims to accommodate the two identities in question.

The response towards the statement *The image of Muslims is as good as other migrant groups in Australia* discerns reflective judgement. Whilst a sizeable majority of participants indicated good feelings and acceptance of Muslims, they are conscious of their negative image largely perpetrated by the media and other political forces. A total of 53% disagreed with this statement; only 13% agreed, and 2% agreed strongly. This view was stated more strongly in response to the statement *Australian TV and newspapers show Muslims in a fair way*. The percentage of those expressing strong disagreement/disagreement (50%) was the highest. A total of 15% agreed, and 35% were neutral. These results make a strong statement about the role of the media in perpetuating a not too inclusive place for Muslim in multicultural Australia. Although vulnerable at a developing age to all kinds of information, a sizeable group of respondents communicated their awareness of a kind of a bias against the Muslim community that they largely attribute to the media.

Perception of Muslim attributes

The global picture shows that the differences in perception between Muslims and mainstream Australians is deeply divided. And yet these views are not uniformly displayed between them with regard to either positive or negative clusters. With a handful of exceptions, the surveyed participants were slightly more critical of Muslims than Muslims were of the mainstream society (see also Chapter 18).

In order to assess more closely the cultural religious divide, a list of 15 attributes was presented for a response as to whether Australian students of non-Muslim background, associate each of the characteristic traits with Muslim, Christian, or non-religious communities. (The latter two groups were included in order to serve as a baseline against which to compare perceptions of Muslims.)

For many attributes, there was little difference in the perceptions of the religious groups, but on some the Muslims stood in sharp contrast to the others (Figure 14.8).

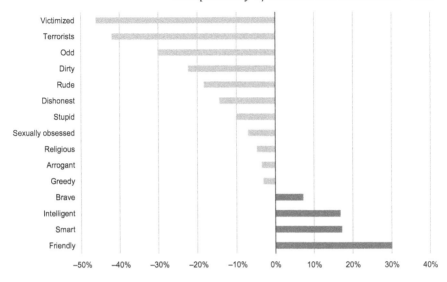

Figure 14.8 Differences in proportion of positive responses to perceived attributes of Christians compared to perceived attributes of Muslims

There is also a discerning fine-tuned position in terms of Muslims perceived equally as being victimised (46%) and as terrorists (43%). Whatever political leaning one may hold, discerning a judgement by solid majorities reflecting two opposite attributes is largely encouraging. Making a subtle difference between the positive image of innocent victims and the negative one of unprincipled culprits is hardly a uniform branding of Muslims. On the negative side, the majority surveyed associate Muslims, in descending order, as being friendly, smart, intelligent, and brave. With regard to negative attitudes, those who associated Muslims with being odd, dirty, rude, dishonest, stupid, sexually obsessed greedy, or terrorists was the largest.

Religion was another attribute that also drew a strong response in attributing it equally to both Muslims and 'their own Christian Australian compatriots'. The association can be interpreted either as a positive or negative, depending on one's interpretation or motive.

In order to highlight the differences between how Muslims were perceived compared to how Christians were perceived, the differences in proportional responses were ranked (Figure 14.9).[5] Muslims were perceived (in decreasing order of importance) as more victimised, terrorists, odd, dirty, rude, dishonest, stupid, sexually obsessed, religious, arrogant, sexually obsessed, and greedy than Christians, while Christians were perceived (in decreasing order of importance) as more friendly, smart, intelligent, and brave than Muslims.

With regard to gender differences, boys perceived Muslims to be significantly more 'dislikeable' (mean score 0.27) than did girls (−0.22) ($F(11915) = 121.4, p < .001$). Boys also perceived Muslims to be significantly

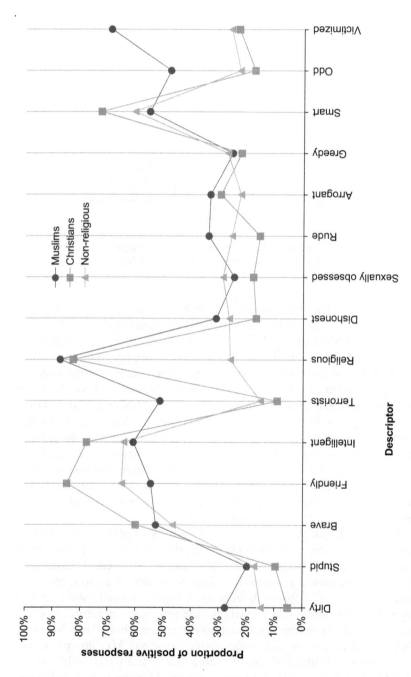

Figure 14.9 Proportion of positive responses to attributes of selected religious groups

less 'virtuous' (mean score −0.22) than did girls (0.18) ($F(11915) = 76.6$, $p < .001$). These findings show that the two Christian groups resembled each other in being more inclined than the non-religious to ascribe both vices and virtues to Muslims. This could mean that for the non-religious, the matter of religion with Muslims was not an issue, whereas for the Christian groups it was.

Conclusions

This survey revealed a trajectory of unexpected findings of attitudes, feelings, and 'like-minded' shared values between mainstream and Muslim cultures as perceived by mainstream Australian students. The cultural and historical differences between Christian and Muslim communities are too wide to make a definitive statement or a complete reconciliation. In equal measures, students are divided in the degree and nature of social harmony, compatibility of core values, tolerance, and allocation of positive and negative attributes towards Muslims in Australia.

A major finding revealed that boys were largely less accepting of Muslims and Islam than were girls. Interestingly, boys agreed more than girls with the statement 'Most Muslims treat women with less respect than do other Australians' – clearly a view not founded in direct experience. A significant difference was also found between boys (mean score 9.6) and girls (8.6) with respect to social distance from Muslims, including aspirations to friendship, neighbourhood, and intermarriage. It was shown that boys significantly desired not only more social distance in general than did girls but proportionately more from Muslims than did girls.

On the question of the relationship between attitude formation and religious friendship, the following was revealed: those with mostly Muslim friends agreed more than those with mostly non-Muslim friends that 'Some Muslims face discrimination because they dress differently' and that 'A person can be both a good Muslim and a loyal Australian'. Those with mostly non-Muslim friends agreed more than others with the following statements: 'Most Muslims treat women with less respect than do other Australians; Australian TV and newspapers show Muslims in a fair way; and Movies show Muslims in a fair way'. There was also a strong tendency for the two Christian groups – Catholics and other Christians – to be significantly less well-disposed towards Muslims and Islam than were the non-religious.

On two statements, all three non-Muslim affiliates – Catholics, other Christian denominations, and secular/non-religious – differed significantly from another. On the statement 'Muslims threaten the Australian way of life', all disagreed, but to different degrees, non-religious most, Catholics next, other Christians least. On the statement 'Most Muslims treat women with less respect than do other Australians', they all agreed, 'other Christian' most, Catholics next, non-religious least.

Goodwill towards the Muslim community resonated with more participants than otherwise. There were twice as many respondents (35 per cent +

7 per cent contrasted with 19 per cent + 2 per cent) who believed that most Australians have good feelings for Muslims. And subsequently it is correct to conclude that they are perceived as being accepted in the wider main-stream society. Those who expressed neutrality (38 per cent) may want to seek a wider occurrence or firmer evidence of this reality.

State school students felt more positively about Muslims and Islam than did private school students. Of particular interest, state school students endorsed the statement *Australian schools should teach more about Muslims,* whereas private school students did not. However, for many attributes, there was little difference in the perceptions of the religious groups, but on some attributes, Muslims were perceived (in decreasing order of importance) as more victimised, terrorists, odd, dirty, rude, dishonest, stupid, sexually obsessed, religious, arrogant, and greedy than Christians, while Christians were perceived (in decreasing order of importance) as more friendly, smart, intelligent, and brave than Muslims.

It was found that a clear majority of Australian students (64 per cent) felt that they have learnt little or nothing about Muslims at their school, with over a fifth strongly disagreeing with the proposition. A mere 2 per cent felt they could give the most positive response. The small response (16 per cent) by those who learnt a lot about Muslims at their school is under-standable. Similarly, a large percentage of respondents (49 per cent) disagreed/strongly disagreed that they understood Muslims better since being at their school. The absence of Muslim students from a large number of non-public schools in regional Australia may have contributed to the direction of responses, although having Muslim friends does not make a significant difference. The survey found that students tend to disagree with the statement *Australian schools should teach more about Muslims.* What, then, is the role of schools in promoting intercultural understanding? Is there a role for school-based interfaith programmes, intercultural studies, and student welfare programs? Does the school curriculum matter? If not, why not? How can it be made more effective? The survey shows that many students think that Muslims are unfairly depicted by the media. Given that we cannot change the media (nor should we), students can be taught to observe it critically.

Acknowledgements

Figures 14.1 and 14.2 originally appeared in 'Research note' *Intercultural Education* in July 2016; Figures 15.3 and 15.9 in *Islam in the West: Perceptions and Reactions* (Oxford University Press, 2018).

Notes

1

2 A pilot study was conducted at 9 schools with 552 students in 2012, and a short form survey was conducted at 13 schools with 682 students.

3 This comment might be taken in two ways depending on whether the media image is assumed to be accurate or not. If accurate, then it is a negative comment; if inaccurate, it could be taken as at least neutral, and possibly as expressing solidarity – 'Muslims are okay; it's the media I don't like'.

4 Scales of this kind (known as Likert scales) can be readily converted into scores measuring the intensity of agreement. This is particularly useful for performing statistical tests of significance. In this study we have scored as follows: *Strongly disagree = – 2, Disagree = – 1, Neutral = 0, Agree = 1, Strongly agree = 2*. This was the basis for computing the mean response for each question.

5 Differences were calculated, as in the following example: 69% of respondents regarded Muslims as 'victimised' as compared to 23% who regarded Christians as 'victimised', hence the difference was 23% – 69% = – 46%. All differences were significant at the 5% level on paired t-tests. No analogous comparison was made between Muslims and non-religious, as it was considered unnecessary since perceptions of non-religious resembled perceptions of Christians.

References

Aly, W. 2006. 'War has lured bigots out into the open', *The Age,* 31 July.

Ata, A. 2009. *Us and Them: Muslim-Christian Relations and Cultural Harmony in Australia.* Brisbane: Australian Academic Press.

Ata, A. 2014. *Education, Integration, Challenges: The Case of Australian Muslims.* Melbourne: David Lovell Publishing.

Ata, A. 2016a. 'How Muslim students' knowledge of Christianity is related to their attitudes to mainstream Australia and Australians: A national survey (project report)', *Social Science (Europe),* 4(3): 800–805; doi:10.3390/socsci4030800

Ata, A. 2016b. 'How Muslim students perceive of Australia and Australians: A national survey', *Journal of Intercultural Communication,* (41) (July); ISSN 1404–1634.

Ata, A. 2016c. 'Research note: How Muslims are perceived in Catholic schools in contemporary Australia: A national survey', *Intercultural Education,* 27(4): 337–351.

Ata, A. and Batrouney, T. 1989. 'Attitudes and stereotyping in Victorian secondary schools', *The Eastern Anthropologist,* 42(1): 35–49.

Bastian, B., Lusher, D. and Ata, A. 2012. 'Contact, evaluation and social distance: Differentiating majority and minority effects', *International Journal of Intercultural Relations,* 36: 100–107.

Benard, C. 2015. 'Moderate Islam' isn't working', *The National Interest,* 20 December, pp. 1–2.

Dunn, K. 2004. 'Islam in Australia: Contesting the discourse of absence', *The Australian Geographer,* 53(3): 333–353.

Gordijn, E., Koomen, W. and Stapel, D. 2001. 'Level of prejudice in relation to knowledge of cultural stereotypes', *Journal of Experimental Social Psychology,* 37: 150–157.

Habtegiorgis, A., Paradies, Y. and Dunn., K. 2014. 'Are racist attitudes related to experiences of racial discrimination? Within sample testing utilising nationally representative survey data', *Social Science Research,* 47: 178–191, Amsterdam: The Netherlands

Hargreaves, Julian. 2016. *Islamophobia: Reality or Myth?* PhD thesis, Lancaster University.

Hirst, John. 2016. *Australian History in 7 Questions.* Melbourne: Black Inc.

Kabir, N. 2007. 'What does it mean to be Un-Australian? Views of Australian Muslim students in 2006', *People and Place*, 15: 62–79.

Lepore, L. and Brown, R. 1997. Category and stereotype activation: Is prejudice inevitable? *Journal of Personality and Social Psychology*, 72(2): 275–287.

Muslim Community Reference Group. 2006. 'Building on social cohesion, harmony and security', Canberra, Dept of Immigration and Citizenship (series)

Nelson, N., Dunn, K. and Paradies, Y. 2011. 'Australian racism and anti-racism: Links to morbidity and belonging', in Mansouti, F. and Lobo, M. (eds.) *Migration, Citizenship and Intercultural Relations: Looking through the Lens of Social Inclusion*. Farnham, Surrey: Ashgate (pp. 159–175).

Pedersen, A., Walker, I. and Wise, M. 2005. ' " "Talk does not cook rice": Beyond anti-racism rhetoric to strategies for social action', *Australian Psychologist,* 40(1): 20–31.

Pew Research Centre. 2006. *Conflicting Views in a Divided World*. Washington, DC: The Pew Global Attitudes Project.

Pew Research Center. 2008. 'Global attitudes and trends', *Unfavorable Views of Jews and Muslims on the Increase in Europe: Ethnocentric Attitudes Are on the Rise in Europe*. Washington, DC, 17 September.

Rabasa, A. and Benard, C. 2014. *Eurojihad: Patterns of Islamist Radicalization and Terrorism in Europe*. London: Cambridge University Press.

Walton, J., Paradies, Y., Priest, N., Wertheim, E., and Freeman, E. 2015. 'Fostering intercultural understanding through secondary school experiences of cultural immersion', *International Journal of Qualitative Studies in Education*, 28: 216–237.

15 Compatibility of Muslim and Australian identities as viewed by Muslim Australian students

A national survey

Abe W. Ata

Islam is the third largest religion in Australia, after the Christian denominations and Buddhism, and the Muslim community is one of the fastest growing, having nearly doubled in size between 1996 and 2001 (Australian Bureau of Statistics, 2001). Many are school students, and of these, many are at Islamic schools. This is fortunate for the purposes of the study. It affords us ready access to respondents (it would be invidious to seek out only Muslim students in a religiously mixed setting), and it presents both a challenge and an opportunity for reaching a target audience.

Muslim schools in Australia are newcomers on the national scene, most having been in existence for only the last 15 years. In Victoria alone they employ about 400 teachers, serve 5000 students, and obtain \$32 million a year from state and federal governments. But Irene Clyne of Melbourne University found that although they may promote a moral outlook, cultural identity, retention of the mother tongue, and religious practice, many parents expressed concern that they might not be a wholesome alternative to secular education (2000, 2001).

The Age (31 July 2005) found that education departments have little knowledge of the curriculum content in Muslim schools for junior grades, the quality of education on offer, or religious views propagated. It stated that 'there are concerns among former teachers and members of Melbourne's Islamic community about the overall quality of education the 600-plus students receive. . . . Muslim extremists were posing a problem for "vulnerable and impressionable youth" . . . . [A prominent Muslim leader says that] the proliferation of Islamic schools is causing concern in the Muslim community. . . . They are accountable to nobody but themselves'.

In a recent survey, *The Great Divide: How Westerners and Muslims View Each Other*, the Pew Research Centre found that reciprocal opinions held by these two groups varied markedly amongst the surveyed societies – one which was a major driver behind the current project. The survey revealed that Muslims were more positive than the general public in their adopted country about the way things are going for them and their future, but many worried about the future of Muslims in their country of origin. Their greatest concern was unemployment. Islamic extremism emerged as the number two concern. By and large, however, several advocacy groups, human rights advocates, and others within the mainstream society do not regard most non-Muslims as hostile towards Muslims. Their commitment and advocacy are inarguably genuine. Their knowledge of what constitutes Muslim self-identification or, for that matter, the self-identification of Christian minorities in Muslims countries, is often incomplete. This in fact constitutes much of the blurred vision and misconstrued attitudes between both communities Muslim-Australians and mainstream Australians. Little is known, for example, that being identified as a Palestinian, Lebanese, Egyptian, and the like entails that one's identity is synonymous with affiliation to a particular religion (see also, Sklare, 1957). In such countries the law dictates that all Christian and Muslim citizens must identify 'their' religion in their passport. Whether they attend a mosque or a church is immaterial and instantly defaults to adopting one's ancestral religion. In extreme, but not unusual, cases, to claim irreligiosity (or secularism) is a punishable offense.

Australians and other Westerns may find this reasoning odd at best. To them Christianity and nationality are distinct, separate, and hence a private matter. To be a secular humanist posits that human beings are capable of being ethical and moral without religion or a God.

A pioneer Muslim writer drives this point further. Muhyi points out that 'Islam is not merely a body of religious doctrine and practice; it is also a form of social and political organization [whereby] most (minority) Christian sects are also governed by religious law. In the Middle East there is no clear distinction between religious and secular life' (1959, p. 51). To Australians and other Westerners who are brought up in a secular state, the complex web of religious and civil authority amongst Muslims and minority non-Anglo Christians appears incomprehensible.

There is little published research, however, beyond the Pew Center's, which has examined specifically the extent to which false facts relate to attitudes of Muslims towards Australia (Rabasa and Benard, 2014). Much less is reported on what may constitute negative attitudes towards Australia that could be predicted from the scale of our knowledge, whether fashionable or well-worn. It is held that many of the false beliefs play a crucial role in perpetuating negative attitudes, legitimising social distance, and justifying blatant and subtle prejudice (Pedersen, Walker and Wise, 2005; Eagly, 1992). In other words, false beliefs interlink with generalisable attributes and stereotyping, extending the portrayal, and the like. More to the point, we know from our previous work with non-Muslim students that there is goodwill but much ignorance towards Muslims (chapter 14). At the same time, we know little about the opinions of Muslim students. For consistency, policy makers should be informed by the viewpoints of both groups. On the basis of this comparison, there is much commonality in our respective findings and much common ground on which to build.

Results from studies on anti-prejudice education showed that participants believed that factual information about out-groups is crucial in challenging negative feelings and improving positivity towards them (Pedersen, Walker and Wise, 2005; Dunn, 2001, 2004, 2005). Several researchers from Europe and Australia, for example, found that that low- and high-prejudiced people share the same knowledge of cultural and ethnic stereotypes of minorities, thus signifying that the level of knowledge and depth of prejudice are independent of one another (Gordijn et al., 2001; Augoustinos and Quinn, 2003; Lepore and Brown, 1997). This could, however, relate to the validity of the test itself. Gordijn et al. argue that the measuring instrument may be insensitive enough to detect finer 'differences in the knowledge of cultural stereotypes as a function of level of prejudice when the free response method' (2001, p. 157).

The aim of this presentation is examine the nature and extent to which Muslim Australian students, and by implication, the broader Muslim community, perceive their dual identities as compatible; the ease of integrating Australian/Western values and mannerisms into their lifestyle; transmitting their own into various secular, cultural, social and political aspects of the mainstream society; the issues, barriers, and challenges they face; the pressures and stereotypes that hinder their full acceptance as citizens; and the perception and experiences of adversity and coping with unwelcome reception, as well as their struggle against apathy and misunderstanding.

Extracted in this chapter are selected results of a five-year-long national survey of 430 Years 11 and 12 Muslim students in 10 Muslim high schools. The current study drew its survey sample primarily from Muslim denominational schools. It can therefore fairly be said to represent how the overwhelmingly Muslim student community views mainstream Australian society.

The current study follows a previous national survey on attitudes of Australian students towards Islam and Muslims – hereafter referred to as 'The Companion Study'. The two studies are largely complementary in the sense that both explore how one community perceives the other.

Survey method and sample characteristics

The survey unit was the high school student. Over 430 completed questionnaires were obtained from students at eight schools (six high schools and two community schools, i.e. those which involve a partnership between the school and other resources) in Victoria, New South Wales, Queensland, and Western Australia. South Australia, Northern Territory, Australian Capital Territory, and Tasmania did not take part for logistical reasons. Two schools catered mainly to students of Turkish background.

Schools were requested to survey Year 11 students, these being considered mature enough to give informed answers, yet unencumbered by Year

12 exams in each selected school. The survey was administered to eligible students present on the day of the survey. Even so, four of the schools chose to administer the survey to Years 10 and 12.

The percentage of female participant students (57 per cent) was slightly higher than male students (43 per cent). Almost the entire sample (93 per cent) declared themselves to be Muslim; the remainder who were also of Muslim descent chose not to do so in writing. We do not know the circumstances of those who gave 'Other' (i.e. not Muslim) as their religion. It is possible that some were children of interreligious marriages, and others just rebellious. There were more students born in Australia (61 per cent) than overseas (39 per cent). However, the percentages of fathers (3 per cent) and mothers (9 per cent) born in Australia were significantly lower.

On many questions, between a third and a half of the sample was neutral, indicating that they neither agreed nor disagreed with the statement (Figure 15-1). This could signify honest ignorance of the issues or, alternatively, lack of motivation. This contrasts with The Companion Study, which found that a considerably higher proportion of neutral responses given by non-Muslim students to comparable (and in some cases identical) questions concerning Islam and Muslims. This suggests that Muslim students are either more informed about or more motivated to comment on the position of Muslims in Australia than are non-Muslims – understandably so, as they are commenting on their own community, not someone else's.

Table 15.1 Survey participant characteristics

Sex	*Male*	*43 per cent*
	Female	*57 per cent*
School gender composition	Co-educational school	90 per cent
	Girls/boys only school	10 per cent
place of birth	Australia overseas	61 per cent
		31 per cent
Language spoken at home	Another than English	93 per cent
	English only spoken at home	7 per cent
Religion	Muslim Not declared	93 per cent
		7 per cent
Parents born in Australia	Father Mother	3 per cent
		9 per cent
Metropolitan (Sydney, Melbourne, Perth, Brisbane, Adelaide) Rural		100 per cent None
Religious background of friends of participant	Muslim Non-Muslim	66 per cent
	Half Muslim, half non-Muslim	3 per cent
		31 per cent

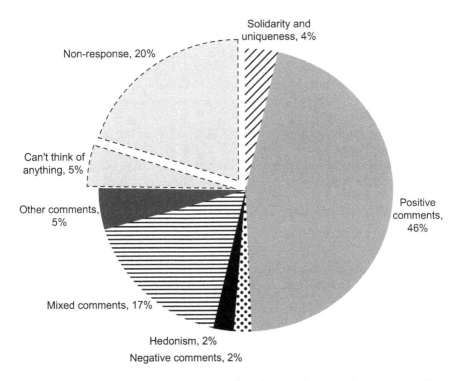

Figure 15.1 Responses to the question 'What do you like most about non-Muslim Australians?'

Note: Apparent errors in addition are due to rounding

N = 431 (Inc. non-response)

Words that are liked most when you hear the word 'non-Muslim Australians'

Box 15.1   Selected responses to the question 'What do you like most about non-Muslim Australians?'

- Their curiosity to always try and learn about others.
- Their struggle in asking a question to Muslims about religion.
- I like how it's not obvious what religion non-Muslims came from.
- How they seem so interested about Islam . . . and how they are fascinated when they discover the truth.
- They are underestimating most of them and are good to get advice from.

- Some of them are nice but other judge Muslim Australians by what they see in the media.
- They want to live in a country that is multi-cultural and everyone is treated the same.
- The general non-Muslim Australian community is extremely gentle and understand that Muslims are not 'terrorists' and it's just a "media story".
- Some are friendly – they know how to have fun without getting into trouble.
- They want to know the truth but they do not have the initiative to seek the truth.

Note: All quotes above are verbatim.

Words that are liked least when you hear the word 'non-Muslim Australians'

Combined, the majority of negative categories, including racism, ignorance, and other judgmental criticisms, are reflected in the responses here quoted verbatim – reflecting fear and anger that the society at large is Islamophobic (see also, Brasted, 2001; Briskman, 2015; Hargreaves, 2016; Poynting 2002; Poynting et al., 2008).

When asked what they like least about non-Muslim Australians (Figure 15-2) roughly one out of three (27 per cent) gave a 'no response', whilst 6 per cent could not think of anything – a significantly smaller percentage than that in the previous finding. 'Racism' drew the next highest response (19 per cent); 'ignorance' 14 per cent; 'being judgmental of Muslims' drew 13 per cent; 'other negative comment including meaningless life, disrespectful, selfish too relaxed, overreact, denigrating our clothes, and abusive' consisted 12 per cent; and other comments including 'they don't drive good cars like us in Lebanon, freedom of women, complain a lot, because they are pigs' drew only 6 per cent.

Moderate Muslims who keep their faith on a personal level to avoid bringing religion into politics and who feel embarrassed at violent actions taken under the banner of their religion are in particular need of such an endorsement (Muslim Community Reference Group, 2006; Asmar, 2001). Absence of a religious hierarchy – one that is similar to the Catholic one with the Pope at is pinnacle – has prompted many moderate Muslims to take matters into their own hands and become more organised. For a self-serving extremist minority of a mainstream society, it may be politically convenient to demonise others on the basis of race or religion, but it never defeats their own phobias (Parliamentary Joint Committee on Intelligence and Security 2006).

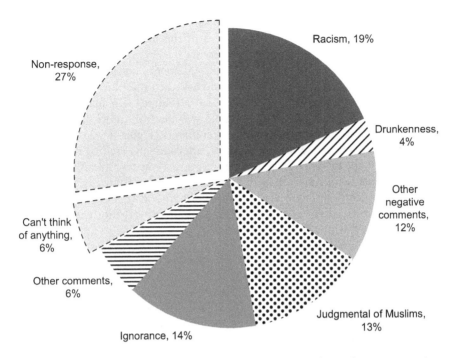

Figure 15.2 Responses to the question 'What do you like least about non-Muslim Australians?'

Note: Apparent errors in addition are due to rounding,

N = 431 (inc. non-response)

Attitudes

Respondents were presented with 18 statements concerning subjective attitudes towards Islam and Muslims and asked to rate their agreement on a 3-point scale of 'Agree' to 'Neutral' to 'Disagree'.

On many questions between a third and a half of the sample was neutral, indicating that they neither agreed nor disagreed with the statements (Figure 15-3a). This could signify honest ignorance of the issues or, alternatively, lack of motivation. Interestingly, the proportion of neutral responses was less than that of non-Muslims to comparable (and in some cases identical) questions concerning Islam and Muslims (Ata, 2007). This suggests that Muslim students are either more informed about or more motivated to comment on non-Muslims than the converse.

How students differ in their attitudes

So far we have explored the attitudes of the sample as a whole. But does this mask differences within the sample? For instance, do boys differ systematically from girls in their attitudes towards Islam and Muslims? To answer this and similar questions, we used statistical techniques to determine if there were significant differences in the mean attitudes of all the demographic groups measured in the survey.

Respondents were presented with 18 statements concerning subjective attitudes towards Islam and Muslims and asked to rate their agreement on a 3-point scale of 'Agree' to 'Neutral' to 'Disagree'. On many questions between a third and a half of the sample was neutral, indicating that they neither agreed nor disagreed with the statements (Figure 15-3). This could signify honest ignorance of the issues or, alternatively, lack of motivation. Interestingly, the proportion of neutral responses was less than that of non-Muslim mainstream Australians to comparable (and in some cases identical) questions concerning Islam and Muslims (Chapter 14). This suggests that Muslim students are either more informed about or more motivated to comment on non-Muslims than the converse.

Gender differences

Boys and girls differed significantly on 3 out of 18 statements (Figure 15.3a). This contrasts with the findings of a survey of non-Muslim students (How Australian Students see Islam and Muslims: A National Survey submitted by Abe, March 2007), in which boys were found to differ significantly on 16 out of 23 questions. Boys agreed significantly more than girls with the following four propositions:

Most non-Muslim Australians want good relations with the Muslim community

On the statement *Most non-Muslim Australians want good relations with the Muslim community* the dominant response was neutral, but of the minority who took sides, those in support outnumbered those opposed by 1.6 to 1 (Figure 15.4). However, a different pattern emerged relative to *Most Muslim Australians want good relations with the non-Muslim Australians*. Those in support outnumbered those opposed by 14 to 1. When this finding is taken in conjunction with that of the previous question, it implies that Muslims are perceived to be keener on good inter-communal relations than are non-Muslims (it is not known if the small minority [4 per cent] who disagreed did so because they consider Muslims' perceived standoffishness to be good or bad) (Figure 15.5).

Respondents overwhelmingly agreed with the following statement 'A person can be both a good Muslim and a loyal Australian', with those in support outnumbering those opposed by 24 to 1 (Figure 15.6). This contrasts with the identical proposition put to non-Muslim students, which found that those in support of the statement outnumbered those opposed by 6.8 to 1. (Ata, 2007).

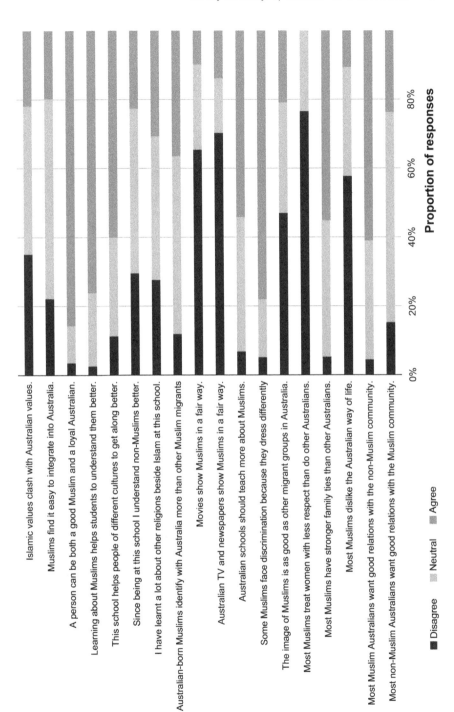

Figure 15.3a Proportion of responses to attitude questions

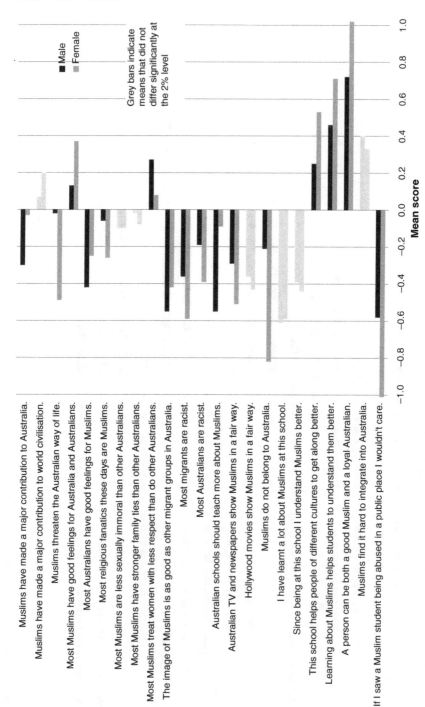

Figure 15.3b Mean attitude scores by gender

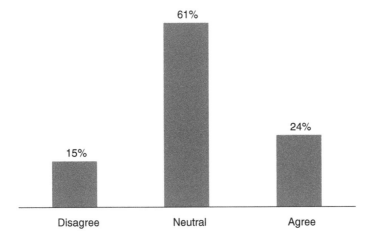

Figure 15.4 Responses to the statement 'Most non-Muslim Australians want good relations with the Muslim community'

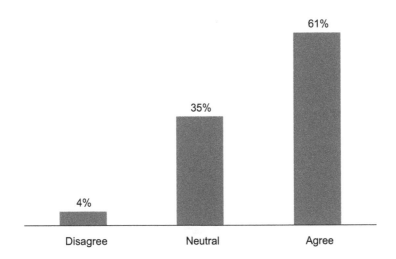

Figure 15.5 Responses to the statement 'Most Muslim Australians want good relations with the non-Muslim community'

2 Muslims are discriminated against

Respondents overwhelmingly agreed with this statement. Some Muslims face discrimination because they dress differently, with those in support outnumbering those opposed by 15 to 1 (Figure 15.7). Respondents overwhelmingly disagreed with the statement that Australian TV and

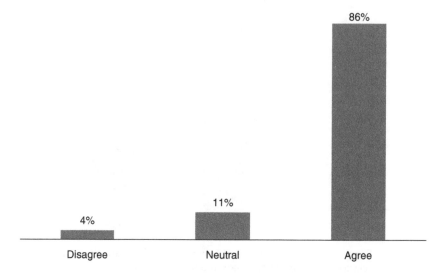

Figure 15.6 Responses to the statement 'A person can be both a good Muslim and a loyal Australian'

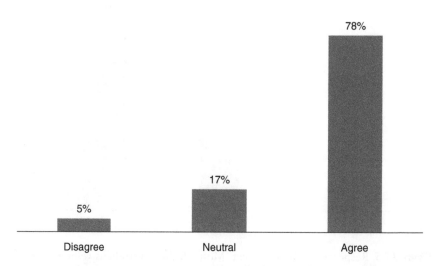

Figure 15.7 Responses to the statement 'Some Muslims face discrimination because they dress differently'

newspapers show Muslims in a fair way, with those opposed outnumbering those in support by 5.1 to 1. In a previous survey Ata (2007) found that respondents strongly disagreed with this statement, with those opposed outnumbering those in support by 3.3 to 1 and 36% were neutral (Figure 15.8).

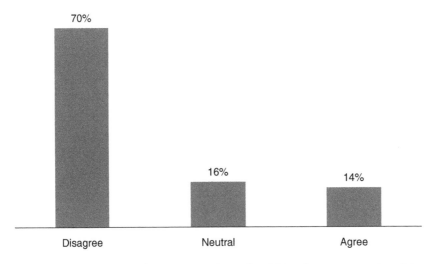

Figure 15.8 Responses to the statement 'Australian TV and newspapers show Muslims in a fair way'

3 The image of Muslims is as good as other migrant groups in Australia

Respondents overwhelmingly disagreed with this statement, with those opposed outnumbering those in support by 2.3 to 1 (Figure 15.9). Respondents overwhelmingly disagreed with the statement *Movies show Muslims in a fair way*, with those opposed outnumbering those in support by 6.7 to 1. In the previous survey Ata (2007) found respondents strongly disagreed with this statement, with those opposed outnumbering those in support by 4.2 to 1 and 47% were neutral (Figure 15.10).

4 Islamic values are compatible with Australian values, code of conduct, and behaviour

Respondents overwhelmingly disagreed with the statement *Most Muslims dislike the Australian way of life*, with those opposed outnumbering those in support by 5.5 to 1 (Figure 15.11).

Respondents were divided on the statement *Islamic values clash with Australian values*. Some 43% were neutral, but of those who took sides, those opposed outnumbered those in support by 1.6 to 1 (Figure 15.12). Respondents were divided on the statement *Muslims find it easy to integrate into Australia*. Most were neutral, but of the minority who took sides, those opposed roughly equalled those in support. This contrasts with the identical proposition put to non-Muslim students, which found that those in support outnumbered those opposed by 4.2 to 1 (Ata, 2007). Apparently non-Muslims think

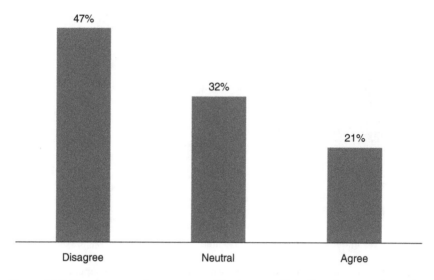

Figure 15.9 Responses to the statement 'The image of Muslims is as good as other migrant groups in Australia'

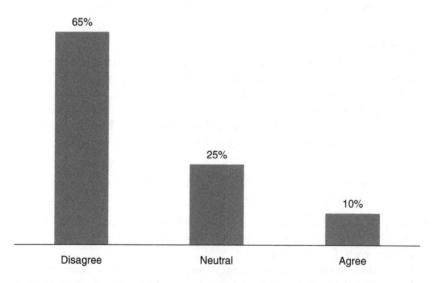

Figure 15.10 Responses to the statement 'Movies show Muslims in a fair way'

that Muslims find it harder to integrate than do Muslims themselves (Figure 15.13). Respondents overwhelmingly disagreed with the statement *Most Muslims treat women with less respect than do other Australians,* with those opposed outnumbering those in support by 10 to 1 (Figure 15.14).

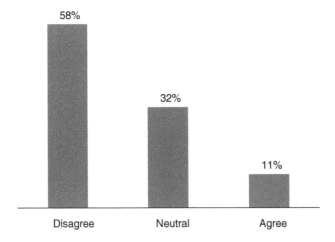

Figure 15.11 Responses to the statement 'Most Muslims dislike the Australian way of life'

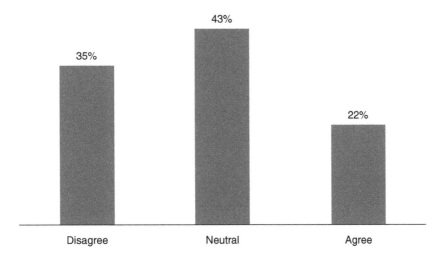

Figure 15.12 Responses to the statement 'Islamic values clash with Australian values' (N = 420)

Perceptions of Australians

Respondents were presented with a list of 15 attributes and asked whether or not each applied respectively to 'Muslim Australians' and 'Other Australians'. Note that the requested comparison was limited to Australians and made no mention of Christians. So while our findings may be coloured by international politics, every attempt was made to avoid this.

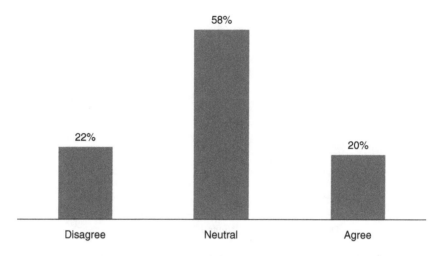

Figure 15.13 Responses to the statement 'Muslims find it easy to integrate into Australia'

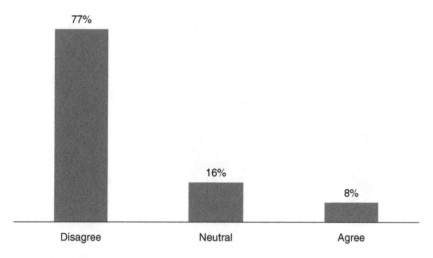

Figure 15.14 Responses to the statement 'Most Muslim Australians treat women with less respect than do other Australians'

Muslim Australians were perceived (in decreasing order of importance) as more devout, brave, honest, respectful of women, tolerant, clever, and generous, while other Australians were perceived (in decreasing order of importance) as more impolite, greedy, selfish, arrogant, violent, immoral, stupid, and fanatical than Muslim Australians.

Overall results regarding positive and negative attributes

For many attributes, there was little difference in the perceptions of the religious groups, but on some, the Muslim Australians stood in sharp contrast to other Australians (Figure 15.15).

In order to highlight the differences between how Muslim Australians were perceived as compared to how other Australians were perceived, the differences in proportional responses were ranked (Figure 15.16).[1] Muslim Australians were perceived (in decreasing order of importance) as more devout, brave, honest, respectful of women, tolerant, clever, and generous, while other Australians were perceived (in decreasing order of importance) as more impolite, greedy, selfish, arrogant, violent, immoral, stupid, and fanatical than Muslim Australians.

Because some of the attributes were quite similar to one another, and hence the responses to them statistically correlated, we used factor analysis[2] to 'collapse' them into a smaller set of attributes, termed factors, with little loss of explanatory power. By reducing the amount of data, this simplifies the analysis considerably and can throw a light on the underlying explanatory links.

Factor analysis reduced the perceptions to the following factors:

- Muslim Australians: Five significant factors jointly explained 61% of observed variance, of which the first factor explained 19%.
- Other Australians: Three significant factors jointly explained 46% of observed variance, of which the first factor explained 16%.

The fact that no single factor explained a high proportion (say 40% or more) of the observed variance shows that in this case data reduction was not possible or helpful. This is not unusual or unexpected; in all likelihood, it means only that perceptions, while differing between Muslim Australians and other Australians, vary a good deal between respondents for reasons that have little to do with their demographic characteristics.

Conclusions

The general picture that emerges from analysis of the data in this project is somewhat daunting and yet provides information that is relevant to ongoing debates and public concerns, such as social integration, cultural harmony, religious tectonics, and fragmentation of values.

Findings in this chapter and Chapter 14 reveal unequivocally that cultural background and religious affiliation are strong indicators of the individual's attitudes towards and behaviour and knowledge of the other, in this case, Australia and mainstream Australians.

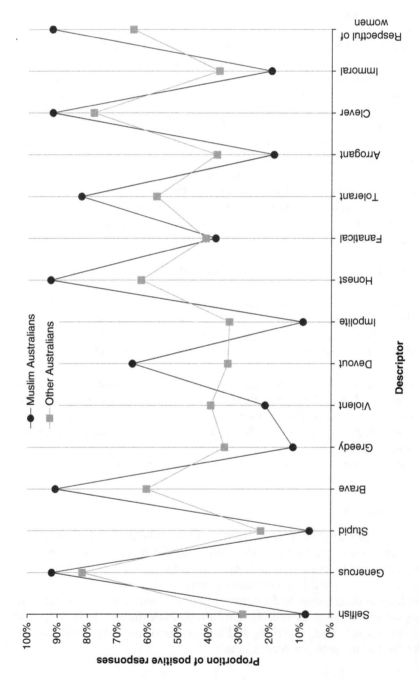

Figure 15.15 Proportion of positive responses to attributes of selected groups

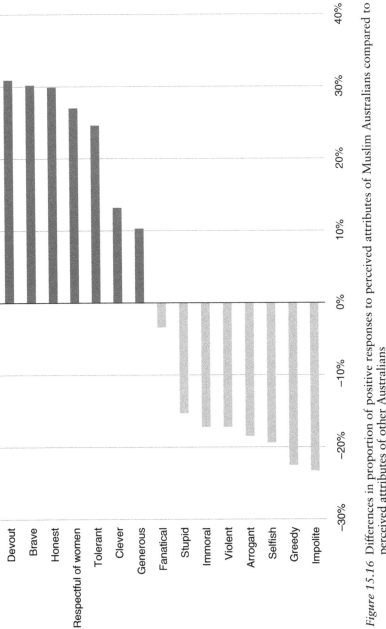

Figure 15.16 Differences in proportion of positive responses to perceived attributes of Muslim Australians compared to perceived attributes of other Australians

A sizable proportion of the students found themselves caught in the middle of two cultural traditions and wonder if their growing community is being accepted by mainstream society.

In Australia, the separation between one's religious and public identities is a cultural and political given. Many Australians may have been influenced by Christian values, but, unlike citizens of many Muslim countries, their identity is not exchangeable with their religious affiliation. That said, significant differences between the two religions, Christianity and Islam, are not to be side-stepped. This could lead to a false sense of security. Differences in the interpretation of social values and way of life, individual accountability, consensual decision-making, and attitudes towards implementing moral imperatives do exist. It is feasible that we should be able to acknowledge them, respect them, and address them without necessarily aiming for compromise.

Clearly much work is needed to bring about a remedy. Providing awareness sessions to students and parents which address critical social, religious, and cultural issues, including stereotyping and inclusivity, freedom of expression and the media, sexual permissiveness and conservativeness, secular and religious identity, individual and community basic rights, and social justice and foreign policy, is one of several measures to take.

There are clearly grounds for this belief. Because in most Muslim countries the mass media is controlled, the question of why Australian television does not help change the negative image and dispense with some honest remains a moot one. The perception that local television is market oriented and is not a free medium to educate the public but is dedicated to the perpetuation of social structure remains strong.

Moderate Muslims who keep their faith on a personal level to avoid bringing political issues into and feel embarrassed at actions made under the banner of their religion and are in particular need of such an endorsement. Absence of a religious hierarchy has prompted many moderate Muslims to take matters into their own hands and become more organised. For a self-serving minority, it may be politically convenient to demonise others on the basis of race or religion, but it never defeats their own phobias (Windle, 2004; Wise and Ali, 2008).

Another major finding was linked to their views regarding the way Muslim schools promoted intercultural understanding. Once again, the survey found that students were equally divided on statements that their school teaches them. The degree to which Muslim students feel that their school is appropriately educating pupils about Australia and Australians was an important predictor of certain levels of tolerance (Ata, 2009, 2016, 2016a, 2004; Simkin and Gauci, 1992). This suggests that the atmosphere created by the school can lead to increased acceptance of mainstream Australians, rather than the level of pure factual knowledge. Therefore, it is not just a matter of knowing more facts about religious and cultural congruence, but perceiving that the school cares enough to educate students on these issues that are important, as well as acknowledging worldview differences.

The need for all Australian schools to teach more about Muslims (and indeed beyond such as Christian Arabs and the like) is quite justifiable in the instance. Several students who participated in this survey expressed their satisfaction at understanding non-Muslims better since being at 'this' school. This was the belief of the majority of those surveyed.

One of the critical steps is to engage with educational curriculum consultants nationally and at a state level. They may propose inclusion of subjects relating to their current and eventual contribution to the building of multicultural Australia; the diversity of Muslim cultures and diverse Christian (and Jewish) minorities in their countries of origin; the emerging identities of children within Christian-Muslim marriages; and their willingness and eventual participation in the cultural, artistic, literary, and political expression of the mainstream society (Ata, Bastian and Lusher, 2009; Asmar, 2001).

That said, significant differences in the teaching and attitudes between the two religions are not to be side-stepped due to a false sense of security. Differences of interpretation towards social values and way of life, individual accountability, consensual decision-making, and attitudes towards implementing moral imperatives do exist. It is feasible that we should be able to acknowledge them, respect them, and address them without aiming at a fine compromise. Not because we no longer need a dialogue, but because these different approaches have concrete implications to both communities living together in a shared place. Professor Robert Manne has on several occasions referred to this capacity of accommodating many cultural and religious expressions – within a single language, law, and polity – as multiculturalism.

Acknowledgements

Figures 15.1, 15.2, 15.3a, 15.15, 15.16, and associated analysis all originally appeared in *Islam in the West: Reactions and Challenges* published by Oxford University Press India in 2018. Due acknowledgement is reserved to Oxford University Press and to the *Journal of Intercultural Communication* publishers referencing various *figures* in 'Research Note: Islam' (July 2016).

Notes

1 Differences were calculated as in the following example: 65% of respondents regarded Muslim Australians as 'devout' as compared to 34% who regarded other Australians as 'devout', hence the difference was 65% – 34% = 31%. All differences were significant at the 5% level on paired t-tests.

2 Factor analysis is one of several statistical techniques collectively termed 'data reduction' methods. As the name implies, factor analysis aims to reduce large datasets, ones with many variables, to simpler datasets that capture most of the information present in the original but with fewer variables, termed 'factors'. Each respondent is assigned a score on each factor. The numerical value of the factor score ranges from +1 (high) to –1 (low) to 0 (neutral).

References

Asmar, C. (2001). A community on campus: Muslim students in Australian universities. In S. Akbarzadeh & A. Saeed (Eds.), *Muslim communities in Australia* (pp. xii, 244). Sydney: UNSW Press.

Ata, A. (2004). Cross religious misunderstanding or a clash between civilizations in Australia. *Current Dialogue,* (44).

Ata, A. (2005a, January–February). Beyond the Stereotypes. *Quadrant,* No. 413, *XLIX.*

Ata, A. (2005b, January). Cross religious misunderstanding or a clash between civilizations in Australia. *Current Dialogue.* WCC Geneva.

Ata, A. (2005c). Dynamics of the interfaith marriage: The Australian Christians and Muslims. *Eastern Anthropologist, 50,* 187–199.

Ata, A. (2006a, January 16). Acknowledging differences in Australian society. *Australian e- Journal of Social Debate.* https://www.onlineopinion.com.au/view. asp?article=4043

Ata, A (2006b, Summer). Demonising Australia's Christian and Muslim Arabs in Cartoons. *COMPASS, 40,* 31–34.

Ata, A (2006c, November 17). Lost in translation: Australia's top cleric. *Australian e- Journal of Social Debate.* https://www.onlineopinion.com.au/view. asp?article=5167

Ata, A. (2007, March). *How Australian students see Islam and Muslims: A national survey* (unpublished). Department of Immigration and Citizenship.

Ata, A., & Furlong, M. (2006). Observing different faiths, learning about ourselves: Practice with inter-married Muslims and Christians. *Australian Social Work,* 59(3), 250–264.

Ata, A., 2009. *Us and Them: Muslim-Christian Relations and Cultural Harmony in Australia,* Brisbane: Australian Academic Press .

Ata, A 2016. How Muslim students perceive of Australia and Australians: a national survey, *Journal of Intercultural Communication,* ISSN 1404–1634, issue 41, July.

Ata, A 2016a Research note: how Muslims are perceived in Catholic schools in contemporary Australia: a national survey, *Intercultural Education* 27 (4): pp. 337–351.

Ata, A., & Batrouney, T. (1989). Attitudes and stereotyping in Victorian secondary schools. *The Eastern Anthropologist,* 42(1).

Ata, Abe, Bastian, Brock and Lusher, Dean. 2009. ' Intergroup contact in context: The mediating role of social norms and group-based perceptions on the contact–prejudice', *International Journal of Intercultural Relations"* 33 (6): 498–506.

Augoustinos, M., & Quinn, C. 2003. 'Social categorization and attitudinal evaluations: Illegal immigrants, refugees, or asylum seekers?' *New Review of Social Psychology, 2,* 29–57

Australian Arabic Council. (2001). *Increase in racial vilification in light of terror attacks: Sep 2001.* Melbourne.

Australian Bureau of Statistics. 2001. Census reference and information. Canberra: https://www.abs.gov.au/websitedbs/censushome.nsf/home/historicalinformation2 001?opendocument

Briskman, Linda. 2015. "The creeping Blight and Islamophobia in Australia", *International Journal for Crime, Justice and Social Democracy* 4 (3): 112–21.

Brasted, H. (2001). Contested representations in historical perspective: Images of Islam and the Australian press 1950–2000. In S. Akbarzadeh & A. Saeed (Eds.), *Muslim communities in Australia* (pp. xii, 244). Sydney: UNSW Press.

Bullivant, B. M. (1987). *The ethnic encounter in the secondary school: Ethnocultural reproduction and resistance: Theory and case studies.* London; New York: Falmer Press.

Bullivant, B. M. (1988). The ethnic success ethic challenges conventional wisdom about immigrant disadvantages in Australia. *Australian Journal of Education,* 32(2), 223–243.

Cahill, D., Gundert, A., Australia. Bureau of Immigration Multicultural and Population Research., & Australia. Dept. of Immigration and Multicultural Affairs. (1996). *Immigration and schooling in the 1990s.*Canberra: Australian Govt. Pub. Service.

Davis, R., & Stimson, R. (1988). Disillusionment and disenchantment at the fringe: Explaining the geography of the one nation party vote at the Queensland election. *People and Place,* 6, 69–82.

Department of Education. (1997). *Multicultural policy for Victorian schools.* Melbourne.

Department of Education. (2003). *School circular: 075/2003. Advice for schools in dealing with the international situation.* Melbourne.

Department of Education and Training. (2000). Racism. No way: Anti-racism education for Australian schools. Retrieved 17 January 2006, from www.racismnoway.com.au/

Department of Education Employment and Training. (2001). *Guidelines for managing cultural and linguistic diversity in schools.* Melbourne: State of Victoria.

Donohoue Clyne, I. (2000). *Seeking education: The struggle of Muslims to educate their children in Australia.*

Donohoue Clyne, I. 2001. Educating Muslim children in Australia, in S. Akbarzadeh & A. Saeed (eds.), *Muslim communities in Australia* (pp. 219–244). Sydney: University of New South Wales Press.

Dunn, K. (2001). The geography of racisms in NSW: A theoretical exploration and some preliminary findings from the mid 1990s. *The Australian Geographer,* 32(1), 29–44.

Dunn, K. (2004). Islam in Australia: Contesting the discourse of absence. *The Australian Geographer,* 53(3).

Dunn, K. (2005). Australian public knowledge of Islam. *Studia Islamika: Indonesian Journal for Islamic Studies,* 12(1), 1–32.

Dunscombe, R. (2004). *Heinemann media 1. Units 1 &2.* Port Melbourne, Vic.: Heinemann.

Eagely, A. H. 1992 'Uneven Progress: Social Psychology and the Study of Attitudes', *Journal of Personality and Social Psychology* 63 (5): 693–710.

Galbally, F. (1978). *Migrant services and programs: Report of the review of post-arrival programs and services for migrants* (No. 06420362840642912246). Canberra: A.G.P.S.

Goodall, H., & Jakubowicz, A. (1994). *Racism, ethnicity and the media.* St Leonards, N.S.W.: Allen & Unwin.

Gordijn, E., Koomen, W, Stapel, D. 2001. Level of Prejudice in Relation to Knowledge of Cultural Stereotypes, *Journal of Experimental Social Psychology* 37, 150–157

Hargreaves, Julian.2016. Islamophobia: reality or myth? PhD thesis, Lancaster University

Human Rights and Equal Opportunity Commission. (2004). *Ismau listen: National consultations on eliminating prejudice against Arab and Muslim Australians.* Sydney: Human Rights and Equal Opportunity Commission.

Kalantzis, M., & Cope, B. (1984). Multiculturalism and education policy. In G. Bottomley & M. M. De Lepervanche (Eds.), *Ethnicity, class and gender in Australia* (pp. xi, 218). Sydney: George Allen & Unwin.

Lepore, L and Brown, R 1997. Category and Stereotype Activation: Is Prejudice Inevitable? *in* HYPERLINK "https://www.researchgate.net/journal/0022-3514_Journal_of_Personality_and_Social_Psychology"*Journal of Personality and Social Psychology* 72(2): 275–287

Muhyi, I. 1959. 'Women in the Middle East', *Journal of Social Issues*, 15 (3:)51

Muslim Community Reference Group. (2006). *Building on social cohesion, harmony and security*. Canberra.

Omar, W., Hughes, P. J., Allen, K., & Australia. Bureau of Immigration Multicultural and Population Research. (1996). *The Muslims in Australia*. Canberra: Australia Govt. Pub. Service.

Parliamentary Joint Committee on Intelligence and Security. 2006, *Review of Security and Counter Terrorism Legislation*. Canberra: Parliament of Australia.

Park, R. E., Burgess, E. W., & McKenzie, R. D. (1925). *The city*. Chicago: University of Chicago Press.

Pedersen, A., Walker, I. & Wise, M..2005. "Talk Does Not Cook Rice: Beyond Anti-Racism Rhetoric to Strategies for Social Action", Australian Psychologist 40: 20–31.

Pew Research Centre. (2006). *Conflicting views in a divided world*. Washington, DC: The Pew Global Attitudes Project.

Poynting, S. and Mason, V. 2008. "The New Integrationism, the State and Islamophobia: Retreat from Multiculturalism in Australia, *International Journal of Law, Crime and Justice*, 36 (4, December): 230–46.

Poynting, S. (2002). 'Bin Laden in the suburbs': Attacks on Arab and Muslim Australians before and after 11 September. *Current Issues in Criminal Justice*, 14(1), 43–64.

Rabasa, A. and Benard, C. 2014. *Eurojihad: Patterns of Islamist Radicalization and Terrorism in Europe*. Cambridge University Press, NY.

Rieder, J. (1985). *Canarsie: The Jews and Italians of Brooklyn against liberalism*. Cambridge, MA: Harvard University Press.

Said, E. (1981). *Covering Islam: How the media and the experts determine how we see the rest of the world*. New York: Pantheon Books.

Said, E. (1995). *Orientalism*. New York: Penguin.

Simkin, K., & Gauci, E. (1992). Ethnic diversity and multicultural education. In R. J. Burns & A. R. Welch (Eds.), *Contemporary perspectives in comparative education* (pp. xlv, 432). New York: Garland Pub.

Sklare,M. 1957. "The Function of Ethnic Churches". In Religion, Society and the Individual, J.Yinger (ed), pp. 459–60. New York: McMillan.

Speck, B. W. (1997). Respect for religious differences: The case of Muslim students. *New Directions for Teaching and Learning*, 70, 39–46.

Windle, J. (2004). Schooling, symbolism and social power: The hijab in republican France. *Australian Educational Researcher, 31*(1), 95–112.

Wise, A. & Ali, J. 2008. *Muslim-Australians and local government [electronic resource] : grassroots strategies to improve relations between Muslim and non-Muslim-Australians : final research report*. Canberra: Department of Immigration and Citizenship

16 Integration, identity, and the community

The case of Germany and France

Claudia Postelnicescu

During the migration crisis in 2015, the European Union faced one of its most difficult moments by far; migrants from the Middle East, Asia, and Africa unknowingly unleashed old fears for Europeans, and hence populism and terrorism – with its new forms – emerged stronger in Europe at the same time, adding to the political crisis of the European Union. Nonetheless, political and legal consequences followed: the predictable and historical fracture between Central and Eastern member states and its Western member-states regarding the common policies on migration and asylum, the failure of the legal architecture of the Dublin agreements regarding asylum seekers and refugees, and the dysfunctionalities of the Schengen agreement of free movement among European member states. The impact of these consequences is going to reshape the European Union in the following years and the power structures between its member states.

Although migration and populism are not new phenomena in Europe, the questions raised are different in this age; hence, this chapter proposes answers to these dilemmas: Will Europe survive in the age of global migration as a diverse, open society? Why do national sentiments and national identity need to be defended, and how is this conflicting with the respect for diversity and individual freedoms of those belonging to a minority? What and who represent the always elusive and mysterious European identity? Is the failure of a common European identity understood as shared solidarity a legitimate preservation of national identity or a lack of common political culture?

The adequate responses to these questions will determine the future of the European Union and, at the same time, the adequate approach to the integration of the new migrants and refugees who arrived in Europe in the context of the failure of multiculturalism and the resurrection of identity politics.

The new populism has thrived on the remnants of multiculturalism, so it is worth asking why identity politics matter so much in a globalized world and in a unifying European space? Who is responding to the appeal to nostalgia of a safe nation-state within a fortress single nation without new immigrants? Why is this new populism gaining momentum throughout

Europe? The assumptions of this chapter are that populists thrive in times of crisis, fear, and chaos, and the phenomenon is nothing new, but trends that are counter to diversity and integration of migrants have become more solid in recent years. Since Brexit, with its popular vote of the British people to no longer be a part of the European Union, and the very nationalistic stance of Hungary, who jeopardized European unity in the refugee and migrant crisis by building fences to keep the refugees outside its borders, the return of the nation-state appears to be stronger than the predictions of its end.

Moreover, the demise of multiculturalism challenged the defenders of diversity and open door policy towards the migrants and refugees; hence, a new approach based on the assimilation of and compliance to liberal values is adopted in many European countries. However, in the coming years we will either see a common European conscience grounded in civic values, which may not be properly represented by their elected politicians and the bureaucracy in Brussels, or a more politically fractured European Union, with many countries falling prey to new populists.

The discussion about the demise of multiculturalism started when leaders like Angela Merkel, David Cameron, and Nicolas Sarkozy publicly noticed the failure of this approach to integrating migrants, although signs of fatigue and inefficiency of multiculturalism in responding to both the needs and rights of the members of the host societies and minority communities were obvious much earlier (Kymlicka 2016). The migration crisis in 2015 only accentuated the strain between individual rights and core values of the European countries and the expectations of the newcomers. The unfortunate correlation of the migration crisis with terrorism, particularly the phenomenon of the lone-wolf terrorist, acting alone on the soil of Europe, emphasized once again the complete structural flaw of multiculturalism.

Ever since, a new approach to diversity considering both the national ethos, patriotic sentiments, and the particularities of other communities to curb their inherent tension (Etzioni 2009) was advanced by politicians. In many states across Europe people live with different creeds, religious beliefs, traditions, and lifestyles, as liberal democracies have allowed collective identities to manifest. The result was that in Britain, the Netherlands, Germany, France, and Belgium, minorities did not embrace the host culture, lifestyles, values, and freedoms – they governed themselves according to their own. Inevitably, tensions rippled, and we have witnessed many: the lack of identity of the second and third generations of immigrants in multicultural states who became terrorists, acting with limited resources, but a strong fanaticism. They found in the violent ideology of the brutal *Daesh* something missing within themselves. The expression of a modern identity politics that is similar, in its own way, to the identity politics practiced by European populists: terrorism with a political agenda is not a manifestation of Muslim culture as opposed to populists' narrative that vilifies the immigrants and Muslims in Europe. Those who are European citizens turned into foreign fighters for *Daesh* feel profoundly rootless: there is no cultural identity, no political affiliation, no sense of belonging, no identification with the hedonist lifestyle of the European youth, no sense of self. In this huge vacuum, radical Islam and its jihadism found their perfect niche, and their success proves that, although elusive, identity is essential, especially in conflicting and paradoxical environments, when the self of the individual (Taylor 1992) is in tension with the ethos of the nation (Etzioni 2009). The phenomenon of the so-called 'foreign fighters' for the terrorist movement *Daesh* are Europeans, born and raised in Europe, who prefer to embrace a foreign culture of death instead of that of their own adopted and adopting country. If some European states fail to have a common liberal culture to be embraced freely by the immigrants, it is no surprise that Europeans cannot find a common European identity. Furthermore, it means that ideas and abstract laws cannot unite or give a common purpose to different people if there is a lack of emotional bonding and deep attachment to something more profound. The only common emotion people feel together is during football championships when flags, anthems and the favorite teams win for the country. Although these championships provoke intense sentiments, it remains fleeting, lacking solidity and consistency, hence nothing remains to keep the bond after the game is over.

Defenders of multiculturalism and diversity such as Will Kymlicka consider that populists are allergic to the 'moral relativism'[1] that constitutes the core of the multicultural approach, but in fact both, populist and multiculturalists share a tunnel vision about the reasoning behind the affiliations people form with each other and with the community or the nation. The multiculturalists defend diversity by betraying the idea of individual rights and freedoms to favor collective rights and freedoms, while the populists defend the nation-state and nationalism by doing the same, favoring collective rights at the expense of individual rights. The only difference rests on the rationale behind their approach and how they justify their position: multiculturalism is the opposing view of the national identity ethos, which can be only one, integrative of all the others, while a diverse society is one where many different identities are represented regardless of their connection or integration into the national ethos. When politicians recognized the failure of multiculturalism, particularly in Germany and Britain, populists felt vindicated and a surge of far-right parties emerged stronger than ever. The fact that communities of immigrants lived their own lifestyles, their own traditions, their own religion, their own habits with no attachment to the host society justifies the negativity against immigrants in the discourse of the populists. The defenders of multiculturalism consider that the very concept of 'integration' is dismissive of the identity of the immigrants, which affects their self and view of themselves (Taylor, 1992), while many directly bring fascism and racism into the debate, with the consequence of no real debate taking place and an ongoing crisis in finding policy solutions.

European identity and the lost sense of belonging to a political community

The definition of a common European identity concerned many philosophers and political thinkers, for obvious reasons: the very existence of the European Union as a supranational structure required complicated questions about how people will relate to more than one attachment beyond the nation-state. One of the few important questions was raised by the philosopher Jurgen Habermas, one of the strongest advocates of the European Constitution and European identity: 'Should citizens' identities as members of ethnic, cultural, or religious groups publicly matter, and if so, how can collective identities make a difference within the frame of constitutional democracies?" What Habermas envisions here is a post-national constitution, based on common values and principles that can elicit strong sentiments and attachments, hence the various Europeans from national states will commit enduringly to a 'constitutional patriotism' (Biró-Kaszási 2010) born out of a political understanding of what Europe is and what being a European means, based on the same 'political culture'. However, this idealism failed, as Europeans are still attached to their own national identity and identity is still perceived in nationalistic terms, rather than as a patriotic constitutionalism or, at least, a common 'political culture' able to facilitate the connection with a European identity. Not surprisingly, Viktor Orban, the prime minister of Hungary, declared in Poland in May 2018, that the European Union must renounce its 'delusional nightmares of a United States of Europe'. The supposition advanced by Habermas that people can and will connect with a common identity grounded in a political affinity with a community was contradicted by others, who noticed that identity comes with a sense of belonging and attachment to a particular political project. The inaccurate use of the term 'identity' was noticed by David A. Hollinger (2006), who proposed a move towards the idea of solidarity, as 'an experience of willed affiliation'. While I agree that 'identity' has become a messy word in the modern world, I prefer the term community, although it might not suffice; people can experience solidarity and other affiliations to a community, not in an abstract sense to an idea, but to a real connection with the political body for the members to share that belonging. The fact that communities developed as isolated enclaves within the host society proves that this assumption is correct.

The critical moment of the summer of 2015, when massive waves of migrants and refugees arrived on the shores of Europe, proved that there is not enough affinity among fellow Europeans to compel them to share resources and compassion with others, regardless of whether these 'others' are counterparts near the border or complete foreigners. On the contrary, the idea of membership of a community or, at least, of a shared affiliation, showed to be stronger and reunited the Central and Eastern Europeans on the one side and Western Europeans on the other, which is historically not surprising. There was also a tendency towards regional alliances within a few core states, rather than a supranational over-regulated entity. This fracture in solidarity is reflected in the debate about the two-speed or multispeed Europe white paper circulated by the European Commission following the disagreements in reaching a common EU migration policy. The dissensions among member states do not allow the European Union to move forward in its objectives united; hence, the non-solidary states will be left behind to catch up on the 'core' states at their pace, but to allow the core to push forward on a common agenda.

In a very rigid understanding, diversity is a threat to national identity and to a common European identity that already is weak and volatile, with no clear components. I would argue that the demise of multiculturalism has been accelerated or partially caused precisely by the lack of a strong foundation for national identity, either from fear of resurrecting old nationalisms and to make more fragile the vulnerability of the immigrants, or from a reluctance to openly embrace a national identity with all its components – traditions, lifestyle, religion, laws, and culture, which allowed for particular alternative ethnic and cultural identities to emerge as isolated islands inside the host society. The same conclusion seems to be that of the UK's government that discovered 'pockets of monoethnicity and monoculture', communities that did not have any common values with British society and no emotional bond with the host society or, at least, a functional one, such as language. The unfortunate correlation of high immigration, economic crisis, and terrorism impacted further on the lack of commonalities between people of Britain, so the obvious lack of sound social identity prepared the ground for the exit from the European Union, which has calmed the anxiety about immigration for the time being but will not solve the anxieties about how Britain integrates its Muslim immigrants into a society that has nothing to offer those who value traditions and religion, patriarchy, and inequality. Despite the tradition of monarchy rendered to a mere display of esthetics and charities, the British society has expelled religion and all the common values of Christianity and replaced them with a set of rules that cannot form a system of collective values. The monarchy could not be the sole unifying cultural institution, as the immigrants have no loyalty to the crown and the queen.

Meanwhile states like Poland, the Czech Republic, Slovakia, Hungary, and Romania to some extent claim openly their Christian heritage and values to be the core of their national identity and require the immigrants to respect those values before being granted any kind of status of belonging to the nation and openly disregard diversity. While Britain was very multicultural and diverse, with equal political opportunities for all minorities, it failed in developing a common identity, a British one, with loyalties to the British state, but a rather created a fragmented society, where the national citizens feel discriminated and forgotten, while priorities are given to the immigrants, perceived as the vulnerable ones. The multicultural policies across Europe have reached a stage where everyone feels resentful: immigrants for being vilified and the natives for feeling ignored. In Germany immigrants feel entitled and discriminated at the same time, while in France and Belgium they are ghettoized. One of the most powerful acknowledgements of the paradoxical situation created by multiculturalism belongs to the former French president, Nicolas Sarkozy, who said on French television, in 2010, that 'we've been too concerned about the identity of new arrivals and not enough about the identity of the country receiving them'. The social and political trends that followed these declarations emphasized that multiculturalism was toxic for both the host societies and the immigrants, and it did not save either of them, although many concessions have been made to accommodate and respect cultural diversity. The paradox here lies precisely in the lack of respect for our own European values, which immigrants have perceived and appropriated: if we do not value ourselves, why would the others value us? This psychological assumption is universal and functions with individuals, with communities, and with nations.

National identity continues to be a sensitive subject and reflects in the post-modern era the relationship between individuals and the nation in the age of globalization, with the prediction of 'the end of the nation-state and the rise of regional economies' (Ohmae 1995); precisely these perceptions are implicitly mirrored by the newcomers, as they assimilate the value the citizens attach to their citizenship (Fukuyama 2006).

East vs. West: national identity as the new fracture among European states

Why has multiculturalism failed? Contrary to the idealistic view of Europe as one continent with one culture, a single market, the same values, and the same core freedoms, in fact, many member states were consistently against rendering their sovereignty and national identity irrelevant and transferring all decisions to Brussels, to a forum of bureaucrats and politicians. At the same time, those states opposed to multiculturalism from the beginning were quick to emphasize that there is no terrorism within their national territory because their citizens share a sense of belonging to the national identity and to cultural and religious beliefs that are common. Their position was against Muslim immigration or any migrants that were not Christians or of Christian heritage. The political declarations of the Czech prime minister and president Milos Zeman and the Hungarian prime minister Viktor Orban during the migration crisis were undoubtedly against Muslims. They were joined by Slovakia and Poland with whom they form the regional coalition Visegrad Four. Initially, Romania rejected the quotas of refugees per country imposed by the European Commission, but later it adjusted its approach after the European Union decided to pursue a legal case in the European Court of Justice against Poland, Hungary, and the Czech Republic and there were experts pointing to breach of the European law. The fact that the European common asylum policy was founded on the principle of solidarity in order to align asylum procedures in the member states to enable an efficient and adequate response to any asylum seeker or migrant and have 'effective mechanisms of sharing the burden with member countries that are located at the outer borders of the Union or are exposed to a larger number of migrants, refugees and asylum seekers' (Maldini and Takahashi 2017) felt as a betrayal of common European principles and shared effort, and a lack of unity in terms of showing compassion to refugees and people in vulnerability.

The crisis of solidarity and disagreements among European countries over the best policy to tackle increased fluxes of refugees and migrants have highlighted the lack of common values and guiding principles among Europeans. What intellectuals and philosophers hoped would unite Europe, either a common constitution and a 'constitutional patriotism' (Habermas 1992), either shared solidarity (Hollinger 2006), or the Eurozone, have all failed for the time being. There is no sense of what it means to be European, there is no common conscience or identity; as it was founded mainly as an economic project, the European Union failed to arrive at the moment when it is a real community of people sharing the same ideals and a patriotic attachment to the European Union, assumed as a political community with common values and a political project that grows organically and embrace all Europeans.

The hindrance of the European identity is the volatility of both concepts together, identity and European. People do not feel a strong attachment to ideas, but to emotions, and there is little emotion and attachment to Europe and its founding values: Christianity is despised, the superiority of its culture is despised, the European heritage is despised. The reasons are multilayered and reflect the postmodern soul that avoids connections and disregards strong emotional bonds with a particular nation, religion, or culture. Globalization and the free movement of people have facilitated this new 'identity' of the wanderer, the global citizens, who do not feel attached emotionally to any country or idea of community; therefore, abstract concepts like patriotism for a political project were bound to fall on deaf ears. At the same time, there is the countertendency to the postmodern souls, the traditional ones, for whom the nation still holds emotional bonds with the individual, although its political appeal has weakened in the last two decades. In the words of Francis Fukuyama (2006):

> If postmodern societies are to move toward a more serious discussion of identity, they will need to uncover those positive virtues that define what it means to be a member of the larger community. If they do not, they will indeed be overwhelmed by people who are more sure about who they are.

However, a certain nationalism that appeals to the emotional connection with the nation is not only enduring, but healthy, in the words of one of its defenders; the nation-states retain spiritual components that could be equally valid for a common European history (Manent 2006). A healthy nationalism may allow for the expression of particular identities within the same nation, but it requires confidence and the dissipation of any fears about nation and the security of its citizens.

The obvious paradox in multicultural societies has proved that the distrust and contempt towards the national identity leads to a weak collective identity (Fukuyama 2006). It also generates the abandonment of certain values that will enable the preservation of national identity in fear of not offending others' identity. The case of Britain today, with a failed multiculturalism, a fractured identity, and an immense amount of resentment from the British population, and the abandonment of Europe, is the best example of the end road of not respecting your core founding values as a nation. In a strange way, the liberal democracies have embraced multiculturalism by betraying their core liberal values for the sake of not denying the values of immigrant communities, which has often proved profoundly illiberal.

However, there is a stark distinction between Western European states and Central and Eastern European states who are more than reluctant to abandon their culture, traditions, and identity for the benefit of immigrants. Hence, there is no surprise that those states favor Christian immigration and limited numbers of migrants and refugees, and they are willing to fracture the European Union into a two speed entity or the core and the periphery of the European Union to stand by this goal, of maintaining their national identity, often through a highly charged nationalism and populism rampant these days in Hungary, Poland, the Czech Republic, and Slovakia, but also spreading to Austria, Germany, Sweden, Netherlands, Italy, and Greece.

Therefore, the ongoing migration crisis has unlocked old wounds between the European member states regarding the attachment and solidarity to the European Union and has fractured the unity among Europeans, with new alliances, but also disputes. The summit of ministers of the interior from the European Union in Innsbruck, Germany, in July 2018 generated a new common approach from Austria, Germany, and Italy for an anti-migration agenda, which is once again a new trend that opposes, in the case of Germany, the position of Angela Merkel with that of its opponents, while Italy, who was left alone with Greece to handle the worst part of the first large wave of refugees in 2015, with its own limited resources, has remained bitter and enraged about the lack of solidarity between Europeans. Italy and Greece had to sustain alone the requirements of the Dublin agreement and the consequences of not being able to respect the EU law and breaching the Schengen agreement. In fact, the conditions of the Dublin agreement as such have obliged Italy to consider all the refugees and asylum seekers as country of first entry and to process alone all the applications, with sparse resources and breach of the rights of the refugees and asylum seekers agreed in international law and conventions. The recourse of this situation is that many refugees and asylum seekers have decided to legally pursue the abuse of their human rights and dignity, and a consistent case law on this matter is rising in the European Court of Human Rights.

The migrant and the populist: archetypes of new politics in the age of global migration

The figure of the migrant is as old as the Bible; we have been raised to learn about the Jewish people forced to flee Egypt and find their own land. Since the ancient times of the beginning of Christianity until the formation of the state of Israel, the Jew was the familiar migrant in most parts of Europe. Hence, migrants and migration are not a new phenomenon, although the current global migration with its increased flows of people is entirely new and unexpected for some. Equally, the figure of the populist is nothing new also, although in old times we might have other names for the reactionary, the bigot, the hateful, the defender of the status quo, the cunning politician who finds the usual scapegoat – they are well portrayed in literature, if we look only at Shakespeare's plays.

The novelty of the current and future populism stems from a few assumptions that we had about our modern politics: 1) we thought that after the violent nationalisms of the twentieth century no dark ages would ever be experienced by humankind, at least in Europe after Hitler and Nazism; 2) we thought that liberalism was the status quo and the liberal values represented the core of our political systems and liberal democracy was the natural choice for a political regime; 3) we thought that democracy and constitutionalism with guarantees for human rights and human dignity has sufficient immunity to authoritarianism and the return to an illiberal political arrangement; and 4) we thought that the transparent process of the law and regulations adopted in the European Parliament and the decision-making process of the European Commission would reduce the democratic deficit of the European Union, but apparently it has only enlarged the gap between the political elites, bureaucrats, and the people. The debates about the future of Europe, the identity of Europe, the democratic process, and the involvement of citizens in the decision-making process in Brussels are many and recurrent.

Populists are usually opportunists who have the uncanny ability to speculate on fears and vulnerabilities. During crises – and Europe had many in the last decade – people turn towards those who respond well, at least rhetorically, to these fears. It is the classical dark case of Germany before Hitler came to seize power to restore the lost faith in the German identity, Germany's future, and the Germans' confidence in themselves as a nation after the defeat and shame of the First World War. People nowadays, in

Europe and the United States more prominently, but also globally, are ridden with anxieties about the future and economic insecurities and inequalities; hence, the time is ripe for the charismatic, problem-solving leader who will promise everything, regardless of whether it will be delivered or not. In this context, new populist parties have appeared across Europe, in countries that seemed safeguarded against this virus, but they are spreading fast everywhere in Europe. Their main agenda is national, with an emphasis on stronger national sentiments, stronger national identity, and a rejection of foreigners and an aggravated Euroskepticism.

In recent years migration has become the most important topic for national politics, and that has fueled the rise of many new populist leaders, building on the resentment of people to the policies of political elites in Brussels and at home about handling immigration, welfare, education, and healthcare. The populists from the UK Independence Party (UKIP) party have consistently made immigrants the scapegoats of all failures of British politics, and ultimately it was nationalism that took Britain out of EU by pushing on the emotional triggers and vulnerabilities of the common people. Although the advocates of the Remain campaign, the pro-Europeans, have appealed to the connections and similarities between Britain and the rest of the European states as one European family, there was no sentiment for the British people that they belong to Europe and that they share a common nationhood, or at least a common public spirit and a civic demos.

Is it possible at all to have such a common spirit when countries are so keen on their own identities? The whole legal process and decision-making of the European Union prove that is not possible. The failure of the common EU migration and asylum policy is redundant, as it has never worked, since the first debate on the common asylum policy in 2005. Inevitably, countries prioritize what is perceived to be their national interests, and with populists at the top government keeping immigrants and refugees outside Europe has become one of their most important goal. As a consequence, as long as national agendas take priority, there is no real possibility to achieve a common understanding of what a European demos might be.

Immigrants were always treated as minorities, and access to citizenship was conditioned heavily in all European countries, the exception being those born on the European territory. When multiculturalism failed to offer those second- and third-generation immigrants a real new identity, the political elites realized that citizenship without attachment to common values was empty and hollow, hence the many changes in their policies: Germany and Britain now openly require immigrants to speak fluently the national language and to conform to liberal democracy's values and freedoms, rejecting any previous compromises for accommodating diversity. The tension between nationalism, populism, radicalism, and the open society with its freedoms and diversity has never been more profound.

Conclusion

While Europe has struggled to integrate more states within the union, a few member states have struggled to find their own identity after decades of submission to the Soviet Union. This simple yet heavy discrepancy makes Europe today a fractured project, along the same historical divisions. At the same time, the project of the European Union to become a supranational body on many levels generates reluctance, anxiety, and hostility, as those states are aware of the dangers of a supra-regulated entity, which renders national sovereignty irrelevant. The reverse of this process will signify a weak European Union unable to face united the many contemporary threats from terrorism to global markets, climate change, cyber wars, and the use of artificial intelligence to influence national elections.

However, the positives of any crisis are that it emphasized what is flawed, and there is a tremendous opportunity in these times, for the next 10 years, to overcome discrepancies and generate the European identity through its common public spirit and civic engagement. Many European and global concerns have the ingredients of becoming key aggregators for such a public conscience: migration, racism, hate of minorities, corruption, freedom of speech, the impact the laws and agreements decided by political elites have on people. Across the globe there have been many significant protests against corruption, which prove that there is not only an emerging European conscience, but a global one.

The rise of the politics of fear will consolidate the power of the populists leaders and in the flux of new waves of migrants and refugees, they will continue to hold strongly to the power in many European countries, with migrants and migration being the perfect tool for cynical populist politicians. As Europe has always struggled with conflicting visions of its identity, at least there was a search for an unifying idea, but now and in the coming years Europeans will be divided between their solidarities (Postelnicescu 2016). The European project was bold in its assumptions that national identities will merge naturally into the European one, and that is yet another contradiction of the core of the founding values of liberal democracy: that values can be imported and implemented easily. Too many failures have proved this assumption terribly wrong. However, we can envision that populists everywhere will be opposed by those who cherish the freedom of expression and the fundamental human rights, those who stand against hate speech and point to the fact that populism in power always fails people, depriving them of the most essential rights.

Considering that global migration to Europe has just began, the trends are here to stay. What will be gained in the sense of a common shared European consciousness and civic spirit may be lost at the political level, with states being divided between a core and peripheral alliances. The fracture favors further populist parties that will use the disappointments of the European integration to accelerate the gain of power in the national politics, particularly on topics that have to do with sovereignty, common foreign policy, and common migration policy. Member states have a strong aversion to having their security policies dictated to them by Brussels. The result may be that people will require more accountability from the politicians, including those proposed to be elected for the European Parliament. Isolation only on national political themes is no longer possible in the digital borderless society, and people will require to know why there is no sense of unity and security among Europeans.

The struggle to find a common European identity, flexible enough to allow Europeans and immigrants together to find a common purpose, might prompt many to realize that the denial of the Christian roots constitutes a solid source for the European identity; after all Christians, Muslims, and Jews have often shared together a common sense of solidarity, compassion, and, ultimately, European identity.

Note

In this chapter I use the terms refugees and migrants, with refugees used in the sense defined by the Refugee Convention in 1951 and migrants referring to any person who travels to Europe with the scope of immigration for various reasons – political, economic, and personal. The distinction is important, because refugees are protected under international law, while migrants often fall under the laws and regulations of the state where they immigrate, although under European law (Dublin agreement) there are clear rules of processing requests and offering a status to third-party nationals.

References

Barber, N.W (2002). *Citizenship, nationalism and the European Union. European-LawReview: Oxford Legal Studies Research Paper pp 241–259*, https://ssrn.com/abstract=2256427.

Biró-Kaszási, Eva (2010). *Habermas on European Constitution and European Identity. Journal of Social Research & Policy*. No. 1, December 2010.

Chayes, Sarah (2018). *Fighting the Hydra: Lessons from Worldwide Protests against Corruption*. Washington: Carnegie Endowment for International Peace.(54 pages).

Etzioni, Amitai (2009). Minorities and the national ethos. *Politics*, 29(2).

Fukuyama, Francis (2006). Identity and Migration, *Journal of Democracy* 17:2 pp 4–20, National Endowment for Democracy and the John Hopkins University Press, Baltimore.

Habermas, Jürgen (1992). Citizenship and national identity: Some reflections on the future of Europe. *Praxis International*, 12(1).

Habermas, Jürgen (1995). Multiculturalism and the liberal state. Address. *Stanford Law Review*, 47(5), pp. 849–853.

Hollinger, David A. (2006). From identity to solidarity. *Daedalus*, 135(4), pp. 23–31.

Kymlicka, Will (1995), *Multicultural Citizenship*, Oxford: Oxford University Press, p. 113–I updated in the paper

Kymlicka, Will (2012). Multiculturalism: Success, failure, and the future. In Migration Policy Institute (ed.), *Rethinking National Identity in the Age of Migration*. Berlin: Verlag Bertelsmann Stiftung, pp. 33–78.

Kymlicka, Will (2016). Defending diversity in an era of populism: Multiculturalism and interculturalism compared, published in Meer, Nasar, Modood, Tariq, Zapata-Barrero (2016). *Multiculturalism and Interculturalism: Debating the Dividing Lines*. Edinburgh: Scholarship Online.

Maldini, Pero, and Takahashi, Marta (2017). *Refugee Crisis and the European Union: Do the Failed Migration and Asylum Policies Indicate a Political and Structural Crisis of European Integration?* Communication Management Review Paper, Department of Communication Science, University of Dubrovnik.

Manent, Pierre (2006). *A World beyond Politics? A Defense of the Nation-State*. Princeton: Princeton University Press.

Ohmae, Kenichi (1995). *The End of the Nation State. The Rise of Regional Economies*. New York : Simon & Schuster.

Postelnicescu, Claudia (2015). *Romania si criza migratiei. Contra UE, de mână cu Viktor Orban. Expert Forum*. Policy Brief no. 39.

Postelnicescu, Claudia (2016). Europe's new identity: The refugee crisis and the rise of nationalism. *Europe's Journal of Psychology*, 12(2).

Taylor, Charles (1992). *Multiculturalism and the "politics of recognition": an essay*. Princeton: Princeton University Press.

17 The integration puzzle

Exploring challenges and hindrances when fitting immigrants into the Swedish labour market

Agneta Moulettes

With an overall aim to discuss current labour market policy and how it contributes to transforming unemployed immigrants into commodities, the analysis in this chapter will draw on ideas from critical theory as I see it as potentially insightful lens for bringing to the surface epistemological misinterpretations and power asymmetries between labour market intermediaries and unemployed immigrants.

This chapter is positioned in the realm of immigration, and in particular the discourse of labor market integration. It takes its point of departure from the Swedish labor market policy and politicians concern how to come to terms with unemployment and how to integrate immigrants into the labor market.

An expected shortage of labor in the European market due to a decreasing population poses a challenge for politicians, who have to negotiate between companies' growing demand for skilled workers, on the one hand, and, on the other, a promise to their voters to limit immigration of non-Europeans and the influx of refugees. The difficulty faced by immigrants in entering the Swedish labor market is a well-known problem among politicians, and the effort how to solve the issue has long been on the political agenda. What has made matters more complicated is the huge number of refuges that arrived in Europe as a consequence of recent conflicts in the Middle East and parts of the African continent. With a total number of 165,000 Sweden was, for instance, one of the European countries that received the most refugees in 2016 (Migrationsverket, 2018). This, in turn, has made people more concerned about the economic burden that immigration involves than the contribution that immigrants may bring to society in the long run. Besides a growing competition on the job market, the immigrants' situation is further complicated by society's request for language skills and legitimate documentation of education and work experiences.

In spite of a massive critique against current labor market policy, and regardless of an apparently huge interest in integration issues and a fairly extensive documentation of immigrants' situation in previous studies (Bakshi, Hatlevall and Melchert, 2009; Dahlstedt and Bevelander, 2010;

Moulettes, 2015; Guilherme Fernandes, 2015), little scholarly attention has been directed towards professional labour market intermediaries and their work assisting unemployed immigrants entering the Swedish labour market. Besides a few reports investigating the involved actors' fulfilment of the government policy (e.g. Jansson and Kilsved, 2013; Lundgren, 2009), costs in connection to the integration of refugees (Ruist, 2018), and unemployment among highly educated immigrants (Ljunglöf, 2018; Joyce, 2018), the main interest has focused on the existence of discriminatory practices among employers and unemployed immigrants' feelings about being excluded from the labour market (Rydgren, 2004; Wiesbrock, 2011). Considering the hitherto fairly limited number of scholarly studies on labour market integration, I contend that the labour market intermediaries' role in the integration process deserves more scholarly attention.

Although I am aware of the existence of success stories, this chapter will mainly focus on challenges and hindrances that labour market intermediaries are encountering in their work. The interest in unemployed immigrants is due to the fact that they constitute those who are the most exposed to unemployment (SCB, 2017a), and as a consequence are often exhorted to take part in labour market activities. Another reason is that immigrants' knowledge and work experiences often are treated with suspicion and considered inferior in comparison to the native population. I will therefore counterbalance labour market intermediaries' view with immigrants' experiences of labour market activities. With an overall aim to discuss current labour market policy and how it affects immigrants' employability, I will draw on ideas from postcolonial theory, as I see it as a potentially insightful lens for bringing the legacy of the colonial mindset to the surface. As critical management scholars (e.g. Prasad, 2012; Jack, 2016; Jack and Westwood, 2009) remind us, postcolonial theory aims at highlighting that organizations maintain their embeddedness in Western rationalities characterized by national, cultural, and racial hierarchies.

Viewing the labor market discourse through the postcolonial lens

Said (1995) made Westerners aware of the way colonial ideas have influenced our perception of the world. What has made Said's ground-breaking book, *Orientalism*, survive for forty years is most likely because he managed to capture the essence of the colonial strategy and delineate the consequences that still haunt us today. His work informs us that colonialism was one of the most profound and significant experiences that shaped Europeans' perception not only of Orientals but also, and perhaps mainly, of themselves – as well as Orientals' perceptions of themselves (Fougère and Moulettes, 2012). As argued by Said, the imperialist powers needed to create the Orient as an "Other," to define themselves as the centre. To achieve success in this endeavor required a colonial strategy that systematically led colonizers to see themselves as superior and colonized people to see themselves as the inferior. The reason why he analyzed Orientalism as a discourse was because it was the only possible way to understand "the systematic discipline by which European culture was able to manage – and even produce – the Orient politically, sociologically, militarily, ideologically, scientifically and imaginatively" (Said, 1995: 3). Orientalism sought to establish approval for its rule of the Orient by producing a binary division in which the Orient in contrast to the Occident is ascribed negative stereotypes. Hence, while the Occident (Europe/the West) is characterized as rational, virtuous, mature, ambitious, normal, and modern, the Orient (the rest/the non-West) is characterized as irrational, depraved, childlike, different, and old-fashioned.

From a postcolonial or post-Occidental (a concept coined by Mignolo, 2011) perspective, it is not the fear of difference per se, but rather the fear of the superiority that the others may possess and of the threat this may pose to our image of cultural identity that causes ethnocentrism and the exclusion of those we perceive as different. Positioning culture as both resemblance and menace, Bhabha (1994) argues that "the colonial mimicry is the desire for a reformed, recognizable other, as a subject of a difference that is almost the same, but not quite" (p. 86). From this standpoint, therefore, the notion of a homogeneous culture needs to be continuously repeated to be kept alive.

A reason why the image of cultural homogeneity has become important in today's society is probably people's enhanced vigilance to keep the discourse of cultural difference and the classification of people by race, ethnicity, geographic origin, gender, and the like alive in times of increased migration and external pressure and uncertainty. It is plausible that labor market intermediaries' subjective notions and pressure from the environment to keep the image of cultural homogeneity alive may affect their mindset and actions. As Meyer and Rowan (1977) argued, organizations are likely to mirror the myths and values of their institutional environment, and irrespective of whether they wish to conform or not, people consequently contribute to the reproduction of the dominant discourse.

Methodological considerations and research technique

I present myself as a Swedish woman with a critical view on the way the world is discursively divided into one superior West and one inferior non-West and who wishes to destabilize the taken-for-granted assumptions embedded in mainstream perception on culture. To do so, I will use critical discourse analysis (CDA) because it focuses on the language and the ideology behind the presumption, dissimulation, or manipulation of knowledge that shapes people's mindsets (Winther Jørgensen and Phillips, 1999; Zanoni and Janssens, 2001). Drawing on postcolonial theory, my intention is to use CDA to explore how the binary system is expressed in private service providers' discursive accounts. To support my argument I will include immigrants' views of the help they are offered by the system.

The chapter is written from a Swedish perspective and draws on interviews gathered among nine private labor market intermediaries (seven women and two men) from eight different companies and interviews with six immigrants from Hungary, Bosnia, Peru, Latvia, France, and Ghana. The interviews lasted between one hour and two and a half hours and were transcribed word for word. Since they were conducted in Swedish I only translated the parts I thought could be useful for this text. In addition to the interviews various documents (e.g. Swedish Codes of Statutes, public authority reports, pamphlets, home pages, newspapers, and TV news) have been collected and some of it used in the analysis.

As the research was exploratory in nature, I wanted the interviews to be respondent-driven rather than interview-driven. They were performed, therefore, as conversations instead of conventional interviews based on structural questionnaires, which meant that I had prepared only some broad questions that covered the main purpose of the research. The choice of interview technique can be seen as a disadvantage, as it does not guarantee that it will provide a cohesive pattern. However, this can be seen as one of the advantages, as it also may provide information that would not be discovered in traditional interviews that uses structured or semi-structured questionnaires.

Background: labour market assistance in Sweden

The first step toward the creation of a public employment agency was taken in 1940 with the establishment of the Labour Market Commission. The aim was to help people earn their living during World War II. Over time, the commission's activities continually developed to reflect changes in the labour market and society.

A significant change in the public labour market intermediaries work routines came in the early 1990s when new public management was implemented by the Swedish right-wing government. The neoliberal ideas that began to flourish in Europe in the 1970s were now regarded as a way to come to terms with a bureaucracy that had long since been considered to have grown out of proportion (Green-Pedersen, 2002). Another change came in 1993, when the employment agency's monopoly expired and the government opened up the establishment of private labour market agencies (SFS, 1993: 440). As a result Sweden has witnessed a growing number of private businesses engaged in labour market services aiming at helping unemployed in finding jobs.

In 2011 the total number of actors within the private sector reached 958 allocated to seven different programs (Jansson and Kilsved, 2013). Due to a massive critique for being ineffective, the labour market policy programs have been reduced and the service is now given by approximately 170 private businesses that have a contract with Swedish Public Employment Service (SPES). They offer the unemployed tailor-made assistance in developing application documents (e.g. CV and personal letters), job searches, coaching in interview techniques, vocational guidance, language training, and motivational training.

Constructing "the helpless Other" to justify the image of the expert self

A common denominator among the private service providers is their positive attitude to their work and achieved results. They all described their achievements and how they have managed to help their clients to find jobs or traineeships. As a consequence of earlier critique against the services provided by the coaching and matching businesses, more time is now spent on individual activities. This means, for instance, that they spend more time helping clients in general, and immigrants in particular, to write CVs and application letters. As Sara, a self-employed coach, said, "There's a lot of ignorance amongst them. Many of them do not know how to write a proper CV," and as Lisa, a manager at a local office, pointed out "Who wants to hire someone who does not have a proper CV?" They also insisted that it is a challenge to make the clients write a personal letter marketing themselves instead of using the traditional model starting with a "Hallo, my name is XX and I'm from YY". As Hanna said "You cannot start a letter by saying that you come from Syria. You must show that you have a certain competence . . . and that you know the codes."

Implicit in the service providers' discursive accounts, one can discern a tendency to define the unemployed immigrants as ignorant and an attempt to make them break with their past to become integrated into Swedish society. And to get a job, you apparently have to know how to write a professional CV and a selling letter that makes the employer believe you are a "real Swede", who knows the language and the codes. It makes sense that competence is central, but if name and place of origin do not matter, why should it matter if someone mentions them? As one of the coaches commented, "Some of them are proud of their origin." Irrespective of the good intentions behind the advice to leave out names and places, it seems as if immigrants are expected to cast off their cultural identity and adjust to the dominant rules. From a postcolonial perspective, the persuasion to make immigrants deny their origin could be interpreted as a modern way to exercise power over minorities (Said, 1995).

The activities were criticized by immigrants who felt they already knew how to write letters and CVs. Philip, a system programmer who had lost his job when the company decided to outsource his department, told about a situation where a coach tried to convince him about the importance to learn how to write CVs. "I objected", he said, "and told her that I know that by now and that it isn't by learning a different model that I will get a job". To him this was a pure waste of time that would not get him any closer to a job, and, as he said, "rather a way for the coach to earn her living by justifying her expert knowledge". Interpreted through a postcolonial lens, it could be argued that a construction of unemployed immigrants as helpless is a way to defend the notion of differences in favour of the natives.

Constructing "the Other" as a burden or as an asset?

In spite of their good results, they all agreed that immigrants' lack of Swedish language skills is the major hindrance to getting a job. This is evident from comments like: "There are no jobs for those who cannot speak Swedish", "It's always the language that is the hindrance.", and "If I was to mention only one obstacle for obtaining a successful integration it has to be the language." The examples of immigrants they believe have difficulty finding a job due to the lack of language skills are manifold, and a reason that some of them gave is that they must be able to read instructions. Lisa questions the authorities and their inability to understand how important the Swedish language is:

> The language is a problem definitely. . . . It's no problem for me to make them understand. It is a problem that many authorities believe that those who don't know enough Swedish can work in the industry. But no, they must be able to read security regulations.

Even if local language skills, without a doubt, are valuable assets, the request of being fluent in the Swedish language, which has become increasingly important, requires serious reflections. First, as it is not mandatory to show the employer that you have read the security regulations; the question is, how many Swedish industry workers have read them? Second, it is hard to believe Swedish language skills have the importance that people like to think they do, considering that many immigrants with a Swedish academic degree constitute an important part of the unemployed or are stuck in low-skilled jobs. Because, as the following examples indicate, there is no guarantee that Swedish language skills will end in a job:

> I have a guy from Finland with a doctors' degree in neuropsychology. He speaks Swedish of course. . . . I have a woman from Pakistan. She came here six years ago and has a master in chemistry from a Swedish university. She speaks four languages, Dari, English, Swedish and a local Pakistani language.
>
> (Adam, coach at a local office)

And if it does lead to a job, it is likely to be a job for which they are overqualified:

> One of my clients was a woman from Iraq who had studied psychology and social work. Her husband had told her that she had to start all over as her education had no value in Sweden. I helped her to get a job in the child care sector. But she was integrated and modern. She didn't have a veil and stuff.
>
> (Maria, coach at another local office)

The examples indicate that the hierarchical ordering of countries (Hofstede, 2001), which places Western countries like Sweden at the top and non-Western countries like Pakistan at the bottom, is equally valid in terms of education. Even if immigrants have a Swedish university degree, there are many reasons available to separate them from the native population e.g. their education is not at the same level as the Swedish education, they do not know enough Swedish, they are not integrated and modern enough. Maria's explanation that the Iraqi woman got the job because she was integrated, modern, and did not wear a veil reflects the impact of the social disadvantage that the headscarf is causing to the woman who wears it. Her statement mirrors the impact of a colonial mindset (Said, 1995) and the link between the fear of difference (Bhabha, 1994) and what it may mean for our supposed cultural identity.

Third, in spite of the argument that many immigrants do not have the level of Swedish language skill needed to get a job, there are many companies that recruit employees directly from countries outside EU. This has, for instance, become a common strategy for companies within the computer business, the health care sector, and the catering trade. One example is a private company in geriatric care that recruits nurses from the Philippines while they, as they say, cannot find nurses in Sweden. Another example is the pizza restaurant whose owner claimed that, "I cannot find employees in Sweden so I have to recruit people outside of Sweden and the EU. It is very important that I am allowed to do that. We would not survive economically if we couldn't" (Aktuellt, 2018).

Scrutinising the recruitment discourse, there seem to exist two groups of job-seeking immigrants – one group that already lives in Sweden and one group that lives abroad – where immigrants in the first group are considered as a burden and immigrants in the latter are considered an invaluable asset. Thus, it could be argued that immigrants who come as refugees or to connect with their families may be perceived as a threat, as they have the intention of staying permanently. They are likely to be perceived as a threat to the dominant value system as long as they constitute a minority group in the margin of society and are believed to pass on their culture to their children. On the contrary, those who are directly recruited by companies come as expatriates with no intention to spend the rest of their lives in Sweden.

Like the Philippine nurses, they often leave their families behind, live close to their workplace, and will probably not spread their culture and value systems while working here. Because of that, they are considered an asset to society rather than a burden.

The myth of the passive welfare beneficiary and the superior self

The opinion that people from so-called underdeveloped or developing countries seek refuge in the West to live off the welfare system is shared by many people in Western societies, including Sweden. Hanna considered the lack of work motivation to be one of the major challenges in her job. To illustrate what she seemed to interpret as an aversion to working, she recounted the following story about a man who had been her client for quite some time.

> I recall this man who had been in Sweden 15 years without a job. He had applied for more than 80 jobs. He was not motivated. My colleague used to say "I cannot be in the same room as this person". He was so extremely negative. It didn't matter what we said. He infected the whole group. I took him aside and told him that I can't help you if you don't believe I can. In the end we became so tired of him that we gave up.

One thing that can be noticed in this sequence is how she reconstructs her experiences using a rhetoric that lay stress on the inferiorization of the client. With emphasis on the negation she apparently interpreted his fifteen years in Sweden and eighty job applications as a sign of work aversion. Like her colleague she had obviously lost her patience with him because he never got a job, and on top of that was "so extremely negative". She might be right in her conclusion, of course, but she did not ask herself if his lack of motivation and negative attitude were due to the fact that his applications always were rejected. Why would he send all these applications if he was not interested in finding a job? Is it not more likely that he had lost his motivation to a system that he found inefficient? Could it not be that he felt discriminated by the employers who rejected his applications? Reasons like these did apparently not cross her mind. Instead she seemed to take for granted that it was his own fault that he was unemployed and therefore needed to be corrected for his bad behavior. Interpreted through the post-colonial lens, it may be argued that her conclusion that he was to blame reminds us of a modern version of colonialism (Prasad, 2012). Similar to the colonizers' mission to civilize the colonized, it has become a common instrument in the integration policy to reform the immigrants (Moulettes, 2015).

> Lisa, who was keen to point out that she manage to get most of her clients into work, admitted that she had never been able to find a job for a Somali.

Lisa: I don't think there is anyone who has managed to get a Somali into work. Ever. I don't know anyone.

I: But do you think it only depends on them?

Lisa: No, now I sound like a racist and that's awful. But if we talk about financial support . . . they have never had so much money in their whole life. They are very happy with the situation and find ways to survive. . . . They are used to living on nothing.

Lisa was quick to correct herself when she realized that her comment could be perceived as racist. She is nevertheless convinced that they are happy with their situation as unemployed as they had "never had so much money" and "are used to living on nothing". Conclusions like Lisa's where immigrants are regarded as passive welfare seekers, content to live on the margin in a foreign country, shows that our colonial past still influences our way of thinking about non-Westerners as poor and inferior (Said, 1995).

Commodifying the others

In their investigation of the job and development guarantee program, Jansson and Kilsved (2013) found that seven out of ten jobs do not come from the SPES where all vacancies normally have to be announced. Referred to as "hidden jobs" they explained that when private service providers inform the employer about the possibility to obtain financial compensation, these jobs are cobbled together as a solution by assistance from the SPES. They further explained that what normally takes a week for the SPES to administrate is approved by the union within the hour.

The possibility to engage the unemployed is appreciated by the private service providers, as they see work training as an efficient way for unemployed in general, and for unemployed immigrant in particular, to find a full-time job. According to Mats, the owner of a coaching business, "it's always better to have a job as a trainee even if it doesn't correspond to the education and what they want to do . . . and eventually it may lead to a full time employment". Maria shared this view while she thought it is an opportunity for small businesses that, in contrast to large companies, cannot afford employing people. "It's an advantage for employers to engage trainees as they are cheap", she said and added that "There are businesses that operate entirely by engaging cheap labour." When asked if she did not see a risk that it would have negative effect on the wage development, she replied, "I don't think there is a risk of wage dumping. I rather think it is a way of helping people. It's cheaper and easier for the employers".

In contrast to Maria's confidence that the system functions faultlessly, Adam suspected that immigrants' applications are ignored in the recruitment process. "There's no way I can prove it", he said and continued that, "It is probably true also for age and perhaps even for gender." Adam, a university-educated pharmacologist, immigrated to Sweden in the late 1980s from an English-speaking country. He worked as an external communicator until he lost his position some years ago when his last employer decided to reorganize the company. After three years without work he was finally offered a job as a coach and is now helping academics in their search for a job. Maybe his earlier experiences as an unemployed immigrant with an academic degree in his fifties have made him sensitive to employers' treatment of immigrants. At least, this is an impression that his story about one of his clients communicates:

> It happens quite often that they don't get a job that matches their academic education. The Iranian chemist who got a PhD from England . . . he has been in search of a job for ten years. . . . It's a smart guy, but he is 57 and too old. He lives with his son because he cannot afford independent living. Now he is applying for a job in the Gulf States. Identity is equally important . . . and he takes pride in his PhD.

What Adam is implying is that people who do not accept being excluded from the labor market because of age and ethnical background start looking for jobs in other countries.

Adam's suspicion that immigrants are discriminated against is corroborated in a recent survey (Joyce, 2018; SCB, 2017b) which shows that it is harder for an immigrant with university degree to get a job than for a native Swede with only a primary school education. It turned out to be true also for those who have lived in Sweden for more than twenty years. According to statistics only six out of ten highly educated immigrants have a qualified job. Instead of taking advantage of immigrants' competences, they are offered jobs for which they are overqualified, while those who lack higher education are offered traineeship (Aktuellt, SVT, 2018). As Hussain, a gardener from Syria, asked in front of the TV camera: "Why just traineeship? I only get traineeship. Traineeship, traineeship and traineeship. Why not a proper job?"

The critique against traineeship was shared by unemployed immigrants in my study. Approaching his retirement Philip, who had taken part in several coaching activities and traineeships, declared that he was no longer prepared to work without a decent salary and concluded that:

> We are treated as commodities . . . as long-term unemployed you are sent to one coaching agency and to one company after another. The only difference between the jobs we do as unemployed is that we do not get a proper salary and are denied the possibility to affect our situation.

It needs to be pointed out that the conditions do not apply to immigrants alone, but to all groups (young, old, female and male) who find themselves out of work. It is my contention, however, that society sees more obstacles and problems when it comes to guiding immigrants out on the labour market than any other group. It is taken for granted that differences in upbringing, lack of education and Swedish language skills, and professional variations are insurmountable obstacles. It is in these taken-for-granted perceptions and treatments of "the Other" as a commodity without the power to decide their future that the colonial legacy becomes apparent in its modern variation.

Conclusion

The aim of this chapter was to discuss current labour market policy and how it affects immigrants' employability. To do so information was gathered mainly among private labour market intermediaries, but also among immigrants and in some cases in media texts. The findings indicate that the private labour market businesses emphasize deficiency discourse, where unemployed immigrants are often perceived as helpless and in need of special aid to become integrated. To most of the service providers it was especially challenging to help the immigrants with the documentation and to motivate them to apply for jobs. The assumption that immigrants are ignorant and in need of more help to write CVs and application letters compared to the native population may be true in some cases, for example, for those who have recently arrived in Sweden. But considering that many of the immigrants have lived and worked in Sweden for many years and, besides that, often are highly educated, these kinds of statements are inadequate. The blame on immigrants' shortcomings may be a way for the service managers to favour employers' preferences to employ nationals. Even if it is an advantage to communicate in the national language, it is plausible to assume that the request to master the native language sometimes is nothing but a false obstacle intended to favour the natives. From a postcolonial perspective (Said, 1995) it could be argued therefore that private service providers need to construct the immigrants as helpless in order to see themselves as superior and justify their work. The findings further indicate that immigrants concurrently are met with fear and confidence and perceived both as a burden and an asset. At the same time as there is a fear among people that immigrants' who live in the country permanently will spread their aberrant values and seriously affect the dominant culture, there is a confidence that expatriates will have a positive impact on society's economic development without influencing society with their value system. The findings also show how cultural binaries are maintained and reproduced through words like modernity and ignorance. It shows how the connection between employability, modernity, and the veil mirrors the impact of a colonial mindset and what it may mean for our supposed cultural identity (Said, 1995; Bhabha, 1994).

References

Aktuellt, SVT (Swedish Television) June 11th, 2018. Retrieved from: www.svtplay. se/video/18113799/aktuellt/aktuellt-11-jun-21-00-1?start=auto&tab=2018

Bakshi, A., Hatlevall, T. & Melchert, R. 2009. *Matcha eller rusta? Arbetsförmedlingens framtida insatser för nyanlända invandrare.* Sveriges Kommuner och Landsting. Retrieved from: http://webbutik.skl.se/bilder/artiklar/pdf/7164-490-9.pdf

Bhabha, H. K. 1994. *The location of culture.* London, England: Routledge.

Dahlstedt, I. and Bevelander, P. 2010. General versus vocational education and employment integration of immigrants in Sweden. *Journal of Immigrants & Refugee Studies* 8(2): 158–192.

Fougère, M., & Moulettes, A. 2012. A postcolonial reading of Hofstede's culture's consequences. In Prasad, A. (Ed.), *Against the grain: Advances in postcolonial organization studies* (pp. 276–301). Copenhagen, Denmark: Copenhagen Business School Press.

Green-Pedersen, G. 2002. New public management reforms of the Danish and Swedish welfare states: The role of different social democratic responses. *Governance* 15: 271–294.

Guilherme Fernandes, A. 2015. (Dis)Empowering new immigrants and refugees through their participation in introduction programs in Sweden, Denmark, and Norway. *Journal of Immigrants & Refugee Studies* 13(3): 245–264

Hofstede, G. 2001. Culture's consequences: Comparing values, behaviors, institutions and organizations across nations (2nd ed.). London, England: SAGE.

Jack, G. 2016. Postcolonial theory: Speaking back to empire. In Mir, R., Willmot, H. and Greenwood, M. (Eds.), *The Routledge companion to philosophy in organization* (pp. 151–170). New York: Routledge

Jack, G. and Westwood, R. 2009. *International and cross-cultural management studies: A postcolonial reading.* New York, NY: Palgrave Macmillan.

Jansson, B. and Kilsved, H. 2013. *Granskning av upphandling av Arbetsförmedlingen, Svenskt Näringsliv.* Retrieved from: www.svensktnaringslive.se

Joyce, P. 2018. *Rätt jobb åt utrikes födda akademiker En samhällsekonomisk beräkning av en fungerande jobbkedja.* Retrieved from: www.jusek.se/globalassets/rapport_ratt-jobb-utrikes-fodda-slutversion.pdf

Ljunglöf, T. 2018. Arbetslösheten för akademiker. *SACO* 2018–01–30. Retrieved from: www.saco.se/press/arbetsloshet-for-akademiker/

Lundgren, S. 2009. 22. Jobb- och utvecklingsgarantin – en garanti för jobb? *Riksrevisionen.* Retrieved from: www.riksrevisionen.se/PageFiles/1663/RiR_2009_22.pdf

Meyer, J. W. and Rowan, B. 1977. Institutionalized organizations: Formal structure as myth and ceremony. *American Journal of Sociology* 83: 340–363.

Mignolo, W. D. 2011. *The darker side of Western moder- nity: Global futures, decolonial options.* Durham, NC: Duke University Press.

Migrationsverket. 2018. Retrieved from www.migrationsverket.se/Om-Migrationsverket/Statistik.html

Moulettes, A. 2015. The darker side of integration policy: A study of public employment officers' discursive construction of female immigrants' employability. *Journal of Workplace Rights. SAGE Open* 2(5). Retrieved from: http://journals.sagepub.com/doi/abs/10.1177/2158244015575631

Palenga-Möllenbeck, E. 2013. New maids – new butlers? Polish domestic workers in Germany and commodification of social reproductive work. *Equality, Diversity and Inclusion: An International Journal* 32(6): 557–574.

Prasad, A. (Ed.). 2012. *Against the grain: Advances in postcolonial organization studies.* Copenhagen, Denmark: Copenhagen Business School Press

Ruist, J. 2018. Tid för integration – en ESO-rapport om flyktingars bakgrund och arbetsmarknadsetablering. *Rapport till Expertgruppen för studier i offentlig ekonomi* 2018(3). Regeringskansliet. Finansdepartementet.

Rydgren, J. 2004. Mechanism of exclusion: Ethnic discrimination in the Swedish labour market. *Journal of Ethnic and Migration Studies* 30(4): 697–716.

Said, E. 1978. *Orientalism, Western conceptions of the orient*. London, England: Penguin.

Said, E. W. 1995. Orientalism: [Western conceptions of the Orient]. Hammondsworth: Pengiun.

SCB. 2017a. Sysselsättningen bland utrikes födda fortsätter att öka. *Statistiknyhet från SCB* 2017–08–29 9.30. Retrieved from: www.scb.se/hitta-statistik/statistik-efter-amne/arbetsmarknad/arbetskraftsundersokningar/arbetskraftsundersokningarna-aku/pong/statistiknyhet/arbetskraftsundersokningarna-aku-2a-kvartalet-2017/

SCB. 2017b. *Sämre matchning på arbetsmarknaden för utrikes födda*. Nr: 60 Published: 2017–10–04. Retrieved from: www.scb.se/hitta-statistik/artiklar/Samre-matchning-pa-arbetsmarknaden-for-utrikes-fodda/

SFS. 2014. (Svensk författningssamling [Swedish Code of Statutes]). Lag 1993: 440; om privat arbetsförmedling. October 2014. Retrieved from: www.riksdagen.se/sv/Dokument-Lagar/Lagar/Svenskforfattningssamling/Lag-1993440-om-privat-arbet_sfs-1993-440/

Wiesbrock, A. 2011. The integration of immigrants in Sweden: A model for the European union? *International Migration* 49(4): 48–66.

Winther Jørgensen, M. and Phillips, L. 1999. *Diskursanalys som teori och metod*. [Discourse analysis in theory and method]. Lund, Sweden: Studentlitteratur.

Zanoni and Janssens. 2001. Deconstructing difference: The rhetoric of HR managers' diversity discourses. *Organization Studies* 25(1).

18 How German non-Muslim university students see Islam and Muslims

Abe W. Ata and Klaus Baumann

Since 2015 the number of asylum-seeking arrivals to Germany from predominantly Muslim societies has exceeded 1 million, elevating the Muslim population to 6.5 million, as reported by the Pew Research Center. Not surprisingly, attitudes towards Muslims and asylum seekers have recently loomed large in the public debate and media forums presenting a range of mixed feelings about diversity and national identity. The community at large is increasingly asking the question: At what point is a country like Germany able to preserve its national sentiments and identity while at the same time promoting diversity and multiculturalism? The proposed study will measure the attitudes and perceptions of a group of mainstream tertiary students towards members of the Muslim community.

The study will further explore the link between attitude formation, the media and socio-political forces, and how those attitudes overshadow mainstream core values, diversity, social integration and cultural harmony. As well, this study will make key curriculum recommendations and explore predictors that will either bring about or retard social integration. A total of 2000 participants from universities in Germany, France, Holland and Britain will form the basis of this field research using a structured questionnaire as the main instrument for data collection, cross-tabulation and comparative analysis. In this chapter, we are presenting results of a pilot study conducted at the end of 2018 and the start of 2019.

The study of acculturation, and by implication integration, social harmony or lack of it arguably dates back to the 1930s, when sociologists and anthropologists coined the term and explicitly explored acculturation at the group level. They were followed in the 1960s by psychologists investigating acculturation at the individual level. Berry (2008) famously developed his influential fourfold model. He identified these as follows:

> *integration* which results in the maintenance of existing cultures and behaviours while *peoples engage in day to-day interaction within an evolving civic framework;*

separation which leads to avoidance of interaction with the dominant group in favour of holding on one's own psychological and cultural qualities;

assimilation whereby minority groups lose distinctive core cultural and behavioural features, and gradually absorb those of the dominant ones;

marginalisation resulting in cultural and psychological loss of immigrant communities, along with their exclusion from full and equitable participation in the larger society.

For all its elegance, however, Berry's model has come under criticism for its static approach. The field is now characterized by lively debate, with more complex, dynamic models competing for relevance. These newer models seek to answer such questions as how acculturation happens and why biculturalism is so hard to sustain. In recent years, this debate has largely focused on Muslim migrants' integration and social harmony in European and other Western countries. Others, however, believe that the majority of European Muslims are neither well integrated nor radicalised. Benard and Rabasa (2014) point out that for the minority amongst second-generation Muslims who are disaffected, some find it difficult to live within both the traditional culture of their parents or the modern Western culture where they reside.

A large amount of previous work revealed that majority and minority status groups differ in their focus during intergroup interactions.

First, whereas majority group members are generally self-aware of their own prejudice towards the minority groups within contact situations, minority group members tend to be more concerned about being the targets of such prejudice.

Second, minority group members tend to think of themselves in terms of their own group membership more than majority group members and tend to be aware of their group's devalued status (Habtegiorgis, Paradies and Dunn, 2014).

Third, the intergroup attitudes of minority group members are often based on the anticipation of prejudice from the majority group, whereas intergroup attitudes of majority group members tend to be based on their own perceptions and beliefs (Konig, 2005).

Research suggests that social media – one of several social-psychological factors – influencing fact-driven attitudes – contributes to developing a negative perception of Muslims, often portraying Islam in direct conflict with the values and traditions of Western cultures; that terrorism and Islam, for example, are synonymous; or that Germany/Europe and Islam are incompatible and that their worldviews are irreconcilable (Ata, 2014, 2009; Lewis, 1994). In Germany, in 2017– 2018 this has been epitomized by the reiterated debate in politics and society of whether Islam belongs to Germany.

In 2008 the Pew Research Center reported that growing numbers of people in several major European countries reveal that their "opinions of Muslims also are more negative than they were several years ago" (ibid, p. 1).

The UK was particularly shocked that British-born second-generation Muslim youths of Pakistani and Jamaican descent, with good education and job prospects, were the perpetrators. These events raise fears that second-generation Muslims living in isolated urban communities are becoming alienated from democratic societies and may be developing closer sympathies with extremist Islamic movements. For some observers, disaffected Muslims in France, the UK or the Netherlands are seeking to create a society entirely separate from the mainstream (Bawer, 2007).

Due to these developments, European countries which used to be relatively homogeneous in their cultural heritage, historical traditions, ethnic composition, language, lifestyles and religious faith – such as Denmark, France and Sweden – have become far more socially diverse today (Hunter, 1998).

In spring 2006, the Pew surveys compared public opinion in four European countries (Britain, France, Germany and Spain) alongside Muslim minorities in these countries, reporting that both groups perceived a sense of growing Islamic identity and concern about Islamic extremists. The majority of Europeans expressed doubts that Muslims coming into their countries wanted to adopt their national customs and way of life. A subsequent Pew survey reported that many Europeans also viewed Muslims in an increasingly negative light, especially in France, Germany and Spain (The Pew Global Attitudes Project, 2008). As mentioned earlier, the incidence of radical protest involving intercommunal violence and cases of outright terrorist incidents involving small groups of militant Muslims lend further plausibility to the divergence argument – a term that means deviation from the common standards or norms (The Pew Global Attitudes Project, 2006; Coolsaet, 2008)

The Pew Center reported in 2006 that Muslim practices of forced marriages, polygamy, domestic violence and honour killings, as well as patriarchal beliefs about the traditional roles of women in the family and the symbolic wearing of the hijab, niqab and burqa, have proved controversial by conflicting with the more egalitarian gender roles, the liberal social values and the secular legal frameworks prevailing in Western countries (Roggeband, 2007).

Equally important, there is little published research examining the extent to which false facts relate to attitudes of Muslims towards Germany. Much less is reported on what may constitute negative attitudes towards Germany that could be predicted from the scale of our knowledge, either fashionable or well worn. It is held that many of the false beliefs play a crucial role in perpetuating negative attitudes, legitimising social distance and justifying blatant and subtle prejudice (Ata, 2009; Ata and Batrouney, 1989). Such studies on anti-prejudice education show that participants believed that

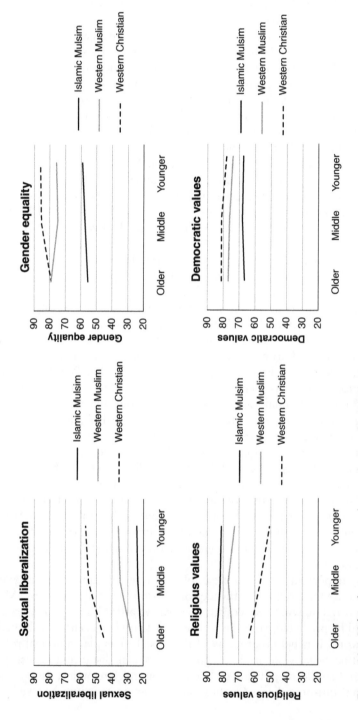

Figure 18.1 Values by age group and type of societal-religious identity
Source: pooled World Values Survey 1981–2007

factual information about out-groups is crucial in challenging negative feelings and improving positivity towards them.

Drawing on the findings of available literature in this area, we will examine if a relationship exists between prejudice and fact-driven knowledge of Muslims on German university campuses. In other words, are negative attitudes towards Muslims strongly correlated with false beliefs?

In this proposed study we are concerned with understanding what may drive negative attitudes and behaviours of mainstream European students towards Muslims and Islam. Specifically, we will identify, measure and interpret the knowledge, values and attitudes of tertiary students in Germany towards the Muslim migrant community and Islam. It explores the link between the media, political forces and attitude formation and the extent to which these factors shape mainstream core values, social distance and broader concerns towards 'the outsider'.

Examining issues surrounding religious matters in present-day Europe presents a difficult and sensitive task. And yet this presentation provides a stepping-stone on that journey, especially for those who wish to develop a better and broader understanding of Muslims within the broader German cultural and religious traditions – a German society where the separation between the religious and secular identities is a cultural and political given.

This project will subsequently fill in a big void in the literature. It will explore the nature of the problem and its causal factors and the predictors of what may constitute negative, and positive, attitudes towards Muslims, which we may predict from the scale of 'our' knowledge. We will look behind the walls and explore the issues challenging the mainstream German/European community and their struggle to achieve integration of the Muslim community and accommodation of Western values and lifestyle mannerisms.

Survey method and sample characteristics

The sample comprised 404 student participants mainly from Freiburg University with a sizable proportion from universities in Karlsruhe, Bremen, Stuttgart, Koln and Hamburg in Germany. The sample formed the basis of this field research using a structured questionnaire as the main instrument for data collection, cross-tabulation and comparative analysis.

The research instrument is a structured questionnaire comprising 90 variables consisting of open- and closed-ended questions. Combined, they will elicit precise and free-associated answers reflecting demographic attributes, perception and attitudes, knowledge and behaviour beliefs and opinions.

Where appropriate, the survey was administered in classrooms in consultation with the teaching scientists. Participants who volunteered were briefed in German on the rationale and aims of the survey. In conjunction, a number of volunteer participants were randomly selected from the student bodies from the various university campuses.

The survey of this pilot study was administered in German with an English translation to male and female students who are 18 years and over, these being considered mature enough to give informed answers. Participants with a Muslim affiliation were provided with a slightly varied version of the questionnaire to allow for follow up with a meaningful statistically valid comparative analysis. This will be part of the main study, too.

• Percentages are rounded

Findings and discussion

Three open-ended questions were put to respondents and the answers coded into a manageable number of categories, as shown here. Naturally, this entailed a degree of subjective judgment.

Table 18.1 Survey participant characteristics

Male	174	43.1%
Gender Female	227	56.2%
Other	3	0.7%
Christian	358	88.1%
Religion Other	4	1.0%
None	44	10.9%
Germany	370	91.6%
Place of Birth Europe	20	5.0%
Other	14	3.5%
Undergraduate	291	73.3%
Level of Education Postgraduate	102	25.7%
PhD/Post Doc	4	1.0%
Older (22+)	165	41%
Age Younger (18–21)		
Germany	330	82.3%
Place of birth (Father) Europe	34	8.5%
Other	37	9.2%
Germany	337	83.8%
Place of Birth (Mother) Europe	30	7.5%
Other	35	8.7%
German only	296	73.3%
Language spoken at Home Other	19	4.7%
German + other	89	22.0%
Mostly Christian		86.0%
Mostly Muslim		0.5%
Religion of friends Half and half		1.2%
Do not know		3.0%
Other		8.7%
Yes		35.9%
Having Muslim neighbours No		64.1%
		Total = 404

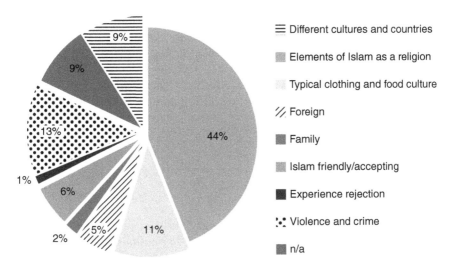

Figure 18.2 Responses to the question 'What are the first words that come into your mind when "Muslim" is mentioned?'

What are the first words that come into your mind when 'Muslim' is mentioned?

When asked for 'the first words that come [to] mind when the word "Muslim" is mentioned', the largest proportion of responses (44%) was associated with various elements of Islam as a religion. A smaller percentage (9%) indicated 'different cultures and countries'; 11% related to food and clothing; 13% mentioned violence and crime. Only 6% mentioned Islam as a friendly or accepting reality – a response trend which is also reflected in the survey results obtained from Australia high school students (Ata, 2014).

Box 18.1   Selected verbatim responses (first words)

Headscarf, Koran, Good Eating, Turkey, Immigration, Religion, Islamist, Uncertainty, Qur'an, Kerchief, Believer, Conservative, Women's Rights (Discussion), Prayer, Believer, Intolerant, Women's Discriminatory, Mosque, strong faith practice, conflicts, fundamentalism, believers, veiling, headscarf, migration, no respect for women, discriminated against, Islam, Palestine, Interesting Culture, AVICENNA and AVERROE, INTEGRALIST ?, petroleum, panarabism, strict culture, disrespectful, medieval islam, faith, mosque, turkey, family, prayer, kerchiefs, no pork, danger to women, strict religion, Allahu

Akbar, paradox, tolerant but not if majority, victim, Muhammad, mecca, headscarf, no alcohol, 5-time prayer, kebab, tamil, warrant, fugitive or turk, dirty, stupid, terrorist, danger, turban, warm land, unknown, headscarf, pray, headscarf, mosque, no pork, Ramadan, Mecca, bad press, Turkey, Koran, Muslim, Other Religion, headscarf, kebab, mosque, Other Religion, Afd, Mohammed, Mecca, Religious, Lent, Great Family, Allah, Science, Burka, Quaba, Hijab, Sharia, Religious, Integration, Family, Allah, Arab. Food, yufka, east, mistaken belief, legalism, uncertainty

What do you like most about Muslims?

When asked what they liked most about Muslims, just under one third (33%) offered a positive comment, of which 11% alluded to courage (this compares to 44% who gave a positive response in a similar national survey in Australia focusing on 17- to 18-year-old students in high schools, equivalent to *gymnasiums* in Germany) (Ata, 2014). However when the responses 'integrated well' (8%) and 'normal, everyone is different' (17%) are calculated as positive, the total becomes 58%. Some 7% of respondents gave superficial or facetious comments, or explicitly stated that they could not think of anything they 'liked most about Muslims' (not to be confused with a non-response, which might signify simply lack of motivation to respond). Just over a third of respondents (33%) gave no response.

Box 18.2   Selected verbatim responses (like most)

Hospitable, No difference, Hospitable, Generous, Strong family bonding, Bringing together interesting aspects of countries of origin, Family spirit, Courtesy, Not enough contact, Often very religious and family, Often very open to other people, Connection v Religion and modern culture, Intercultural, Courtesy, Good character, Friendly, Respectful, Very friendly, polite, hospitable, Very reflective about beliefs and social issues, Do not know, Stupid question, Integrated, Just like others, Mix of cultures, New to know, The food, Full and Confident expression of Faithfulness, Kindness, Hospitality, Eating, Courtesy, Willingness to help, Everyone Individual, Kindness Openness to others, Togetherness, Willingness to help, Culturally diverse, Family bonding, Acceptance of the Christian religion, Friendly, Sense of family and community, Will to integrate most, Friendly, polite, hospitality, g fellowship, community, warmth, family sense, diverse perspectives, likes, friends, no idea, insight into other culture, good values (honor, family), high status of religion

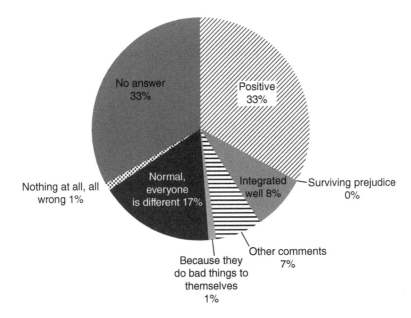

Figure 18.3 Responses to the question 'What do you like most about Muslims?'

What do you like least about Muslims?

When asked what they liked least about Muslims, just under two-thirds offered a comment of some kind (Figure 18-4). Nearly a third (32%) mentioned attitudinal issues, including an inability to integrate, being strange or an inability to speak German. Another group (12%) mentioned 'the way they treat women' or alluded to domestic violence. The remainder stated extremism and hatred (2%), crime or criminal lifestyle or simply there was 'nothing' they did not like about Muslims.

Those indicating neutrality, or who explicitly stated that they could not think of anything they 'liked least about Muslims' (not to be confused with a non-response, which might signify simply laziness), comprised 8%. Just over a third of respondents (40%) gave no response.

Selected verbatim responses (like least)

Low value of women, superiority, isolation, demarcation, image of women, father as head, lack of integration/openness towards Germany, no idea, dirty, cultureless, if they are too strict, narrow-mindedness, image of women incompatible with, European, lack of openness to non- Muslims, Too little free exercise opportunities for young Muslims, Lack of integration, isolation in religious circles, Few want to integrate, Lack of tolerance of other beliefs, Intrusiveness, Problems with integration, group formation much

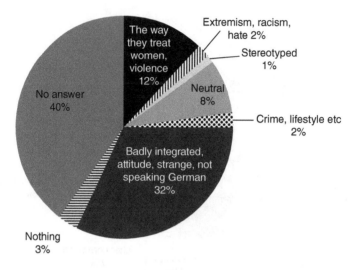

Figure 18.4 Responses to the question 'What do you like least about Muslims?'

among themselves, Nothing, Urgent relig. Laws on state laws, Integration culture partly absent, Veiling, Directness, Loud talking, Representation in victim role, represent all German as racists, Bad integration, no learning German, Arrogant, Do not integrate, Partly parallel society, misogyny, honor killings, If to radical, only in their group, no willingness to integrate, reservations, missing, openness, some not interested in integration, parallel societies, no difference, dealing with women, like us, Muslim, too loud, restriction of women in their appearance

The reference to extremism and terrorism has in recent years been at the center of the public debate. Even where consensus exists, the problem is recognized as complex. The causal factors – psychological, sociological, historical and institutional – that give rise to violent extremism combine with and interact in ways that make it extremely hard to predict which particular individuals will succumb. According to US researchers Denoeux and Carter, 'There can be no general theory about "why and how the turn to [violent extremism] occurs," because the answer to that question will vary from one setting to another' (2009, p. 84). The Edmund Rice Centre (2005) listed several falsehoods held by the mainstream community about Muslims. They contend that such falsehoods have long-term implications, in that they are negative and passionate reactions. For example, words like *jihad* have come to overshadow what is a religion of many perspectives. *Jihad* does not mean 'holy war', but refers to 'any action by which one makes sincere and conscious effort for a collective benefit', and wearing a *hijab* is a testimony of faith, not subjugation. It is pointed out that differences in worldviews between the two societies and their traditions will continue to exist.

Rabasa and Benard (2014) have challenged the widely held view that violent extremism is born of 'relative deprivation', 'religion' or any number of other causes. In Benard's words,

> If we take a closer look at 'moderate Islam' we find that one slice of it – the 'aggressive traditionalist' slice – incites not violence against the West, but rejection of Western values, modern life and integration. It demands of its followers that they be in the West but not of it, that they maintain emotional, social and intellectual separation.
>
> (Rabasa and Benard, 2014, p.1)

And it is this sense of separation that makes violence possible.

That said, this analysis does not attempt to expand this already-extensive body of knowledge, a task better tackled by national agencies with an international remit.

How do male and female students differ in their attitudes?

So far we have explored the attitudes of the sample as a whole. They covered a range of themes including cultural pluralism, the media, religious education, civic engagement, spiritualism and interfaith dialogue, the role of women, asylum seekers, sexual abuse, mental health, mixed marriages, identity, social services and institutions, conversion to and from Islam, tolerance and factionalism, apologists and the faithful, schools and universities, challenges and future directions.

The attitudes of the sample as a whole may mask differences in the attitudes between male and female students within the sample. For instance, do male respondents differ systematically from female respondents in their attitudes towards Islam and Muslims? To answer this and similar questions, we used statistical exploration to determine if there were significant differences in the mean attitudes of all the demographic groups measured in the survey. The result is outlined here.

Significant differences were found between the responses of male and female students (Table 18-2). Males and females in this instance differed significantly on the following statements.

These findings show that male students were less accepting of Muslims and Islam than were female students. Interestingly, male students agreed slightly more *but not significantly* than females with the statement 'Most Muslims treat women with less respect than do other Germans'. Taken in totality however the results (Figure 18.5) show a third of the respondents agreed with this statement and were almost equal in proportion to those who disagreed (32.5%) and those expressing neutrality (31.7%). This finding was corroborated to a small degree by the findings in the survey's open-ended questions, in which only 12% identified 'sexism' when asked what they liked least about Muslims. Note that we are not suggesting that either

Table 18.2 Gender differences on select statements of attitudes

Males agreed more than females with the following statements:	Females agreed more than males with the following statements:
• Muslims threaten the German way of life. • Most religious fanatics these days are Muslims. • Most migrants are racist. • If I saw a Muslim student being abused in a public place I wouldn't care.	• Most Muslims have good feelings for Germans and Germany. • This university helps people of different cultures to get along better. • Learning about Muslims helps students to understand them better. • A person can be both a good Muslim and a loyal German. • Most Germans have good feelings for Muslims.

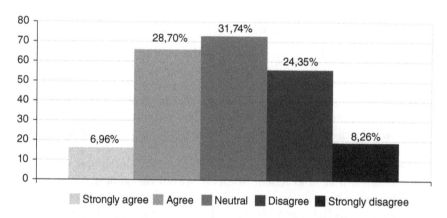

Figure 18.5 Responses to the statement 'Most Muslims treat women with less respect than do other Germans'

men or women are being treated with less respect, only the possibility of this being true and our concern with the wording of the statement. It is important to stress here that a low level of significance between the two subgroups is of little or no value, given the sample size and sensitivity of the p-value to it.

Conclusions

This survey revealed a trajectory of unexpected findings of attitudes, feelings and knowledge of Muslims in German universities. The themes addressed and the cultural and historical differences between mainstream and Muslim communities continue to be too wide to make a definitive statement or a

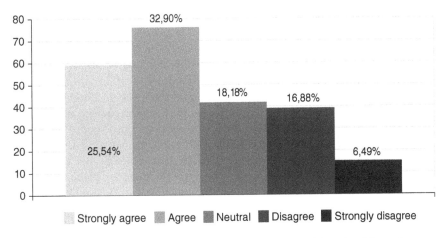

Figure 18.6 Responses to the statement 'German universities should teach more about Muslims'

complete reconciliation, but given the alternatives, a creative dialogue must continue. Just like mixed marriages, certain differences between the two cultures and faiths may be identified without being fully reconciled. A starting point towards this end is identifying misconceptions, misgivings and the roots of grievances.

Three open-ended questions were put to respondents and the answers coded into a manageable number of categories, as shown. Naturally, this entailed a degree of subjective judgment. A few negative stereotypes and the relatively new presence of the Muslim community in Germany tend to suggest that non-Muslim students may not be fully informed, given the privileged academic environment they inhabit, while the existing multicultural posture of educational policy suggests otherwise. Variations in responses between male and female, religion or non-religious affiliated, also revealed a high level of significance. The findings show that a sizeable proportion of students are generally ignorant about Muslims and Islam, and few believe that universities are filling the gaps in their knowledge. While non-Muslim students agree that acceptance of Muslims does not come easily in Germany, the school does not emerge as a site for change.

The survey found that students are divided in the degree and nature of prejudice and tolerance towards Muslims. One of the main findings was with regard to gender differences, where boys were less accepting of Muslims and Islam than were girls. Interestingly, boys agreed more than girls with the statement 'Most Muslims treat women with less respect than do other Germans' – clearly a view not founded in direct experience.

It was found that with German students, a clear majority (74%) felt that they have learnt little or nothing about Muslims at university. Respondents tended to agree that German universities should teach more about the Muslim community, with those in support outnumbering those opposed by three to one. The absence of Muslim students from a large number of non-public schools in regional Australia may have contributed to the direction of responses, although having Muslim friends does not make a significant difference. Ata and Baumann (Chapter 18) survey of 400 mainstream students in six German universities bring to the surface new findings as to how Muslims are perceived as an integral part of the German society; the positive and not so positive attributes that the local media portray about them; their contribution and loyalty; the conditions that encourage their integration, acceptance or rejection on campus and in the mainstream society that are accepted and rejected on campus and beyond; the degree to which they are marginalised; and the extent to which the university is positioned to fill the gaps in their knowledge and equality.

References

Ata, A. 2009. *Us and Them: Muslim-Christian Relations and Cultural Harmony in Australia*. Brisbane: Australian Academic Press.

Ata, A. 2014. *Education, Integration, Challenges: The Case of Australian Muslims*. Melbourne: David Lovell Publishing.

Ata, A. and Ali, J. 2018. *Islam in the West: Perceptions and Reactions*. New Delhi: Oxford University Press(global).

Ata, A., Bastian, B. and Lusher, D. 2012. Contact, Evaluation and Social Distance: Differentiating Majority and Minority Effects. *International Journal of Intercultural Relations*, 36, 100–107.

Ata, A. and Batrouney, T. 1989. Attitudes and Stereotyping in Victorian Secondary Schools. *The Eastern Anthropologist*, 42(1).

Bawer, B. 2007. *While Europe Slept: How Radical Islam Is Destroying the West from Within*. New York: Anchor.

Benard, C. and Rabasa, A. 2014. *Eurojihad: Patterns of Islamist Radicalization and Terrorism in Europe*. New York: Cambridge University Press.

Berry, J. W. 2008. Globalisation and Acculturation. *International Journal of Intercultural Relations*, 32(4), 328–336.

Bowen, J. R. 2008. *Why the French Don't Like Headscarves: Islam, the State, and Public Space*. Princeton, NJ: Princeton University Press.

Coolsaet, R. 2008. *Jihadi Terrorism and the Radicalisation Challenge in Europe*. Aldershot: Ashgate.

Denoeux, G. and Carter, L. 2009. *Guide to the Drivers of Violent Extremism*. Washington: USAID.

Edmund Rice Centre. 2005. *Debunking Myths about Muslims in Australia*. ERC, Strathfield, NSW.

Gordjin, E., Wigboldus, D. and Yzerbyt, V. 2000. Emotional Consequences of Categorizing Victims of Negative Out-group Behavior as In-group or Out-group. *Group Processes and Intergroup Relations*, 4, 317–326.

Habtegiorgis, A., Paradies, Y. and Dunn, K. 2014. Are Racist Attitudes Related to Experiences of Racial Discrimination? Within Sample Testing Utilising Nationally Representative Survey Data. *Social Science Research*, 47, 178–191.

Hunter, S. 1998. *The Future of Islam, Clash of Civilizations or Peaceful Coexistence?* London: Praeger.

Hunter, S. 2002. *Islam, Europe's Second Religion: The New Social, Cultural and Political Landscape.* London: Praeger.

Israeli, R. 2008. *The Islamic Challenge in Europe.* New Brunswick, NJ: Transaction Publishers.

Konig, M. 2005. Incorporating Muslim Migrants in Western Nation States – A Comparison of the United Kingdom, France and Germany. *Journal of International Migration and Integration/Revue de l'integration et de la migration internationale*, 6(2), 219–234.

Lewis, B. 1994. *Islam and the West.* New York: Oxford University Press.

Pettigrew, T. F. and Tropp, L. R. 2006. A Meta-Analytic Test of Intergroup Contact Theory. *Journal of Personality and Social Psychology,* 90(5), 751–783.

Pew Global Attitudes Project. 2006. *Muslims in Europe: Economic Worries Top Concerns About Religious and Cultural Identity.* http://pewglobal.org/reports/display.php?ReportID=254

The Pew Global Attitudes Project. 2008. *Unfavorable Views of Jews and Muslims on the Increase in Europe.* http://pewglobal.org/reports/display.php?ReportID=262

The Pew Research Centre. 2006. *Conflicting Views in a Divided World.* Washington, DC: The Pew Global Attitudes Project.

Rabasa, A. and Benard, C. 2014. *Eurojihad: Patterns of Islamist Radicalization and Terrorism in Europe.* London: Cambridge University Press.

Roggeband, C. 2007. Dutch Women are Liberated, Migrant Women are a Problem: The Evolution of Policy Frames on Gender and Migration in the Netherlands, 1995–2005. *Social Policy & Administration*, 41, 271.

Tropp, L. R. and Pettigrew, T. F. 2005. Relationships between Intergroup Contact and Prejudice Among Minority and Majority Status Groups. *Psychological Science*, 16(12), 951–957, 20 December.

Index